A SPIRIT LOOSE IN THE WORLD

A SPIRIT LOOSE IN THE WORLD

BY BENEDICT REID, OSB

HARBOR
HOUSE (WEST)
PUBLISHERS

Library of Congress Catalog Card Number
93-061087

ISBN 1-879560-20-8

Manufactured in the United States of America

1   2   3   4   5   6   7   8   9   10

Book and Cover Design by Soozie Bing
Cover Photo by Father Jude Bell, OSB

ABBOTWORD

In the early Middle Ages, some monks practiced a strange form of asceticism; they wandered from place to place, from shrine to shine, and from monastery to monastery; they gave up the comforts of a permanent home in order to be with Christ on pilgrimage. Abbot Benedict Reid has a permanent home (Saint Gregory's Abbey) and for years he has lived a cenobitic way of life (stability in a community) but given a sabbatical he was bitten by the bug of pilgrimage and wandered from site to lovely site in North America.

The book you have in your hands is more than an account of his travels; it is also a reflection on the way God is working in the lives and activities of ordinary and colorful people. Abbot Benedict discovers and comments on the omnipresent God in many persons, institutions, and places.

Abbot Benedict is curious about life, its problems, and its surprises. He entertains us with his comments on the dangers, choices, and conundrums of life. I find his account refreshingly honest, especially when it leads to a description of an abbot in a hot tub!

These pages indicate that Abbot Benedict has an ecumenical spirit. His mind is open to the many veins of thought present in the world today, both in society at large and in the churches. He looks for the broader, the world-wide picture of spiritual and theological movements. His sabbatical travels are anything but a rest for his mind; they bring him into contact with the thoughts of many friends and congregations. He receives wisdom from others but he also shares his own.

Take a ride in the van with Abbot Benedict! You will find yourself experiencing new places and seeing the God who drives all of us on our pilgrim way.

Abbot Jerome Theisen, OSB
Saint John's Abbey
Collegeville, Minnesota
(now Abbot Primate of the male Benedictine Communities,
 headquartered in Rome)

FOREWORD

One could probably make a rather noble list of Benedictine abbots who earnestly desire some practical, workable insights into monastic community leadership more respectful of modern man's levels of education and sophistication.

On a somewhat smaller piece of paper would be the roster of Benedictine abbots who have spent several months "tootling" about the highways — and especially the byways — of our nation, as sole proprietor of a "Winnie."

A little register or sales slip from K-Mart would be enough for the names of Benedictine abbots completely open to the world's craziness, and able to theologize on it so readily and cogently.

For the names of Benedictine abbots who are happy to remember the time they drove, on purpose, into an "alternative dress" colony, and stepped, shorn of their sartorial impediments, out into the sunshine, to join those good people in the pristine glory of a newborn man of God, you would need only one of those tiny slips the dry cleaner pins to the fly of your trousers.

The list of Benedictine abbots who, in their travel memoirs, offer a brief dissertation, with spiritual application, on humanity's excremental detritus, would fit quite comfortably on the "Inspected by No. 8" confetti you find in the pocket of a new garment.

It is a rare privilege to read this most extraordinary journal of the only man in the worldwide community of St. Benedict whose name would appear on all five of those above-mentioned lists.

Frank Mulligan
Friend of the Abbey
Author of *A Lector's Guide to the Episcopal Eucharistic Lectionary*

APPRECIATION

After God, it would be almost impossible to list the people who made this sabbatical journey possible: my community, friends and donors, those whom I visited and gave me a word or a snack for my travels, the unknown strangers who helped me, and some who didn't, including those I saw only briefly in a glance. All were part of the journey. These notes are a grateful, if inadequate, appreciation and offering. Particular thanks are due those friends who at various times helped bring my scrambled notes into readable form. One special friend, Charlene Bollman, brought unusual editorial skill and deep commitment to the theme of the book. Without her profound faith investment you would not now have this book in your hands.

Anyone who is interested in the human journey is also due my appreciation. We are fellow believers, fellow travelers, sharing a faith in the mystery of life. We are friends, even if we have never met, and we belong to the one human community. I thank you all and pray for you.

POOR RICHARD'S PRINTER

Every would-be author must know the frustration of attempting to get his work published. For me, the possibility of the Notes ever being formally published never occurred. How then did this manuscript happen?

I am a list maker and as I thought about the possibility of a sabbatical, I started to make some notes. Friends and other travelers contributed their ideas and these, too, became part of my thought lists. Once the decision was made that I would take a sabbatical, the task of organizing my abbatial duties required more lists. Part of this included letting the extended members of our monastic family, the Confraternity, know that I would be away from St. Gregory's. The easiest way to do this was through our Confraternity Letter. Thus, the first formal writing evolved. There were others who needed to be aware that things at the Abbey were OK but I would be unavailable for the usual conferences, confessions, and simply their general visits. Since the abbot usually writes at least one of the articles for the Abbey Letter each year, it seemed like a good idea to use the opportunity to not only inform people but also to let them know I would be away from Three Rivers. Both the Confraternity and Abbey Letter allowed me to clarify more of what I hoped the sabbatical would achieve. Mostly, it was simply going to be a time of being open to the Spirit and trying to see where and how it was active.

Just before my departure, a friend gave me a travel diary. For a time it was a good place to make quick notes — the odometer reading, names of people and towns, highway numbers, and occasionally a very sketchy thought. It never really was a travel diary but a good place to make lists. Soon I found its pages getting full — not of writing but of the little lists I made of things to do, people to see, the day's itinerary, articles I wanted to purchase. It was a handy storage place and more often than not, I kept very brief notes thinking that I would refer to them later. I began to think about the possibility of writing about the journey not as a book but as a series of mimeographed notes which would be given to friends and benefactors. Thus it was that the early typed pages were often referred to as Notes.

As the journey continued, I often found myself not writing any notes for several days. Then when I did, my reminders were written on the back of sales slips, scraps of brown paper bags, 3 x 5 index cards, gas receipts, and occasionally, an actual piece of paper. Whatever was handy was OK. There were times when I was in a location for several days and it was there that I often wrote the longer sections. Sometimes I returned to a familiar location such as a relative's home where I could rethink the past few days. Staying for an extended time in an apartment in San Francisco not only allowed me to spread out my things but also to leave the writing and return to it at will. But the writing could just as easily have been one of the evenings in a camp area or my room in Rome or England. These Notes and their reflections became my traveling companion and I allowed them to flow or not to flow as the Spirit directed. I didn't have any format in mind but simply wrote as I experienced the thought. Without planning it, a pattern developed in my writing. I went from commenting on the travel and people around me to sections which later would be identified as reflections.

When I returned to the Abbey, visitors often would ask about my sabbatical. I knew I had the piles of paper — ideas now on very roughly typed sheets plus all those slips and scraps. Several volunteers came to the rescue. Since none used a word processor or computer, the manuscript became more typed sheets. Over time, many different people played an important role in their development: a member of my community, a published author, a seminarian, a nun, an Abbey guest, another friend, and a member of our Confraternity. Busy lives and simply the roughness of my writing never allowed any of them to take it to the final stage. I was very appreciative of all that they had done to contribute to the project but its completion simply wasn't that important to me. And, I fully understood the demands their positions required.

Several months after my resignation as abbot, I was preparing to go to Seabury Western Seminary to teach for the fall term. In getting ready for my class, the two plastic bags with the manuscript came to my notice. A friend who was visiting St. Gregory's asked if there was anything I needed, and innocently asked if I needed any typing or anything done. I mentioned the Notes and she agreed to take a look at them. She didn't know what she was getting involved with. And, in truth, I didn't know either.

First came the job of sorting out what was actually my work and what had been the suggestions of the others who had worked on various parts of it. Then the discovery was made that 40 pages were missing. These were found in still another pile at the Abbey. For the first time, the thoughts were being transferred from typed sheets to a computer and I was confronted with a whole new language which I didn't understand and didn't particularly want to learn. (I am not known for my love of computers — although I do appreciate them.) I received the first pages and edited them. They looked pretty good to me. Since we were doing the manuscript in pages and not as a whole, I didn't comprehend how it really would look. Before I received the second draft, my typist asked if it was all right to make suggestions. Sure. Why not.

Draft number two almost had more comments and suggestions on it than typed script. She was serious and I was forced to read and think about what it was that I really was saying. And finally, the format was agreed upon and formalized.

Draft numbers three and four were still more refinements, more clarification, more details. Was I sure I turned north out of Washington, D.C. or did I actually head south. We sat with an atlas, a road map, and the Notes. Draft five arrived and for the first time, I saw the document in its entirety. I could not believe I had written that much. My comment on the last edited sheet to her was, "My God. Who wrote all of this?"

The sixth draft was to be the last major revision. Slowly it was nearing completion. Hereafter, it would only be minor changes. But I was still very skeptical that it should be published. Several people who visited the Abbey asked about the sabbatical and I allowed them to read the rough draft. Partly because of their reaction and the work that had been invested in the manuscript, I decided to try to bring it to completion. The seventh draft was the last one before sending off the prospectus.

What a transformation it had made: hand written slips and scraps of paper to roughly typed sheets to retyped script to an Apple computer and laser run hard copy. All total some 5000 sheets of paper. Finally, some 150,000 words of script were reduced to one simple double-sided 3.5 inch diskette. I held in my hand a square piece of modern data-filled plastic that weighed less than ounce. A journey which took me to three countries and over 14,000 miles of motor home travel in the US covering seven months, now was ready to be sent to a publisher. Could the right one be found?

Was the process of clarifying the journey worth the investment of time and energy people gave me? Did I believe that I had something to share with readers? I am no great author. My style is not refined. Perhaps the message is unique — a perspective of what it was and is like to attempt to travel with the Spirit and to remain open in a variety of situations and circumstances. Most enthusiastically I can encourage others to do the same. The Spirit is there — within each of us. The key may be daring to discover a slightly different way to venture with the Spirit. Some friends and a poor Richard's printing process are sure to be at hand.

The further adventure of finding a publisher, Harbor House, with an extraordinary spirit-filled family and staff was further confirmation that the Spirit is indeed drawing like-minded folk together. The invitation is there. Why not join others for the new and unfolding chapter of the Spirit joyously loose in the world.

Richard Preston Benedict Reid, OSB

CONTENTS

INTRODUCTION i
The Sabbatical Idea
  Purpose; Organization of Notes; Preparations; Pilgrimage Van; Departure

BOOK ONE 1
BECOMING FREE IN THE SPIRIT

Chapter 1: The Journey Begins, The Middle America Loop.....................3
  McHenry, Illinois; The Community of St. Mary; Left Brain; State Parks;
  Eucharist; New Melleray; Winnebago; A Small Parish; Anniversary;
  Crisis of Faith; A Cathedral; Spring Liturgy

Chapter 2: Going Deeper with the Spirit – Listening to Change 13
  Depression; A Sunday; New Harmony, Indiana

Chapter 3: The Spirit – East and West 17
  Osage Monastery; Saint William Laud Parish; The World; Northwest Texas;
  Copper Breaks and Santa Rosa

Chapter 4: The Charismatic Spirit.......................................21
  Pecos Bendictine Monastery; Where are those shirts?; Diet; The Aquarian
  Conspiracy; Santa Fe Anywhere

Chapter 5: Desert Spirit..27
  Christ in the Desert; Santa Fe Revisited; Ethan Simmons; O.A.R.;
  Desert Inn; Truth or Consequences; Michigan Friends;
  The Pony Express Drop; The Thunderbird Shop

Chapter 6: The Spirit Imprisoned, Yet Free 37
Maximum Security Prison; The Servants of Christ; Arcosanti

Chapter 7: The Spirit of Pentecost 43
Sedona; Hurt Pride in the Coconino National Forest; U-Haul and
the Spirit; Humprey's Peak; Justification; Droppings;
The Ponderosa Fountain

Chapter 8: The Spirit of Creation 49
Sheila; Grand Canyon; Monument Valley; Natural Bridges; Lake Powell;
Golden Eagle; Hanksville; Capital Reef; Bryce Canyon; Arrested;
Zion National Park; Desert Storm; Las Vegas

Chapter 9: The Golden Spirit 59
Gypsy Moth Inspection; Barstow, California; Sky High Ranch; Bob;
The Paulists; The Freeway City; You *can* go home again; St. Alban's;
Family Picnic; A Day in the Country; Old Friends; Culture; Olympic
Village; A Meditation; Huntington Beach; House Mass; Kaaren; The
Art of Living; Santa Barbara; San Luis Obispo; The Coastal Paradise,
Harmony; San Simeon Castle; Plaskett Creek Campground; Trolls

Chapter 10: Spiritual Roots 77
Camaldolese Hermitage; Jack Daniels; Sunday; The Link

Chapter 11: The Expanding Spirit 83
Esalen; Stephen; N.L.P.; A Day at Esalen; Some N.L.P. Principles;
Hypnosis; Busing Dishes; Sea Otters; Yoga; Breathing; James Bupp;
Stephen Revisited; Community; Richard Price; Spin-Offs;
Sin at Esalen; Carmel; All Saints; Ordinary Prophets

Chapter 12: The Spirit of St. Francis 95
San Francisco; Pascal Redburn; Zen Center; Father Kappes;
The Episcopal Cathedral

Chapter 13: Connections in the Spirit 99
Incarnation Priory; Robert Hsi; Sausalito; Michael; John; St. Mary
the Virgin; June Singer; Linne; Ghost Busters; St. John's Parish;
Mariana; Departure; Fleur de Lys; John

Chapter 14: The Mountain Spirit 111
Taking 80 Home; Lake Tahoe; Reno

Chapter 15: Native American Spirit 115
Rolling Thunder; Geoffrey; The Sunrise Service; Mala Spotted Eagle;
Lemoille Canyon; Recreation

Chapter 16: The Persevering Spirit 121
Prayers and Music; Genesis Community; Salt Lake; The Bishop
of Salt Lake; High Desert; Zazen on the Desert; The Eldreds;
Sioux City;Forest City; Labor Day Weekend; Father Wiedrich;
DeKoven Revisited;Returning

Chapter 17: The Eastern Spirit 131
Toledo; Cleveland; Mysticism; York; Laura; The Jameses; The Jesuits;
Off the Road; Bethlehem; ESMA; Nockamixon; Temple Bells

Chapter 18: Brotherly Spirit 139
New Hope; Philadelphia; Sunday; Julie

BOOK TWO 145
THE SPIRIT OF THE ETERNAL CITY

Chapter 19: Kindred Spirits 147
TWA 260 and 840; Phyllis; 2:30AM/8:30AM; San Anselmo; My Room;
Living in Christ; Art; True God. True Man; Shopping; Liturgy;
Sister Joan; Relaxation; Asceticism; Digestion; The Vatican Museum;
St. Paul's; The Romanian; The Monk and the Poor; A.I.M.; Zen Buddism;
Lay Monks; Shopping; More Canon Law; Oblates; The Anglican Centre;
An Attempted Summary; Statements to Communities; Varia; Women;
The Last Supper; Departure

BOOK THREE 173
SPIRITUAL ROOTS

Chapter 20: Our Nashdom, Our Home 175
Heathrow; Nashdom Abbey; Depression; Sunday; The Guest Lounge;
The Confessor; Haircut; TWA; Interviews; Exercises and Sitting;
Margaret; The George and Lion; The Younger Ones; Wednesday Night
Prayer Group; Peter Lang; 10 Acorns; The Elders; The Retreat;
Incarnation; Leaving for Alton Abbey

Chapter 21: The English Spirit at Alton Abbey..............................187
The Party; The Sermon; Alton Abbey; The Church; Wivelrod;
The Retreat; St. Luke; Departure from Alton; Peter and Martin;
Sunday; Flight 155

BOOK FOUR 195
THE FAMILIAR SPIRIT

Chapter 22: The Spirit of Friendship 197
Philadelphia, USA; Bishop Dimmick, R.I.P.; Adjusting; MAC; Robert;
Holograms; Suppers; Bishop White; St. Mark's; Voting; The Possible
Society; The Wizard of Oz; Liturgy; The Child; Sunday

Chapter 23: The Reflective Spirit..205
The Last Night; Departure; Father Fox

Chapter 24: The Inner City Spirit..207
Newark Abbey; The George Washington Bridge; Peter and Griffin;
Orlando; Liturgy in the City; Dr. Holder; More Holograms

Chapter 25: The Spirit at Rest..213
Going West; All Saints; All Souls

Chapter 26: Hearthfire Spirit 215
Return; Hearthfire Lodge; The Election; Paul Solomon

Chapter 27: The Historical Spirit..219
Shenandoah Valley; Holy Ghost Abbey; Waterford; Brown and
Margaret; Trespasso; Frederick, Maryland

Chapter 28: Spirit of Liberty 225
  Kennedy Center; Watergate; Vietnam Memorial; Lindsay;
  Henry and Sally; Jean; Bill and Sally; Shalem Institute

Chapter 29: The Unsettling Spirit – A Time of Change and Growth 233
  Baltimore; The Hermit; Pendle Hill; New Directions

Chapter 30: Winding Down – Discerning the Spirit 241
  Winding Down; First Presbyterian Church; The Country Club
  Patriarch; The Last Night

Chapter 31: The Spirit – Life's Companion 247
  Summary

APPENDIX 251

Appendix 1 253
  Week of Review; January 23-27, 1984

Appendix 2 255
  Some Thoughts on the Position of Superior of the Community
  by Fr. Anthony; January 23, 1984

Appendix 3 257
  Excerpt from Confrater's Letter, Spring 1984

Appendix 4 258
  "On Sabbatical," reprinted from The Abbey Letter, Spring 1984

Appendix 5 260
  The Twelve Steps

Appendix 6 261
  Living the Rule of St. Benedict
  Paper given at a Benedictine Conference in New Harmony, Indiana 1984

Appendix 7..274
A Talk by Abbot Benedict to Senior Members of a Religious Community

Appendix 8..276
Sermon delivered at Church of St. Joseph the Evangelist
San Francisco, California; August 10, 1984

Appendix 9..280
Message of the Congress of Abbots to The Benedictine Communities, 1984

Appendix 10...282
Communal Process for Conflict Resolution

Appendix 11...284
Appreciation and Reflection
Delivered to Congress of Abbots 1988

Appendix 12...286
Text of Confraternity Letter; March 14, 1985

Appendix 13...289
"On Sabbatical," reprinted from The Abbey Letter, Easter 1985

Bibliography...293

INTRODUCTION

Life is a pilgrimage to God. It is also a pilgrimage with God. God is our traveling Companion. On our journey we come periodically into a sanctuary. One may think of this as the Church, or one's family and friends, or as the inner place of one's heart. The interplay of these two themes, the journey and the sanctuary, is our human way of understanding the mystery of life. To make the journey in peace and in union with the Lord of the Journey is the spiritual art.

As a Benedictine monk, and at the time of this writing, Abbot of St. Gregory's Abbey (a small monastery of the Episcopal Church just west of Three Rivers, Michigan), I was privileged to examine these basic themes during a sabbatical from Easter to Advent, 1984. These notes, tracings of the Spirit, are a comment on this seven-month journey. I apologize for any mistakes in names, places, and details which I cannot always verify. Christian faith colors these reflections, but at times they are just mine. Our common humanity may make these reflections of interest to others, whether of the same faith, or another, or even to some who have no faith-label for their life. My answer is that many people realize that they, too, are on a pilgrimage, and that the world itself in its movement toward the fulfillment of its purpose in creation, is experiencing a profound journey, full of excitement, dislocation, and violence. No doubt there are principles on this journey we can discover as guidelines. Perhaps this personal account will permit the reader to identify his or her own story with mine.

THE SABBATICAL IDEA

The idea of a sabbatical emerged in 1982 while I was pondering the requirement of the constitution of our monastery that an abbot submit his resignation at age sixty-five. For me, this would be in April, 1986. I broached the idea of a sabbatical to my community, to my advisers and friends, and found no strong disapproval, although many were simply too busy even to consider the possible worth of such a plan. This struck me as important. Do we all need time away from our regular work to give us perspective — and don't know it? Some with whom I discussed the plan found the idea of a sabbatical stimulating for their own reflections about life. Plus, the desire to escape is in all of us. Finally, for me it grew in meaning as the right event.

PURPOSE

My purpose in taking a sabbatical was three-fold: to allow my community some time without my leadership, since I had been their superior for more than 28 years; to allow myself some unpressured time; and to discern, if possible, some tracings of the Spirit for the future of this world.

ORGANIZATION OF NOTES

These notes have at least three levels. First, they contain organized materials, such as position papers for my community, or talks and retreats given along the way (see Appendix). Second, they contain a running account of the people and events I experienced. And third, because one is fascinated by the various meanings of such happenings, they contain reflections which I have indented. I also have supplied subject headings in case the reader may wish to return to a particular portion of these rambling accounts. This is something of the human way of making sense out of life. In the Bible, inspired though it be, we see the same process at work in the collection of documents, reports, stories, and reflections. As part of the organized materials which amplify this account (the first in outline form), is a statement I made to my community during our Week of Review which was held in January, 1984 (Appendix 1). Section I refers to the voluntary yielding of my Chapter rights during my sabbatical, so that the common life could proceed without the problem of an absent vote (each community is governed by the permanently committed persons called, collectively, the Chapter). Section II describes my two-fold purpose for the community and for myself. Section III expresses my intention to interview the brethren so that we might resolve any matters from the past which might mar our time apart. (In fact, I did not fulfill that last intention very well. Even a monastery can be a busy place, and time and leisure for shared reflections are not always easy to find.) Section IV is Fr. Anthony's statements on three monastic issues. Appendix 2 represents the position paper of our Prior, Fr. Anthony, in which he explained how he saw the basic situation of the Abbey, and how he proposed to handle things while he was in charge.

The next document is a copy of our Confrater's letter for Spring 1984 (Appendix 3). This letter is mailed several times a year to that larger part of our family known as the Confraternity. This group is composed of people who support the Abbey with special prayer intentions and the desire to live their life according to the Spirit of the Rule. Then follows my article from the spring issue of the Abbey Letter (Appendix 4). Next is a copy of the Twelve Steps used in Al-Anon (Appendix 5); followed by a paper entitled, "Living The Rule of St. Benedict," delivered at New Harmony, Indiana (Appendix 6); then a talk given to the seniors of a religious community (Appendix 7); a sermon given at St. John's Parish in San Francisco (Appendix 8); and a copy of the message from the Congress of Abbots (Appendix 9). These are followed by some reflections on communal conflict resolution (Appendix 10). Appendix 11 is a reflection and appreciation delivered at a later Congress of Abbots where I was aware of the feminine issues within the Church. At the conclusion of the sabbatical, I wrote two additional items: Appendix 12 is the Confrater's letter, and Appendix 13 is my article for the Abbey Letter.

PREPARATIONS

I had the work of slowly removing myself from the operation of the monastery.[1] The internal affairs were in the experienced hands of Fr. Anthony. Even so, he and my secretary had long lists of matters that might need my attention. For my personal correspondence ,we worked out a system whereby letters and gifts would be acknowledged; anything marked private would be forwarded to designated places. I also planned to phone at least once a week.

Finally, I sent out a limited mailing which included a picture of the van which friends had provided, along with a Jubilee card which summed up the significant dates of my life — birth, monastic profession, appointment as Prior, and subsequent blessing as the first Abbot of St. Gregory's Abbey. On paper, anyway, I had transferred my work to others. Now I had to squeeze myself into a "mobile cell."

PILGRIMAGE VAN

The small motor home, which I prefer to call a van because it sounds less pretentious, had a beginning odometer reading of 634 miles. After delivery to the local dealer in Battle Creek in February, I had put some three hundred plus miles on it in a shakedown process. So I began the sabbatical trip with a reading of 990 miles. The van, called a Phaser, is a unit manufactured by the Itasca Division of the Winnebago Corporation. Since its appearance on the market only a short time before, it had caught my eye as remarkably suitable for my purposes. The unit begins life in France as a small Renault truck with a four-cylinder diesel engine with turbo boost. The Winnebago people then add a thoroughly modern living section. If one is gadget-conscious, it is an example of "amazing grace" with hundreds of little systems that make up a very convenient (when functioning) traveling companion. If you are not into camping, or RVing (recreational vehicle living) you would be amused and impressed with what is available. Starting with the driver's seat, one has controls for all of the up-to-date systems one is accustomed to on a car: a very good AM/FM radio with cassette player, air conditioner, an individual day's mileage recorder, cruise control, and power steering. In addition, the motor home unit usually has two batteries (one of which operates many of the interior systems). Warning lights on the dash give important information on the functioning of all these systems. Behind the driver's section there are two seats which

---

[1]The Benedictine vocation in the Church (since the 6th Century) emphasizes a vowed life (Stability, Conversion, Obedience — which includes poverty and chastity) in Community, whose main work is the corporate offering of the Church's prayer and the Eucharist on a daily basis. Time is also provided for personal prayer, Scripture study, and personal spiritual exercises. Silence and a degree of separation from the busyness of the world do not exclude a ministry of hospitality to guests and retreat groups. If the monastery is small, the brothers or sisters (in the case of a convent) do much of the household work themselves. In larger houses there may be schools, parishes, publishing departments, or other extensive ministries. While offering occasional outside ministries, the communal life of prayer in the monastery is itself the main contribution Benedictines make to the Church and to the world.

make into a bed, a neatly designed Pullman-type bathroom (small, of course), a kitchenette with two propane-fueled burners, refrigerator, a sink, a wardrobe (not high enough to accommodate a monk's habit), and a rear dinette area which can convert into a bedroom. The van can store 16 gallons of water or be connected to city water. It has a furnace with an electronic ignition and temperature control. One handy feature is a monitor control panel which contains a digital clock (with an alarm to awaken you) and readings on the water and propane supply.

All in all, it is extremely well-designed and functional. But one does have to develop some mechanical ability. This is not my usual area of expertise, but I enjoy it if I have plenty of time to learn. And, of course, there is not enough storage space. I had it in several local shops, including the research and design department of Skyline in Elkhart, Indiana, whose president (a personal friend) and staff were most accommodating and generous. With the addition of a number of storage and convenience gadgets, it proved to be a delightful traveling companion, allowing me considerable freedom to move about and park where I chose. But it took me a month to discover how to make it all work.

DEPARTURE

In the last days before departure, which included the busy days of Holy Week and Easter, I merely threw items into the van. There was no time to pack neatly, although I will not agree, as some of my brethren charged, that the windows of the van were blocked with luggage.

I departed on Easter Tuesday, April 22, about noon. My first stops were local — obtaining traveler's checks, saying goodbye to various friends, one of whom, Dave, a Three Rivers gas station owner, had kept my previous "high top" camper functioning. That first motor home, the gift of my natural brother Bob, had been my introduction to the highway travel world. Now it was to be sold.

BOOK ONE

BECOMING FREE
IN THE SPIRIT

CHAPTER I

THE JOURNEY BEGINS:
THE MIDDLE AMERICA LOOP

McHENRY, ILLINOIS

I headed west, through Chicago and beyond, to a northern suburb, McHenry, where I knew the priest, Marion Mailey. I attended her evening Eucharist, gave a short homily to a small group, and had a leisurely supper with her. We shared news of mutual friends, the state of the Church, and world events. Thus began my personal research of what is going on in the world today.

> A person of faith sees life differently, looking at it in its relationship to the whole pattern of life and its source. And if that person happens to be a woman, she brings to that faith a special quality of feeling and respect for life. The Church is still getting used to this new ministry of the woman priest. I believe it is an enrichment and a blessing for the Church.

THE COMMUNITY OF ST. MARY

The next day, I was at the DeKoven Foundation in Racine, Wisconsin, a part of the Western Province of the Sisters of St. Mary. For about 18 years, I had been the Chaplain General to the three Provinces of this Order, the oldest in the Episcopal Church. At DeKoven, the small community has attempted a freer and more personal way of life, qualities now being explored generally in the Religious Life. The Divine Office[1] (the daily prayer of the

---

[1] The Divine Office (Opus Dei) refers to the official prayer of the Church in contrast to individual devotions. It is normally offered as worship in a parish church, a cathedral or a monastic choir — although it may also be said by an individual or small group. It is taken from an established service book as the *Book of Common Prayer* in the Episcopal Church. Monasteries and religious houses are able to offer a more extensive version of the Office. Such official prayer is found in all religions in one form or another. In previous times people were more accustomed to attending the Office in the church or in gathering together for a family version of such prayer. Our Lord himself was familiar with the regular prayer services of the synagogue or temple. In Chris,t the faithful now see the Office as a share in the dialogue between our Lord and His Father. The Early Church inherited this practice and added to the general use of the Psalter, New Testament readings, hymns, and Collects which reflect the unique role Christ has brought to the prayer of the Church. Down through the ages, the Church has added feasts from the lives of the saints or new insights into events of Christ's life. The names by which the various parts of the Office are designated, point to the time of day or night when they are offered. Hence, Lauds is prayed at daybreak, the Little Hours (Terce, Sext, None — coinciding with the third, sixth, and ninth hour of the sun's travel through the day), Vespers toward the end of daylight, and Compline at the end of the day.

Church) and the Eucharist, both from the current *Prayer Book* in the Episcopal Church, are offered daily. But the setting is simpler, combining silence and music, with an occasional experiment in dance. Some of the sisters also like to do folk dancing for recreation. They have a regular flow of outside people — clergy and laity — attending retreats, conferences, and classes, or receiving counseling. It is always stimulating to share their life and to try to help them discern the worth of their various experiments. Here is a valid attempt to renew the Church, to re-image it. Guests cannot help but pick up this new image. This is, of course, going on throughout the Church. I saw this in talking with the leader of the Midwest section of the Brotherhood of St. Andrew who was attending a retreat with his group. At DeKoven, I sensed the blend of traditional faith and practice with various elements of renewal movements: Cursillo, Faith Alive, Charismatic Movement, group therapy models, and different kinds of recovery programs (such as Alcoholics Anonymous). This mix, meeting more of our needs today, is slowly reshaping our way of living the Gospel.

Adaptation is a normal process in the Church. For instance, Scripture and traditional theology need constant interpretation so that today, people whose lives are rapidly changing can understand and apply their teaching. For example, some theologians and liturgists, as well as those concerned with social issues, see the power of language affecting how we speak about one another (sexism, minority issues, cultural prejudices), and also in how we speak about God. To refer to the Divine solely in masculine terms is to limit the breadth of qualities in the Creator of life, and to send an unbalanced message to human beings — who then may extend that unbalance into creation (pollution, exploitation, consumerism, etc.). I am fully aware of the issue of inclusive language, but I have not found an easy way to incorporate the concept into readable prose. Another example of adaptation touches what is known as the Anglo-Catholic interpretation of the Church. This is the position of those Anglicans who see their tradition as fully connected with the historical Church since the time of our Lord. Now, we are examining that Catholic interpretation to discover what is permanent and what can be adapted. Sacraments, Creeds, and the hierarchy of the Church are permanent. Scripture is still the inspired Word of God. But today groups studying Scripture in a systematic way and using it in personal devotions probably are absorbing the teaching of the Bible more effectively than through sermons. More than instruction, people may need a strong sense of God's Word within them, empowering them to get through their very complex lives. All Christian denominations, and other religions too, are working at this principle of adaptation. Part of the direction of adaptation is in the interest of helping us live with people of faith everywhere in the world.

Christian communities, parishes, groups of faithful, wherever the test of old and new Christian ways can be made, are extremely important for the sake of shaping the life of the future Church. Certain fundamentalist groups resist this work of adaptation.

In Milwaukee I visited the mother house of the Western Province of St. Mary. Here is another aspect of the Church's life. The main house has been sold and the members are moving in various directions — some into a small house nearby, some into a Church-oriented retirement facility, and still others into a modern version of the life of the hermit. With our attention being drawn toward the process and values in our personal death and dying, and toward hospice work, as a natural result of the lengthening of life, our awareness of the normality of death as part of life has deepened.

We need to learn how to go through the death process, whether personal or institutional, without guilt or a sense of failure. Why some groups do in fact die and others learn how to adapt toward new life is not clear. Perhaps there are principles of adaptation to be learned. In any event we often notice that the ending of a way of life is really the ending of a particular way of ministry. The Church should be the supreme guide through such changes in ministry, painful as they are.

It will be interesting to see what kind of new life and ministry will emerge from the long years of fidelity these sisters have practiced. There can be no doubt that the Lord will honor their commitment.

LEFT BRAIN

On my way toward western Wisconsin, I was amused to discover how often I stopped at discount stores. There was always just that one more item that I needed to make the van more functional. This was fun, but I detected a certain compulsive itch to exercise control over all of the systems which made up my rolling traveling companion's "personality." I realized that I had numerous lists: shopping, repairs, letters, bookkeeping, my diary, etc., all designed to help me keep abreast of the many details involved in such traveling. Some commentators call this the work of the left brain, the organizing and controlling part our mind. Up to a point, it is necessary.

But we may be facing the impasse of an exaggeration of such left brain control in our Western culture. The truth is that anxiety and anger are not far beneath the surface when our control is frustrated.

STATE PARKS

I stayed in my first state park, Blue Mounds, Wisconsin. Here, in my gratitude to those who have made such accommodations available, I propose the following modest instruction for RV travelers: For varying rates, some as low as $2.00 (if one is a senior citizen and not using electricity) one can have a clean parking site with access to fresh water, often a hot shower in a heated washroom, garbage disposal cans, all surrounded by the natural beauty of woods and lakes. In such a place, one may take time over bookkeeping, say the Divine Office (the official Prayer of the Church, normally offered in choir or the parish church), putter with the needs of the van, and tidy up things that have been left on the floor or thrown on the second seat. Then, after a simple supper, one can take a walk and finally get ready for bed, holding a cup of hot cocoa and watching the sun set. Sometimes deer will enhance the picture. Remember to keep the flashlight handy, put your glasses out of the way so that you don't roll on them during the night, open the window a crack, try to resist adding one more item to one of the lists, and go to bed. In the morning, heat up the coffee (which one can do practically while still in bed) and sip that first delicious cup of hot, black "grace," and ponder the coming day. Then, after The Morning Prayer Office, one is ready to move. Check the departure list, which can be lengthy, especially if you have been hooked up to electricity or water. Look under the hood at the brake fluid level and walk around the unit and see that you are clear to move. Look inside, too, to see that everything is well-anchored. A rolling home is an awkward thing to manage when you are locked into the driver's seat and things are spilling out of closets or off shelves. Also, see that your snack tray is replenished, that you have some money in your wallet, there is fresh water in your plastic containers, letters to be mailed are on the dash, and addresses you might need for the day are handy. Finally, return the daily trip odometer to zero. It does become routine, a comforting pattern for the journey.

> But watch your disposition if something doesn't go right. Then you must work on your attitude. Try to be at peace, even if you are waiting for a tow truck, as I did one day.

EUCHARIST

Sometimes, when I have found myself in one of these parks and at some distance from friends or a town with an Episcopal church, I have offered the Eucharist very simply in the van. (Normally one is supposed to have at least one other person.) Some bread and wine, the *Prayer Book*, and a heart full of gratitude make a good celebration.

One morning when I awoke the weather had slipped back into early spring, down to 45 degrees. I hurriedly got out the owner's manual, read the instructions on the furnace operation, put these into practice — and it didn't work. However, as my brethren will attest, I am not famous for my ability with mechanical details. A second time through the instructions revealed my mistake, and, Alleluia, I had heat. Marvelous!

NEW MELLERAY

After breakfast in Blue Mounds State Park and some tidying up in the van, I was on my way. By mid-afternoon I had arrived at New Melleray Abbey, southwest of Dubuque, Iowa, and was warmly received by the previous abbot, David, who was acting guestmaster. Although they were remodeling the guest department, he gave me a room. (Monasteries are always remodeling something.) The church, too, had been recently redesigned by Frank Kacmarcik, a well-known liturgical designer. It is serene, even severe, allowing the stone structure of the building to stand out. I was invited by the present abbot, Brendan, to sit beside him in choir, with the use of one of their traditional cowls, a long, flowing garment that covers the habit or work clothes.

At supper in the guest dining room I sat with one of the monks, Frederick (who is undergoing cancer therapy), with his sister Martha, and the abbot. The talk ranged over various male/female issues of the day, therapy, Jungian ideas, and politics. Then we attended a lecture by a canon lawyer, Ladislov Orsy, S.J., a Hungarian, and a long-standing teacher at Catholic University in Washington, D.C. He was commenting on the new code of canon law for the Roman Catholic Church. He observed these points:

> Religious (monks and nuns) have their charisma from the Spirit, not the law; but as loyal sons and daughters of the Church, they try to live under the law; still, no reform has ever come from law however necessary it is for the general life of the Church. Vatican II renewal is highly evident in the new code (there is more freedom and autonomy given to local authority). There are some striking phrases such as, "All Christians..."; "...all people of faith." The next code cannot be delayed another sixty years (the Church is changing too fast); the practice of obedience is changing because of the higher level of education of those coming to maturity in the Church.

Some may ask why Anglicans should pay attention to this new Roman code. My answer is that the Roman Church is the strongest Christian group in the West, and their decisions warrant our serious study. Besides, one day we will be back together — probably with a considerable change of structure.

At Compline that night, a guitar accompaniment to the Psalms in a half-lit church made a very restful closing of the day. Sleep that night was not long enough. I rose for the Vigil at 3:30 AM. This Vigil, or Matins, begins the monastic day of prayer. The various times of prayer, called an Office or Little Hours, follow intermittently throughout the day. In between are periods of personal prayer and work. This Vigil was a peaceful recitation of the Psalms and readings, all flavored with Easter themes. Afterwards, I had some coffee and did my own lectio (a personal and prayerful reading of Scripture). After the Office of Lauds we had the Eucharist. I was not invited to join the brethren in Communion. This is the painful result of our division in the Church which I accept as my part in the penance needed to heal the brokenness. But after another session with the canonist, there was a small group discussion in which they showed me great respect and trust by including me in sensitive and honest talk about departures from the monastery, formation problems today, the place of psychology in the monastery, and the use of group processes in communal life. Here the openness was like Communion of a different sort. After lunch I had a talk with the previous abbot, David, who had preceded me at an alcoholic treatment center which we both attended. Each of us had been there on behalf of a member from our respective communities. We compared notes. How startling it was to deal with an alcoholic problem in a Religious community; how embarrassing it was to discover one's own blindness (and in my case, my survival pattern, enabling me to live from childhood on with an alcoholic father); and yet, how profoundly impressive was the recovery regime with its emphasis on powerlessness, turning one's life over to God, honesty and the daily application of reality principles. We compared the AA program (Appendix 5) with St. Benedict's Rule, Chapter 7: On Humility. Then we speculated on how this might become better understood in community.

> For all of us, there is always the usual resistance and denial until the crisis of death makes us look honestly at our life. It is still hard to convince the average Christian that death and resurrection are the underlying realities of daily life.

David and I also talked quite frankly about communal life: how to deal honestly and lovingly with the weaknesses of the brethren, What are the best kinds of group processes? Can outside facilitators help? Is all of this an American phenomenon? David acknowledged that European Cistercians conclude that Americans are immature and sentimental, yet he felt that they, too, would come to some of these same ways of promoting conversion and spiritual growth. But how to promote this when individuals today are much more independent, sometimes blindly so, even aggressively defensive? It was enlightening and comforting for me to be able to compare notes with people in the same monastic tradition who are grappling with today's problems. I pondered all of this as I drove westward.

WINNEBAGO

It was now early May, and I was in Forest City, Iowa, where the Winnebago Corporation has its main office and factory. Even though I had no reservation for service, Roger Lunning, the man in charge of Customer Service, was cheerfully accommodating. I only wanted some minor adjustments made — a few more storage racks installed and an awning added. This was my fifth shop and by now I had come to appreciate that each shop had special abilities and limitations. The farther away from the manufacturer one gets, the less likely it is that one will find a complete service shop — especially in a situation where the engine and chassis are from another country. Frustration can easily arise. This raises the question: how to remain calm when one is faced with one's dependence on many machines and gadgets, all requiring constant maintenance? I was learning to come to peace of mind before entering a shop.

and, or

Today, if you do not know how to maintain this state of peace, you have a constant battle of fearful negotiation. So much of life seems to be win/lose. This robs us of peace. In many ways the van was one of my spiritual directors, revealing my inner condition. (This is something of a Zen idea.) If one can use such personal discovery as an invitation to practice peace, one is rewarded with many opportunities for spiritual growth. The modern world can be a good school of Christian growth.

I stopped at the corporate headquarters of the company and thanked various people who, at that level, had helped me acquire this vehicle. It is fun for me to meet such people, trying not to take them beyond the limits of their corporate responsibilities. They are usually willing to do all that they can. If you work with people in a modern corporation in a courteous way, they respond with courtesy and helpfulness, telling you when they can go no further. If you approach the corporation as an "enemy," it can be stubborn and impersonal. Charity, as usual, can do wonders.

A SMALL PARISH

After leaving Forest City, I traveled south to Perry, Iowa (St. Martin's), where I knew the priest, Willa Mikowski, and her husband, Anselm. I had met them previously in a parish in Michigan where I had ministered on occasion. Here again was a woman priest, doing a splendid job, getting the life of the parish onto a smoothly running basis, as well as opening up new levels of pastoral ministry. Of course, Willa had previous professional experience in a medical career. But her faith and pastoral skill promise many blessings for that parish. She described her recent Holy Week and Easter Services as a true participation in the Lord's Passion, alternating between the liturgy and visits to the hospital to see her husband, who for a time was in critical physical condition.

> This is an important part of Christian faith: to see the connection between life and liturgy. When we view the passion of the world, we see constant opportunity to share in Christ's redeeming life. As St. Paul notes: "We who live are constantly being delivered over to death for Jesus' sake, that the life of Jesus also may be manifested in our mortal flesh." (2 Cor. 4:11)

I visited several parishioners, and received many gifts and kindnesses from them (a batch of home-baked cookies is a delightful treat on the road). These people are the backbone of the Church. Their theology may not always be "correct," nor their attendance at church consistent, but their faith and steady support of the local Church make them Christian heroes. When I am preaching and see their expectant faces, I am filled with the desire to tell them that they truly are the Lord's beloved. When the faithful are bathed in God's love, they respond most gratefully. I also met with the Perry ministerial group and was impressed with how much we are sharing the same faith. There are, of course, denominational problems on the organizational level, but God's people are definitely being drawn together in their faith experience.

In Perry, I was able to finish my paper, "Living The Rule of St. Benedict," which I was to deliver in New Harmony, Indiana, at a conference on the Benedictine Life. Doing this paper (Appendix 6) gave me the opportunity to review my 36 years in the monastery.

> Perspective provides the meaning to our ordinary zig-zag path through life, clarifying the evidence of God's guidance, strengthening our trust and commitment.

ANNIVERSARY

I left Perry on May 9th, the 33rd anniversary of the dedication of our abbey church at St. Gregory's, and the 15th anniversary of my abbatial blessing. While driving, my thoughts were meditations: painful ones as I remembered mistakes I had made, grateful ones for God's gracious love, appreciative ones for my brethren who probably think that they never fulfill my expectations. Leaders often stay ahead of their communities. I made new resolutions to appreciate the brethren. Such reflections are part of the gift of a time of sabbatical.

CRISIS OF FAITH

In Des Moines, I talked with a friend whose life had come apart completely — his marriage, his business, his health. But what a miracle that he is still able to keep the Lord at the center of his struggle.

> What would our life be like without God's gift of faith? And it is the local parish which feeds that faith as one makes life's journey, unpredictable in glory and sorrow as it is.

In Davenport, the cruise control on the van was repaired. It was assuring to see this repair done in a well-organized shop with experienced mechanics. A previous RV shop had fiddled with it, failed to repair it, and charged me for the time spent. I am never quite sure how to be firm with people who fail in their responsibility. It is difficult for me to combine such firmness and inner peace; perhaps this is one result of the uncertainties of growing up with an alcoholic father.

A CATHEDRAL

My next stop was Peoria, Illinois, where I appeared, unannounced, at the cathedral. Bishop Parsons and Dean George were most gracious and lent me two typists to do the New Harmony paper in final form. (I have learned that one can never really finish a paper. There are always new thoughts and new interpretations of old ones.) Their copier effortlessly turned out 36 copies.

These people on the hierarchical level are another part of the Lord's Body who constantly serve. The strain on them can be heavy. And the rewards? There is not enough return, financial or in appreciation, to pay people for such service and the burden they carry. Why aren't we more grateful? I encourage you to drop an appreciative note soon to your bishop and priest and their staffs.

SPRING LITURGY

One morning after leaving Peoria, I found myself driving through the countryside of central Illinois, alongside the freshly plowed fields. The birds were singing, the diesel engine was humming, farmers were driving their tractors, and the sun was shining. Even the country roads knew what was most important: they went around the farmers' fields — even if they had to so somewhat abruptly. Here was a liturgy of praise and peace. And it was not organized, it was just happening in some kind of annual rhythm of the earth with man as priest of creation. By evening I was in Walnut Point State Park, Indiana, on a site near the lake, awning stretched out, chair in the shade, watching the birds. What could be more peaceful?

CHAPTER 2

GOING DEEPER WITH THE SPIRIT—
LISTENING TO CHANGE

DEPRESSION

Why did a quiet mood of depression come upon me? Was it an unanswered puzzle about an oil leak which so far had not been corrected? Was it the natural let-down after some three weeks away from my monastic brethren and routine? Was it the lack of my usual responsibilities or role as abbot? We often understand ourselves only in our work. At such down times we usually focus our attention on small annoyances, or the body claims undue attention. I reminded myself of my intention to be at peace, but the mood was heavier than the intention. I drifted off in a nap. I awakened to the same mood. But I made supper, said the Office, listened to some music, and did my day's paperwork. Routine is often the best thing we can do in such circumstances. It is a small act of faith in the order of things before the mysterious forces within and around us which defy understanding or control. The monastic discipline, or the routine of any persevering person, is a valuable stabilizing function in life. After reading some pages in *Blue Highways*, enjoying the travels and reflections of another wandering philosopher, William Least Heat Moon, I went to sleep.

A SUNDAY

Rain in the night reminded me of being stuck on another occasion, so I moved the van. I had my breakfast of an orange and a cup of coffee, and said the Morning Office. It was Sunday, so I decided to worship with some fellow Christians. Sure enough, on driving to town I located the local Christian Church. No particular denomination. I began to appreciate what most laypersons go through. How can I sit in the back and not be noticed? Why don't they make those teenagers ahead of me behave? Is that man over there asleep or meditating? Look at her, she seems so self-righteous. The hymns were old fashioned, the prayers although familiar, were dominated by the minister. The sermon was professional, perhaps for having been preached before. It was Mother's Day, so occasionally "she" was brought in. Then there was a typical Protestant Communion Service with the Scripture reading and the passing of the grape juice in small cups. Finally, the offering and some closing prayers. I had the feeling that the people were not much involved, but how does one measure the hidden work of grace? Even so, I had been with God's people, and we had worshiped Him as best we could.

NEW HARMONY, INDIANA

By evening I was in New Harmony, Indiana, the small southern town on the Wabash River which had seen two remarkable Utopian communities more than 150 years ago. First, there was the George Rapp group, Lutherans from Pennsylvania, who with typical German efficiency turned a frontier village into a highly organized farming and industrial town. Their skill in crafts and communal organization reminded one of the Quaker and Mennonite traditions. They were replaced by Robert Owen, an English industrialist and idealist who brought in a new group of people: educators, scientists, humanists. Jefferson would have been pleased. But for all their idealism, talent, and determination, neither of these groups could withstand the forces of mass production, the inevitable goal of industrialism. These Utopians attempted to keep man superior to the machine. They failed. And we continue to fail. Now, in Alvin Toffler's phrase, the "third wave" is upon us, and future shock intensifies.

> The agricultural and industrial revolutions (the first and second waves) are struggling with old principles and tools, to face the new problems of a new age — an age of instant information and unexpected intimacy, forcing people of diverse values and cultures up against one another.

A living descendant of the Robert Owen's family, Kenneth Dale Owen, and his wife, Jane Blaffer, and the state of Indiana, plus various foundations and people of vision, have taken up the goal of restoring New Harmony. They seek to make of the town a living museum, not only of the past, but of the future, too. Philip Johnson's roofless church, Richard Meier's high-tech Visitors' Center, and Evans Woollen's Inn and Conference Center make New Harmony an extraordinary interplay of the old and the new. Visitors, craftsmen, artists, and writers gather in New Harmony to enjoy the ambience of yesterday and to dream new dreams for tomorrow. It is a place, a holy place (I cannot avoid the phrase) of richness, showing us that America has its own baroque quality of life.

The Canterbury Trust in America, located in Washington, D.C., has as its purpose the welfare of Canterbury Cathedral in England — its life, buildings, and meaning as a symbolic center for all Anglicans and people of many faiths. They have sponsored several conferences on the Benedictine life because the Cathedral was established and served as a monastic and ecclesiastical See by Benedictine monks. It was the life of these monks, lived in cathedral monasteries, that infused the Benedictine spirit into the Anglican Communion. *The Prayer Book*, the standard book of services and prayers used by all Anglicans, reflects the monastic emphasis on the Office (Morning and Evening Prayer) and the Eucharist. The conference in New Harmony from May 13 to 19 was a continuation of the "Benedictine Experience," as some recent conferences at Canterbury have been called.

Samuel E. Belk, Milo Coerper, Elizabeth Swenson, and their staff, came to New Harmony to coordinate the talents of invited speakers and those attending the conferences. There were monks, nuns, and people knowledgeable of the Benedictine way of life, mingling, praying, working, and studying. Mrs. Jane Owen acted as a co-sponsor. Her charm, generous hospitality, and deep spiritual insight made her a special presence of rare faith and wit. Her feeling for history, art, various aspects of the world's cultures, individual people, and for the essential spiritual quality of creation make her a worthy patron of Christian and Benedictine life.

> A person of firm faith is a special witness in a deeply troubled and complex world.

The Rev. James Daughtry of Washington, D.C. and his able assistant, Fr. David Clark, provided the daily services of prayer and the Eucharist, a central quality of Benedictine life. Br. Andrew of St. Gregory's and I had papers to read. The day was apportioned like a monastic horarium: time for prayer, study, lectures, manual work, meditation, and recreation. The silence after Compline may not have been strictly practiced, but the monastic aura flavored the whole time together.

> If indeed we are on the edge of another dark age, a darkness that may be deceptively well lit with intense excitement, even violence, then the life of faith which St. Benedict organized in small communities of prayer has a new chapter to be lived.

Unfortunately, I had to leave the conference before it was over. But it gave me a hint of the genuine widespread interest in the Benedictine way of life.

On a beautiful May morning, I left New Harmony early and effortlessly drove the van for a 560 mile trip, mostly on freeways. I learned how to work the tape player. Listening to Samuel Barber's "Adagio for Strings" (while moving along a freeway on cruise control) on a sunny day in spring must be one of the loveliest gifts of our modern culture. Let's appreciate the good things of our time.

CHAPTER 3

THE SPIRIT—EAST AND WEST

OSAGE MONASTERY

I arrived at the Osage Monastery west of Tulsa, and was given a place to park the van. Again, I had not told them the exact day I would be arriving, but they were gracious in the extreme. Sister Pascaline, the sister in charge, was away at the time, but the others, including Jim Connor, their resident priest and a Cistercian, all made me welcome. This monastery is largely staffed by Benedictine Sisters from St. Louis, responding to Vatican II's encouragement to explore East/West religious dialogue. Osage Monastery, although quite new, has already received visits from Fr. Bede Griffiths (a Benedictine who has spent more than 25 years in India), from Buddhist monks, and from others interested in such exchange. This monastery is a monastic ashram (a kind of spiritual village) which is open to people of all religions. Some of the community have spent time in India and themselves hosted many from India.

> Why is it necessary for us to study Eastern religions? This is an honest and serious question. One answer seems to be that, through the Easterners' highly developed and ancient spiritual techniques, they have something to teach us Westerners: a way of reintroducing us to our own mystical tradition. This has been largely dormant in the West in the last few centuries.

Then there is the current world situation. As East and West meet politically and economically, we need to know one another in our faith experiences. Even so, we can be patronizing about other faiths. We believe that Christianity is the complete revelation of God. But do we fully understand that revelation? Isn't it possible that God has shared that revelation of Himself with other peoples? An Eastern inner experience of the Spirit and a Western Incarnational theology may be parts of the same whole truth. Some commentators like to think of the Western emphasis on Christ the Word as an aspect of revelation particularly suited to our Western minds, attuned as they are to the material and its organization. Perhaps the Eastern emphasis on Spirit, pursued beyond the material and its organization, beyond concepts or words, is part of the manifestation of God we have not fully appreciated. Now we have the chance to enrich our experience and our theology of God through prayerful and respectful acquaintance with Eastern tradition.

Osage Monastery, a name that honors its American Indian neighbors, blends Eastern ashram living with the Western monastic tradition. The emphasis is on prayer and simplicity, with freedom for solitude within communal life. I was to meet something of the same combination among the Camaldolese in California. The Osage Monastery is open to visitors of all religions. The name in its logo form, O + M, "... represents and forms the sacred Eastern word for the Ultimate; the Manifested One as well as the Unmanifested Mystery beyond creation" (their brochure). There is a common house and some small hermitages for the use of the community and guests.

The Divine Office of the community has elements of both East and West. It was quite easy to pray in this way if one is ready to use times of silence for simple awareness of God's presence. Compline, for instance, was simply a short text in honor of St. Mary with a time of meditation.

Those who do not wish to observe complete silence can join the community at meals where the talk is a lively exchange about ordinary events — the dogs, neighbors, weather, little human stories. It is always a hallmark of true spirituality that it fosters true human living. At one Eucharist, Fr. Conner asked me to give the homily. Communion was always offered. On Sr. Pascaline's return, we had a good talk. She gave me good suggestions on persons and places where the East/West work is occurring. I already knew some of them. Bede Griffiths had visited St. Gregory's. I had met and enjoyed Abbot Thomas Keating (another Cistercian) at a conference of the American Benedictine abbots. I knew Fr. Panikkar from an East/West conference in Vina, California, and had read Merton's Asian Journal.

One of my reflections:

> Hindu and Buddhist ideas probably will appear odd to us in the West as long as we remain intensely involved in the build-up of the industrial revolution (interesting how the word "revolution" need not always connote violent change). As we move beyond an industrial way of life, we will regain more appreciation for leisure and spiritual growth. Even now, are we not seeing a recovery of the contemplative life? Moving through the decline of intense industrialization into the information and service revolution, we may find that this East/West blend is a more natural milieu for spirituality as a normal part of culture. Each person could be taught to explore the indwelling presence of God through silence and meditation. Then a personal and inner experience of God would strengthen ordinary life, protecting it from a mindless, collective, herd-like group life.

SAINT WILLIAM LAUD PARISH

My next stop about 90 miles east of Dallas, Texas, was in St. William Laud parish in Pittsburgh. Fr. Blankenship, an old friend, was the priest. He had generously supported my sabbatical pilgrimage and I wanted to repay him in some way. I arrived in time to preach on a Sunday and meet his people. On the following Tuesday, I gave a Quiet Day (a time set aside in the parish for spiritual talks and private reflection) for local clergy and laity. I realized that I get enthusiastic about sharing God's love, and this communicates to people. They are grateful. But I admit I was not ready to bring my recent experience from Osage into any kind of connection with parish life. It may take time, and the present culture will no doubt have to undergo more change. I had some marvelous days with Fr. Blankenship, who is a good cook and a great pastor. His people respond to his love. Saying the Office regularly with him, eating his good cooking, listening to his stories, hearing him play the piano, doing a Quiet Day for people in the region, showed me the pleasant side of Christianity. Father B. is what many in the Anglican tradition would call "a good Catholic priest."

> His loving heart warms his sense of discipline and his rather strict teaching. How does this fit with my intuition regarding continued changes coming in the Church? I believe that Catholic truth, in the fullest form, does fit with universal truth. It is not always easy to see how it is to be applied to contemporary problems. For example, it is not easy to establish a Catholic position in regard to the extraordinary new areas opening up in medicine and biology. It often comes back to the priest's ability to love his people in their struggle in uncharted waters.

Fr. B. is a person who has done this for many decades. The warm appreciation of his people shows that.

THE WORLD

After too short a time with Fr. B., I drove into Dallas/Fort Worth to give the van its 3,750 mile check-up. I was quickly brought back to the world of negotiation. A verbal agreement over the phone with the service manager of a large dealership proved to be unreliable. He couldn't take me that day. I stayed in a nearby motel for too much money. Too much, that is, compared with my usual state park fees. I did enjoy a good shower and some TV, but the traffic and the tension were not pleasant.

It turned out that I could not be accommodated on the next day either. My peace was being tested. On my way to the outskirts of town, I spied a wooded lot just off the busy avenue. I drove in and tested it with my "feelings" barometer which gave me general clearance. So I stayed there that night. I have to admit that occasionally I had feelings of anxiety, with stories of what happens in large cities looming up in my imagination. But I also saw several firsts: a scissor-tailed fly catcher, a roadrunner, and a lizard. My Scottish ancestry would have approved of the price — even if some of my friends would have disagreed with my judgment. Anyway, the service manager eventually did fit me in. There were no major problems.

NORTHWEST TEXAS

By noon I was on my way westward, climbing into the high desert country. As I passed through Amarillo I remembered my time there in the army some 40 years before. Then we used to say that there was nothing between Amarillo and the North Pole but a barbed wire fence — and even that had lost its barbs. Of course, that was coming out of the minds of unappreciative GI's. Even so, it was in that olive-drab world that I first turned inward and discovered my inclination for prayer. The Amarillo of the 1980s was a modern, freeway-dissected, shopping-center, high-rise-bank, urban-suburban complex. Only in the back streets could one see the small, wooden, dusty cottages of yesterday.

Moving on westward, with only a short stop at a K-Mart, I again had the pleasure of listening to music — this time Bach — as I drove through the desert plateau. My altimeter seemed to lag but it was over 3,000 feet. While having a snack at a rest stop, I saw a Bullock's oriole, more scissor-tailed flycatchers, and other small birds that defied identification. I am still at that stage in bird watching where I panic once I suspect that something is a sparrow or a warbler. And then you learn that in the fall there is a category known as confusing warblers — well.

COPPER BREAKS AND SANTA ROSA

That night I stayed in a wonderful state park known as Copper Breaks. It is situated in a low canyon of rock outcroppings which the Indians used as a camp. I enjoyed my mobile home with all of its conveniences, allowing me to look out the window on the natural countryside, or providing an instant home after a walk. Here in the West, a late afternoon walk often favored one with the quiet magic of a soft sunset. How calming were the vast stretches of land and sky, perfumed with the smell of pine and sage.

The next day I drove on to Santa Rosa, New Mexico. North of town some seven miles there is a man-made lake developed by damming the Pecos River. The bare hillsides were dotted with Juniper and Piñon pine. I couldn't help remembering the problem some Indians have with the government in its pine-clearing policy in parts of the West (see Rolling Thunder section, p. 115). The next morning, Sunday, I had the quiet joy of saying Mass on some rocks amidst the junipers. Birds provided the choir, the sunrise was the reredos. My mystical bent (I'm half Irish), the memory of the Indians, the sense of the earth and prehistory — all moved me to a deep feeling of kinship with the Lord of Creation. Perhaps it is because I was born in Denver that I have a deep response to the West, its space, its quiet, its peace. The mystery of the Divine is all around. No wonder so many of the Lord's prophets were trained in the desert.

CHAPTER 4

THE CHARISMATIC SPIRIT

PECOS BENEDICTINE MONASTERY

That Sunday afternoon, after climbing up to 7,000 feet (and the four cylinder diesel engine did labor at higher altitudes), I arrived at the Benedictine Monastery of Pecos, near Santa Fe. Again, the warm welcome. What a blessing it is to belong to the Benedictine family! Anywhere in the world, I always receive a friendly reception. St. Benedict has his own, quiet, ecumenical movement. I remember some years ago on my way home from Rome, my stop at Montserrat, a very old Benedictine monastery in the Catalan district of Spain. As soon as I conveyed that I was an Anglican and a Benedictine they graciously received me. I was moved when, sitting in the front guest row of the Basilica during Mass, the kiss of peace from the community came to me. It went no further in the congregation as that it was not a general practice at the time.

The Pecos community is out-and-out charismatic. To the initiated this means speaking in tongues, wordless humming, being baptized in the Spirit and other practices far outside the usual middle-class experience of most of us. This is only a superficial view. The leadership of the Charismatic Movement has a deep theology of the Spirit and a profound commitment to the Lord. I have been involved with the Charismatic Movement for many years, being invited to confer with leaders as a kind of consultant. They respect my experience as a religious leader with a long tradition, and I respect their genuine faith and love. So, I am always at home with them.

At Pecos I met a friendly community of about 30 people. I enjoyed their way of prayer, which is a combination of psalms, hymns, guitar accompaniment, silence, prophecy, free prayer, and a long exchange of the kiss of peace. Communion was freely offered. In this atmosphere one can experience a very warm and healing love. The Charismatic Movement has brought theology and the experience of the heart together within the traditional structures of Western Christianity.

WHERE ARE THOSE SHIRTS?

In the midst of my stay at Pecos, I became aware that I couldn't locate one piece of my luggage, the shirt bag. Suddenly I was caught in one of my compulsions. Where were they? I made several trips to the van which was parked outside my guest room. I inspected and reinspected my luggage. I thought. I tried to remember. I tried to forget. Gradually it became clear that I had left it at Fr. B.'s rectory in Texas. A phone call verified this. He promised to forward it to my California stop. Then, the compulsion left and I was free to attend to my visit at Pecos. I had a vivid mental flashback. Many years ago while playfully displaying some toy rings I had taken to a convent, I passed them around for the sisters to laugh at. They all came back except the one that said, "LOVE." For quite a while, this upset me. It took me a long time to see the joke on myself. I still get caught up in such silly annoyances. As a person committed to poverty, I can get very attached to certain things in my life. But I also have the sense that these compulsions tend to die down (unless they are very deep) as a person gives himself to the adoration of God. I think of compulsions and neuroses as little backwater streams of the larger river of Love. The more we love, the more we are healed.

DIET

I took advantage of the serious nature with which this community approaches nutrition to get some information on my own diet. I am not inclined to cook complicated meals on a two burner stove with unrefrigerated ingredients. I don't care that much for food, its preparation, or the cleaning up afterwards, so I tend to look for easy menus. Of course, Americans on the move have access to many snack foods. But we all know that most of them are hazardous to our heath, if not to our pocketbook.

So I began to compile my list: wheat germ and shredded wheat (even for snacks). The sisters at DeKoven had given me three large buckets of granola. Soy beans, nuts, peanut butter, and cheese all provide protein. Dried fruit is good, but it "loosens you up" which can be a problem when traveling. Watch out for saturated oils, salt, fat, sugar. Those Snickers™ bars under my driver's seat may have to go — once I've eaten the last one, of course. This diet lasts only a few days before I'm invited to a friend's house for a balanced meal, or I stop at a restaurant. But it does raise the question: in our modern way of life, what is the best diet for us?

AQUARIAN CONSPIRACY

One of the books I have been enjoying is *The Aquarian Conspiracy* by Marilyn Ferguson. It is a masterful gathering of reports on breakthrough discoveries by artists, writers, and scientists, some of them Nobel prize winners. The various discoveries of these brilliant people point out that the human race is indeed evolving, and faster than ever before. Sometimes this amounts to recovering ancient wisdom that primitive people had possessed quite naturally. Extrasensory perception is one example. Sometimes it amounts to finding whole new gifts of our humanity. Such a find is the deeper understanding about the nature of human body cells. Apart from their own marvelous ability to develop complex organisms from simple ones (as in the birth and growth of a human person) these cells seem to be open to our choices. Whether we love or hate, our cells try to obey. I admit that reading such books and speculating on the implications of our life profoundly stimulates me. I see the possibility of choosing and creating new ways of sharing the gift of life, God's greatest gift to us. Now God seems to be allowing us to shape the very gift itself.

Can one increase the speed…and depth of human growth? *Aquarian Conspiracy* would say, "Yes." Some obvious ways are the following: Take advantage of wisdom from the past. An example from the Rule of St. Benedict is "seek peace and pursue it." Know your personal history and seek out opportunities for human growth. At one time in history, the wheel on which this van rides so marvelously was a breakthrough invention. This history also includes gifted people who knew how to penetrate the mystery of life. Along with Christ as the supreme example of one who reveals the mystery of life, Who is the Mystery in Himself, we can also think of other great religious leaders. But *Aquarian Conspiracy* would have us see ourselves as persons of great potential vision.

> What is the secret? To be aware that the infinite source of life is within us. Then, in that awareness, learn to focus on the simple things of life. Learn to pay attention to what you are doing at this moment. Do it. Know that in the doing you are connecting with the Indwelling God. We all do this often without conscious awareness of the principle. But we often get blurred and out of focus because we don't consciously practice the principle. By focusing our ordinary attention, connected with the Indwelling Divine, on some simple object or act, we can be lifted into a new and deeper awareness. This is a growth step, a new kind of consciousness, a larger experience of life, a transformation and appreciation of a center within, which is beyond our little, ordinary self. It doesn't matter whether what we focus on is an ordinary object like a cup of coffee or an extraordinary event like a sunset. It can be a pleasant experience or a deeply painful one. The point is to form the triangle between our ordinary self, the immediate object of our experience, and the Divine. God does the rest.

But do we need to go through all of this intricate thought process? Can't we simply live and do the best we can? Yes, but then we should not wonder if after many years there seems to be no real growth in our enjoyment of life. How often have I "rediscovered" what I really knew because I keep losing it through merely thinking about it? Growth requires a stretching and willingness to *become* what we already *are* — human beings filled with the Spirit of the Living God.

The Charismatic Movement is one way of staying in touch with the Indwelling Spirit. I believe it is a valid way that fits some people. We need many ways for many people. One must find one's own special way, the way that spiritually renews one again and again.

One of the brothers at Pecos took me on a bird walk and I could sense his gentle spirit. He showed me the property and the buildings of the community, in the process allowing me to meet him in a human and enjoyable way. Others treated me with kindness, if only with a smile. One person discussed the experience of the recovering alcoholic as a paradigm of human healing. Healing is an important part of the Pecos ministry. Today the amount of damage found in human beings in the Church is incredible, to say nothing of the brokenness in the world.

Later, I talked to Abbot David, the spiritual leader of this remarkable community. He is obviously a deeply and theologically informed person with an intense commitment to the charismatic way. He responded to my questions about the essentials for Christian community today. He felt that a mixed community of men and women was important now. This is a position that most religious communities are just barely beginning to consider. He wondered if traditional forms of the monastic life could work any longer. He said that prayer and a prayerful communal consensus was the way to let the Spirit guide the community. He emphasized the importance of solid theology, especially the theology of the Spirit and the essential connection between experience and theology. Perhaps his emphasis on the importance of depth psychology might puzzle some. The rationale is that the experience of the revelation of God's nature simultaneously reveals the mystery of human nature. If deep knowledge of humanity is neglected or rejected, one is liable to do strange things in the name of God and religion. A religious war, or just an intense rejection of another person, might well be unconscious confusion with one's own weakness or pain, transferred to someone else. And it can be done with fierce religious conviction, Bible quotations and intense self-righteousness.

> We have reached the stage on this earth when we cannot permit such violent projections. We cannot have several religious systems in the world, each absolutist, bent on eliminating the other. To treat anyone as an enemy is eventually to become an enemy to oneself. The situation with the super powers is an example. If one wins then the other must lose. Apparently, the Gospel teaching to love one's enemy is more than piety. It is the law of reality. That law is verified, whether on the inner, unconscious level, or on the international, political level.

A school to train spiritual directors has developed from the Pecos community's blending of theology and depth psychology. There is a growing need for such skilled people. Pecos also has a busy paperback distribution ministry, providing this new viewpoint to ordinary people who are struggling with their faith. Pecos is doing an important work.

SANTA FE ANYWHERE

From Pecos monastery I drove west into Santa Fe, New Mexico.

> The neon signs,
> The well-known shrines,
> The traffic lines,
> Fast ways to dine,
> The urban wine,
> Anywhere, anytime.

This is cynical. One *can* find the historic old town. There are also special places where creative people work. But the old love for life has been weakened. Urban living, smooth as muzak, flows precariously on top of violence and despair.

A few miles off the main road or out of the city, you can also find life as it was two hundred years ago. Living then wasn't comfortable but it was connected with the earth. Now the car and the time schedule lock one into the franchise motel, the shopping mall, the quick food stop. America anywhere.

What kind of catechism does it teach? What effect does it have on us? We don't know. We take it for granted. Not even the Churches or the human service agencies can overcome the powerful myth of the commercial world. What is the hidden mysticism on which commercialism feeds? The more you consume the more you are. Everyone wants to be more. Is the promise fulfilled? Try to pray in a shopping mall. To whom do you pray?

All of this is very unfair to Santa Fe. But it somehow fits the sociology of America. I should have allowed Santa Fe to charm me, but I was eager to move into the desert.

CHAPTER 5

DESERT SPIRIT

CHRIST IN THE DESERT

Fifty miles or so northwest of Santa Fe along Highway 84, with the shacks and the junk fallout from the urban center gradually diminishing, you pass the town of Abiquiu. Then you come to a desert museum. This is a place where the local birds, animals, and plants are all displayed and labeled. It is a good introduction to the arid kingdom. Maybe the city, too, should have its own interpretive museum; educating, and warning, the uninitiated what to expect.

Just past highway marker 298, turn west. The pavement ends and for some 12 miles you are on a dirt entrance road to the monastery of Christ in the Desert. This is a foundation from Mt. Savior, a Benedictine monastery in New York State, and at the time of the sabbatical, a member of the Olivetan Congregation. (Most Benedictines belong to a group of monasteries known as a Congregation either by national origin or by the way they interpret the Rule of St. Benedict.)

Sometimes the road was a pleasant trek across sage-covered plateaus; sometimes it dipped precipitously into the canyon along the Chama River. The van needed its low gear, and in bad weather it never would have made it. Eventually, I came to a gate, the end of the road. This was the monastery, the last pocket of private land in a government tract of wilderness. Passing through the gate I was confronted with a sign that stated: "No Vehicles." Huuuuuuuummmm. I parked and began to walk. The guest house (which displays the brethren's crafts for sale) was empty. I walked on and saw the adobe church George Yakoshima designed. It had a cruciform plan with a higher glassed-in clerestory section in the center. Finally, I found Br. André, who received me cordially. I had a vague agreement with them that I could come by some time. Now was the time, and they accepted that. From meetings of Benedictines, I had known Br. Philip the Superior, and some of their community had visited us at St. Gregory's. I was given permission to bring the van up to an adobe cell and unload. What should I take out? Over the next few days, it took me several trips back and forth to the van (returned to the gate parking area), to get the appropriate list of articles for "simple" living: a flashlight, shaving kit, hiking shoes (OK for church, too), alarm clock, an extra jacket (it can get cold here at night, even in summer), a spiritual reading book, binoculars, a bird book, and work clothes (over which one wears the cowl for certain services in the church).

My cell was an adobe room which measured about 9' by 12' with a stone floor, small wood stove, front door with a half window and another window at the back. After dark, light was supplied by kerosene lamp. The room had a desk, chair, a simple prie-dieu (prayer desk), some wooden hooks for clothing, and a "sculpturesque" adobe bench, the bed. On the bed was a foam pad (not thick enough) and some blankets and a pillow. After a few days, it became quite comfortable. The walls were white and on one hung a crucifix, making the space a place of faith. The wooden beamed ceiling had an upper layer of smaller stakes arranged in a basket-weave pattern. Nearby was a bathroom unit. One adapts and soon I was at home.

Outside, the apparently random cluster of buildings seemed miniature in the vast landscape; we were in a river valley with stone cliffs on one side, and on the other, miles away, distant mountains. I looked and looked and looked, drinking in the space, the beauty, the solitude. What an immense glory! Simplicity. Soon, I found my binoculars and noted a Western blue bird, some kind of blackbirds, ravens which soar more than regular crows, a Cassin kingbird, a chipping sparrow, violet green swallows, a Mexican jay, and purple finches.

At Vespers I was given a cowl and a seat among the brethren. The altar was in the center under the large glass clerestory. The brethren and guests sat around the altar with no distinction between them. The Grail translation of the psalms with Gelineau-type melodies were used with guitar accompaniment. The simple melodies seemed appropriate. Later, I met the community in the kitchen. They were all wearing a bluish blouse, the main habit of the community. I, too, was given one. The gathering was informal and friendly. "How good and pleasant it is when brothers live in unity," the words of the Grail Psalter 132. In a separate building across a Zen-like garden from the church were the kitchen, refectory (dining room), and the vegetable-growing sun porch. In the dining room, simple wooden benches and tables were the natural furniture. The brethren and guests, some of them women, gathered in the kitchen and served themselves a hearty soup, bread, apple sauce, cookies, and iced tea. As we sat down to eat, a tape recorder with some Chopin music was turned on. Delightful. Suddenly I had the image of how rich the simple life could be — living close to the earth and the simplest kind of furnishings with touches of the richest gifts from the culture.

> But when these rich gifts are piled too high, and come too often, we lose the capacity to enjoy them. We need to be aware of how much the human person can see and hear. Too much is too much. And on reflection, we realize that someone else in the world has too little.

The guests joined the brethren in this human liturgy of renewing our life at the common meal. Among the guests was a Carmelite nun from California. Later, we did the dishes — monks and guests — socializing in this other sanctuary, the kitchen. Then Compline. Afterwards, in the cool dusk, I walked back to my cell, shrinking smaller and smaller into the vast space of the desert canyon. One could feel the call of the hermit. O Solitude! It makes for an awesome sense of God's Presence.

My room was still pleasantly warm, the adobe having soaked up the heat of the day. I lit the kerosene lamp and did some reading, occasionally meditating on the shadows the lamp cast on the wall. Then bed.

I was up for 4:00 AM Vigils. The psalms were sung by one brother to simple Gelineau tunes. Kerosene lamps were the only light. The darkness forced one to hover close to the light.

Have we lost the sense of light and dark in our 24-hour electrically lit life?

Then a simple breakfast of juice, bread and peanut butter, and coffee. On returning to my cell, I took a "meditative" nap, musing and dozing. This may not be real prayer, but it is a kind of faithful and childlike resting in the Lord.

At Lauds, 6:00 AM, the use of a guitar was a haunting accompaniment to the universal themes expressed in the psalms. The light was appearing at the top of the cliffs, seen through the high central windows of the church.

Around 8:00 AM, the Office of Prime was followed by Chapter, a gathering of the community to discuss its daily affairs. I was given the opportunity to explain my sabbatical and views on the general picture in the Church and world today. Some of the brethren asked questions; all gave me courteous attention.

After Terce, I walked with Br. Jeremy, who had been a member of the Word of God community in Ann Arbor, Michigan. The Word of God community was one among the many Christian charismatic communes around the country. What a shift of emphasis from charismatic to contemplative, two aspects of God's life in the Church! Br. Jeremy showed me the small but adequate library, gift shop, novitiate, and the various workshops where some original and beautiful things are being done in weaving and carving. People drive a long distance — and over that road — to buy these items. Then there are carpentry shops, fields, and gardens. All of the various buildings were separated by a short walk from each other.

While we were touring them, there was a partial eclipse of the sun. An odd, filtered light washed the landscape as if one had put a dark lens on the camera of one's eye. Coyotes in different canyons howled — a special touch to this primitive place. But the conversation Br. Jeremy and I had about relationships in community was far from primitive. We discussed the questions: How to love one's neighbor? How to be honest? How to maintain one's necessary independence and be at peace in the struggle — a struggle which did not always produce understanding and charity?

The contemplative life must be founded on the hard rock of the reality of the nature of God and of human beings. It takes "tough love" to live at this level of simple reality.

After the Office of Sext, we had a lunch of salad, lentil loaf, spiced tomatoes (in the Southwest the tomato is almost a sacrament), bread, potatoes, and tea. Then siesta. I didn't awaken for the afternoon work period, but when I did emerge from my cell, I wandered around, looked at birds, took some pictures, and chatted with various people. The silence was not rigid.

One of my chats was with Ellen Berg, a resident hermit. I wanted her to be in touch with a woman from a Quaker background who lives near St. Gregory's and aspires to the hermit life. As I talked with Ellen I was impressed with her warmth and her focus on God in a direct and loving way. But this is a calling, a way of living consciously and directly with the indwelling Lord. There are techniques and attitudes to be maintained in this special vocation, but in time it all blends into a simple way of love. I raised the question of the so-called "secular hermits" in today's cities, many single people who live out lonely lives. Could they learn to be at peace, centered on God? Probably only a minority will see this vision. Most will allow the media to provide their direction for life. But who will monitor the media? A hermit always has a spiritual director and some faithful friends with whom to share the mystery of simply living with God. Later, I sent Ellen a copy of *The Aquarian Conspiracy*.

> We need people of faith, meditating on the implications of the fascinating breakthroughs of our times.

As I was walking back from the weaving shop where Ellen has her hermitage, I saw a file of people coming up from the river. Now what? They turned out to be members of an anthropological research group who wanted permission to camp nearby. They intended to scale the mountain across from the monastery to a part of the Indian ruins of the Gallina tribes. The Gallina Indians had lived at the same time as the Anasazi cliff dwellers but had made their homes of circular formations of rock on the plateaus. Where had they come from? What had been their culture? Are we perhaps recovering a true appreciation of the wisdom of these people who learned to live at peace with the earth? With permission granted by one of the brothers, the research group returned to their raft and floated a short distance downriver, out of sight, where they made camp. The next day they made their hike. I wished that I could have accompanied them.

Vespers, supper (music — Dvorak's "New World Symphony" — how appropriate!) and Compline. Then, I stood outside a long time in the dusk.

> The layered canyon walls,
> The signature of the centuries.
> The raven soaring along the cliffs,
> Edging the mind of God.
> The softening blue sky,
> The piñon and sage covered valleys,
> Melting to a quiet silhouette
> Of light and dark.
> The mood of dusk,
> Washing the mind in silence,
> Nourished by peace,
> Breathing with the Ultimate.

The next day, the Feast of the Ascension, we rose somewhat earlier to do three nocturnes (three portions of psalms and readings) at the night office. Afterwards, following the course of the sun, the usual gentle rhythm of silence and prayer, Lauds, Prime, Terce. Mass today reflected the day's theme. We had more music and a homily. From the homily my own meditation went something like this:

> The risen Lord departs from us in his human form in order to return to us as Spirit. But can we ever expect the world to reflect this mystical reality? Only when all humans are enlightened. Let us not expect the kingdom in this world too soon; there is much work for justice and truth to do.

After Mass I developed a simple, seven step formula for the average person to keep in mind in his or her daily life. I am intrigued with the spiritual potential in people. None of us is working at anything like our real capacity.

Monday:	You *are*, you *live*.
Tuesday:	*Become aware* of other people and things. They are.
Wednesday:	You are *being led* to God Who is in everything and everyone. Hear, see, touch, smell, taste Him.
Thursday:	God is *Love*.
Friday:	God *gives* you Love, forgiving you everything else.
Saturday:	Now *you are Love*. Forgive yourself and others of what is not Love.
Sunday:	*Be* Love. *Give* Love. *Share* Love.

A slight rain raised the question of the condition of the road. Twelve miles of mud could defeat a 6,000 lb. van. Would it not be enjoyable to stay here longer? But I have other places to visit, other people to see. Left brain, right brain, teeter totter. As it turned out, the rain stopped.

In the early afternoon I was invited to a communal picnic. We had charcoal barbecued chicken, corn, potatoes, salad, beer and soft drinks, brownies, and watermelon. It was pleasant just to chat with the brethren on the simplest kind of human subjects: humorous events, odd people, old stories, other days.

On Friday after Mass, I departed. Even a few days in a place gives me a real taste of its spirit. Sometimes I feel like a robber, coming in and stealing what others have accumulated over many years. Perhaps a pack rat is a better simile. I always leave a blessing and a very warm affection for those who have taken me intimately into their life. I stopped at the gift shop and selected a ceramic bowl to send to Fr. B. in Texas. It is a strange trinity I live: tasting deeply of the present, looking ahead to my next stop, and sending notes and gifts of appreciation to those I have just left. The drive out was easy. Why is a return trip shorter? Because it is more familiar?

SANTA FE REVISITED

Back on the paved road I returned to Santa Fe. There I tried to locate Cynthia Stibolt whom I had met through Fr. Moore of St. Mark's, Philadelphia. She was one who understood the themes of *Aquarian Conspiracy*. But she was not home. I did not feel I could take the time to look up other people and groups in the area. I was badly neglecting Santa Fe.

Some people say that there are various places in the world that seem to attract spiritual energy. Whether this is true or not there are some fascinating things going on in the Santa Fe - Albuquerque area. Apart from artists and Christian groups, there are Moslem and Buddhist centers, and what we might call "new age" gathering places. These are the places of various experiments in cross-culture blends. No one has the formula, and many of these experiments no doubt will disappear. But the attempts are important. For my interest in such things, some of my friends think I am eclectic, pluralistic, or worse, unorthodox. I am only looking for clues on how the people of this planet can live together in peace and fulfill their potential.

On the freeway, I headed south to Albuquerque. Such effortless driving, sometimes with music, makes for long thoughts and quiet meditations.

> Driving a car through the countryside or in heavy traffic may well be one of modern man's spiritual exercises. Can one pray, can one be centered inside this complex machine, moving intricately among other human beings, equally armored in their motion crafts? If you listen to yourself, you will hear spontaneous expressions of praise, thanksgiving, confession and intercession. These too, are prayers.

ETHAN SIMMONS

In Albuquerque, I found Ethan Simmons, the son of a woman who writes to me at the abbey. He worked at a bookstore near the campus of the University of New Mexico. I knew he was a kindred spirit by the way he recognized me although he had never seen me before. We had written, but I appeared incognito, in work pants, a colored Tee shirt, and moccasins. "You must be Father Abbot," he said, making my day. From his bookstore I was able to send the book, *Rolling Thunder*, to a young monk at Christ in the Desert who had shown interest in Indian affairs. While Ethan finished out his workday, I did some shopping, replacing the van compass which had apparently overheated and lost its "mind," found some refills for my Bic four-colored pen, and added a new door pocket to the van. Later Ethan and I had a leisurely supper at a nearby restaurant where we discussed various aspects of his spiritual journey. He honored me by being quite open about himself. I learn from people's stories. Here was a highly intelligent and spiritual person who did not feel at home in the ordinary parish of any denomination. This need not be seen as a judgment, either on the person or the Church. And today it is not at all uncommon. The Church is not the only way in which sincerely spiritual people find their guidance. He had been to

India and was quite sensitive to, and well informed about, Hinduism. Intriguingly, it is Hinduism that attracts many modern physicists as they attempt to find a compatible philosophy for their scientific discoveries. Ethan was also conversant with other religious systems and ideas. He had been a language specialist in Korea during the war, then a computer programmer. He was quite sympathetic with current ecological and holistic health concepts. One might say that he is a brilliant "drop-out." Or he might be seen as a minor prophet, waiting for the times to catch up. We were simpatico, to use the Spanish phrase. It is not that I want to shed my Christian theology and monastic vocation. Quite the opposite. The original monastic charisma (gift) has to be on the edge of the culture —(a liminal role), to witness to a reality *beyond* the culture. Besides, I feel a strong desire to pastor people of any faith, or no faith, in their human journey. As people see the spiritual nature of that journey then I am fascinated with the common ground we share.

I slept on the floor of Ethan's small apartment, had coffee with him in the morning, and talked more. Can such a person find a place in the normal economic/political world? It seems to depend on how human that world can be.

> Here is a challenge for our time, or any time: How to be fully human (which includes some kind of spiritual awareness)? How to help fellow pilgrims with whom one can share without imposing on them? For me, Christ is the outward sign, the Sacrament, of God's Love. I long to share that. But I also must respect the other person's way to God, however different. And I am excited to see God at work in all of us, gently accepting us where we are, being anonymous if necessary, leading us to the divine. I am sure I will continue to meet, and learn from, more Ethans.

O.A.R.

I left Albuquerque on Saturday morning, drove east on I-40, up another thousand feet (easy to do in this region), and turned south on a state road. Finally, I found Tajique, the post office address of the Order of Agape and Reconciliation, a small community in the Episcopal Church. The surrounding country was mountainous, with cattle farms in the valleys. Four miles off the paved road, 7,000 feet up the Manzano Mountains, was the main house and a set of buildings that make up the O.A.R. Center. Fr. Cyril and Sr. Mary Michael Molnar, a married couple, received me most graciously, although again, I had only sent a vague notice that I would be in their area about this time. I was given a room on the top floor of the central house, immediately adjacent to the chapel. In just an overnight stay I was able to sense the ambience of this unique community. Very human and informal in one sense, but very traditional in their Western spirituality and worship. Their uniqueness includes an appreciation of the importance of male/female qualities in community, of solitude, and of human hospitality — the work of the Spirit for our day. This is another form of the charismatic life.

Fr. Cyril is a highly intuitive person, deeply informed theologically, and a man of prayer. Sr. Mary Michael is a more "natural" kind of contemplative who knows quite clearly that she fell in love with God. This doesn't prevent her from arguing with Him at times. Both of them are sure that God has guided them in their venture. There were a few other guests. These included: Father Weaver Stevens from an Episcopal Church in the Los Angeles area; Emerson, a lay person from the Albuquerque area, a very committed and knowledgeable Christian: and a layman who helped maintain the place when the Molnars were in their other center in Costa Rica. On that Sunday, another guest came to Mass, Steve Makara. He, too, was a pilgrim. His present work was farming and doing research on the actual image and materials of the miraculous "painting" of Our Lady of Guadalupe, the focus of the popular Mexican devotion. His remarks reminded me of the recent studies made of the Shroud of Turin. Science and mysticism are drawing closer and closer. The O.A.R. Center, like other prayer centers, draws people who share an interest in mysticism.

I talked candidly with Fr. Cyril and Sr. Mary Michael about their future. They do not have the clear tradition that I enjoy in the Benedictine life. Will they grow? Where should they be? Does their special vocation need clarifying? These are all large questions with no simple answers. On the other hand, they enjoy certain freedoms that my vocation doesn't include — except in this unique sabbatical time. We need to stay in touch with one another. There is room for many different kinds of vocation, "In my Father's house...."

I love such adventurous people and long to help them. Perhaps I could at least help them find more care-taking persons who would occupy the lovely mountain retreat at Tajique while they are in Central America doing some important ecumenical work. We had a wonderful lunch and more good talk. Celebrating, eating, talking, and being silent are all ways in which we share God's love.

DESERT INN

I departed in the rain and drove southwesterly. The landscape was infinite as usual, only distant mountains touching the sky. A few houses, a few cars, the thread of the road, all lost in this space. I wanted to spend the night in this expanse so I finally found an obscure turnoff and drove about a mile into the desert. A little parched piece of desert became my "inn." My imagination produced antelope, but actually I only saw a jackrabbit. The silence was huge, the emptiness full. I finished Vespers, had a cup of soup and crackers, and some pickles. Not a very good diet but enough for me that night. One car drove by. After some reading, I said Compline and went to bed. The wind stirred up some dust dancers.

The next morning at sunrise, after watering the nearby bush, I simply stared at the distance. Then I felt moved by an Indian practice to face north, east, south, and west, praying to the Creator. I returned to the van, heated the coffee, and said the Western prayer of Lauds. One rancher drove by, looked and kept on. I, too, was soon on my way.

TRUTH OR CONSEQUENCES
At the town of Truth or Consequences, New Mexico (the story of that name must be intriguing), I phoned the Abbey, two time zones to the east. Talking to various brethren brought into focus the old items on my mental list. One brother had left. This hurt, but I was determined to refrain from making too much comment. It feels somewhat like being on a spaceship, periodically checking in at home base.

A little farther south I took a diagonal shortcut southwest to connect with I-10 at Deming. I saw some turkey vultures and some hawks, not too sure which ones. I also listened to a Beethoven piano concerto, had some granola bars and an orange, and said some of the Little Hours on my "dashboard prie-dieu" (a little shelf that allows me to prop the Office book on the dash and still keep an eye on the road while saying the Office).

MICHIGAN FRIENDS
At Willcox, Arizona, I stopped to see Father Bud Williams and his wife Joan. They had lived near Detroit for many years and he had visited St. Gregory's. After retiring he was ordained and now had charge of the mission in this town. We talked Michigan. He gave me a report from some other friends, the Perretts (also formerly of Michigan) who had just sold their ranch retreat in the nearby Chiricahua Mountains, near the Apache Indian Cochise's hideout. In fact, at the time they were back in Michigan. After a welcome supper (my snacks on the road are never quite balanced) I moved on to Tucson and stayed at a motel — not nearly as pleasant as my Desert Inn.

THE PONY EXPRESS DROP
The next day I met William Johnson and his wife Doris. They had been storing my mail. After saying Mass at their parish, Grace Church, I spent the night with them. We had a delightful Mexican supper at a nearby restaurant. William is another Michigander, ordained a deacon many years ago who has been faithfully serving the Church. I was impressed with his quiet and generous service to the kingdom. He knew many of my old friends in the Catholic movement of times past.

THE THUNDERBIRD SHOP
While in Tucson I visited the Thunderbird Shop, where my abbatial cross had been designed and executed by Frank Patania. His unique design of the abbot's cross, the gift of David and Charlotte Risto (he was our business and farm manager at one time), has caught the eye of many. Frank's father came from Italy, where he was a silversmith. As he grew up in the Santa Fe area, he taught his son the craft. Frank and I talked over refreshments in a charming courtyard adjoining his shop. These "patios" must surely be one of

the most beautiful landscape gifts given us by the Spanish. Later as he polished my cross, we discussed art, the Southwest, and Indians. He agreed that there was indeed a special spirit about the Southwest.

> I wondered. Was it because the Indians, and later the Spanish, had lived out their faith here? Or, are there places in the world that are, in fact, more intensely spiritual? No one can answer those questions. But you can't help being aware of the mystery that broods over the area. And this in spite of, or underneath, the rampant commercialism that makes America the envy and the agony of the world.

CHAPTER 6

THE SPIRIT IMPRISONED, YET FREE

MAXIMUM SECURITY PRISON

Leaving unseen many friends and places of interest, I moved on to one of the most provocative experiences so far. I went to Florence, where a correspondent friend was being held in maximum security. After preliminary clearance I was admitted to see Paris Carriger, an American Indian on death row. He and I had been writing for some time, but this was the first time I had seen him. I was impressed. He was clean (cleaner than I was), very intelligent, and deeply involved in a number of social justice causes outside the prison. His co-workers in these causes were professional people of academic or legal standing. He has kept himself busy writing to these people, to foundations, handling hundreds of thousands of dollars on paper, all to promote programs connected with prisoners or justice. One such program STOP, (Service to Offenders Program), had just lost, by disappearance, one of its secretaries, along with some $16,000. Paris was not bitter. At times he mentioned anger and his need to keep busy, but in general his manner was in sharp contrast to his surroundings.

Our conference room was drab and depressing. On the wall outside it was someone's comment: "P.C. Sucks." I wondered why it wasn't removed. Some of the attendants were very human and courteous; others seemed to be robots. What a world. I didn't want to offer Paris any advice. He seemed to be doing well enough without it. He had been recently baptized. I prayed with him and left.

On the way to the parking lot I retrieved my van keys from the front gate attendant. After a few pleasantries I sensed that he was capable of more serious questions. I ventured one: What did he think of Paris? He said that he knew him well. The attendant had worked in all departments of the prison. We moved from one question to another, covering a wide variety of subjects — the definition of happiness, what is success, the influence of parenting on criminals, alcoholism (both of us discovered ourselves to be children of alcoholic fathers), frustrations with all institutions (spiritual or secular), the pain of losing one's ideals. I was amazed. A real philosopher at the front gate. He was careful not to make direct answers to my questions about Paris. But I couldn't escape the impression that there was a definite concept, sociopath, used by professional people about a person on death row. This describes a person who cannot, or will not, live peacefully in society, and has no remorse for any serious hurt he has done to others. Well, I can find a streak of that in myself. But the impression I had from my time with Paris, and now the opposite impression, equally convincing, that I was receiving from a highly intelligent and compassionate person, simply did not fit together. Do any labels really fit?

A letter Paris had written to me came to mind (printed as written):

Dear Brother Benedict:

My instinctive reaction to being judged by a guard, any guard, is distaste. Competency to judge aside, there are some basic realities. First, there is no such thing as a cop who knows me well. I won't permit it. Knowledge is a weapon in my world, in the world that the cops and I share. In their eyes there are two kinds of prisoners, one is submissive and easy to manipulate and challenges no one's right to stand in judgment of other men. The second type of prisoner is pure trouble to systems devised to subjugate without honor through the use of psychological violence and more. The words written on the wall "P.C. Sucks" when translated means "protective custody sucks" and in general it is intended as a warning and may in fact have been written by a guard as easily as a convict and, is in fact just as probable. I suspect that if you had gone to those who held keys over Jesus they would have had compelling reasons for why they were right and I would bet that most of the teachings he presented would have been viewed in the light of the psychopathic judgments of the day. No my friend, I do not like being judged anonymously because I value those who have paid the price of learning to know me. The price is not cheap; it cannot be paid in coins made to meet the concepts of worth of others. The only coin redeemable with me is the willingness to meet and share as equals, perhaps not to agree but always to respect. That is a coin I have never seen paid by any guard to any prisoner. It is understandable.

The first need of man, any man, is to justify himself. No guard can say, "This convict is a great and good man, but let's execute him anyway." My friends are my friends because we share a vision of the possible that is the most difficult to attain. One of my friends is a former professor of psychology at Stanford University and presently is a professor of psychology and law at the University of Michigan. If you wish to understand a professional opinion from one who is qualified to label me, I suggest that she and her husband and perhaps even her children are most qualified to give it. I am a man who has lived within sight of the gas chamber for 12 years knowing that guards will be the factual hands that take my life. Whatever I am, I am unable to call those men friends or allow them to see what hurts me or brings me shame.

. . . Further, there is the backdrop of the right wing vision that is held by most of this state as it is exposed in the 10 year fight over the Martin Luther King holiday. Those people argue that the vision they hold is not racist. I tend to listen less to what a man says and look to see where he spends his money to see what he values. My mother's people have long understood the power of white words. For me, I notice that the black population in this state is approximately 7% of the whole, yet the prisons are just over 45% black. Why is that? I notice that if you are convicted of killing a white in this state the odds are you will get the death penalty for it, but the historical numbers say that if you kill a black in this state there is almost no chance of you being given the death penalty. In fact that average time given to he who kills a black is just over 5 years. These numbers are not the whole story but they are enough of it to suggest to the wise man that visions of reality shape the acceptable and after reflection, I prefer my vision to those who have judged me.

I wish you Peace, Dignity, Love,

(signed) Paris

A further irony. If Paris is released, or if he is not, it may have little to do with actual justice. Some line of argument, some lawyer's ploy, some set of circumstances, may start a movement in the penal system which cannot be reversed. But on the human side, both Paris and the attendant, while being on the opposite side of the bars, had come to some kind of peace in the midst of this strange penal process. Both had gained a degree of freedom. That is surely the supreme achievement for any human being who must live out his life within the limitations of a fallen society.

THE SERVANTS OF CHRIST

As I drove to Phoenix, downhill to about 1,000 feet, it was hot outside, and also inside my brain, trying to sort out Paris' situation. I was soon enveloped in the lush oasis of Phoenix, where I found the address of the Servants of Christ, a small religious community in the Episcopal Church. One of their members, Br. Samuel, had spent several months with us. So, it was a joy to see him again and to meet the two other members of his family, Fr. Lewis Long and Fr. Cornelius de Rijk. They readily took me in and I was soon carried along by the familiar rhythm of prayer, silence, and good talk. Br. Samuel kindly did my laundry, arranged with a parishioner to cut my hair, and otherwise took care of my practical needs. We had some good talks about the religious life, formation, architecture, and fund raising; all issues a community must face. The answers are never simple and require a special kind of patient faith. I remembered our own early days and how we pondered these matters.

The poor head fumbles with the mystery of establishing a community. Meanwhile, God does the work. Of course, not every community succeeds, and even if it does, it must go through considerable pain.

> This sabbatical is no doubt offering me some relief from the stress of living by faith while managing a community. This is no different from the stress any human being experiences. I was also gaining some perspective on what is worth worrying about. Nothing, really.
>
> There is a saying, "Experience is what you get when you are looking for something else." So I consider that in the 36 years of my monastic life I have at least gained some experience. And I've had a lot of fun, met some wonderful people, lived with some very understanding brethren, and learned to appreciate the real freedom that God gives us. All of this is His love.

The two Fathers also took me out for a tasty Mexican meal. Why is such food so good? But I admit that I couldn't finish the beans and the rice.

ARCOSANTI

From the nurturing of living in community for a few days, I again moved into the mainstream of my journey. Going north from Phoenix, one has to climb several thousand feet. The little four-cylinder diesel heated up, but made it. At Cordes Junction I turned off the freeway and began looking for the publicized "City of the Future," Arcosanti. Since it is only two percent built, it isn't obvious on the landscape. But eventually, off to the east on the edge of a barren and rocky ravine, I saw it. It was all a series of cement arches, square chunks of buildings with large holes cut into them, cranes poised purposefully, and lumps of building materials piled around.

One might have supposed that some great spaceship had crashed. Actually, a great earthship is being readied to lift — to lift men's minds and imaginations into a new way of life for tomorrow — if there is to be a tomorrow. Some believe that unless we take serious steps to arrest urban sprawl with all of its fallout, there may not be a tomorrow. Phoenix spreads farther and farther into the desert and may run out of water. Anthropologists speculate that this may have been the fate of the abandoned Aztec cities.

I joined a small tour, and in spite of two very uninterested small boys, found the description and the philosophy fascinating. The concepts were originated, or at least were perfected and brought into a master plan, by Paolo Soleri, who came from Italy and has lived in Arizona since 1956. For a time, he had worked with Frank Lloyd Wright, then struck out on his own. Soleri's vision is based on the need to re-collect the city's functioning center, leaving the best outlying land for food production and recreation. Such a center attempts to use all of the earth's resources — sun, water, air, earth — in a harmonious, interconnected whole. With only a small part of the full plan now established there is still a feeling of excitement. Art, crafts, music, young people, all seem to be part of this experiment. Windchimes jingling (cast on the site), ceramics, music festivals, the young architects of tomorrow working hard to release Soleri's dream in the rock canyon and the disbelieving general public's dull imagination, all set up a special vision-chime of its own.

After the tour I walked around, took a few pictures, had a delicious ham and cheese sandwich and a beer at their cafeteria, gazed out through a huge circle on the desert landscape, looked down on the growing fields in the valley below, and dreamed my own dreams. Such is the power of Arcosanti. It may be full of mistakes and it may never get finished, but it is alive with potential vision and much hard-headed analysis for our time. I rethought our own architectural plan, wondering how it might be made closer to the earth and closer to human nature. Arcosanti was another expression of Christ in the Desert, although the theology was more humanistic. What a lovely preparation for Pentecost.

CHAPTER 7

SPIRIT OF PENTECOST

SEDONA

Continuing north, I found the desert plateau land gradually developing some deep canyons. The traveler is being prepared for a much grander canyon. Turning off the freeway one finally comes to Sedona. What gorgeous red rocks and a charming town of artists, retirees, and old sets for Wild West movies. But it is being eaten up by the shopping center dragon, even though dressed now in a Western-Spanish-Indian motif. I stayed the night in a crowded state park and dented the side of the van on a dumpster. My romantic images of Sedona were dented, too. I do admit that I was impressed with the bold design of the Chapel of the Holy Cross, a strong, cement form rising up out of the rocks above the valley.

The next day, the Saturday before Pentecost, I found the old site of the Spiritual Life Institute where some years ago a group of hermits had lived. Condominiums were filling what used to be a quiet space for prayer. I was not angry. There are just many different worlds, "In my Father's house...." Personally, I prefer Arcosanti to this.

HURT PRIDE IN THE COCONINO NATIONAL FOREST

By now I was feeling the mystery of Pentecost. Was I to celebrate it with some of the faithful, or as a hermit? Coming out of beautiful Oak Creek Canyon up to some 7,000 feet in lovely forested and open range country, I noticed barbed wire fencing alongside of the highway. But periodically there were gates on which a sign read, "Please Close." That gave me the idea that they were expected to be opened. About eight miles short of Flagstaff, I found a road in, even without a gate. I turned off and saw a beautiful ponderosa pine forest. That tug of solitude. So, I looked for a side road so that I would not obstruct anyone. This found, I began some delicate maneuvering among the pines to squeeze the van into a site. The way was narrow. A rock tipped me to one side. There was a terrible scraping. I finished the few feet remaining to the opening. Then I stepped out and looked at the van.

Nothing wrong up high. Whew. But down low, the right rear fender had been ripped off. Damn! Near the offending tree I gathered up the three pieces of damaged fender and put them inside. The scar was jagged. My solitude and my piety were going to cost me. I was depressed.

At this moment I determined to do something positive with my hurt pride. I read one of the books I had brought, *Love Is Letting Go of Fear* (Gerald G. Jampolsky). All right, damn it, I will put this to work. The teaching on the page I was reading encouraged me to let go of pain, let go of fear. Think only of love. So I got out a pad of paper and began listing the things I ought to let go of: my embarrassment and annoyance at yesterday's denting of the van on the camp dumpster; my anger today at ripping off the fender; my frustration at not having reserved a houseboat at Lake Powell (which was one of my plans while in this area); my needling anxiety about the finances of the sabbatical (the van was not fully paid for); the uncertainty about other finances at the Abbey; the hurt over losing the brother who had recently left; the deep frustration I carry when the community is not even able to discuss long-range visions for our life; my loneliness when I cannot share my ideals with others. This was my Pentecost preparation, to let go of all of this. I settled down for the night in the forest, awaiting the dawn when I could offer the Eucharist.

The next morning the temperature was down to 45 degrees, but clear. In the van, I read the opening prayers and lessons for the feast. Then I took my Communion kit to the nearby rocks and selected a suitable natural altar. As the sun rose I slipped out of my clothes and faced the warmth of a new day. I put the bread (which I had bought from the bakery at Arcosanti) on the stone. The wine was in a small cup. I prayed the Prayer of Thanksgiving. Sometimes I faced all four directions as I prayed for the world. A piece of bent fender stood off to the side as an icon of all that is bent in the world. My list of what I was letting go of was there, too. I adored my God in the ancient sacrifice of the Lord of Creation at 7,000 feet surrounded by towering pines. The wind blew gently and I thanked the Spirit for the healing gift.

Back in the van I had breakfast and then carefully groped my way back to the main road. In Flagstaff I looked up the RV dealers to see if any were open. None was, except —

U-HAUL AND THE SPIRIT

I never connected the Spirit with U-Haul. But they proved to be timely friends. Being Sunday, the regular mechanics were not on duty, but a lone attendant lent me a rubber hammer to do what I could with the fender. What a release it was to do some pounding! Then I began to think about my wish to have a houseboat on Lake Powell. So far I hadn't been successful with the big Del Webb corporation in even getting a reservation. So about noon I went off to the local Episcopal parish, Epiphany, and came in at the coffee hour. The Rector, Fr. Gutmacher, couldn't help, but a lady (there are always a few who know everything) introduced me to a layman who gave me the name of William Sturm in Page, Arizona. Over the phone Mr. Sturm, who turned out to be a faithful churchman, promised to do what he could. My spirits were lifting, so I stopped in at a Big Boy restaurant where they advertised an all-you-can-eat breakfast. I celebrated the Spirit with two platefuls of eggs, potatoes, muffins, peaches, bacon and ham, and milk. It was a great feast, during which I said None. Then I set out to find a place for the night. I instinctively avoided the in-town RV parks. After moving out of town, I found another dirt road, always a good sign.

HUMPHREY'S PEAK

After a few uphill miles I found my spot, a quiet grove amidst tall pines, on the lower slopes of Humphrey's Peak. There followed a pleasant afternoon of sitting in the sun, listening to some classical music from the university station at Flagstaff, and reviewing my Owner's Manual. After actually driving the vehicle for some time, there are always items one needs to remember and understand anew. I had forgotten that one should let a diesel engine idle for a short time after starting and just before stopping. I don't think I really registered the point that one should put pressure on the foot brake before setting or releasing the hand brake. And I finally figured out how to flash the turn signals without actually locking them into their permanent turn position. All small details for Pentecost, but as Paolo Soleri says in his book, *Arcosanti, An Urban Laboratory* (which I had bought), "...do not look for the Spirit where matter is frowned upon." Then my morning *lectio* in, *Love Is Letting Go of Fear,* had pointed out that you can change problems — in your head. Instead of problem solving (left brain work) one can use a "problem dissolving" approach. After my mental struggle with the fender, I decided that fixing my attitude was more important than fixing the fender. Another gift of the sabbatical. So I fixed my attention on the Lake Powell situation, imagining the Spirit working on that for me, then I went for a hike. I saw some beautiful tree swallows, a gorgeous Western tanager, a humming bird, brown creepers, jays, doves, and flycatchers.

JUSTIFICATION

Here I am on the mountain, enjoying the glorious sunshine, the ponderosa pines, the birds, the freedom, when the radio news reports a fragile peace in Lebanon, continuing war between Iran and Iraq, budget problems (our economy affects the whole world), and intense negotiation in Congress over aliens (mainly the Hispanic question). How can one justify being so detached and so happily occupied with simple beauties? The Church itself and my own community are working with serious questions — questions that evolve into other complex questions. The human journey involves endless problems. Some people would even question the worth of the monastic life. What good is prayer amidst so much need and conflict? My name was mentioned in two dioceses as a candidate for bishop. Why wouldn't that be a way to help resolve the problems? It might be for someone else. For me, a contemplative, the heart of the human problem is the heart itself. Or you could call it the mind, the intuitive, faith-centered part of the mind. I am exploring the possibility of a depth of freedom that penetrates (not disregards) problems.

> Can we choose to meet the day's events — some of which are indeed scary and burdensome — as opportunities to be guided by the Spirit? Perhaps the Spirit works intimately within our human faculties; guiding, nudging, leaning, whispering, pushing, laughing, holding his/her breath, weeping, rejoicing. If we learn to live with the Spirit we learn to choose life and love. Nothing else.

45

But will this work in the "real" world? That depends on which side of your brain asks the question. No, it will not solve the left brain's problems. But it will open fascinating doors and pathways through problems when we are in tune with the One Who dwells within all problems — waiting to be recognized. This does not remove the Cross; rather it sees the Cross as God's way of infusing divine energy into the worst of our human condition, into death in all its various forms. If you can change your mind, your heart, you can change the world. Ask Dame Julian (14th Century English mystic).

DROPPINGS

Meanwhile, as I was "dissolving" my Lake Powell questions, I noticed what any hiker will see, the droppings of animals. Here were deer droppings, here rabbit, here something I couldn't recognize. These are part of the sign language to a student of animals, telling what animals are present.

> Downtown, one of the human animals I overheard at the grocery store used a four letter word, not "droppings," when confronted with a frustration in his shopping list. Across the street at the mental health clinic, the same word is used to describe the feelings of one who has suffered child abuse, a breakdown of a marriage, the loss of health, frustration over work, alcoholism, the invasion of violence into a life. Up here on the mountain, droppings tell that animals are present. Down in the town it tells what animals have hurt other animals. Can we teach the human animal not to hurt its fellow animals? Or can we teach a human animal that you can choose not to be hurt, or to hurt anyone else; that you can, in fact, choose to love — no matter what others do. Droppings are an interesting sign language.

THE PONDEROSA FOUNTAIN

From looking down low, I turned my gaze upward. Standing at the base of a tall ponderosa pine I looked up its trunk, toward the sky, now filled with millions of little fingers of greenish light. The sun shining through the many needled branches made them like a fountain. The memory of the fountains of far away Rome came to mind, splashing or waving languorously. The ponderosa did not move. Or did it?

> Modern physicists tell us that everything is moving. What we call movement is only "faster" movement, or visible movement. But everything is moving, except the Unmoved Mover, the source of all the fountains.

Looking up the tree trunk, from within the fountain, one was caught up into the quiet surge of greenish light that splashed against the vast fountain of the blue sky. We are part of the fountain when we let the life force movement of the fountain of life carry us, flowing, into the Source. Then a big-eared squirrel chattered at me, returning me to the present. All in all, a good Pentecost.

On Monday, I determined to continue the observance of Pentecost in my prayer although our Ordo (the daily schedule of prayer through the year) returns us to the ordinary liturgical usages through the year. I left the forest grove early because I wanted to get back to U-Haul. There I was turned over to Bob, an older foreman of the shop who delights in telling you how terrible your situation is, how it can't possibly be fixed. Then he sets out to fix it. He did a real plastic surgeon's job on the fender. That inexpensive Coconino site only cost $35. I had a few other items to be attended to, including an extension to the shower hose, allowing me in a private camping site to stand outside the unit and rinse down. And the U-Haul people were very accommodating in letting me use their telephone for credit card calls. By Monday afternoon the van was fixed, with only a few old-age wrinkles remaining.

CHAPTER 8

THE SPIRIT OF CREATION

SHEILA

Several phone calls to Mr. Sturm in Page clarified that none of his friends had a houseboat available. It was the tourist season. So I went back to work with Del Webb, the big developer who has brought so many projects to the Arizona scene. But it is terribly hard to make arrangements over the phone for something you have never seen or done. However, in Phoenix an angel named Sheila, one of the phone hostesses for the Lake Powell marinas, became a personal friend. She listened to my plaint: in fact, since March, I had been trying to get a boat. Whether it was Sheila's intervention, or just a lucky cancellation, I did get a reservation for a houseboat for four days and nights. Ah, one of my dreams was coming true. I love space, I love water, I love the wilderness. Lake Powell had them all. This vast body of water was created by damming the Colorado River — that great river which cut the Grand Canyon, the river that had made it possible for Indian tribes to live in the arid desert, the river that was explored by the Spanish, the Mormons, and finally just after the Civil War, the American military commander, Major Powell. The area has a romantic story (if you happen to be one of the winners) or a tragic one. The Indians, some of whom had already left the area for an unknown reason, were overwhelmed by an aggressive, industrially developing wave of adventurers and settlers. And so, a little over a hundred years later, I will be able to coast the vast waters of Lake Powell in a houseboat. Again, I felt like a robber.

GRAND CANYON

I began my love affair with the Colorado River by a visit to the Grand Canyon on the Monday after Pentecost. Unless you know the geology you cannot be prepared for the sudden shock when you drive out of the high desert, park at an overlook, and walk to the South Rim of the canyon. An immeasurable view overwhelms you. Two billion years of rock formations lie before you. Five thousand feet below flows the powerful Colorado. Vistas of many-colored layers of rock retreat in miles of colored glory. Visitors of many nations and languages stand mute at this wonder of the world. Cliff swallows and swifts slide crazily off the air above the plateau into the abyss. On the precarious ledge, towhees scratch the ground. Gray-headed juncos hop about, unaware of the nearby grandeur. Ravens alone seem to know where they are; they sail and soar, and in this kingdom of rock and sky, "caw" their lonely cry.

That night I stayed in a nearby camper area and returned the next day for a short hike and more silent gazing. I wanted to say Mass, so in the evening I chose a jutting formation of rock. The quiet Liturgy was enacted in a slowly purpling sanctuary as the sun set. Just at the moment of consecration, a group of sunset viewers came out from the hotel. I moved away from their lookout place and continued. The "congregation," intent only on the outer view, were unaware of the invocation of the source of this awesome display of nature and of the responding sacramental action going on in their presence. After I finished the Eucharist I joined them, their chit-chat incongruous with the sublimity around them.

> But if you can't comprehend something, what else do you do? Don't most people move through the mystery of life, chit chatting?

The guide for the group was an American Indian in a National Park uniform. He was friendly and well informed, but I couldn't help wondering what he really thought. (It reminded me of the time during World War II when I was appointed to supervise some German prisoners of war who were to do some house cleaning in one of the barracks at an army camp. Their discipline and military bearing contrasted sharply with the sloppy, casual manner of those who had conquered them. I wondered then, as I wonder now, what the conquered people thought.) This young Indian guide, part of a conquered people, had aspirations to get more college education and eventually teach Anglos something of his people's dignity and wisdom. I pray that his heart will not be broken in the process. On the other hand, maybe the Anglos are at last waking up to the fact that they desperately need some wisdom if they are to survive. Can a Space Age people gain wisdom fast enough?

MONUMENT VALLEY

The next day I drove northeast, over the upthrust of the earth that over millions of years had forced the river to cut deeply into the earth on its way to the Gulf of Mexico. Toward the end of the day, I found myself on the Navajo reservation in a mysterious area known as Monument Valley. Here in the desert, a few buttes starkly stand out against the sky, broad and meditative. While the Grand Canyon was sunk into the ground, here the aspect was of lonely, upthrusting sentinels.

The camp on the reservation where I stayed had a visitors' center where the Navajos displayed their jewelry. I couldn't decide what was authentic and fairly priced, so I bought nothing. Perhaps I was put off by the clash of cultures: the young Indians listening to rock and roll (not much else on the radio up here) and the timeless beauty around me. Later in the day, a young Indian girl came to the camp, selling jewelry. I felt moved to buy something. I selected a blue beaded, Juniper berry necklace. As my brethren know, I like jewelry. But it is usually worn in fun. However, I was willing to have a modest memento of this culture. I asked the price and she said that it was three dollars (later I priced this elsewhere at two dollars). I gave her five dollars. She said she didn't have the change. I felt the chill of uncertainty within me. Then in the awkward silence she did find change, asked me if I had any candy, and explained that she was helping her father buy a new pickup truck — certainly a necessity in the desert. But I was disappointed. What had we done to the Indians? We had taught them our "wisdom." Could we learn theirs? Later in another park, discussing this with an Anglo ranger, he reacted quite differently and straightforwardly asked, "When you were a child, didn't you find ways to make money?" I realized that I was idealizing the Indians, projecting on them something of my own romantic need. I am always having to withdraw such expectations.

The Indian campground was not in good repair, but the scenery dwarfed that problem. Besides, out in the desert, maintenance is not easy. Space, huge forms of rock, sky; these brooded hauntingly, eternal. And these were enough to generate a genuine religion, no matter what the theologians call it. It was a space that called you to an awareness of nature and its source; all was reduced to the irreducible.

NATURAL BRIDGES

As I slowly proceeded to my appointment on Lake Powell, I stopped at another park, Natural Bridges, Utah. Here a smaller river had cut through the sandstone in a meandering pattern. Gradually, that meandering had worn through certain thin spots, aided by the grinding power of gravel-laden water, until a breakthrough created a new path, often leaving an arch overhead. One could see the Grand Canyon principle at work on a smaller scale. The Indians had left this area, too, but something of their spirit remained. There were, however, some disagreeable gnats that bit and stung. Paradise always has some practical reminder that all is not perfect. But I am sure that the gnats are performing some part in the over-all ecology of the region.

> What we call "perfect" is probably some abstraction that edits reality according to our taste.

I stayed in Natural Bridges Park inexpensively. I have what is called a "Golden Age Passport" which (being older than 62) entitles me to half fare in all National Parks, National Forests, and certain other federally administered recreation areas. In criticizing the middle class way of life, in all fairness I ought to acknowledge its benefits, of which this sabbatical is an example. My various credit cards also make it fairly easy to move about and get gas, overnight accommodations, gifts, even cash. A modern, middle class nomad has access to considerable service as he travels. I have met some people who live in their trailers, going south in the winter and north in the summer, with trips in between to wherever they please. They say they can live for about $1,000 per month. That doesn't permit much fancy living, but for some, life in natural areas is much fancier than the urban life.

LAKE POWELL

Sixty more miles, over apparently lifeless desert, halfway between Page, Arizona and nowhere, one comes to Hall's Crossing on Lake Powell. A number of marinas dot this lake which otherwise seems part of the deserted landscape. Even the many people who take advantage of this wonderful recreational facility "disappear" once they are on the lake.

At the marina I found a boat partner, another person who wanted to tour the lake and share expenses. "Ned," he called himself, had ridden a motorcycle from California. I looked at him carefully and decided to trust him. Was it the look in his eyes? A look that seemed intent on the same mystery of space that attracted me. Was it his quiet courtesy? It felt like I was in the presence of a kind of monk, a single person who had worked through the surface questions of life, and come to the essence. I felt a kinship.

We rented a 36 foot houseboat and about noon began a new adventure. A houseboat is something like a van, only bigger and more spacious. It holds 120 gallons of gasoline, propane to fuel a stove, an oven, a water heater, and a refrigerator (which didn't work — I put ice in it), pull out beds, drinking water, and water pumped from the lake for washing and plumbing. Decks fore and aft (you have to learn some nautical terms) give plenty of space for enjoying the scenery. The kitchen is modest but adequate. The houseboat is powered by two 70 hp motors and steers by a marvelous ship's wheel.

The check-out procedure seemed simple enough. It was only later that one tried to remember what the dock hand had said. We had a map of the lake, a compass, and gorgeous weather. Lake Powell is an extensive waterway in the Glen Canyon. It soon became evident that it was hard to determine which were the real side canyons and which were mere indentations. There were some marker buoys, but they did not always match the map. After a little way we decided to have lunch. We thought you could just let the boat drift without the motors but it was not like a parked car. As we were eating sandwiches and having an iced drink, we noticed that we were drifting towards one of the shores. Almost all of them were rock lined. We started the motors and began a short course in using two motors, sometimes reversed, steering with and against the breeze, but a houseboat is not simple to maneuver. Before we were clear we had bumped one rock. Later we learned that we had bent one propeller. Our deposit began to shrink before our eyes.

However, we were pretty good on open water and we did find a lovely canyon called Moki, a jumble of the Spanish and Indian languages. It reminded us of those who had lived here under extremely harsh conditions. Many of the canyons have almost vertical rock cliffs, a talus base (rock that has splintered from the cliff), and many intricate little bays and inlets. What a world. I tried to write a haiku:

> Water flows,
> high sky hovers,
> red rock mediates.
>
> and

Water and sky try to touch,
rock intervenes,
the rock wren twitters.

Well, I am not a poet. But the essentials of water, sky, and red sandstone were primitive and powerful. Wherever I turned there were new combinations of this trinity. A few powerboats and other houseboats occasionally came by, but for the most part it was a private glimpse of the eternal.

After a few days, Ned and I became a reasonable team — reasonable for inexperienced water travelers. He did the cooking; I washed the dishes — which dried themselves in the desert air. I tidied up deck ropes and did other household chores, but we didn't spend much time on such things. The weather and the scenery were too alluring. Figuring our gas mileage was confusing. We had 120 gallons of gas. We had two RPM instruments which told us how fast the motors were going and how many hours had been clocked. But what is an "hour," that is, at what RPM? We became so confused that the next day we decided to return to the marina and get further instructions — plus, a few more items I wanted from the van (the houseboat had no deck chairs). For all of our anxiety, we discovered that we had used only eight gallons of fuel. So, we returned to the lake with more confidence.

This time we headed northeast some twelve miles. Again the main channel was fairly easy to read, and all the side channels were attractive. One had to choose. Without having to work too hard at navigation, we could move along at about four MPH enjoying the moonscape views. We turned in at Forgotten Canyon. The map said it had pictographs but with all of the fantastic weather marks, rock splits, and water stains, it was sometimes hard to tell what we were seeing. Picasso would have loved the designs — great, sprawling, exaggerated figures, human and animal. No matter whether any human had actually drawn them, one's imagination enjoyed them. At the base of a cliff we found a short strip of sand which became our campsite. Our anchoring technique was to plant two rope-attached, arrow-shaped anchors at about 45 degrees each side in the sand on the beach and let the pull of the boat dig them in deeper. It works. But the beaching and departure processes were always tricky. One can never calculate the wind direction in a canyon. Once you lose momentum, you simply have no control. You drift and swing. Ned and I called instructions to one other as if we knew what we were doing. But we never became proficient at handling the boat near shore, and it can be somewhat unnerving to jump from rock to rock with an anchor while your shipmate frantically manipulates the steering and motors. Once successfully beached, we celebrated with cold ginger ale! Even if one loses a pair of glasses overboard, as I did, there is a happy sense of achievement in getting one's boat secured for the night.

At dusk, some kind of gnats came out, but they soon disappeared. The bats swooped. The stars were stabbing bright in the clear air; a few birds chirped; some unidentified noises, but mostly an awesome quiet. And in the quiet, huge forms of rock brooded over us. The blue-green water and the high cliffs gently faded into purple, touched with washes of the setting sun. Then a deep evening solitude. After the first few nights, we slept on the deck and watched the stars and the bats, dancing a million miles apart.

The morning is a gentle invitation to watch the sun reappear and start washing the world with light from the tops of the cliffs to their sides, and finally into the deep gorges. As we drank coffee on deck, watching this cosmic scene felt like being at a grand opera — really grand. Ned did not bother me when I said the Office and often just listened as I prayed a psalm. I never asked him about his religion, if any, and he never inquired about mine. We had agreed just to share these few days and not invade one another's life. I was grateful not to have to get involved in any theological discussions. The scene had its own eloquence.

The next night we went to Knowles Canyon. There one could easily see the restored Anasazi ruins and the pictographs. It was hard to imagine how the Indians managed to live, but when life is reduced to the bare minimum, one can focus on essentials. Art was obviously part of that minimum.

> I pondered whether we modern people could ever recover such simplicity without abandoning our position on the evolutionary ladder. Luxury and pleasure have such a hypnotic pull. Can a people choose to be simple, and yet at home with our complex technology? This is an art we have not learned.

After Knowles Canyon we decided to come back toward the marina. About an hour later, we beached on a sandy cove. Again, it was tricky but we finally stabilized the houseboat. The water was perfect, the air dry, the sun hot. We slept on the deck for a last look at the stars.

The next day we left our beach early to get back by the check-out time, 9:00 AM. However, we found a stranded man and his wife in an expensive powerboat which had run out of gas (at least we hadn't done that). He was embarrassed. Feeling very superior, we towed them to the marina. After gassing up we returned our boat to the main dock. There the efficient management group checked us out. I knew when the young man raised the motor from the water that I would have to make my confession.

"Ah, you hit a rock," he observed.

"Well," I replied, "the rock just jumped off the shore and banged into me."

He smiled. Nearby the young woman supervisor smiled too, and very professionally said, "Rebuild."

My Scottish heart sank. But when she named a figure of $17.50, I relaxed. Not bad. So I paid the bill out of my deposit and left the office — very relieved.

Saying goodbye to Ned was as easy as meeting him. We had grown close but had hardly discussed our lives. Words can often cover over the mystery of life. Our common love of the beauty of the area had opened up a bond between us which could not be expressed. We both understood. We thanked one another and parted.

I bought ice and more diesel, and headed back out of Hall's Crossing. I reflected that the Grand Canyon had been a vast view of a magnificent sunken carving of the earth. Monument Valley had been a view from the bottom of the desert looking up at the lonely rock sentinels that stood spare and isolated. Lake Powell had been a water adventure at the base of rock cliffs. What a triple imprint on the imagination.

GOLDEN EAGLE

In the midst of these thoughts I became aware of a duel ahead in the air just above the desert floor. My tape of Chopin's vigorous music was the perfect accompaniment for a contest between a golden eagle and a raven. The raven chased the eagle, which maneuvered easily and effortlessly, occasionally rolling completely over. Here was the drama of life on a bare stage. Nature was the Creator's Sacrament, gorgeously beautiful, but ruthless if the rules are disobeyed. Rock and sky and creature conflict, all moving beautifully to Chopin.

HANKSVILLE

I continued north on Highway 95 through the Henry Mountains of southwestern Utah. This bleak, desert town has one unique feature: a gas and food store hollowed out of a rock, very comfortably cool inside. Even the usual tourist mementos looked attractive in this wilderness. What had life been like here 50 years ago?

CAPITAL REEF.

Turning westward from Hanksville, I soon came to my destination. Capital Reef State Park shows one more aspect of the two-billion-year drama of the upthrust and erosion story. Here the interesting feature was that the jagged rock cliffs overlooked a lush valley. It was part of a water-pocket formation which held the water in the rock, letting it gradually seep out. Some Indians had lived here, but the Mormons developed the real potential when they came through in the mid-1800s. They developed irrigation ditches which watered orchards, hay fields, and gardens. This was a far-Western version of the New Harmony Utopian experiment. The Mormons never gave up, and Utah is marked with their industry and communal consciousness.

BRYCE CANYON

Going north and then south to negotiate some high mountain ranges, I came to Bryce Canyon National Park. Here the story was different. Delicate fingers of red and pink sandstone standing file upon file in Gothic-like rows gave the impression of a cathedral. Again, the various languages I heard revealed visitors had come from many countries.

ARRESTED

Driving from the camp to the rim of the canyon, I eased past a stop sign in a casual manner. I hadn't seen any hazards, let alone the park ranger. But, he saw me! He stopped me and gave me a lecture about the need for caution with so many people about. I felt like a small boy — or maybe a parishioner receiving a sermon. However, he was compassionate and only issued me a warning. Later that evening as I was saying Mass on some rocks away from the camp, I was amused at the Gospel (Matthew 10:17) which said that the faithful would be arrested. Of course, I was not a martyr but there are interesting connections with the Bible if you are doing your lectio daily.

After leaving Bryce, I went through more Mormon towns with their cultivated fields and orchards. Wherever they could find water they made good use of it. Not far away (50 miles is nothing in this part of the country) I arrived at my next wonder.

ZION NATIONAL PARK

Zion combined huge cliffs with stream-filled little valleys. It was refreshing to bathe in the Virgin River, some of which is fed by weeping springs coming out of the rock. Here, too, the deer were quite tame. One tour bus arrived with travelers from Pennsylvania. These Western parks were indeed part of a worldwide pilgrimage for people from all over the world.

DESERT STORM

Another 40 miles and I came to the city of St. George (one wonders who named it) at the southwestern tip of Utah — an interesting example of a modern city arising out of the desert. After some shopping, I headed to nearby Snow Canyon. There I had a lovely private site, picnic table, waste disposal, shower, and drinking water — all for $4.50. As I was sitting outside the van enjoying the shade from the awning and a cool drink (the temperature was over a hundred degrees), I became aware of some gathering clouds. But it wasn't until the awning began to flap noisily and some drops of rain touched me that I took the situation seriously. Quickly I folded up the awning — by now a familiar operation. Then the wind rose and the rain came. It rained hard and I had a firsthand experience of the power of water. It beat on the sandstone rocks around me and soon rivulets were draining off the rocks, then small waterfalls. Just beyond the van a little creek, muddy and strong, began to pour by my camp. I could see how with enough time the Grand Canyon could be shaped by this carving process. It was a good opportunity to take a shower and enjoy the storm all around me. Finally the rain ceased but the creek continued to flow. I waded in and watched it carry away the fine sandstone that had come down from the higher rocks. Later, when it had ceased flowing, I could see the watermarks on the sand, exactly as one sees them etched on the hard rock of the national parks. These sandstone formations were laid down by an ancient sea which left its signature.

LAS VEGAS

Soon I was out of Utah and dropping in altitude — and gaining heat. I took a side road toward Lake Mead, hoping to repeat my Lake Powell experience, at least with a swim. The bleak desert and the heat dissuaded me. The stick-on thermometer fell off the dash at 110 degrees. So I ended up in Las Vegas. I remembered being there over 40 years ago. Then I had visited a convent which was just off the Strip (as the main street is called). The roulette wheels and the callers naming the winning numbers were mixed in with verses of the Office as the sisters prayed (windows open, no air conditioning then). Well, what a change!

I found an inexpensive motel and took advantage of the booklet of tickets provided by the management. Walking the Strip was like being inside a neon sign. All was flickering light as far as I could see. The people were moths, caught and mesmerized. The rich and the poor (judging by their dress) were equal; all hovering near some mysterious flame — money. My booklet gave me two dollars, which I changed into nickels. I, too, was soon worshiping, watching the pears and apples roll by, mentally trying to arrange a favorable combination. Sometimes a few nickels would return to me, but the two dollars went quickly. Around me were mostly old ladies, working their right arms with determination. Nearby were green-covered tables where various card games were being played. I had no nerve even to try; I would have been eaten up by those clever dealers. They hardly smiled. I tried to let the scene open up illusions of grandeur and power. I couldn't get addicted. It was fascinating, amusing, sad. I know this is called "Sin City." I was not shocked. Just sad. So many people, casino workers and visitors, all looking for something they knew they would never possess or have very long. But the looking was hypnotic.

As I approached a change counter, a woman worker stepped outside her booth. "Are you quitting?" I asked.

She looked at me with a wistful look. "I wish I were," she said. Her face underlined the statement.

I used another ticket to have a meal with an ice cream for dessert. I tried the most exotic casino I could find, Caesar's Palace. The expensive illusion wouldn't work for me there either. If it could be taken as a cheap arcade, it could probably be enjoyed. But the place is run with such grave zeal that lightheartedness, like Dante's hope at the Inferno's entry, must be abandoned.

The next day I moved westward. I was fully aware that it was summer in the desert. I had forgotten that there were so many mountains. At one point, some 50 miles west of Las Vegas, I had a long hill to climb, from 2,000 up to 4,700 feet. The engine thermometer climbed also; it moved to the red mark on the gauge, and I was not yet at the top. Finally the summit came and I could coast down the other side. The little diesel engine with its wonderful gas mileage record did have its limitations. Again, I turned on Chopin and celebrated the conquest of one more range of mountains.

CHAPTER 9
THE SPIRIT OF THE GOLDEN STATE

GYPSY MOTH INSPECTION

At the California border I was confronted with an inspection station. "Oh well, they're probably after the big trucks," I thought. No, they wanted me.

The pleasant young woman surveyed my van professionally and calmly said, "I'll have to do a gypsy moth inspection." Was she joking? No, she wasn't. In all good humor she asked me to take the camp chairs out of their storage bag. She peered down the hollow metal legs. "Good place for moths," she explained. She crawled under the van. The moth apparently lays its eggs in dark places and then hopes for exposure to vegetation when the eggs hatch. The state of California doesn't want that to happen. A few years ago they lost millions of dollars from a fly infestation. Well, I got through.

BARSTOW, CALIFORNIA

In Barstow I met my nephew and his wife, Neil and Bonnie Randolph, and their four lovely daughters. I have known Neil all his life and had a feeling for his sensitive and fun-loving nature. By now he was about 49, had experienced open heart surgery and already was looking at the last chapters of his life. It is for people like this that I long to find a simple formula of wisdom. For most people, living is a hazardous affair. Learning to live with trust and skill and humor may be the wisdom.

One of the daughters did my laundry. After 4:00 PM, I was immersed in the family — the dogs and cats, news, preparations for dinner, reports from various family members, inconsequential chit-chat, the touching of tender points of people's lives — the evening ritual of any family. I wondered, what is the spirituality that can help such a family focus its life? They do "go to Church," but the world is so pressing and so complicated. I wondered. I enjoyed the family ritual but a part of me kept wondering.

After supper we went for a drive and saw some of the outstanding features of Barstow. It was a railroad town but now the railway cars and their destinations are being handled by a "classification" program. A computer reads their car numbers and directs them to the correct train. We drove eastward and saw a large solar energy installation, a series of mirrors that reflect sunlight and heat on to a single element which then converts that light and heat into electric energy. This is the exciting part of the future. The dangerous part? Technology seems so good — at first.

I asked Neil and Bonnie what they saw as the most significant changes since they had become adults. They commented on the breakdown of the family, the lack of commitment to children, the loss of community. Bonnie worked in the mental health department of town; Neil with a nearby newspaper. They saw, and they, too, wondered.

SKY HIGH RANCH

After breakfast with Neil and Bonnie, I left Barstow. A short drive through the high desert brought me to Lucerne Valley. I parked on Old Woman Spring Drive and asked the location of Sky High Ranch, a conference center where individuals and groups come to learn new ways of experiencing human growth. It is not a church organization, but it is exploring many of the aspects of our humanity which I believe the Church will one day have to understand in order to help people attain deep prayer and maturity. Looking at such centers is part of my sabbatical search.

I found the address and made my way out of Lucerne Valley and up the mountain to Sky High. A conference was in progress so I left and drove to another site a few thousand feet up the mountain. There it was cooler, and I spent a restful time amid the Juniper trees and rocks. I worked out my finances from Lake Powell, did some reading, a little hiking, had some simple meals, and spent a quiet night under the stars. This is the advantage of being independent.

The next day I returned to Sky High Ranch. The conference attendants had left and the staff and a few long-staying guests were unwinding. I was given a room and access to the pool. In the desert, water is a symbol of refreshment and life. One can understand the significance of water in the Bible much better after a desert experience.

At 5:00 PM, we had a prayer session which consisted of listening to a tape on which the "OM" sound had been repeatedly recorded in soft and louder versions. The twelve or so people gathered "tuned into" this OM sound in any way they chose. In spite of some self-consciousness (although I had met this same technique at Osage Monastery in Tulsa), I did find it relaxing. Supper was eaten in silence until the dessert course. Then we chatted. I discovered that they were impressed with a monk and abbot, and I felt that I was with people whose values essentially were mine. They were loving, courteous, intelligent, and deeply committed to prayer. Every time I fell into conversation with any of them, I found this to be true. Instinctively I felt that their meditation and their commitment to the deepest human values brought them very close to my own ideals.

I talked with Michael Sanders, the director, asking all the questions that interested me after some 36 years in community. Despite the differences in our theological premises, I felt real kinship with his ideas. Theologically, he had difficulty with the concept of Christ as the only one who has full access to the Divine. He also thought that the doctrine of sin was a self-perpetuating negative teaching and he saw Christianity as polarizing, separating those who are "in" from those who are "out." In my younger days, I would have argued with such ideas. Today, I take them seriously. I believe we have limited the concept of Christ and of His Way. Now we are faced with the need to discover the universality of Christ. I also see the need to be as serious in our Christian way as these people at Sky High are in their way about prayer and human growth.

I was particularly interested in Michael's idea of how to handle conflict in community. Rather than negotiate or psychologically analyze a given conflict, their way is to "resonate." By that he meant to be together and to move to a place of union, deeper than the disagreement. This is not a resolving of differences, but a dissolving of differences. To resonate, or as they say, "share energy," at a level where there are no differences, is a possible model for handling conflict on a worldwide basis. But how far all peoples must go to reach that kind of understanding!

Michael did agree that people in conflict should communicate and not let misunderstandings fester. And he favored group exercises as a basis for growth, rather than mere ideas and discussions (see Appendix 10). The basic life of the community, meditation and work (including daily chores and conferences), constitutes their way of spiritual transformation. The phrase "secular monastery" is even used. I find this interesting. There is something universal in the idea of a monastery. As long as there is some kind of spiritual basis for the idea, I have no difficulty in accepting this usage. I felt that Michael was, indeed, a kind of unlabeled abbot, the spiritual father of a family.

After supper, I helped with the dishes. Then several of us were invited into the meditation room where a tape of a modern jazz group called Fresh Aire was played. The music was meditative jazz, or what in my earlier days I might have called progressive jazz. The room was covered with a soft, purple carpet, the walls were light blue. Besides the four-speaker stereo system, the only furnishings were many pastel colored pillows. After the music had been playing for a time, the light dimming in the twilight, a few people began to move rhythmically and finally to dance independently. It was like a very personal interpretation of the music, aerobic in style. I did not dance, but I was delighted with their free response.

After the music, I sat on the patio and watched the last colorings of the sunset. Then I went to bed. I awoke the next morning at about 5:30, sat out on the patio overlooking the valley, and watched the sun rise. It was a good time to say Lauds.

At 6:00 AM, there was another prayer session. This was simply a time together in silence in the meditation room. After a half hour, some went for a walk in the desert. Later, the other three guests and I had a private breakfast while the staff were having a meeting/breakfast. The four of us discussed all kinds of subjects: Jung, evil, wholeness, culture, Indians, etc. It reminded me of conversations I had at New Mellery Abbey in Iowa. All people of prayer seem to be free to look at life with a fresh insight, born of their own inner growth.

Before we could solve all the world's problems, I was called to work. I had volunteered to work, partly because I wanted to see the community more closely and partly because I wanted to reduce the fee I would be charged. I was put in the laundry. After a large two-week conference of 45 people, you can imagine the amount of soiled sheets and pillowcases, towels, and other linen. After about 15 minutes of instruction, I was put in charge of two washers and two dryers. At home my brothers would laugh because I am not famous for my knowledge and skill with practical things. I threw in my own laundry and went to work. It was fun. And I did a lot of laundry, browsing through a book between loads. People would pass by and cheer me on.

> Community is a matter of working together and encouraging one another.

Then, a late morning silent meditation, lunch, and some goodbyes. I had been touched and moved. With a more conscious attention to Christian theology and liturgical practices, I could see Sky High Ranch as a valid way of life. It has a right to be what it is and the Church can learn from such places without giving up its own truth.

The 45 mile drive across the desert was an opportunity to reflect further on my Sky High experience. All experience needs reflection. In an hour or so I began to come to small towns and finally to Yucca Valley. Here in the midst of the high desert was suburbia. The shopping centers, banks, franchise chains, bold signs, all geared to the mobile, consuming society. On one level it is fun and convenient; but in terms of the object of Sky High, the real transformation of humanness, it seemed terribly shallow.

Dropping down into Palm Springs, I saw another energy experiment. Pacific Gas and Electric has set up a series of propellers, maybe as many as a hundred, all generating electric power from the wind. Intriguing technology. Of course, what they need to develop in the Southwest is some technology to produce water.

BOB

In a short time, I arrived at my brother's residence in a mobile home park in Palm Springs. Bob, the second oldest child, the oldest son, managed the family affairs when my alcoholic father could no longer function. Like many in the area, Sahara Park is occupied by retirees. They have a real community, sharing their skills and their friendship. For a modest fee, an ex-plumber might keep everyone's plumbing working. With all of the available recreational facilities, they seemed happy and fairly healthy. Old age, and eventually death, were facts they had to accept. In July, in 115 degree heat, many of them had escaped to cooler places. A few remained and the pool became a welcome gathering spot.

Bob and I talked about the family, five brothers and a sister, about each one's life situation. He had his own interpretation, his own frustrations, and his own plan — if only they would listen to him. As we spoke of the various members of my family (two living brothers — one deceased whose wife and two daughters remain — a sister, and all their children and grandchildren), I recognized the familiar refrain: "So and so is a good person, but if only he would change in this important way, he or she (and the family) would be much happier."

The same type of analysis goes on in my own community. I suppose it is typical of the human family. I would guess that behind the scenes one hears the same reflection at the United Nations.

Over the years, Bob's careful shepherding of the family finances had helped us maintain a reasonable middle-class style of life. Some members appreciated this; some seemed to feel some resentment. Such is human nature. Bob had given me the previous camping van which by now had been sold by my gas station friend, Dave, in Three Rivers. Bob helped with the present van, too. I was grateful for his part in this marvelous gift of freedom which the van afforded me.

Bob has a friend, Louise, who lives across the street in the park. Louise, Bob and I spent many pleasant hours together. We went up a nearby mountain, San Jacinto, where the elevation brought one into a cool, mountain temperature and environment. We also went to a Fourth of July fireworks display, as well as having meals together under a large tree in the yard. In this kind of community, such friendships are frequent and enriching.

THE PAULISTS

While in the Palm Springs area, I visited the Society of St. Paul in Palm Desert, just a few golf courses away. They are a community of men in the Episcopal Church. Previously, they had lived in Oregon but had moved to Southern California where they have a lovely retreat house, enclosed behind walls, with a cluster of buildings inside. For the duration of the summer heat they had closed down their retreat program. Br. Andrew (later ordained), then superior, was also the chairman of the Conference on the Religious life, an association of some 20 or more Religious Orders in the Episcopal Church which offers counsel to anyone with questions regarding the Religious Life. Some 40 years ago Religious (monks and nuns) in the Anglican Communion were not well understood and thought to be exclusively connected with the "Anglo-Catholic" movement in the Church. This is the group in the Episcopal Church that treasures and practices the Catholic heritage of Western Christendom. However, this is changing, thank God. More people in the Church are coming to appreciate that the Religious life helps the Church keep an important focus on prayer, community, and commitment. These are important qualities to be preserved in a secular, activist world; especially important for people intensely involved in social issues. In our own guest house I have met people who demonstrated bravely for peace, going to jail in some cases, and then found that they were angry and bitter within. There is an inner arena of peace that first needs development if one is to promote peace in the world.

Br. Andrew and Br. Barnabas were the two I knew best. I was happy to meet Br. Thomas, Br. Frederick, and Fr. Theodore Black (who had tried his vocation many years ago at Nashdom Abbey, our mother house in England, with our own American Founding Fathers who went to Nashdom Abbey for training). After leaving Nashdom, Fr. Theodore had an interesting career and was now back in a Religious house. It was refreshing to slip back into the rhythm of prayer, Eucharist, silence, and talk about community affairs. Br. Andrew was also working in the nearby hospital which features Betty Ford's work on alcoholism.

Again and again, I discovered that Christian life, even ordinary life, comes alive when there is a touch of death. Inevitably, alcoholism leads to death. Death awakens us to the marvel of life. Some do not waken soon enough, but for those who do, life has a wonder that leads naturally to an appreciation for the gift — and the source — of life.

Br. Andrew and I speculated on the direction of the Religious Life, evolving out of its Anglo-Catholic past, and the movement toward a better communication between Religious within the whole Anglican Church. There are also some interesting conferences among Religious, Roman and Anglican, which point to a quiet ecumenical healing of the divisions in the Church. One can see the Spirit drawing us even closer. The world, too, is being drawn closer. Can we live together peacefully? Prayer and the art of community are important ingredients for peace in the world.

After an all too short visit with the Paulists, I returned to my brother Bob's in Palm Springs. On Sunday I was invited to the Episcopal Church where the Rector asked me to read the Gospel and assist with Communion. It is always good to be with people of faith, celebrating together our life in the Lord. I sometimes wonder if our middle-class kind of faith will stand up to the increasing pressures of our time; but there are heroic and loyal people of faith in the pews.

THE FREEWAY CITY

I left Palm Springs and was making my way westward on the freeway to Santa Monica and my other brother's house. This is about a 130 mile trip. Along this strip, developers have built shopping centers, housing, recreation facilities — all for the real or imagined needs of people today. There were only occasional glimpses of hills and fields. The rest was a freeway city. Gertrude Stein said about another California city, something like, when you get there (to Oakland), there is no there there. Many large cities today are a series of small cities, all connected by a freeway octopus.

The flags for the Olympic Games, pointing out the turnoffs for various events, reminded me that the city is for celebration. Old memories of places I had known when I lived here with my family from 1930 to 1940, blurred into a continuous flow. It wasn't as dramatic as looking at the world from outer space, but it was a new perspective. *The Aquarian Conspiracy* notes that the Belgian physical chemist, Prigogine, sees a "similar law of flow" in blood cells or traffic.

Does this mean that there are mysterious principles (mysterious until we discover them) that govern the dynamic interaction of all of life? Does this mean that there really is no such reality as "the secular"? All is part of the Divine way. The so called "secular" is our human way of ignoring the Divine way and seeing life as centered on ourselves. It won't work. It can't work. We are all caught up in the Divine flow of life that centers on God.

No small or large act of selfishness (even an atomic war) can interfere with God's will. And yet, He continues to invite us to share His will. What patience. What a Divine Passion.

YOU CAN GO HOME AGAIN

The financial crash of 1929 and my father's drinking convinced him that we should move from Denver. Mother agreed, and we came to Southern California. My father was still astute enough to pick a desirable location. For about $12,000 he purchased an attractive Spanish, two story, stucco house, 217 19th Street, Santa Monica. At the time of my visit it could be sold for more than a half million dollars. Tomorrow, who knows! Real estate in California is crazy.

After the deaths of my father and mother, my sister Helen lived at 217 with her family. When her husband died and her children grew up, she moved to Palm Springs. My brother Don and his wife Bessie Lou, and their son, took up residence at 217. So there have been many family memories connected with the house. At the time of my arrival, Don was retired but still working as a consultant. Helen was visiting in the house, taking a break from the heat of Palm Springs. We quickly slipped into a comfortable pattern of a leisurely rising time, after which I would either visit friends or do some typing — letters and this manuscript. Then, around 5:00 PM, Bessie Lou, Helen, and I would convene in the comfortable living room, put on some classical music, have a glass of wine, and talk. It became a kind of Vespers. About 6:30, Don would come home and join us. Then we would have a very good supper (Bessie Lou is a good cook) and continue our conversation. Do we have to wait for retirement to have this much leisure?

Of course the neighborhood had changed. A Japanese couple lived next door, assigned by their company to the United States for five years. Their industrious attitude makes them good students of the language and American ways. I caught a glimpse of a nation still moving ahead through the vitality of its people. Would the Japanese ever become complacent, like so many Americans? Some observers of their industrial way of life predict that this will happen. There are other racial groups in the neighborhood. Often, I would hear the lament that other races were crowding out "Americans." With many people being displaced for one reason or another, racial pressure will probably be one of our time's major issues. The neighborhood had its share of horror stories, too — thefts, even a murder. So beautiful Santa Monica is not the paradise it once was.

But human nature has a way of breaking through problems. There were many joggers and walkers out every morning. There is more consciousness of diet and health. And I sensed a strong desire for world peace.

ST. ALBAN'S

My mother had attended St. Alban's Episcopal Church in nearby Westwood. Other members of the family had been associated there, too. I was happy, therefore, to work with the

Rector, Fr. Norm Ishasaki, on a mini-workshop on alcoholism. We had about 17 people and we talked very simply and openly about the whole disease of alcoholism. My own family and my monastic community have had their share of the problem. I learned at a treatment center that information is far better than sermons.

> One of the hardest parts of the problem is living with an addicted person before he is ready to acknowledge that he can't manage his life. Then the family has to find its own way to survive without becoming bitter and hopeless. It does involve the whole family, and eventually, many more besides. What is the full cost to the world of this one disease? But what joy and grace comes to the person and his or her loved ones when sobriety is sought and received!

I had the pleasure of celebrating the Eucharist on St. Benedict's Day at St. Alban's. The faithful few who attended the mid-week Eucharist were surprised to have an actual abbot in their midst. On another occasion, Norman, his wife and I had a pleasant lunch together. I am in awe of the task of shepherding a parish today. On a Sunday I was celebrant and preacher. This was a special occasion as many of my family attended, in contrast to their usual Sunday pattern. One thinks of the fate of a prophet in his own country, but most of my family have come to respect my choice to live the monastic life. They even see me as their "private chaplain" for all of the family matters that require special attention. Of course, I can't always fix everything but they do listen to my suggestions.

FAMILY PICNIC

On the Sunday afternoon following my appearance at St. Alban's, 35 members of the extended family gathered at 217 for a picnic. While such an affair seems haphazard, an important signal is being sent. This is your family. The people know each other in a more intimate way. They need one another. Mackie, my sister's son, brought a movie camera with sound. He arranged each group of the family around its eldest member and had them record who they were and how they were connected in the family. This will be an invaluable story for the children. As I watched and listened to the family, I realized that there is a Reid trait: talking. I smiled to myself, thinking of some of the burden I place on my own monastic brethren.

A DAY IN THE COUNTRY

Helen and I were given tickets to an art display at one of the local museums. It was called, "A Day in the Country," a collection of French Impressionist paintings. I am told that it was the largest collection of such paintings ever displayed in this country. (Simultaneously with the exhibit's tour, a French film of the same title, featuring stunning impressionistic cinematography, was touring American movie houses and being reviewed favorably by art critics.) In my later years, I have come to appreciate art as a necessary way of human understanding. We might think of it as a natural sacrament (or a natural sacramental, as the theologians probably would call it). In any event, man has always used art partly to objectify his inner experience, and perhaps partly, to search for the Spirit within all creation. In the exhibit there was a lovely mood of peace and beauty expressed in flowing energy, not so much as a description of the object but more as the dream-like response to the object. The commentaries noted that France was emerging from the Franco-Prussian War, that it was in need of a way to regain hope, and that it found beauty and mysticism in the industrial development. Trains and stations figured in Impressionistic art, painted in great clouds of steam, meant to evoke the image of a mysterious power. There were also scenes of middle-class picnics at the shore and in the countryside. I thoroughly enjoyed the display and found a deeper response to beauty within myself. The Greeks said that beauty, truth, and goodness were a kind of trinity of reality. I think I would like to learn to paint.

OLD FRIENDS

In wandering around my old haunts, I found that many of the places I thought of as "friends" had changed. I drove by my high school and hardly recognized it. I stood on the corner of Fourth Street and Santa Monica Boulevard, the main downtown intersection, and wondered. I went to my old parish, St. Augustine's By The Sea, and found it locked. Since I had left, the wooden church I had known had burned and was replaced by a modern building. Later, I looked over the palisades at the beach where I had spent many happy hours and found it strangely different. What if I had stayed in Southern California? What if I had pursued a career in these places? No doubt we would have grown together. Now these places were strangers, only barely suggesting memories. Even so, I still say you can go home again. It is good to take memories out occasionally to relive, and reinterpret.

I looked up a few old friends. Alice McCloskey met me at St. Alban's and took me to lunch. We went back over old days when we belonged to a group which called itself "The Black Sheep." In that group we explored "Catholic" ways and thought of ourselves as rather bold and exclusive. We said the Rosary, shopped around for priests who would hear confessions, and located those parishes which offered Benediction. I am sure that my vocation was nurtured by this group. Now, I do not look for these particular externals of Catholic life, but at the time they were important experiences. Being with Alice was like a living link with those days. Alice teaches costume design at U.C.L.A. and is still an active Christian, moving back and forth between the Episcopal and the Roman Catholic Church denomination of her late husband. More and more I see the blurring of denominational lines.

Another friend, Ralph Kiewit, met me for lunch. Quickly we covered names of some old friends, their journeys, and present status. Ralph was obviously doing well financially, having an office in a large bank building, a house in exclusive Malibu, owning an airplane, and property in California, Colorado, and Hawaii. But he was willing to reflect on some changes in himself. He is pulling back from some of the intensity of the business world, using alcohol less, and looking at life more philosophically. I always appreciate such reflections and never try to force theological questions. They tend to come up naturally in older persons.

We live very much in a pluralistic society, probably a preview of things to come throughout the world. Can we develop a way of human wisdom which will attract people of good will to meet and cooperate in stabilizing this global village? This certainly will be part of the next chapter in the human journey.

CULTURE

One night Don, Bessie Lou, Helen, and I went to the Hollywood Bowl for a concert of Wagner, Grieg, and Tchaikovsky. It was a real celebration of the goodness of life. We, like so many others, had a box lunch. Arriving early, we unpacked our picnic of wine and cheese and had a leisurely preparation for the music. One could look around and see what others were eating, speculate on where they lived, listen to different languages, and enjoy the ambience of a summer evening. It was another Impressionistic scene. The music was good — all the richer for being played by a live orchestra. After we got untangled from the traffic, the drive home through parts of Hollywood, Los Angeles, and Beverly Hills was a cultural event in itself. The city is an art gallery of culture.

Of course the dark side is there, too. The crime, the misery, the violence, the poverty. Only when we agree to work together can we overcome the darkness. And it promises to be so until the end of time. Light and dark will continually struggle. How patient God is, allowing us to experiment again and again with darkness — until we discover that it leads to death.

OLYMPIC VILLAGE

TV at this time (mid-July) was filled with preparations for the Olympics. This, too, is a cultural event of real importance because it helps people focus on life, fitness, and discipline. (I was further reminded of this as I was working on these Notes and read Giamatti's book, *Time for Paradise: Americans and Their Games*.) I caught an interesting comment by one of the newscasters. He had gathered some observations from various coaches who were not pleased with the Olympic Village, the place established to house the athletes from all over the world. One observation was something like this: "The Olympic Village is too confusing for my athletes. One needs to focus and simplify life to maintain the necessary concentration."

This almost sounded monastic. In a pluralistic society, one needs a way of centering, focusing, and concentrating on the essentials. To do this there is need for more than the extrovert quality of life, which loves to act, do, work, achieve, control, compete, and to win. The introvert quality helps one to be simple and attentive to the main point of life: to be in touch with the Source of life itself.

A MEDITATION
During my visit in Santa Monica, the van odometer reached the 7,500 mark. I made an appointment with an RV dealer for the designated check-up. On arriving at the dealer's, I discovered that it would take several hours more than expected. Rather than just sit and fidget in the waiting room, I decided to attempt a meditation. An RV dealership's waiting room is not a church, but the mind can make it so. I began with the simple phrase, "God is Love." I repeated this phrase several times until my mind was focused on it.

> Meditation, in its deepest form, is not what we think.

But in this dealership there was not the quiet to permit such a "going beyond." Doors opened, telephones rang, people came and went, little events developed and were resolved (or not). "God is Love" seemed like an unreal fact, disconnected from the rush of activity going on about me. At least my mind was able to see that the God of Love was the ultimate power sustaining all of this surface activity, keeping it in existence. God was the hidden structure and meaning of the doors, telephones, people, and events. Everything fits together in the divine. There was a person in a rented RV who had transmission problems and had to be picked up somewhere in Los Angeles, brought here, and put in a new RV — all in accordance with the original contract and price agreement. This, too, was held in being by the God of Love. The Finnish rifle team who were supposed to bring a letter of authorization from the Finnish Olympic organization allowing them to take an RV for some days of touring had to be handled diplomatically (they didn't have the letter) until the matter was resolved. The computerese the manager spouted on the telephone when programming his computer was a foreign language. The frenzied activity just beyond the wall in the repair shop was a tension which fed on the power of God. I have to admit that the manager was something of a priest, connecting, smoothing, anointing problems, smiling, patiently negotiating, flowing with the momentum of it all. Probably no one was consciously thinking of God, yet all were using His power. Occasionally, a conflict would be dealt with in a jab of anger, but mostly it was an unspoken agreement among the members of the dealership that each problem was part of the overall flow of the day. God's love reflects itself in the ordinary affairs of daily life, the flow of business, the constant adjustments among people, the patience of the managers and the courtesy which oils the grinding of gears among personalities. I was grateful that I knew the name of God, His love, and could see him working his marvelous compassion in daily life. Alleluia. God is Love.

HUNTINGTON BEACH
After Santa Monica, my next base was at Huntington Beach, some 50 miles south on the coast. I drove Helen down and we stopped at her son Mackie's place of business. He employs his wife and various members of the family in a small business that makes O-rings, a type of gasket used in many kinds of machines and tools. It was just such an O-ring

that malfunctioned in the Challenger space ship tragedy. Mackie's almost garage-style operation keeps a portion of the family in existence. Mackie and his wife Shirley, and their three children live in a pleasant California-style house with a swimming pool. I slept in (or on) a water bed. I didn't like it, maybe because it was too unsteady — perhaps it made me feel insecure. Anne, Mackie's sister, and her family live nearby. They visited each other daily. What a grand muddle of people, dogs, children, conversation, TV, going to the beach, eating, and sleeping. Not an introverted household. But underneath the near chaos was a thread of humanness, caring for one another, being responsible for one another. The God of love was here, too. One night we looked at the movie Mackie had made at the family picnic. For all of the imperfections, jumpy photography, and extraneous noises, the theme came through. This is our family. We need each other.

HOUSE MASS

I proposed we have a house Mass on Sunday. I realized that I would never drag them all to Church. And, I wanted to celebrate with this family in as natural a way as possible. On Sunday morning we cleared out the dining area next to the kitchen, and set up a small table — large enough to hold the *Prayer Book*, some bread and wine, and two candlesticks. Somewhat later than planned, they finally straggled together. They were not used to getting organized so early (10:00 AM) on Sunday. There was even a couple who had just dropped in, friends of Anne's family, who had to be introduced to the idea that they were suddenly in Church. With everyone seated around the table, little Charles wandering around among them, we started the ancient Liturgy. I tried to explain as I went along, making connections with all of the activity we had enjoyed in the last few days —people, dogs, children, conversation, life at the beach, eating, and sleeping. In the Eucharist we were continuing all of that, but focusing on the One Who gave it all to us to enjoy.

I had various members of the family do the readings. We got a little exchange going about the lessons, but not much. We prayed for the family, for friends, for the world. At the Offertory it took a little while to locate a suitable piece of bread out of the bread bin. Then the Prayer of Thanksgiving. At Communion time I passed the bread among them, my sister Helen handling the chalice. She was the eldest, the one who holds the family together. Afterward we had the kiss of peace, a real release of tension. Mackie made another movie of this event for the future. Then we had doughnuts, fruit, and coffee. I was very pleased to be able to let the family see itself in this setting. Many of them thanked me and said it was very special. A few said they really must get back to Church. I'm not sure that will happen. But the God of our family was clearly more visible that morning.

KAAREN

I left Huntington Beach on Monday morning. All week long I had been negotiating with Kaaren, my late brother Jack's daughter. She wanted the children baptized, but she was married to a Lebanese man who was loyal to his Church. So we had tried to get in touch with the local Maronite bishop to see if we could do this together. I stopped at her mother

Doris' and phoned again. No, the bishop would not be available in the time we had. But he had agreed that we would do it together, if all could be worked out. Another example of the ecumenical drawing together. Kaaren and I were disappointed, but we had tried. She is a lovely girl, now a mother of three (another coming), and holding a vast kingdom together — Lebanese and American, business and family life, all on very little money. She also had some of the Reid energy and intuition. Her life, at this time in history, is a fascinating mixture of old traditions and new possibilities. Can she retain her joy of life? That is a question we all face.

In talking with Doris, I became aware again of how vulnerable our older people are. She lived alone in a nice enough neighborhood, but she was afraid of the violence, wanted bars on the windows, didn't go out much, and felt oppressed by much of life today. These older ones are middle-class hostages, people who are suffering more than we recognize. And if they live in downtown areas of big cities, they are often virtually recluses and prisoners in their apartments. To undo this situation is to face the whole redoing of our society.

THE ART OF LIVING

As I drove up the coast toward Santa Barbara to visit a nephew and his family, I pondered my time with the family. It was good to see them. I couldn't unravel many of their problems. I could love them and encourage them, but I could see that many of their life situations were the result of their conscious or unconscious choices. An idea took shape. We need a book describing the art of living in the city today. This would include many practical items such as how to deal with insurance, house repairs, managing one's finances; but it would also have small bits of wisdom, attitudes necessary to live happily. Of course, such a book would not solve all of the problems, but it could serve as a guide for those who wanted to chart a reasonable course through the maze of today's urban life. The Church has a "book," of course, but it needs practical application for those who never read it.

SANTA BARBARA

After many pleasant glimpses of the ocean, stopping a few times at familiar surfing beaches, I came to the charming city of Santa Barbara. In the downtown section you can only build or remodel in the Spanish style. Here I spent the night with my nephew, his wife, and their two boys. They are examples of the best of the younger generation — bright, sensitive, managing fairly well economically, in touch with new ideas of ecology and peace. Unlike most of my family, they are also active in the Church. The Church has a challenge to stay alive for these people without losing the older folks who in their day were the backbone of the Church. I found Scott and Janet open to ideas about meditation, mental peace, inner healing. One day such ideas must become the norm for all people.

I also talked with George Barret, retired bishop of Rochester. It was good to compare notes with an experienced priest and bishop whose active Church career covered some very turbulent times but who remains bright and hopeful. We talked about the early experiments in group dynamics, later movements in the Church, *Prayer Book* revision, women priests, some personalities we both knew, and present problems and achievements.

71

SAN LUIS OBISPO

I left Santa Barbara and drove north. On a sunny day the California coast is beautiful, luring one to stop frequently. I resisted until I came to San Luis Obispo (Spanish for "St. Louis the Bishop"). I wanted to look up an old friend, Dorothy, who had shared the early days in our elitist "Catholic" group in Santa Monica. She wasn't home, so I took the opportunity to visit the old mission of San Luis Obispo. This was one of the string of missions up and and down the California coast founded in the late 1700's by the energetic Fr. Junipero Serra. The whole mission concept of Serra and his companions was a realistic way of creating Christian community in a foreign land. They fostered the arts and crafts, agriculture, the family — all centered on the Church. It was something like St. Benedict's idea, but in this case it was also a conscious tool of the Spanish government, attempting to maintain control of its holdings in the New World. The missions were caught in the political struggle between Spain, Mexico, and finally the United States. For a while the missions became secular settlements, but the Church asked for their return and now is using many of them for modern parish life. Signs at the center — "Youth Center" and "Senior Citizen Group"— indicate the world of a modern mission. I was surprised to hear John Denver's "Anne's Song" coming from the funeral Mass in the Church. No doubt it was a favorite of the deceased. It is a good song.

Then I went out on the plaza of the Church and heard more music. A single guitarist with harmonica propped up before him was entertaining a group seated by an outdoor restaurant along the stream that goes through town. It was too charming to resist. I bought a sandwich and joined the group. The magic of the music, the sunlight, the stream, the people chatting, seemed like blessings coming from the old mission.

Then I went back to Dorothy's apartment and found her just getting out of a cab, very slowly and with a cane. Nothing serious except time had happened to her. She handed me the money for the driver and slowly focused on me. She smiled at her mistake, a gracious acceptance of her infirmity. Then I introduced myself and her whole face exclaimed with joy. I carried the groceries in and she fussed about, asking if the room was all right. Obviously she had grown used to not seeing much. She served a glass of white grape juice in elegant style and we talked about old times. What interested me more was her bright spirit and her faith. She had become a Roman Catholic and now lived near the mission, helping wherever she could. This was her life, and she enjoyed it. She was truly happy. And her humor was not "pious," the twinkle in her eye sparkled when she hit upon some human foible, especially her own. I left her waving vaguely in my direction and smiling — at God, mostly.

> I come back often to a growing conviction about holiness, people who know they are accepted and know that God enjoys Himself in their life.

THE COASTAL PARADISE

After filling up with diesel fuel (the van was getting a surprising 23-25 mpg), I headed toward the coast, away from the freeway. I tried a couple of camping places near the beach, but they were filled. My usual custom is to find a place in the early afternoon before the crowd gathered, but it was now 5:00 PM. The ideal would have been to find somewhere right on the beach. However, this is a rugged coast and there are only occasional coves with sand. Also, access to the beach is limited. You may remember that there had been huge landslides along this coast and it was only recently that the road (US 1) had been reopened at a cost of more than seven and a half million dollars. It is said to be the most expensive highway in California.

HARMONY

Finally I resorted to what had worked in less civilized areas. I took a side road and followed it into the hills, but this, too, was fenced on both sides with hardly a place to turn around. A glare from an old woman in her front yard told me everything. I came back just short of the main highway, and then spotted Harmony. On the old highway, Harmony had been a small but active little town. With the new highway, it had tried to become a center of arts and crafts. But that effort, too, had died. Now it was abandoned. Two cars on the main street, parked in front of a house and a quaint store, suggested that there might be a few people here, maybe. Anyway, I drove up to what had been a brick paved courtyard. A fountain was still bubbling. Little shops and flower gardens opened off the courtyard. It was a set awaiting some actors, and I was the only one. Oh yes, a cat wandered by. So, I parked and had my supper. A door to a public lavatory was unlocked, which was convenient. Once in a while another curious tourist would come by, reach the dead-end where I was parked, turn and depart. I had Harmony to myself.

SAN SIMEON CASTLE

The next morning I enjoyed the ride up the coast listening to one of my new tapes, Andreas Vollenweider playing an electric harp. The music was soft and flowing. The hills were rounded and gentle. The ocean was easy. The sun was warm. No wonder the Indians who lived here grew lazy. Why not? Then I came to San Simeon, a strip of expensive looking motels and shops. What's this? Oh, yes, William Randolph Hearst. He was the grand lord of the publishing business of his time and friend of many notables. The movie *Citizen Kane* was based on his life. As a youngster in Santa Monica I had tried to look over the wall of Marion Davies' beach house which Hearst had built for her. I remember my Jesuit professors at college commenting on their visit with Hearst at his castle. They said you could discuss anything in the world with him — except death. This amused my teachers, accustomed to the deathless atmosphere of philosophical speculation, but Hearst was serious. He did not want to die. Now the fantasy castle entertains tourists. Sitting high on a hill overlooking the ocean, it is impressive. Although I only looked at it from a distance, it seemed to me that it would make a lovely baroque monastery.

PLASKETT CREEK CAMPGROUND

This day I stopped in good time to have my pick of the sites in a state park campground. Then I went down to the beach, only to find that one had to climb down a steep cliff to get there, because storms had washed out the easy trail. I spotted a lovely little cove and descended toward it. In the midst of this exercise, I realized that a certain bush I had been pushing through was probably poison oak to which I am susceptible. Oh well, there was nothing to do but push on, get to the beach, and jump in the ocean, hoping the poison would wash off. The sand, sun, and the brisk water temperature (58 degrees), removed any immediate anxiety about the problem. I thought back to my experience on Lake Powell. Apparently, I am moved by the simple natural elements of earth, water, sun, and sky. Maybe there is a remnant of the primitive in all of us. Do we somehow remember when these elements were the sacraments of God? The setting sun reminded me that I had to climb out of this cove. On top again, I went straight back to the camp and washed my arms and legs. The next morning I was back, standing on the cliff, looking at the ocean. What Divine power did God infuse into this vast creature? Often I tried to leave — but I kept looking.

TROLLS

Later I found that this place was called Sand Dollar Beach and was told that Richard Burton had made a movie here. And it was inhabited by trolls, or at least one troll. I was standing on the cliff, deep in my meditation, when a figure emerged from the bushes. He was young looking but something about his face alarmed me. He came over and began a continuous patter. There was no chance for even a reply or question. He described himself and yet, remained concealed. Everything he said was ambiguous, equivocal. I sensed that he was not really mentally balanced, but I didn't quite know how to disengage. I was afraid. He wanted to sell me some jewelry. I finally just waved and walked away. Back at the camp I asked the camp host about this person.

"Oh, yes," he said. "We call them trolls. They live in the hills. Some are alcoholics. Some are just unbalanced. The authorities know about them and keep an eye on them. If they bother anyone they are taken to jail. They are usually harmless, but their health eventually breaks down."

Trolls? Out here in the sparsely populated coastal area they seem to be manageable, even quaint. Not everyone has to be middle class!

But pack people together in the city and some seem to go crazy. What to do with the urban troll? And how difficult to love such people? They cannot be allowed to destroy life, yet they themselves cannot be destroyed for the sake of other people's convenience. This is a question we face in the world where many people seem quite strange and frightening — homeless. Are there collective trolls, displaced refugees?

Fear breeds control and repression, the precise ingredients which have the world on the brink of extinction. Love knows how to protect life, but not at the expense of human beings, however damaged or different they may be.

The troll at Sand Dollar Beach taught me that I need to grow in love.

CHAPTER 10
SPIRITUAL ROOTS

CAMALDOLESE HERMITAGE
One of the important objectives of my sabbatical was to visit other monasteries and convents, especially the more contemplative type. It is a simple truth today that the Western world is too active, focused on secondary issues, and that we have lost our spiritual roots.

> The life of prayer, lived in community, is an important counterbalance to this loss. Furthermore, contemplatives who are not so absorbed in the immediate needs of people can look ahead and see the obvious, the need to live together in peace. The ingredients are the same, whether we look at a fragmented human being, at a group of people trying to bridge their differences, or at the world which does not know how to live in unity.
>
> The contemplative would say that we can only learn the art of unity from the One God who (for Christians) is also a Divine community.

So, I am always interested in visiting communities of prayer. The New Camaldoli Hermitage is a part of the Camaldolese Order, a member of the over-all Benedictine way of life. They derive their spirit from St. Benedict and specifically St. Romuald (11th Century). Their life features shared liturgical prayer, some common meals and work, and individual hermitages: a synthesis of the cenobitic and eremitic traditions. (The cenobite lives in community, the hermit [eremite] lives alone.) So they also make room for a person who wishes to live a complete eremitic life (there are some recluses on the property), or one who wishes to focus on communal living, or even one who feels called to a special ministry outside the monastery. In this threefold expression of the monastic vocation they are particularly well-suited to the diversity of our times.

Driving along the beautiful and rugged Big Sur coast, I arrived at the turnoff to the Hermitage and began a two mile climb into the hills behind the ocean. I had a letter of welcome from one of the members, but I had no specific reservation. However, I belong to one of the most exclusive groups in the world, the Benedictine "club." All I need do is to identify myself as the abbot of St. Gregory's and Benedictine doors open. This is a tribute to the ecumenical spirit among Anglican and Roman Catholic Benedictines, the result, too, of St. Gregory's credibility over its 48 year history. It also reflects the fact that St. Benedict wrote his Rule in the 6th Century, a time when there was no split in the Christian world, either between East and West or Catholic and Protestant. Benedictines tend to live in that spirit of unity.

Brother Isaiah, the guestmaster, welcomed me and gave me a room with its own little garden overlooking the Pacific. It was a small version of the kind of hermitage each brother has: a unit with a sitting or work area, a sleeping area, a bathroom, a small place for preparing meals, and a prayer room. Outside, within a walled space, is a private garden. Some grow vegetables or flowers; others arrange the garden artistically. Later, just before my departure, I had to vacate my guest room for a scheduled retreat, and I was given an actual monastic unit. As I wandered the grounds, I peeked in a few other units and could see the occupant's personality reflected in the arrangement of furniture. One would be spare and neat, another cluttered and homey.

I remembered visiting a Camaldolese monastery on the island of Majorca some years ago on my way home from Rome. That one, too, was situated on a hill near a coast over-looking the Mediterranean Sea. Each cell had these same areas, with a patio facing the south, worthy of an expensive hotel. After its secularization it had been occupied by George Sand and Chopin in their romantic association. I thought at the time that a monastery is indeed a place of love.

The quiet of the monastery was in contrast to the intensity of the Los Angeles area, especially in its preoccupation with the Olympics. It allowed me to process, very slowly, the many persons, relationships, and situations of my family.

Silence is the womb in which meaning is born.

At 6:00 PM a bell summoned us to Vespers. The church is a large hexagon, divided interiorly into two almost equal spaces, a choir and a sanctuary. The choir contained a series of chairs, arranged in an elongated U shape, with the celebrant's chair closing the U. The guests were arranged parallel to and behind the choir. The feeling was one of inclusion in the choir. The Sanctuary, or rotunda as they called it, was a kind of hexagon in itself, opening toward the choir. During the celebrations of the Mass, after the liturgy of the Word, monks and guests moved into this rotunda, a spacious, altar-centered area with no other furniture. Near the outer wall, carpet-covered low steps lifted up from the altar level. It was a perfect setting for the liturgy.

At the end of Vespers there was the asperges, a sprinkling with holy water of those gathered, then a visit to an icon of Our Lady. (These last two corporate acts are usually connected with Compline, but the monks here do many of the Hours of prayer privately.) Then began the deep silence of the night.

One could enter it as though going into a forest. When you are used to it, you know it as an outward expression of the inner silence, the mysteri-ous sanctuary within, the hidden place of the heart. It is here that prayer goes beyond words, beyond images, beyond thoughts and plans, beyond the ego itself, into the eternal emptiness where the Father eternally utters the Word and breathes out the Spirit. Opening oneself to this triune utterance and breathing comprise the essence of contemplative prayer. All prayer is desperately needed in today's overactive and ego-centered (and therefore violent) world.

JACK DANIELS

Apart from the life of prayer, I had come to visit Jack Daniels. Jack is somewhat like Ethan Simmons, my other friend in Albuquerque, but with a few differences: Jack is a recovering alcoholic, divorced, and at the time of the sabbatical, not a member of the Roman Catholic Church. He is working his way through all of his personal history in the context of prayer, in the Church. This struck me as a fascinating gift the Church can give to this world's pilgrims. Jack was being allowed to live in the community, have his own private hermitage, sit in choir, and work with the brethren. What a gracious blessing the community was giving him. It suggested to me that traditional Christianity can feed and nurture souls, even those whose connection with the institutional church is ambiguous. Jack gave me a full tour of the enclosure. Apart from the church with surrounding hermitages, there was a dining area with kitchen, workshops and garages, an administrative unit, a recreation room, and a library. One interesting item was a video cassette recorder with which films could be shown on a TV screen — but the monks intentionally avoid live TV. There were also tapes of music and renowned spiritual teachers such as Thomas Merton. I remembered a discussion in Rome at a Congress of abbots about the wisdom of allowing the modern communications media into the monastery. Finally, after a heated exchange representing both sides, one person reminded the group that the same discussion had taken place in the 7th Century. The question then was about letting books into the monastery. It all comes down to what use we make of what we let into our lives.

Here at Camaldoli, all of the usual departments of monastic life normally collected together in a tight cloister arrangement, were actually housed in single-story buildings, arranged in an extended order. Farther away from the main buildings were various other workshops. It was interesting to see the organic and historic development of the community reflected in these buildings. An architect had combined traditional Camaldolese arrangements with modern design elements in a master plan.

Jack also took me up the mountain where the community owns several hundred acres containing hermitages, meditation spots, and walking trails. They were fighting a legal battle with a logging company that wanted to cut down some redwoods, those magnificent long-lived witnesses to earth's history. One could also see the moist earth in places oozing down in little landslides, a small example of the recent land slides that had covered the coast highway. It is a fragile part of the earth, sparsely occupied, wild and lonely. One night I saw coyotes and hawks. Just the spot for a place of prayer.

Jack and I talked about the various aspects of his life — his former wife and his children, his journey to India, the alternatives he had for the future — convincing me that he was dealing with himself honestly and faithfully. One time we simply sat in his hermitage in silence. I felt that monastic life helped both of us to be saner.

With some allowance for individuals, the monks rise at 4:00 AM for private prayer, Vigils at 5:45. Later, they gather with the guests for Morning Prayer and the Eucharist. There was Eucharistic sharing — so I was able to receive Communion in true spiritual hospitality. There was a feeling of genuine openness along with an understandable protection of their intense focus on prayer and the interior life. This openness — allowing women sometimes into the refectory, certain guests into the cloister, long-staying guests to live near the hermitages with the cloister — had not come about easily. No doubt there were brethren who disagreed with this trend, but it all seemed to be carried in prayerful hospitality. The community seemed to retain plenty of interior space. In contrast, urban people who have little training in utilizing their interior space are going somewhat mad in their crowded physical conditions.

Meals for the guests were provided in a guest kitchen where soups, salads, bread, and beverages could be prepared. I was invited for the noon meal into the refectory, where the brethren talked. The food was vegetarian and tastefully prepared.

SUNDAY

In preparation for Sunday we had a vigil very early in the morning — at 12:30 AM. It is always exciting to do something like this for the first time. I remembered some years ago being at Montserrat, the ancient Spanish Benedictine monastery, and praying the night vigil prayer. It was fascinating, probably somewhat romantic for me; but one can guess that the novelty soon wears off and it can become routine, even boring. It is just such routine that fosters movement in the mind. The left brain, the active, organizing, common sense part of the mind, has to be occupied, then lulled. Then one moves beyond. Not always, of course. One can cling to the busy part of the mind. One can be frightened of leaving it. Some only know themselves in the busy occupation of practical thinking and doing. Much of the prayer of a monk is routine. His active mind can feed upon the psalms and portions of Scripture used in the service while the deeper self moves toward a simple union with God.

At 9:00 o'clock that morning, Fr. Prior invited me to an informal gathering of a few of the monks. They had a tape recorder and I was asked to give an account of my journey and some of my reflections. This was a gracious act of attention on their part. I tried to give them opportunity to ask questions or offer their own reflections. We had an enjoyable hour.

At 11:00 we had the Eucharist. The 15 or so members of the community were joined by at least 40 or 50 guests, some of them resident guests, others, drop-ins. There was no attempt to screen them according to their denominations. All were invited to participate. They did so reverently. Occasionally two young children whimpered, were taken to a more removed part of the church, then brought back. A man was taking some movie footage. All flowed smoothly into the chanting of the psalms, and a reading from Fr. Aelred Squires, OSB (an author, scholar, and member of the community). The flute solo by the Cantor, the hymns, the easy walking rhythms of the brethren as they moved about in the liturgy, were part of a visual and auditory flow. Then we moved into the rotunda. Again I noticed the simple and sacred space as the Mass continued. I couldn't always understand the celebrant's diction, but the flow and the ritual were an all-encompassing, living symbol of Christ in His members re-expressing His love. The Christian truths, that God gives His love in words that ordinary people can hear and in bread and wine that ordinary people can eat and drink, and that His people are His real presence, are simple and profound. We may miss knowing about them unless His love is kept alive within us. At the kiss of peace we mingled and exchanged an embrace. At Communion, the celebrant stationed himself before the altar where we all filed by for the Body of Jesus. Then we divided into two lines and received the chalice from one side or the other of the altar from two priests. We went back to the choir section of the Church for silence, some closing prayers and a hymn which ended the liturgy. I wandered into the cloister, awaiting lunch, aware as I often am of a quiet gentle afterglow of the Spirit; a lingering blessing within and around one.

THE LINK

At lunch time, the Prior introduced me to a couple and we sat together for the meal, talking about various things. Then the link with my next event opened. The couple had lived and taught at Esalen, the famous center for human development, located just a few miles north along the coast. I had revealed, somewhat furtively, that this was my next stop and was surprised to learn that the Prior, Jack, and some others, took Esalen very seriously. I was afraid they would judge it as being totally secular, as having nothing to do with the Christian journey. I was relieved and pleased that the talk about Esalen touched on human development and spiritual values as a valid connection with our traditional Incarnational theology. Not that everyone would make that connection, but the fact that some of the Camaldolese monks and this couple, who were very serious about the Christian faith, could take Esalen seriously confirmed my intuitive expectation. Between the monastery with its emphasis on meditation, traditional Christian theology, silence, ordered communal life, and Esalen with its emphasis on exploration of the ever-expanding dimensions of human nature, there was obviously a deep connection. One could sense the networking of persons across the gulf that has separated religion from "mere humanism" (as we used to say). The fact that such persons come from very different backgrounds, many with no organized religious affiliations, and yet are converging, is a sign to me that God has decided that it is time for us to be one people on this planet.

Some of the ingredients for this convergence seem to be a recovery on the part of Western Christians of all denominations of the depth of their own mysticism; an increasing awareness of Far Eastern techniques of prayer and insights into the nature of reality; the many strands of developmental psychology, East and West; and a deeper appreciation of the mysterious dimensions of human nature. A hopeful new chapter in the story of mankind is opening up.

After lunch I said goodbye, received a monastery fruitcake as a parting present, gathered my things together in the van, changed into my driving clothes, and eased down the winding hill. Was this another holy and human experience? A further inner and outer convergence?

CHAPTER 11

THE EXPANDING SPIRIT

ESALEN

As I drove along the coast the few miles that separated the monastery from Esalen, I was aware of some mixed feelings. I was excited because I knew I was in for a new adventure. I was somewhat apprehensive because I knew that the pathways of this adventure would not be in accordance with my accustomed ways. I was heading toward a place where emphasis is on the body and on wisdom gained over the centuries from other cultures. It is one thing to think about such an exploration. It is another to do it. The head would not be in control, familiarity would not be one's companion, there may be no friend to rely on. But I wanted to go. Perhaps it would be helpful to quote a description of how Esalen sees itself.

> "Esalen Institute is a center to explore those trends in education, religion, philosophy and the physical and behavioral sciences which emphasize the potentialities and values of human experience. Its activities consist of seminars, and workshops, residential programs, consulting and research."
>
> — (From an Esalen cookbook.)

This sounds easy; a little stretching, maybe, but nothing unusual, I thought. How mistaken I was!

I turned off the highway and headed down a steep road to a gate where a young woman directed me to the office. I began to sense the gentle ambience, people in informal clothing or swim suits, strolling about the green lawns. Wooden buildings were randomly scattered. From the number of cars, one would guess that there were several hundred people here. At the office I showed my letter of acceptance and my receipt for one of the programs, "Experiencing Esalen." I was told my room number and the location of the first meeting that Sunday evening, then was given meal tickets and a map of the grounds. The friendly people, the lovely grounds, and the magnificent ocean just over the edge of the cliff were creating a calming effect.

STEPHEN

How shocking, then, was the loud laughter coming out of the room I was assigned. I checked the number again. Yes, it was room 33. I walked in to meet Stephen, a 42 year old Chinese-American from Oakland. He was laughing *too* loudly. I introduced myself. This hardly registered with him. Then he said, "They're *nude*," and again broke out into nervous laughter. I had heard about the nudity at Esalen but had determined to see how it fit with the general program. Stephen, I discovered, had registered as I had, and then had gone out on the lawn. Below him was the swimming pool, and there definitely were some nude men and women swimming. He had retreated to our room where I found him. I tried to help him see this in perspective. There was no nudity on the upper level of the office, the dining room, and deck. He didn't have to get involved if he didn't want to. At this point Dieter, our other roommate, came in. He was from Germany (Esalen attracts people from all over the world) and a teacher of psychology. He sized up the situation quickly and helped calm Stephen. I have since learned that many Chinese are particularly private. Finally Stephen came to dinner with us, and the slow softening process began.

After supper I had a little time before my first session. I decided to take advantage of the hot sulphur baths the Indians had enjoyed a long time ago. Down a path along the cliff was a building with a series of hot tubs. Here, too, was social nudism. It was not in the least offensive. Everyone was talking or just soaking. There was nothing furtive or suggestive. In fact it was much less "sexual" than other gatherings I have attended — some in the Church — where the spoken and unspoken innuendoes were clearly provocative.

Actually, this was not my first experience with social nudism. Some years ago, when the Abbey first acquired the camping van my brother gave us, I began receiving notices of camping places. One of these, in small print, classified itself as a "clothes optional camp." I hadn't caught that. On my way home from a weekend in a parish, I decided to spend the night in a camp before returning to the Abbey. I drove into this camp, paid my fee, and arrived at my site. As I began to leave the van for a walk, I noticed that the people around me, some of them family groups, had no clothes on. Should I go back to the gate and ask for my fee? But the family aspect touched something deep within me. I decided to stay and risk my first experience with social nudism. I took off my clothes in the van and stepped out. For about 15 seconds I was sure that everyone in the camp had stopped what they were doing and turned to look at me. The fact was no one noticed me at all. They just went on enjoying themselves in the sunshine, the pool, and on the volley ball court. I forgot my shyness and began to enjoy myself, too.

Soon I was chatting with others and walking around the grounds quite unselfconsciously. Later, after a swim, I was saying the Office by the pool. A voice said, "Father, when you are finished with your prayers, come over and have a drink." I looked up to see a man smiling. I waved and later joined him and his group. Some of them were teachers at Notre Dame, one a priest, another an ex-nun. But the talk was of Maritain. I have noticed that social nudism fosters an open and honest exchange among people. There is no barrier, no armor, no hiding. I won't pretend that it solves all problems, but it certainly dissolves some. I have seen teenagers happily mixing. Much of the secret "naughty" aspect of sex has been removed by natural, social unclothed mixing.

N.L.P.

On this first evening while enjoying the hot tub with others at Esalen, we were talking about our programs. One very articulate man caught my attention. I asked a few questions and found that he was a Jesuit from India and that he was working on a doctorate in "N.L.P." These letters stand for Neurological Linguistic Programming. Some people may be acquainted with this system through the book, *Frogs Into Princes*. Dick, the Jesuit, talked me into changing my program from the introductory sessions for which I had signed up. I changed it easily at the office, then went to the slide show on Esalen. Later, our first N.L.P. session began. We met our leaders, Eli Jaxon-Bear and Judy Rush, and the 17 or so members of our group. At the beginning, I was somewhat unsure how much to reveal of my monastic and priestly vocation. Over the week it turned out that it didn't make any difference. In fact, as people began to know my position, they often expressed gratitude that one in my theological situation would take Esalen seriously. It reminded me of the time, many years ago, when I was talking to Mies Van der Rohe, the late architect who was one of the great men of our time. He was interested in doing some architectural work for St. Gregory's because in his early days in Europe, the Church and the artist had drifted apart. Both were the poorer for it.

I have the impression that the Church must take the latest discoveries regarding human nature very seriously. We can have reservations, but we dare not be facile in our rejection. I was able to convey this attitude to the people at Esalen. After our session, about 10:00 PM, I again went down to the baths. This became a nightly ritual. How restful. Often the moon and the stars were there to pour their wonder over us as we soothed muscles and mind. That night, back in our room, we did not discuss our different programs. Stephen was restless, but quieter.

A DAY AT ESALEN

My day began about 6:30 AM. I would say Lauds, then go down to the dining room for a cup of coffee. At 7:15, I went to our meeting place, a charming house where Fritz Perls (the late giant of the Gestalt movement) had lived. It had a main room, two bedrooms, and a marvelous deck overlooking the Pacific. There for a half hour, some of the group sat in silence. At 7:45 we did some moderate yoga exercises. How centered is the body — and therefore the mind, according to the Eastern point of view. Breakfast was usually rather simple. The diet at Esalen was mostly vegetarian with emphasis on wholesome foods: whole grain breads, granola, honey, bear mush (a natural cereal), and for lunch and supper, vegetables and glorious salads from the community's own garden, tastily prepared. I grew to love it. From ten o'clock to noon, we had our morning teaching session. Lunch followed, either in the main dining area or on its adjoining deck. I took a nap, then walked, and wrote in my journal in the van which was parked outside our room. At 4:00 PM, we had our second session which lasted until 6:00. This was followed by supper, then busing dishes — which was my way of repaying for the considerable scholarship aid I received.

It was rewarding to see how the permanent staff people and the working scholars actually did the chores together. (A working scholar is someone who spends a month or so at Esalen, working and attending workshops.) It was a happy atmosphere. People were friendly, cooperative, yet direct when something needed attention. I finished the kitchen work in time to attend our third session at 8:00 PM. After that I spent some time in the baths before bed. It was a full day, stimulating and relaxing.

SOME N.L.P. PRINCIPLES

Without trying to do full justice to this workshop, I will outline some recurring themes:

First, over the years, all of us consciously and unconsciously have developed reactions and responses to life, forming *inner maps*. At one time these maps worked effectively, but may not do so now. For example, in my case, as a child I developed a way of dealing with my alcoholic father which protected me from his unloving behavior. This was not conscious. It was a way of surviving. The result was a set of habits which prevented me from talking honestly with people, from allowing myself to feel what was too painful, and from trusting. These survival habits were no longer serving me. In fact, they were getting in my way. The N.L.P. program can teach a person how to break such habits down into small pieces and redo them in a more positive way. I now see ways in which I can empathize with people in their pain without feeling obligated to relieve it (unless they themselves ask me to do so) or to protect myself from it.

Second, we discover that there is an enormous amount of energy stored in our memory of past experiences. If they are good memories, they can be used to strengthen us in our present needs. Painful memories, can be brought alongside the good ones and "dissolved." Then our energy is no longer used to insulate us from our past pain and is more available for life today.

A third area is the signals we all give as we communicate with one another. These signals are not always in words. They are also contained in the way we use our eyes, head, body language (as it is often called), the tone of our voice, or the preference we have for feeling, visual, or tonal language (e.g., "I *feel* your frustration; I *see* what you mean; I *hear* what you are saying.") By carefully listening and closely watching, we can usually discover the other person's language. Then we can communicate better by using their language.

Fourth, traditional therapy attempts to bring understanding to our behavior, offering us freedom to change if we so choose.

Fifth, since each one of us must, in the end, choose his or her own way of life, we can't blame anyone else for it. No matter how deeply influenced by others we were at one time in our life, we are responsible only for our own behavior now. Ruthless compassion, "tough love," on the part of others helps us come to this honesty about ourselves. Anger and resentment on our part are ways of avoiding that responsibility.

If we choose to change our behavior, we need to respect the process by which we were hurt, know what part of us was hurt, perhaps ask permission of that part to look at some alternatives. Without this gentle approach to ourselves we may find that our minds and our wills are determined to change, but some other part of us (probably unconsciously) resists. We are guided by deep habits. We are fixed in our neurotic patterns. One thinks of St. Paul's dilemma in Romans 7:23. Sometimes we may have to search for the "good" which the resisting seeks to hide from us. With gentleness, respect, and alternative ways of obtaining that good, we may reprogram our habits. And we can ask for help from inner allies. (A Christian might see these allies as angels or the Holy Spirit.) Often it is the child in us who has been deeply hurt. It takes a great deal of love and patience to strengthen that child, heal it, relieve it of guilt, forgive it, help it grow up, and to nurture it in its new growth. To see that one really has new choices and that one can learn how to exercise these choices is a great liberation and recovery of self-esteem.

Sixth, we all recognize a recurring mental attitude: "I am impossible. I know about my problem. I get lots of advice. I know that the answer is within me. I don't love myself. I play many roles. I can't make up my mind. I want to be strong. I don't want to continue in this fear. I am afraid of being hurt. I continue to beat myself up." The way we rehearse our problem merely reinforces the inner map we have constructed. This map was my survival once but this map needn't determine my life now. I made a lot of it up. I can remake it. Such realizations need not make me feel guilty. In many ways I am doing the best I know how. And with insight and some skills, I can live differently. I have all the resources I need to live a good life. It is just a question of gaining access to them. Much of the good life is involved with satisfying exchanges with others. But we must study these exchanges. Pay attention to the response we get when we speak. If we get a strange response, a hostile one, a bored one, change the way we are saying what we want to convey. The success of communication is in the response. There is no failure in exchange, only feedback. All problems and limits are opportunities. We learn when we want to learn. We can even learn from the problem. Call it your friend and let it teach you.

HYPNOSIS

N.L.P. principles need development, but one can catch a glimpse of how exciting it is to see doors opening for oneself in gaining new freedom of choice. Another skill we were shown was that of hypnosis. Most of us who are not acquainted with hypnosis have exaggerated notions of what it entails. And when someone reports that while hypnotized he or she walked on live, hot coals, those notions are even more perplexing. Our group leader and one participant had made such a firewalk. No doubt there are various levels of hypnosis. We are all involved in the more normal level of hypnosis every day. It is merely a matter of focusing our scattered attention and in our imagination seeing ourselves doing a particular act. Walking on hot coals is a more intense version of this ordinary skill. We can practice it when we look at one thing in our life and focus our action on that one thing. A small example is to make a telephone call. We focus on the particular skill required to dial the numbers, then *we believe* we will talk to our friend across town or across the nation. The preparation process for hypnosis, induction, is merely a way of getting the active and nervous part of our mind quieted down. We tell stories in a soothing manner, we repeat certain words, we listen to quiet music. Hypnosis is a way of simplifying and focusing our minds, using all the signals our senses understand. In the group we did some simple exercises in hypnosis and looked at ordinary ways we could use it in life.

BUSING DISHES

More than 50% of the cost of my stay at Esalen was provided by a scholarship. So, I was happy to help with the work. I was assigned the job of busing dishes at supper. Wearing an apron, I would bring the dirty dishes into the kitchen from a cart in the dining room, sort out the paper, garbage, silver, plates, bowls and bottles. Another person would put the dinnerware through the dishwasher. I became quite good at this job and enjoyed it. Part of the fun was the spirit of the other workers. Part of it was the general feeling at Esalen that everything we did was a learning experience. I even came to appreciate rock music which the younger workers favored. It provided a rhythmic background for the complex work we were doing. People got to know me in this role and commented on my happy style. Work everywhere was meant to be like this.

SEA OTTERS

This part of the coast is famous as a refuge for sea otters. They are playful creatures who dive in the ocean near the shore, pick up abalone, then float on their backs while they break the abalone shells with a rock. Sometimes they just float and wave their flippers, appearing to clap. They fit the spirit of Esalen. Try as I would, I never saw one. Nevertheless, I think I know them.

YOGA

There were free classes at various times. I attended one of these on yoga, and was surprised to have the instructor spend so much time on breathing. Don't we all know how to breathe? Well, apparently not. We don't breathe deeply enough, deep into our lower bellies, nor do we breath slowly enough. And we don't listen to ourselves as we breathe. This is a Zen point. By breathing and becoming aware of our bodies as we stretch our muscles, we are becoming acquainted with a part of our nature we often neglect — until it cries out in alarm. Why wait for the heart to attack us? Why not be friends with our own body? It has many wonderful secrets to reveal to us.

BREATHING

One of the breathing exercises on the program looked innocent enough. I ended up being a sitter for another person in a room full of "breathers" and "sitters." I couldn't understand why the instructions to the sitters seemed like a veiled warning not to intervene or interfere, just to protect the breather. Protect? Well, the breathers, lying on their backs on the floor, began a more rapid kind of breathing. Then the music came on strong and vigorous. I could sense the tension. After a half hour some were beginning to move on their floor pads. Others remained still. I could see that the intensity of the music was releasing some to get in touch with their unconscious (as I learned later). I was not prepared for this kind of event, but two men from Esalen hovered nearby to lend assistance if needed. The loud music continued, the movements of some increased. Finally, one or two began to moan. I watched and wondered. In a few, the moaning grew louder. Then one man began to twist and churn and writhe. Another was screaming. I looked at the monitors. They were calm, only propping the one up with pillows so that his movements would prevent him from hurting himself, touching the woman in certain places to relieve the physical tension shown in her muscles. After about an hour the music began a subtle shift of mood, becoming more harmonious. Gradually, the intensity of the human movements around me subsided. After an hour and a half the music calmed down to very quiet, soothing, dream-like flow. I was relieved. People began to get up quietly and leave. I waited until the person for whom I was sitting got up and moved to another part of the room to be near a friend of hers. Then I left. I shuddered, said a few inward prayers, and looked at the lovely ocean for assurance that the world was still working. I went down to the dining area and sat in the fading afternoon sun. Wow!

JAMES BUPP

The next day I found one of the Esalen monitors of that "breathing" session and asked him for some explanations. His name was James Bupp. He explained the rationale of the exercise, and I could understand better that it was one way of getting in touch with the unconscious. Some people were relieved, as if they had undergone a kind of inner massage. Others were shown that they needed to do further work on some hurt or damage, stuck deep in the unconscious.

"Why not leave it there?" I asked.

"Fine, if it doesn't disrupt your life," James responded.

But too often we find ourselves doing things we don't want to do, and not doing things we want to do. St. Paul, again. The unconscious stores many beautiful things but also broken things, deep wounds from the past. This, too, has to be redeemed.

In our conversation it came out that I was from Three Rivers, Michigan. James looked at me quizzically. He said that he used to work there — in fact, in a half-way house. Then a half laugh, half embarrassed look came over him.

"Were you there some years ago when I brought a strange young man out simply to stay overnight? He apparently became loud and intrusive, and you, Fr. Abbot, had to calm him down. Later, the next day when I came to pick him up, you gave me a very diplomatic talk on the kind of people the Abbey could, and could not, handle."

I began to recall the incident and we both looked at one another and laughed. Here we were, some eight years later, meeting in a quite different context. If anything, the roles were somewhat reversed. I was learning from him — about the strangeness within each of us.

I also got to know the other man who had worked with James in the breathing exercise. He turned out to be a working scholar, a Roman Catholic priest from London and Ontario, Canada. He was at Esalen for a month.

A third person whom I met, David, was teaching Tibetan yoga. He was on his way out of the monastery at Camaldoli. He talked about the monastic life and the Esalen experience.

> I could see the pain and the yearning, the search to bring traditional wisdom into connection with other cultures and our new insights into human nature. I am convinced that this search will be the essential spiritual work of our time. The empty churches will not fill up until we convey genuine and full wisdom to our people. It is all there in the Gospel, but we don't recognize it or teach it.

STEPHEN REVISITED

As the week wore on I occasionally saw my roommates, Stephen and Dieter. Both were relaxing more. Dieter was obviously getting confirmation of some of the technical information of his field. Stephen was simply blossoming in the friendly atmosphere of the whole place. There was a kind of general healing going on inside him, and one didn't have to investigate beyond that. This, too, was a gift of Esalen.

COMMUNITY

Our workshop group was drawing closer together as we shared the teaching, the more personal matters of our lives, and the new joys of being more honestly human together. The staff and working scholars of Esalen became more of our personal friends, too. Community was building. I could see that community really was possible. But it required willingness to explore and share. I had been reading a book of theology throughout this workshop, just to keep myself in touch with the ideas of Western spirituality. The book discussed the triune God as community and our redeemed life in Christ as a sharing in that community. Here at Esalen, without those words, there was an expression of the community of human beings which must surely be some kind of participation in the Divine community. You could sense it when you went to the administrative office. There was friendliness, graciousness, personal interest, and great patience with people with their endless needs and questions. You could sense it at the front gate where Esalen met the world. The same gracious, personal humanness. I could not avoid the question: Do we do as well in the Church? Or is Esalen, somehow, a part of the Church, too?

RICHARD PRICE

With my penchant for sniffing out the center of things, I gradually worked my way toward Richard Price, one of the co-founders of Esalen, who was in residence. By an arranged agreement, he sat down to lunch with me one day. I asked him questions which he readily answered. I was essentially interested in the life of the inner staff group. He was candid enough to indicate that they had made many mistakes, had been too permissive at times, but by now have come to a way of simply talking openly and honestly with one another. I knew that such open honesty can only be achieved by painstaking inner work. One has to be unafraid to have one's self, any part of one's self, open to others. That only comes after a painful journey of self discovery, growth, and maturity. When he described Esalen as an open market of human exploration, I knew that there were very mature persons maintaining that openness. I asked him how the inner staff managed the complexity of Esalen. He acknowledged that the complexity is a kind of "trinity," the community itself, the programs they offered, and the business side which requires that it made good "cents." Esalen might bring in people of varied experiences and expertise in apparently disconnected value systems, but they must make it work with a solid kind of balance. And there has to be real integrity among the parts of that trinity. While offering programs of inner exploration and growth, the staff itself has to practice these same principles. the business side must be ruthlessly practical, but with a heart. My own support scholarship was an example. I asked him if there were some simple guidelines he could recommend after these more than 20 years of a highly experimental venture. He offered this: There must be no personal harm to anyone. (I recalled that Raj Neesh, a popular and magnetic spiritual leader of our time, had in fact allowed considerable physical harm to come to people under his care.) Each person must have complete freedom of choice; and there is need for a balance between freedom and respect. As he was talking, I speculated that if we could ever convince the world of these principles we would have a workable, non-dogmatic plan for world peace. In my opinion, Esalen was a valid model for a harmonious working together of a pluralistic society.

SPINOFFS

There were some fascinating spinoffs from Esalen. Some people, influenced by Esalen, are in Russia talking with professional people, appealing to common sense and the need for peace. Another group of Esalen-minded people, some 300 generals and admirals, are working on alternative non-military plans for negotiation and encounter in the world.

SIN AT ESALEN

For one raised in a Christian tradition, the question of sin is inevitable. At Esalen, it is never raised as a dogmatic question because there is no systematic theology. But the problem is there because there are people. Little signs remind the participants to be aware of others. There is the recognition that people will misuse the freedom offered. People can come off the highway and steal. One has the feeling that there is an alert awareness on the part of the staff for such misconduct. I never saw any serious violation of the spirit of love, but, as Dick Price intimated, Esalen had been through a too-permissive stage. Love here is more than an ideal. Love is energized with deep understanding and compassion for human nature. In my observation, it is that kind of energy which holds sin to a minimum. I asked my own work-shop leader, Eli Bear, if he thought there was such a thing as objective evil. He played around with the trick of holding the word "evil" up to a mirror — and reading "live." We both knew that this was just a game, played at the edge of a mystery. Finally he acknowl-edged that he really hadn't worked that out. Well, neither have the theologians. I was think-ing of Scott Peck's latest book, *The People of the Lie*, in which he, as a Christian therapist, addresses the existence of evil in the Church. A Christian believes that it took the death of the God-man, Christ, to deal with this mystery and maybe Esalen benefits from Christ's redemption — without actually acknowledging it. Grace is free! However, this large, unan-swered, question did not discount the real accomplishments of Esalen. We must focus on life and its nourishment. Esalen does that magnificently.

CARMEL

I felt the pull to remain at Esalen, but also knew that the benefit of my sabbatical schedule required moving to the next place of grace. I had already stayed beyond my original time of reservation, slept in my van one more night, and had tasted the rich Esalen menu for an extra day. I tidied up the van for travel and headed north up the lovely coastal highway. Again, there were many places where I wanted to stop and just gaze at the ocean/moun-tain/sky picture. Inside, my head was full of the sorting and sifting process from the Esalen experience. It was Saturday and there were attractive restaurants overlooking the sea with people sitting out under umbrellas, enjoying the food and the sunshine. It was a happy scene. I reached Carmel by mid-afternoon and called Shannon Mallory, the bishop of the new diocese of El Camino Real. (The name is that of the road that the Spanish Fathers used in moving from one mission to another along the California coast.) I had met Bishop Mallory in Long Island some years before when I did a diocesan retreat for Bishop Witcher. Something had clicked between us.

A voice answered the phone and informed me that there was a wedding reception for the bishop's daughter. I was welcome to come to the house and take my chances. A wed-ding seemed like an appropriate symbol for me at the time, so I drove out, put on clerical clothing, and joined the group of happy people. The bishop and his wife were most gra-cious in allowing me to join the party. I mingled and soon found out that the groom's ethnic background was Southeast Asian — Burmese, I think. I hoped they might have some Asian dancing but the family had lived in this country for some time and many of their cultural customs had been lost. Even though most of the family were Roman Catholic, they were happy with their son's marriage to an Episcopalian. I got the impres-sion that here was a couple who in their lifetime would be able to move back and forth among Christian denominations.

A member of the groom's family and I fell into a discussion on religion. He admitted that he didn't go to Church much, but that he did remember his Buddhist background in Asia. I encouraged him to recover some of that practice, especially since he felt he was being eaten up in the American business system.

> It showed me again that for religion to be credible, it had to give people the tools to meet their daily needs. However strongly I disagree with the TV evangelists, I recognize that this is what many of them try to do. Without access to some religious tradition, people drift off into secular substitutes, and are eventually cheated of life.

I asked the bishop for his suggestions about church for me for the coming Sunday. He thought that All Saints in Carmel would be handy. I contacted Fr. Fosse and received his gracious invitation to preach. This is risky for a rector. How will an unknown preacher affect his people? But St. Gregory's has a reliable enough reputation for most pastors to take the risk. In any event, Fr. Fosse had known the Abbey from his days in Chicago. I drove out of town and found a quiet place to spend the night in the van. I mused on the Gospel, the feeding of the five thousand.

ALL SAINTS

The next morning I found my way into Carmel proper and put on my habit. Then I met Bob Fosse and we went over a few details about the services. I was to preach at the 8:00 and 10:00 Communion services. When it came to the actual sermon, I found myself filled with an abundance of energy. I tried to connect this energy with the Propers, but it overflowed. I was somehow a vehicle for a powerful flow of God's love and the people responded warmly, some very deeply. I could tell this from their eyes, touches, gratitude at the front door, and at the coffee hour later. I had quite consciously borrowed a few ideas from the recent workshop at Esalen, but the power that flowed through me was more than ideas. Quite simply, I think that the workshop and Esalen in general opened up my own natural energies, and it was this flow that God used to convey His love. I myself was embraced by this grace for the rest of the day.

ORDINARY PROPHETS

I returned to the Mallory's for lunch. A few friends and the family, minus the bride and groom, were helping to eat the leftovers from the reception. After we had eaten and exchanged comments on people and events, the bishop and I withdrew for a private conversation. He was interested in my availability for retreats, even the possibility of opening up a center for spirituality. It was exciting to speculate on what spirituality today might look like. Perhaps it would be some combination of traditional Christianity and the wisdom of other religious traditions, plus certain aspects of the discoveries of a place like

Esalen. Whether I was available or not, I encouraged the bishop to go ahead and start having conferences with the people he had at hand. I remembered Dick Price's phrase, "open market." With some selection and discrimination this could describe the work of the Church. Shannon and I talked about our personal lives, noting the tensions and pressure that anyone in a leadership role faces. I wondered how some of the freedom of my sabbatical might be made a permanent feature of my life. I encouraged him really to care for himself, and for his family. They were planning a family conference at a local center soon. We all need it. I felt that two brothers had strengthened one another. I said goodbye and left the lovely area of Carmel.

CHAPTER 12

THE SPIRIT OF ST. FRANCIS

SAN FRANCISCO

The rest of the drive north had less of the ocean and more of the developed areas connected with the great city of San Francisco. As I moved through what is known as the Silicon Valley, the area where much of the computer chip and electronic industry is located, I remembered that I was looking for someone who has done well in that industry and might take a financial interest in St. Gregory's.

My whole approach to fund raising has been low key. Even at the monastery I have hesitated to launch an intensive campaign, feeling that the way we raise funds must be consistent with our way of life. I had mentioned the subject to various people during my sabbatical, picked up a few names here and there, and played the whole subject lightly, avoiding the huckster's approach. Of course, this style has not produced substantial funds, but at least it has saved me anxious tension. I wasn't sure it was the right time to build. I continued on through the peninsula which protects San Francisco Bay. It is interesting to know that the Spaniards who for years sailed past the mouth of this bay did not suspect the great harbor hidden behind.

PASCAL REDBURN

After some moderate wandering around in the Marina area of San Francisco, I found Pascal's apartment. He had been a member of our community for some years, and after his departure, we had kept in touch. Once before when I was attending an East/West conference held at a Cistercian monastery north of San Francisco at Vina, California, he had provided me hospitality. When I began my sabbatical plans, I induced him to be my northern California secretary and to investigate various places and programs like Esalen for me. While in San Francisco, it was natural that I meet my agent, first thing.

I had not telephoned so he was surprised, but immediately welcomed me, and after a few preliminary exchanges on our mutual state of health, took me to the apartment he had arranged for me. The apartment belonged to a friend who was out of the city. This was thoughtful, providing me a base where I could be private and yet be available for trips in the area and meetings with friends. Pascal shrugged this off as a simple arrangement, but it was typical of his care for me. The apartment had a bedroom, dining and living room, kitchen, and bath. Lovely. Then he took me to an Indian restaurant (Far Eastern) for a delightful supper. San Francisco abounds in unusual places to dine. At a nearby Chevron station he had also arranged a parking place for my van. After supper we parted — I to my new home, transferring what I needed from the van to the apartment and sorting through my mail. The first night in any city for me is always somewhat unsettling, getting used to traffic and city noises. But it was a fairly quiet part of the city near the Pacific Heights area, a pleasant walk from the Golden Gate Bridge.

I spent Monday setting up my desk space. I like a lot of surface area for papers, letters, correspondence. I am a visual person. If things are not within eye reach, I forget them. When I am traveling, I have numerous notes on the dashboard and memos in my pocket daytimer. I also walked through the neighborhood, found a Russian Orthodox Church on the corner, and attended the Liturgy for an hour. It was the Feast of the Transfiguration. The general outline of the Eucharist was familiar, but the long chants and incense rituals with two choirs, deacon, and a priest (and only a handful of the faithful) soon wore me out. An hour later, I left. I wondered how they were holding their people. The leaflet at the door had a familiar plea, to participate more in the life of the parish. In the early 1800s, the Russian Church had come down from Alaska. I have no idea how vital it is today or how it relates to the whole Orthodox world. I know that Orthodox spirituality is profound and ancient, but apart from books, I have had little actual experience of it.

That evening I had supper with Pascal and received more information on the events and people on my list to visit in San Francisco. While I enjoyed walking the streets of the city, I was also getting to know the bus system. For 60 cents and a transfer one can get anywhere in the city. This is in contrast to Los Angeles which spreads out over a vast area.

ZEN CENTER

On Tuesday I walked some 32 blocks downtown, absorbing the refreshingly cool atmosphere, enjoying the shops and public buildings. My objective was the Zen Center. It is a large old house with a temple on the ground floor, room for sitting (zazen), a dining room, and live-in accommodations for staff and students. On the staff I met Kathy, who gave me a tour and an introduction to some of the major Zen ideas. She was an interesting blend of a person who grew up in a traditional Western religious pattern (Roman Catholic), and was now a practicing Buddhist. Her humor and insight into the common elements in Catholicism and Buddhism impressed me. She didn't try to convince me one way or the other. Her comments on breathing and sitting showed me that the weaker side of our Western way of life is our neglect of the body. Certain strands in our ascetical tradition have told us that our bodies are suspect, not to be trusted and, in fact, evil. With that kind of rejection, we are more subject to a tragic split between mind and body. Body-oriented people are now respected, listened to, rewarded. In Western culture, this split has brought us to an impasse. Examples are an economy that is too mind-achievement focused, or international policies which are based on win/lose relationships — leaving the body to the entertainment world, to the commercial world, and to those who pander to physical pleasure.

I was touched by Kathy's recurring theme: living is a matter of enlarging the compassion of the heart. When her family, Italian Catholics, overcame their resentment of her Oriental religious commitment and invited her to a wedding of old friends, they were convinced of her genuine spirit by the way she genuflected, said the rosary, and participated in the Nuptial Mass — from the heart.

I bought a book, *Zen Mind, Beginner's Mind*, by the late O. T. Suzuki, head of the Zen movement in northern California. At another shop I also purchased a round cushion for sitting. I'll try. On another day I returned to the Zen Center for some instruction in sitting and breathing. It isn't easy. In this exercise one gets some surprising feedback on one's whole being — body, mind, and soul. Breathe deeply. Be aware of your breathing. You begin to see the possibility of focusing your life beyond the surface egoism that rules us so much of the time. Since that instruction, I have spent ten minutes a day. We'll see.

FATHER KAPPES

After leaving the Zen Center, I walked uptown to have lunch with an old friend of our community, Father Kappes. At one time, he had been our Confessor Extraordinary (most communities have an outside confessor who provides the brethren access to someone not intimately connected with the family). He had kept in touch with the older brethren even since retiring and moving to San Francisco. He represents the older generation of Anglo-Catholics who have had a hard time adjusting to some of the changes in the Church. I had visited him before and wondered how he was weathering the continued changes. He had invited a friend to his apartment, a former Episcopalian and now a Roman Catholic. We had a happy time touching upon old memories and friends. Eventually, it came out that the friend was a recovering alcoholic. And Father Kappes was attending open meetings of A.A. for his own personal enrichment. This permitted me to recount my recent experience at the treatment center on behalf of one of our monks. I was pleased to see that Father Kappes was brighter, with more humor, and was gaining an appreciation of the conversion element in the A.A. program.

> This provided me one more clue as to how the Church must combine its traditional theology with some human growth practices. For an alcoholic, such practice as provided in A.A. is a life and death matter. It is a recovery from death. Is it not the same with all of us? But the appropriate exercises for personal growth are not so clear for everyone. I believe that the Church must investigate a variety of such principles to offer its people. Is baptism a recovery from death — into life?

While in that area, I visited St. Mary's Roman Catholic Cathedral, a very modern concrete church building, soaring up toward a high cruciform pattern at the center of the ceiling. Many tourists in buses come to see this spectacular building. The "secular city" still prizes its religious centers.

I had supper in my apartment, using some of the ideas I picked up at Esalen — raw cucumber and zucchini slices, an avocado, cheese and crackers, and tea. On other evenings I had marvelous meals at friends' houses. Father Leslie Wilder and John Easton invited me to their apartment which featured grand views of the city. John had been to the Abbey, and our Father Anthony has been to San Mateo where Leslie and John used to minister along with the Sisters of the Transfiguration. So we had many people to remember and many stories to tell. Such evenings have their own kind of magic. Another such supper took place at the apartment of Philip Deemer and Arthur Goldsmith. They have served the Church in a number of ways including some publishing ventures.

THE EPISCOPAL CATHEDRAL

During the first week I had introduced myself to Canon Merriman at Grace Episcopal Cathedral. He very kindly invited me to celebrate at the 11:00 o'clock Eucharist. I arrived early enough to receive instructions. Considering that there were some 15 or so people in the sanctuary along with the choir, it was important to get a sense of their liturgy. I had my own Master of Ceremonies, with mace. As befitting a cathedral, it was grand in every way. Afterwards at the coffee hour, I was able to greet people who had little opportunity to meet a Benedictine. There were friends of the Abbey, too. One, Madeleine Jacobson, was well known by correspondence and support. It was interesting to see how monasticism and life in the world complement each other. Then Pascal and I had a lovely lunch in a well-known San Francisco restaurant. Again, the aura of the celebration seemed to linger as a special gift.

Later that day, we took a delightful trip north along Highway 101 to have supper with Bruce and John. They live in Santa Rosa, some 50 miles north of San Francisco. Bruce works for a number of people, including Pascal, cleaning apartments. He had worked on mine. Now he was entertaining us. Surely, this could happen only in America. We enjoyed a very ample meal with two of their friends and two of John's children. The drive back was suffused by a soft sunset glow.

CHAPTER 13

CONNECTIONS IN THE SPIRIT

INCARNATION PRIORY

Just one week after coming to San Francisco, I went over the Oakland Bay Bridge to visit the Incarnation Priory in Berkeley. This is a very interesting ecumenical experiment which involves members of the Camaldolese Order and some of our own Holy Cross brethren, with the backing of the Roman Catholic and Episcopal bishops. The Order of the Holy Cross has been rethinking their life, now seeing themselves as Benedictines. This is an example of how Anglican Religious Orders, originating in the Victorian era, are now connecting with deeper roots in the monastic tradition. The one I know best on the Roman side of this group is a truly far-seeing person, Father Robert Hale. As a former Anglican, now a Camaldolese monk, he appreciates the special gift that Anglicanism can make to the Western Church. I saw their new quarters, an apartment complex, recently purchased from an Episcopal parish. We sat in Robert's office and talked about the many facets of Religious life today, moving easily from one mountain top to another in the true style of visionaries. Occasionally, someone would poke his head in the door and ask some practical question. Robert would have to scratch his head, reminding me of myself. Later in the week I was able to make a return visit for a day, attend Vespers, Eucharist, and also to have supper and meet more of the community. We had a wonderful time together. Br. William, the Holy Cross Prior, promised to write their superior in New York, Clark Trafton, and see if I might meet him when I was in the East. This promises to be a fruitful exchange between our two communities.

ROBERT HSI

One evening, Pascal and I had the pleasure of being the guests at the house of Robert Hsi, a Chinese-born naturalized American and friend of Pascal through St. John's Episcopal Church. In the past, Robert had been generous to me and now was supporting my sabbatical stay in San Francisco. He is in the importing business and seems to enjoy moving around the world. He is unmarried, but in true Chinese style, is deeply involved with his family. He is always occupied with some gift or favor he is doing for a sister, nephew, or niece. Financially he seems to be well off but the business affairs of such people are always subject to the hazards of international conditions. Robert doesn't strike one as a typical business man. He is childlike, playful, happy-go-lucky about the outcome of his ventures. A member of his business, a young man who was learning the bookkeeping side of things, joined us for supper. Occasionally he would sound a sober note about money but Robert waved it all aside.

Later, we were taken to a Chinese restaurant featuring Mandarin cooking, a business in which Robert still had an interest. The cooks and waiters all seemed to be personal friends, people whom he was helping in one way or another. Robert ordered the meal, several dishes of fish, chicken, prawn, and beef with pea pods. These were piled on top of rice and noodles, a marvelous feast. He talked about his recent visit to the Orient where the Chinese government, knowing his ability with both languages, entertained him. These were some of his impressions:

> China will continue to swing toward the West because its people want a better standard of living. Their growing numbers force them to take birth control seriously. They will work hard to catch up in technology. Hong Kong will be stable for a while because the Chinese government needs it for its own growth. The ordinary people still are not allowed to use the hotels built especially for the foreign visitors. And now that the door is open, it cannot be shut — China, like Japan, will compete fiercely with the rest of the world.

As I looked around the restaurant, and indeed, in all of California, I could see the mixing of East and West in a profusion of races, languages, and cultures. Sometimes there is violence, sometimes distrust. But there is no way to keep the races apart.

> People are moving around the world, either by displacement or by choice. As Wendell Wilkie stated some years ago, it is one world. However much we might question the intense commercialism of the West, the very fact that all nations are being drawn into one economic system is one more practical basis for peace.

SAUSALITO

On a sunny day, I took the bus down to Fisherman's Wharf to wander along the waterfront and enjoy the international shops selling art, fish, kites, cooked food, even boat rides. Many people were enjoying the scene, happy and circus-like. At the appointed time I took the ferry to Sausalito where I was to meet a person who often comes to St. Gregory's Abbey for spiritual direction. The half hour ride was filled with views of the bridge, Alcatraz Island, the San Francisco skyline, and houses tumbling down picturesque hillsides. Hovering and begging, seagulls followed the ferry across. People were happy, enjoying the sunshine and the water. The ferry landed and my friend took me to her house. There she had prepared a lovely lunch of a clear, delicate soup, salad, cheese and crackers, fruit, and tea. We looked over her deck onto the bay with its dancing water and bouncing boats. I eased toward her personal issues which she had discussed with me before. Her husband has an alcohol problem, her job was ending, and she is too old to expect an easy replacement. Her health was reflecting the stress. I listened and offered opinions, comparisons with other lives I knew about, intuitive suggestions, but mostly a listening compassion. She needed no advice, just a sensitive, prayerful, heart. We prayed. Then it was time for me to catch the ferry back.

On the dock, the scene was asking to be painted — Black teenagers break dancing, gulls hovering. I was now filled with the bittersweet of life, the beautiful, the poignant. It is easy to slip into pity, wanting to provide an escape for another person. Zen people talk about "ruthless compassion." It is a quality which shares the pain but stands free enough to allow the person to make the essential decisions which alone will bring one into his new future. I will never see the name, Sausalito, without returning to that bittersweet sense of life.

MICHAEL

That night a member of St. John's parish came to my apartment, bringing supper — salad, soup and bread, wine, and yogurt. And we talked. Michael was wrestling with questions of faith and daily life. It is an old story, and it is unanswerable if one looks for perfection in anything less than God. The Church, its hierarchy and parish life, are not and can never be perfect. But it is normal, especially for younger folks, to want the absolute near.

JOHN

Another day I took the bus across town to meet a priest whose telephone listing caught my eye. I read: "Interpreting Holy Scripture, contemporary theology, depth psychology, and personal experience." My! Here was someone dealing with some of the same ingredients I have been exploring. I met John and was impressed. We talked, ate lunch, and talked more. He gave me some books and some listing of places and people who are thinking in these terms. One sad point was that he felt cut off from the other clergy. Perhaps some of his ideas were undeveloped or would prove to be outside the normal Christian tradition. But to be cut off is sad.

Another telephone listing caught my attention: "Come sing God's Glory. Warm, open community of families and singles worship with deep early Church roots — enlightened preaching — excellent Church School — seminars in meditation, Scripture, personal growth. When we sing we feel God's pleasure." Perhaps non-Californian readers will smile. I applaud any and every genuine effort to bring people into God's love. No doubt parishes will differ, providing for the wide variety of religious taste. We had better be ready for even more variety.

But at the moment, we aren't drawing enough people into the life of grace, the life of the Church, Christ's presence in the world. And we aren't fully aware of the vast dimensions of that presence. The whole exploration of the wisdom of our bodies, the wisdom of ancient cultures, and the wisdom of modern science can enrich our understanding of the Gospel. Dom Gregory Dix, the illustrious liturgical scholar and fellow monk, wrote about the challenge that the Gospel, originating in a Hebrew culture, presented to the Greek-speaking world. The Church finally found a way to understand the Gospel anew. Now, we are faced with the challenge of connecting the Gospel to the wisdom of all cultures. If indeed it is an universal Gospel, it is big enough for the challenge. Are we?

ST. MARY THE VIRGIN

August 15th, a Holy Day in the new *Prayer Book*, gave me the opportunity to visit a nearby parish on this feast of Our Lady. There was an evening celebration and I was invited to be a concelebrant in the sanctuary with the principal celebrant, Jan Griffin. Jan had preached at Grace Cathedral the preceding Sunday. She had belonged to St. Mary's originally, but this was the first time she had been the celebrant at their altar. One could sense the heightened emotion surrounding her presence. There was a good congregation of some 70 parishioners, good music, a fine sermon by the assistant priest, and Jan was competent in every way. I enjoyed being with her. At Communion time, I couldn't help but notice how attentive she was to children at the altar, to particular parishioners for whom this was a special occasion, to those who may have been somewhat uncomfortable. Afterwards there was a parish potluck supper with Mexican food. I sat with Blacks, East Indians, Orientals, Whites, children, and older people. It gave one a glimpse of the real genius of parish life, a meeting place for those who might otherwise be separated. I felt that Our Lady as a universal mother was pleased.

JUNE SINGER

On the following day I drove the van south to the suburbs of Menlo Park and Palo Alto. This is an area where many scientific and educational institutions are located. I did not have time for Stanford University — famous as it is. I was interested in an institute known as the California Institute of Transpersonal Psychology. I know this sounds very abstract. It is a group attempting to blend a number of schools in the psychological world. I had known of June Singer, a member of this group, a Jungian therapist, and a friend through Father Charles Moore, both of whom used to be in the Chicago area. I visited her in her home and checked out a number of my impressions on Esalen, trends in psychology, dreams, human resources in the Midwest, new interpretations of the Myers-Briggs test (which our community took this year). It was reassuring to talk to a person of deep perception and experience and get verification for some of my hunches. She is a convert — to

California. There is no doubt that this land on the edge of the Pacific is a special place for human growth and the mixing of cultures. Some of the results may be a little crazy, but for all that there is solid evidence that a way of living creatively in this world is emerging in California.

LINNE

All too soon I had to leave Palo Alto because I was 40 miles south of my next appointment. I was on the freeway and moving back into the city at rush hour, but the flow was fairly good, with only two slowups. Even so, I was late getting back to the Marina section of San Francisco where I was to meet Linne McAleer, a nurse and practitioner in Trager movement re-education (a kind of massage). I had read about this work in the Esalen catalog and wanted to try it. Linne's name was given me by the administrative headquarters of the Trager Institute in California.

I parked the van, partly blocking someone's drive — always a hazard in this crowded city. I prayed that the homeowners were away or not going anywhere. I was 15 minutes late, but Linne welcomed me in a gracious manner, the beginning of the treatment. She does her work in her apartment, but her equipment and her style are very professional. With a few preliminary explanations of the system, its aims and objectives, she had me undress down to my shorts, and lie on a work table. From then on I had very little to say — unusual for me. Occasionally she would ask me a question or check to see that I was comfortable. The Trager approach is not technically massage but a gentle rocking of the muscles of the body. The intention is to "facilitate the release of deep-seated physical and mental patterns which may inhibit, block, or otherwise distort free flowing motion and full expression. Such blocking patterns often develop in response to adverse circumstances such as accidents, illnesses, poor posture, emotional trauma, stresses of daily living, or poor physical habits."

I was told not to fix the mind on anything in particular, to let her move my body freely, and to be as relaxed as possible. What followed was a gentle rhythmic, rocking of all of the major muscles, starting with my head and then going to all parts of my body. Quiet music played in the background. The session took over an hour. Occasionally, my mind would return to the problem of my van parked in someone's driveway, but I decided I couldn't do anything about that. It was an exercise in letting go. Very Zen.

Afterwards, as we were having a cup of tea, Linne explained to me that this is more than a physical experience. It affects one's whole being. The very cells get the message that life is good. I have often looked at people's faces as I passed them on the street and wondered if they needed that message.

> There are many kinds of quick relief from tension — sex, drugs, alcohol, excitement, escape; but the deepest kind of relief comes when one moves the body in a gentle coordination with mental aims for peace and the life of the earth. It is this total, human ecology that we are re-discovering.

I was grateful to Linne for this further acquaintance with the wisdom of the body. It has its part in our overall need to be loved. And it is from this blessing that we gain new energy to give love to others. Incidentally, the van was not towed away.

GHOST BUSTERS

On a Saturday, Pascal and I decided to take in a movie. I had not been to one since I had seen him some three years before. I have to admit that I am not much of a movie-goer. Well, some friend encouraged us to take in the popular summer diversion, "Ghost Busters." The story: three academic Americans find themselves ousted from their campus employment. They set up an office to investigate paranormal activities. What follows is an insight into such phenomena, at least in the minds that produced the movie. It was fun, crazy, wondrous in terms of the visual effects which now seem to be Hollywood's signature, and a further insight into the pseudo-self-confidence of the image makers. Do we viewers become what we see? But that is to bring far too much speculation and philosophy to the Ghost Busters. We topped the evening off with a quiet dinner at a Mexican restaurant near Fisherman's Wharf. San Francisco has a special charm all its own. I wondered if this is something of St. Francis's own blessing. It is certainly evident in Assisi, Italy, as I remembered from my visit some years ago. These blessings, this ambience, this charm, is part of the peaceful context that helps us live in hope and joy.

ST. JOHN'S PARISH

On Sunday, August 19th, I was invited to preach at St. John's parish in the old mission district of San Francisco. The charm of this old part of the city and its current poverty are a familiar mixture known to many cities. The church building itself with high clerestory windows has an English look. In fact, Emily, an elderly British matron who occupies the front pew, assured me that it looked just like her church in London. At a low moment of St. John's history, when they were threatening to sell it, Emily took the money from the sale of her San Francisco house and applied it to St. John's. Beneath the lovely windows, the church does its best to gather up the lives of its people. The poor, the reasonably well off, the families, the gays, the professional people, and the city's abandoned folk, all gather to do a beautiful liturgy in the best Catholic tradition.

After all of my exposure to various systems of human energy, I found it a challenge to use the Gospel story of the Canaanite woman as a workshop topic for increasing energy and faith. So often a merely intellectual discourse fails to bring the Gospel to life. I walked around; I looked at people; I touched some. I brought in human experience, "Ghost Busters," the baptism that was to take place during the service, and Emily. I sensed the build up of energy flowing among us. It is this flow of energy that makes a powerful pathway for the truth of the Gospel. I invited everyone to recall an experience of separation and another of acceptance. We looked at the energy stored in such memories. Then we watched the Lord work with the Canaanite woman, slowly taking her into the depth of faith-energy until she produced that saving response which the Lord rewarded with the healing of her daughter. (Appendix 8)

A baptism followed. Jesse was a three-year old, full of wonder at the signs and symbols taking place in front of him. He had to be extracted from the ceremony by his mother as an important "call of nature" took precedence, but he was returned and duly baptized and sealed with the Spirit. What an awesome life lay before him, especially if he stayed in this neighborhood. I had encouraged the congregation to show Jesse what baptism meant by the way they treated, loved, touched, held, and lived with him.

> The parish is the second family into which we are born, nurturing us until we are born into eternity.

The Eucharist continued its mysterious weaving of grace and human affairs, working at deeper levels than we can understand, bringing our little lives into the awesome majesty of Christ's own death and resurrection. He tells us and He shows us that everything that happens to us happens to Him, and that everything that happened to Him in His human experience has, or will, happen to us. The words, the altar, the candles, the different roles of the people in the sanctuary and in the nave, are all drawn into a flowing Communion that opens heaven to us.

After the Eucharist, the people gathered at the back of the church for the coffee hour — that extension of the celebration. I met old friends and many new ones. Many were still moving in the energy of the power of the liturgy and the sermon. I knew there was a secret here, but I didn't fully understand it. And I knew I had to be careful not to misuse it.

The celebration continued as some of us moved to a parishioner's house and mingled over a buffet table and wine. It was good to see these people enjoying themselves in a shared faith. Some approached me with serious questions; some came with smiles and an offer of a new dish that appeared from the kitchen. In the midst of all of this, Pascal found me a back bedroom for a nap.

Late in the afternoon we moved to yet another house where we had a supper of lamb, potatoes, salad, French bread, and dessert. In the smaller group we could talk more easily about the state of the Church. Those gathered at this session were all seriously committed to the Church in one vocation or another — a woman priest, a seminarian, those with permanent functions at St. John's, a former Religious — all exploring the other side, the painful side, of the morning's glory. In their opinion, the Church everywhere was fumbling badly. It is easy to blame the hierarchy or the laity or the world, but the fact seems to be that we are in a time of radical transition and no one is quite sure what the Church should be like.

> The Church is Christ's presence in the world, but most of the world doesn't see this. How to make Christ — no, how to let Christ be more obviously present in the members of His Body? I sense that there are

more profound changes in store, much pain, anger, more departures, and yet an inevitable movement of the Spirit, taking us into the future of the Church. What will God's presence look like on the parish, diocesan, and world level? And how will different religions be able to recognize His common presence in all cultures? It is an immense, complex puzzle. We are assured that He has it worked out. We know that it will be part of the continuing resurrection.

MARIANA

On Monday evening I had another view of St. John's through the eyes of its senior warden, Mariana Keene, formerly a member of an Episcopal religious order. Her training in the Religious Life and her care for human beings were being put to good use in the parish, especially in this interim time of searching for a new rector. Her leadership experience gave her a balanced judgment when confronted with differing factions in the parish. For all of her skills, however, she still hankered for a more contemplative way of life. She realized that this did not necessarily mean being in a convent. It did mean that she knew she needed more quiet, more private space, and further opportunity to connect what she was doing with the ultimate meaning of life. Frequently, I find such people. They are often lonely, confused, frustrated, and guilty. What they need is simply private time and space to come to their own level of humanness.

> Just as a business person, or an artist, or a teacher has to focus on and process his or her own way of life, so does the contemplative. And this is doubly hard when the culture doesn't know that there is such a quality of life as contemplation. Of course in some sense, everyone is a contemplative, in that everyone tries to look beyond the immediate and to discover the meaning and source of life. Having gained some access to this source, a human being then finds some way to stay in touch with it.
>
> Symbols and signs are helpful. The Christian contemplative has many effective signs and symbols, culminating in Christ Himself, the Sacrament of God, assuring him of access to God. But the average person, even if baptized, usually doesn't know how to stay in touch with God, and so fumbles in confusion. This is especially true in a large city.
>
> The art of living in the city needs to include attention to the art of contemplation. Such an art needn't involve long hours in prayer. Few urban dwellers could manage that. But it does require the very simple skill of focusing one's life. Some people gain this from daily Bible reading, attending mid-week services, or following personal ways of prayer. All of these are good. They need to be extended so that one is able to meet every event in daily life from a deeper center of faith. This requires discipline.

Most people are not yet convinced this is necessary. I believe we will come to realize its necessity as we witness the middle-class way of life becoming ever more impoverished, limited, and powerless.

In many ways, Mariana has less support to live the life of faith than I do. She experiences more poverty, has less community on a daily basis, and has a far more difficult path of obedience in the maze of secular life. I admire her. We had a lovely meal with two salads, stuffed squash, melon, and coffee. I tried to encourage her in the life of faith she maintained so heroically.

DEPARTURE

My two and a half weeks in San Francisco were coming to an end. I knew this because my orderly mind had already begun to collect things from around the apartment and put them in boxes and suitcases. I finished off some neglected correspondence. And I really knew it when some workmen came in to do a job of rewiring the electrical system, something that had been waiting for months. My lovely space was being invaded. I could feel the urban paranoia.

> Watch out, be careful, be alert, withdraw. Something is going to steal your peace of mind. This is the familiar feeling for the urban dweller. How does one maintain peace and faith in this tension? After a while, the anxiety becomes unconscious. Then we live out of a pattern of distrust and suppose that it is caused by others.

FLEUR DE LYS

Pascal, who had already done so much for me, provided one last gracious gift, an elegant meal in a restaurant known as the Fleur de Lys. Reservations were necessary. It was to be an experience in gracious dining. I was dressed in my habit, an "accident" due to Pascal's request that I come to his apartment so dressed for some photographs. He wanted to draw my portrait. So from there we went to the restaurant, which seemed appropriate for this final celebration.

The maitre d' ushered us to our table, from which we could view the small but beautifully decorated room. Overhead was a sweeping canopy which gave the impression that the room was a large tent. Somehow the acoustics made it possible to talk in a normal voice and be heard, but not overheard. A lavish chandelier in the center hung over a large flower vase, a fountain of color. We had oysters on the half shell. Then I had a green salad. My main course was stuffed squab and vegetables. We were attended by a series of waiters — some brought food, others took the empty plates, still others served water and wine. Through it all Pascal and I talked of many things. We recognized that at the moment we felt like kings. One should feel that way sometimes. Of course we talked about our friends and the Church, a kind of discussion which allows one to do therapy within oneself without being self-conscious. We finished with a chocolate mousse. Then we obtained a copy of the large menu, signed it and sent it off to our mutual friend, Father Blankenship in Texas — whom I had visited earlier in this sabbatical, our mutual friend who was surely there in spirit. A taxi ride home was the ending of an effortless evening of lavish pleasure.

JOHN

The next and last morning, the apartment was dark. No electricity. It seemed a fitting final note for my own sadness at leaving this lovely city. I was fairly well packed. The van had been extricated from the nearby filling station parking lot, and I was doing last minute chores — calling Janet who owned this apartment to thank her; changing the sheets on the bed; emptying the garbage; putting the furniture back the way it had been (I always gather a lot of tables on which I can spread my correspondence); delivering the apartment keys to Janet's friends across the hall — when John came.

John had been hired by Pascal (his gifts never ended) to give me some editorial comment on the article, "Living The Rule of St. Benedict," which had been delivered at the New Harmony conference on the Benedictine life. It is typical of my writing. The reader of these notes will be grateful to John for his comments for he confirmed and clarified what others have noted, especially our Father Jude who has to prepare my writings for publication in the Abbey Letter.

John pointed out, using illustrations, that I jump around from one grand idea to another without much explanation of how connections are made. If my reader has a general kind of mind it works reasonably well, but if one has an orderly mind, intent on specifics, it is disconcerting. I could even convey a certain disregard for my reader, or a personal inner hurt that doesn't expect to be understood. It is a style that also neglects the rules of communication, rules which cannot be avoided if one is to convey one's experience.

> Do I think my thoughts, after some 36 years in the monastery, are worth sharing? If I truly feel that they are, then I must face the obligation of disciplining myself to learn the basic guidelines of the mind and language.

John was compassionate, but firm. Some of my style was unforgivable. One finally comes to the conclusion that the art of living combines an inner experience with an outer form, a form that gives reasonably adequate expression to the experience, a form which can be shared with others. In this sense, style (if it includes the inner experiences and values of life) is everything.

After we had discussed my style, we had a cup of coffee and talked about life. I could see that John, who lives in Wales most of the time, has a real feeling for the dignity of life and for the Church. But he feels that the Church, or Christianity, is dualistic. How often I heard that. I believe that we need to address this accusation seriously.

If there is, indeed, a true basis for dualism, between good and evil, then we seem to have transferred it to good and bad people, good and bad nations. This transferred sense of dualism allows us to practice considerable violence against others, all under the comfortable thesis that we are justified in protecting ourselves and our own (who or whom we accept as good), and rejecting others who do not agree with us (who are obviously bad). This thesis, applied in economic and political affairs, splits the world into good and bad. This is no longer a workable thesis. We must restudy the very roots of the Gospel, as well as humbly listen to other religious traditions. Surely, we will discover a common teaching: evil can be restrained without doing violence to other people; and, good is the essential truth about all reality. We must nurture and encourage good everywhere, throughout the world. As I see it, this is the challenge before the Church today.

CHAPTER 14

THE MOUNTAIN SPIRIT

TAKING 80 HOME

Clarity was a good theme as I moved through the sadness of leaving San Francisco. Soon I was on the I-80 freeway, crossing the bridge, going east. The drive through Sacramento and into the mountains was occupied with an inner sorting and sifting of my recent experience, with detaching, and getting back into the schedule of my sabbatical. I had only ten to twelve days in which to cover the ground between the West coast and Three Rivers, see a number of friends, and get ready for the next stage of my journey — the trip to Rome for the Congress of Abbots. The schedule always required the same discipline as with a diet — you learn to leave before you are full.

LAKE TAHOE

Mountains have a different kind of beauty and strength in comparison to the ocean. Both are mysterious. Back in the mountains I was feeling the strength of their power. They were lifting me to some 7,000 feet. I had called ahead to see if I could chat with Bishop Wesley Frensdorff of Nevada. Even though we would meet the following day in Reno, he arranged for me to stay at the Galilee Church Camp on Lake Tahoe. Lake Tahoe is a large jewel of water in a national forest. The shore has been developed with housing, condominium groups, and shopping centers. And yet, by squinting, one can see through to the majestic beauty of the water, cradled in the Ponderosa pine-covered mountains. The Church camp is on the edge of the lake. I drove in and was welcomed by Ginny, who with her husband directs its year around activities. They welcome any who wish to come. I parked my van near the water and took a swim. The water was brisk but not as cool as the ocean. I met George and Judy, who were putting on the program for this particular week, and John and Mary from the bay area, who were participating. I could sense the informal nature of the camp so I put on one of my Tee shirts. On the front of this shirt it says, "Number One" and on the back, "The Father Rabbit." This last phrase came from a young child to whom I was introduced at Easter time. His eyes widened at being told I was the Father Abbot. "Gee," he said, "the Father Rabbit." Everyone laughed, of course, and now it is part of my repertoire.

After supper I met with the group in the chapel with its glass window behind the altar looking out over the lake. I said a few words about the Abbey and some remarks on prayer. After some singing, George gave a teaching. Then we gathered in the darkness by the lake and had some night prayers.

The next morning I was invited to celebrate the Eucharist by the lake. I tried to incorporate the beauty of the surroundings, the special opportunity (being away from our norm) of seeing our lives anew, and some thoughts about God's love. I did this in an easy, informal manner which is often the style at camps. Music, sharing, a sense of being touched by the Lord, tears, and joy — all were present that morning as the group discovered themselves to be an emerging community. After breakfast, a number of people thanked me for my thoughts and for the Eucharist. I realize that sometimes I can discern a gentle way of the Spirit and can help people move into an attitude of loving trust with God. The summer camps throughout the Church do accomplish a special ministry for our people. It would have been fun to stay and work with George, but I had an appointment in Reno with the Bishop of Nevada.

RENO

The hour's drive down the mountains was pleasant and easy. Reno was far less hectic and bizarre than Las Vegas, possibly because I was seeing it in daylight. Here, too, were the same invitations to gamble, visit the night clubs, and sin big. However, my goal was to meet a person whose name I had heard from many people. I knew he was unusual.

I found St. Stephen's Church, the diocesan headquarters, and sat in the church until he was free. Wesley Frensdorff is a physically small man, but bright and lively in vitality and faith. He is excited about the future. We talked about many subjects but I remember best his energy and adventuresome spirit. Our reflections coincided on many points: we must make room for people practicing different spiritual ways; we need to get reacquainted with our bodies and the earth; we have an opportunity to remodel the Church round a deeper sharing of ministry. He has done a number of innovative things like appointing a respected elder in a community as the authorized distributor of the Sacraments (the Alaska Plan as developed by Bishop Gordon). Innovations work well in a missionary area because they employ the spare resources of people to the best advantage. They often frighten other people. I am convinced that the whole Church is moving toward a simpler way of practicing our traditional theology and sacramental life. We need places and people who can discover how to do that. However brief our meeting, I knew that in Bishop Frensdorff I had met a responsible innovator, a kindred spirit.

Fuffie, his secretary, helped me find an R.V. service shop and a book store. The R.V. people couldn't help me with a minor repair in the van (the backseat/bed was coming loose from the wall), but I did find a copy of *The Aquarian Conspiracy*, which I mailed off to Pascal. I had already given him a copy of *Zen Mind, Beginner's Mind* (an introduction into the Zen mentality), and *Frogs into Princes*, the somewhat zany, but perceptive, comments by two psychologists, Bandler and Grinder, on how we can apply some practical ways of transformation for ourselves and with others. With *The Aquarian Conspiracy*, I was offering Pascal a few fascinating, breakthrough insights by Nobel Prize winners and others who were exploring the changes in the world which require radical new ways of thinking. I wasn't trying to convert Pascal to my view, but rather in the spirit of *Conspiracy*, to breathe with others, and to network with anyone who sees that our time is a special evolutionary moment in human history.

After refueling, getting a Whopper to go, and some ice, I headed east on I-80. The names of the towns must have an interesting history: Sparks, Orena, Winnemucca, Golconda, Battle Mountain, Beowawe. It was later than I had thought and dusk was already setting in. Strange, too, that there were clouds and some lightning. Did I hear thunder? Or was that in my mind because I was headed for the American Indian commune associated with Rolling Thunder?

CHAPTER 15

NATIVE AMERICAN SPIRIT

ROLLING THUNDER

Some years ago, Doug Boyd's book, *Rolling Thunder*, had caught my attention. Briefly, the book described Boyd's interest in Rolling Thunder, a Native American, intertribal medicine man, who had attended a conference at Menninger's Clinic in Kansas. Rolling Thunder had indicated that he could do the unusual things that the conference was studying. But he did them as part of his life, not as a display for conferences. It struck me as an example of how primitive mysticism was still alive on the edge of our culture — for instance, as described in Tofler's *Third Wave*.

As I approached Carlin, Nevada, I had many fantasies running around in my head. I received instructions from a filling station attendant with the casual but unnerving closing, "You can't miss it." What a taunting sentence. If you know where you are going, you can't miss it. If you don't, you can. Or, you begin to develop a sense that you can be "guided" if you listen and proceed carefully. After a few mistakes in the dark, I did find the entrance to Meta Tantay, Walk in Peace, the name of the commune. It was a mere half mile off the freeway. This was my first disappointment. Why wasn't it away from the traffic and the tensions of modern culture? As I traveled the short distance off the freeway, my disappointment grew. What were all of those shacks, junk cars, piles of trash, those hogan-like structures made of all types of plastic and bits and pieces taken from the throw away culture? Oh good, there was a tépee. But my romantic fantasy was crumbling. Rolling Thunder was beginning to do the same work as Zen, detaching me from the surface part of my mind.

GEOFFREY

As I passed through the wooden gate and eased along the road, looking for some sign for a visitor, I saw a man waving me into a parking lot. It was Geoffrey. I produced my letter from the community inviting me to visit if I promised not to use drugs, alcohol, or firearms — or to evangelize. This last request was a sober thought. Later I learned that they wish to respect all religious traditions, but that they expect their own members to be allowed to practice their own Native American traditions without argument or conflict. Fair enough.

Geoffrey gave me a parking site and then chatted with me. He had been here for many years, was a Jew, but now saw himself as a full member of this Indian commune. How often I had met this: a person uprooted from his own religious tradition now embracing a new one. Geoffrey gave me some initial information. He mixed the practical with the philosophical, explaining how they were developing a herd of goats, and in the next breath described the attitude of peace and respect fostered in the group. It was a position of non-judgment. Later in my stay, I heard Geoffrey object strongly to a guest's off-handed statement. I realized that the Meta Tantay people had the same human problem: living up to avowed principles. Geoffrey told me that Rolling Thunder was away on a speaking engagement and using this absence to grieve for his recently deceased wife, Spotted Fawn. I guessed that I wouldn't see the medicine man about whom I had read. Maybe I would catch his spirit anyway.

At 5:00 AM, I was awakened by my mental alarm clock. I made a cup of coffee and said Lauds. Then Daniel, another member of the men's dormitory which was stationed near the front gate, came by to take me to the cook shack. This, too, was a simple wooden building with tables and adjoining kitchen. But it all seemed so disorderly that I wanted to clean it up. People filed in and out. Nothing seemed planned. It was not like a church camp. Daniel introduced me to Mala Spotted Eagle, Rolling Thunder's son, who was in charge during the absence of "R.T." (as they called him). Mala told me that on the first day, it was not their custom to invite new visitors to the Sunrise Service, but that I would be welcome on the second day. I understood this and had another cup of coffee while others went to the ceremony.

After the rather brief time for the ceremony, people filed back in. They seemed rather sullen; no one spoke much. I wondered what kind of spirit they had. Then I remembered our own Abbey guests viewing us as appearing distant in our preoccupation with our own way. I waited to find out more. Breakfast began with the men first. My, this was old style. The food was good — omelette, cereal, coffee. After breakfast, work assignments were made. I was not given anything to do because my stay was so brief. I returned to my van and filled out the form they required of visitors.

The daylight revealed that the appearance of this place was worse than my first impression. Only very slowly, with a change of mind, would I discern some pattern in the rock covered roads, sage brush, and building clusters. An old truck with a painted over "McGovern" sign gave a hint of some people's previous commitments. Of the 30 commune members — men, women and children (some in family units) — only a minority were Indians. A number were German. Many came from other communes. I was to hear fascinating stories of those who had been traveling since the 60s. The social revolution of that time which some have supposed to be over was still evolving.

I did some writing and tidied up the van. Before long it was 11:30, time for lunch. I noticed that my tension was easing. I was learning some names. I was getting beneath the surface in Meta Tantay. The meals were mainly vegetables and salads, but the community was not totally against meat. After the meal I took a stroll toward a nearby stream. I waded upstream and sat and meditated on the past few days. San Francisco, Lake Tahoe, Meta

Tantay. What a combination of experiences. It was an exercise in detachment, my sabbatical Zen. The trick seemed to be to come into a situation, observe, wait, go deeper, wait, and finally receive a gift. I spent the afternoon wading, wandering, looking at the distant hills. Although the camp is some five miles from the small town of Carlin and half of a mile off the freeway, I felt the presence of civilization. Telephone wires crossed the property, power lines penetrated the camp, freeway traffic droned nearby, and overhead airplanes kept me aware of the other world. A few pickups went back and forth on the adjoining property. Later I was told that there was a very profitable gold mine being worked there. In recent times the government had authorized the clearing of piñon pine by dragging chains between bulldozers on large tracts of western land. For Indians this tree has religious and practical significance. The Indians feel that these clearing operations are part of the misuse of Mother Earth. As an Indian asked at a recent conference convened by Robert Redford for corporation executives and Native Americans, "Would you do this to your mother?" The white people see these activities as "development." Two points of view.

Later I went to town to try to phone Bishop Charles in Salt Lake City, advising him of my visit. I also called a friend in Montana, excusing myself from dropping by. I kept running out of time.

After supper, I sat outside and talked with Daniel, another commune sampler but a serious one. He comes from ordinary American stock. Someone has said that the American middle class couple of yesterday worked hard but was amazed, sometimes angry, often confused, in that they had reared a generation of "mystics." But these mystics follow no normal Western way. They often abandon Western versions of religion and move toward gurus from the Far East or those influenced by them. Daniel had found a man who was "awakened" by a Zen Master in Tennessee who had established what is known as "The Farm." There, hundreds of wanderers settled down to practice a kind of American Buddhism. It had moments of glory and times of chaos. The Farm is still going. People like Daniel gained some kind of insight into their spiritual life. Now he was here. He recognized that the years at The Farm with its own discipline and community training had prepared him for this more subtle way of life. Here, inner discipline is important but not enforced. Without it one could not stay, but it took a long time of waiting to discern and follow a way of non-violence and respect.

THE SUNRISE SERVICE

On Saturday morning I was invited to attend the Sunrise Service. Mala met us in the cook shack, picked up a leather drum hanging on a post, looked around, said something indistinct, and went outside. The men followed. I got in line. We walked a short distance to a central point in the camp where a fire was burning. We walked around the fire in single file and took a position in a circle facing the fire. Then the women came, walked around behind us and found places in between the men. Mala, periodically hiking up his pants, gave a brief description of the ceremony, asking us to look at the fire for strength, to pray from the heart, to take a pinch of tobacco and hold it in our hands as a sign of an offering, to rid our minds of evil, and to want only good for others. He began his own prayer which would have served very well in any religious tradition. At the end of his prayer he sprinkled his tobacco on the fire in a circular motion, praying for his ancestors. As he finished, all said an audible, "Ho." It felt like an amen. When it came to my turn I prayed something like this, "God, strengthen the hearts of people throughout the world, that we may live in peace and harmony with you and all creation." I sprinkled my tobacco and the group spoke the "Ho." Some prayed almost inaudibly, others in a firm voice. Then Mala took the drum and explained that we would sing a hymn in the ancient tongue. He beat a simple rhythm and sang, the others joining. I found myself saying 'Yahweh' to the tune. It seemed a universal kind of name. After a short time the singing ceased, the men circled and left the ring. Then the women followed. As I left the Sunrise Service area, I thought that it had some distinct advantages. It was simple, full of symbolism, and helped focus the mind and heart on the best of one's intentions. I wondered whether we couldn't simplify some of our Christian rites, especially for busy people and for families.

MALA SPOTTED EAGLE

After breakfast I had a chance to talk with Mala. It took place in the open, next to the dining room. I sat on a broken-down couch and he occupied a split and weathered leather chair, taken from a car. Not very formal. Of the many questions I would liked to have asked had there been time, I selected three: First, I asked him how the permanent members handled conflict. He explained the simple plan. He (or the leader) would listen to one person in the conflict and then to the other. Then he would attempt to help the two understand one another. If that didn't work, he would resort to the permanent council. Their decision was to be final. Only once did he have to resort to some special healing prayers for an individual. My next question had to do with the convergence of religious traditions in our time. Did he sense that this was taking place? He did, but he also felt that evil powers were building. He sensed that a time of cleansing, what we would call judgment, was coming. It seemed imminent and real to him. Still, he felt that all we could do was be loyal to our own tradition, respect others, and do our best to help people of good will. Even if he did not agree with some of the thoughts or actions of a person, he would help that person if his or her heart was basically good. My third question, put as delicately as I could, had to do with the appearance of the camp. He nodded and very humbly explained that lack of money and manpower prevented them from doing better. I felt ashamed. We have the same problem at the Abbey. Later in the morning, I met Mala walking with a backpack toward the front gate. He explained that he was going to the mountains for a week. That was his way of dealing with his mother's death. I felt drawn to this man, embraced him, and promised to remember his mother. He smiled. He seemed to trust me.

LEMOILLE CANYON

After lunch, Daniel and I drove some 50 miles to a canyon in this area famous for its small glacier. We drove up from five to nine thousand feet. It was an Alpine ecology — high meadows with wild flowers, aspen and pine covered slopes, and bare rock heights provided another world. High up, several small patches of snow indicated the remnants of what was once a large glacier. Daniel was getting very excited. I knew he wanted to have some time here alone, so we found a place to park the van and he took off toward a small waterfall. I stayed in the van, got out my binoculars and looked for animals and birds. I saw what might have been two eagles. It was a beautifully quiet time and I said Vespers. One could easily see why primitive peoples took nature so seriously. I am not sure they were what we call animists (equating God with all natural objects), but I am sure they treated nature far more respectfully than we do.

In due time, Daniel came down from his climb, a bundle of wildflowers and rocks in his handkerchief. He seemed deeply moved and I didn't want to break the spell. We talked a little, but mostly I left him to his inner reflections. I could understand why he was drawn to the American Indian way of life.

On our return we passed through the town of Elko. It seemed such a different place. Natural wilderness and towns and cities seemed to be two different kingdoms. This thought prompted me to ask what Daniel thought about the appearance of the camp, so unlike a town. He agreed that it looked junky. He also agreed that for the Indian this is not the same problem it is for the White. We try to organize, control, and subdue our environment. Meta Tantay gave me a chance to submit and humble my critical mind to the ways of the Indian. We certainly owe them a huge debt of penance for the way we have treated them and their land.

RECREATION

After supper at Meta Tantay, the men gathered in the open courtyard near the cookshack. We talked and joked. There was a new man who wanted to erect a tépee to live in, and there was a lean Englishman, who turned out to be an antique dealer. He had done well selling lace, which had bought him a ticket to America. I had to admire their ability to accommodate a wide variety of guests.

Geoffrey brought his guitar and sang some Western songs. These all had a theme of injustice done to the Indian. Between songs, someone, I think it was the Englishman, said that he hoped it wouldn't rain that night as he was sleeping outside. Geoffrey became quite serious and delivered a lecture on the policy of Meta Tantay. They didn't encourage people to "wish" for any changes in the weather. I didn't exactly follow the logic of the argument, but it had to do with being careful not to attempt to manipulate the weather, or other spirits. He gave examples of how R.T. had to say special prayers to avoid spiritual intrusions into Nature's ways. I felt uncomfortable for the guest and not convinced by the argument.

At least one could say that these people were serious about the fact of evil. C. S. Lewis, in *The Screwtape Letters*, agrees that we have tried to ridicule evil out of existence, thereby giving it more freedom to intrude into human affairs. Later on, feeling uneasy about this episode, I drifted away from the group. Was this an example of primitive superstition? Was it a breach of their own principle of showing respect to all people? Or was it a sobering revelation that I was "soft" on evil powers? In any case, having heard that there was to be no public Sunrise Service on the following morning, Sunday, I decided to say a private Mass in the van. I would put the problems of evil into the hands of the Crucified One. I also wanted to pray for the soul of Spotted Fawn. It was clear to me that however much I admired the people of Meta Tantay, I could never live here. My religious customs had been formed too long in another tradition. They were not forcing me to change and my private Mass was not forcing them to change. The One God could put it all together.

When I came to breakfast I realized that everyone was expected to do the Sunrise Service in the public area, but without the leader. Apparently, they felt that only a male Indian could lead the service. The men were all away this morning. So, before having my pancakes, I went out, stood in line and said my prayer, sprinkled a pinch of tobacco on the fire, circled appropriately, and returned for breakfast. I could pray in this way quite honestly, but I was grateful to have the Mass.

After breakfast and some goodbyes, Geoffrey and I walked to the van. He was much more lively than the rest. I gave him a donation for my visit. He gave me back the bottle of Benedictine which had been taken from me on my arrival. (No liquor was allowed in the camp.) He asked to be put on the Abbey's mailing list. I could feel that he was genuine in his interest in me and the Abbey. He gave me the name of another commune toward Salt Lake City. We said goodbye and I drove out of Meta Tantay. I had very mixed feelings about the whole experience. I certainly learned that I think like a White man. It would take considerable effort for me to live like an Indian. Still, I gained some valuable insights and I certainly respected the Indian traditions.

CHAPTER 16

THE PERSEVERING SPIRIT

PRAYERS AND MUSIC

Driving along the freeway offers one a good time to say the Office. As I roll along the free-way with the Psalter propped on the small shelf on the dash board of the van, I can glance back and forth from the psalms to the road, or refresh my memory of certain prayers from our *Prayer Book*. Between Offices I would play a tape (not much music on radio in eastern Nevada). This, too, was a kind of prayer, mixing the flow of the music and the vista outside with a quiet feeling of gratitude and praise.

GENESIS COMMUNITY

At Geoffrey's suggestion, I turned off the road in a place called Oasis (Nevada) to see a group called Genesis Community. They had a farm and a roadside store featuring natural foods. I didn't have time to make an extensive visit, but I talked with a young woman named Francie who had a table in the store and was working on a bleached cow's skull. She was decorating it with colors and rawhide, and beads. Having introduced myself and refer-ring to Geoffrey, I asked her questions while she worked.

This community had begun in Santa Barbara and had increased its numbers as it gained a clearer understanding of its avowedly Christian principles. Basically, they believed in the divinity of Christ and the inspiration of the Bible, but did not see themselves as con-nected with any denomination. This, too, was a familiar theme which I heard often. They did well on the West Coast, but many members felt a desire to live more simply. So, they traded their land in California for this ranch in eastern Nevada. They had put up mobile homes as the quickest way to obtain shelter. Its appearance was neat and orderly, not at all like Meta Tantay. Francie was charming, friendly, informed, and deeply committed. She said that honesty among the members established the basis on which they dealt with con-flict. Like Mala, Francie felt that there was a quiet kind of convergence afoot among spiri-tually minded persons, but she, too, felt that powers of destruction were building. I was uncertain whether this expectation of coming trouble was a true perception or the result of a more sensitive awareness of good and evil in general. People from the highway came and went; I was aware of a gentle courtesy with which they were met. It told me much about the maturity of this community. Francie promised to put me on their mailing list, and I did the same, leaving her a copy of the Abbey Letter. This is one way that people of good will can be in touch and learn from one another.

SALT LAKE

Soon I left Nevada and became aware of the main feature of western Utah, the Great Salt Lake. In between the hills, shallow pools of salt water (having no place to drain) lay for miles and miles across the desert. It makes one appreciate the courage and perseverance of the Mormons as some 137 years ago they made this harsh environment their home. I would like to have taken more time to look at the numerous shore birds, but I did notice the seagulls which were a great symbol for the Mormon settlers, having appeared to them as a symbol of God's Providence. The state park I had intended to use was closed because of the floods all around the Salt Lake from the heavy snows of the previous winter. So I went into the city and found an inexpensive motel. It was time for a real shower and some laundry after many days of camping and Indian living. I also called another good friend, explaining that I would be unable to visit. I missed seeing many friends and interesting sights but I needed to follow a schedule faithfully or I would not get very far in the time still available. That night I also spent some time puzzling out the system of street designations in Salt Lake City. It is all very orderly and based on the points of the compass but it takes some thinking out.

THE BISHOP OF SALT LAKE

On Monday, my main objective was to visit with Bishop Otis Charles. Twice previously, he had invited me to his diocese to do my Body of Christ retreats. We were well acquainted. This time I just wanted to compare notes since our last meeting. Once we got together, I described the highlights of my journey. He told me some of the turning points in his life. He had made a significant retreat with the Jesuits which had deeply affected him. He had also done an EST workshop, based on the somewhat controversial figure of Werner Erhart. A number of other serious Church leaders have done this program. It sounded something like the work I had done at Esalen.

> Without attempting to justify the general kind of work done at Esalen or est (and many similar programs), I see them as penetrating, sometimes vigorously, through our middle class minds to put us in touch with truths that once were common wisdom.
>
> Our industrial and technological way of life has accomplished marvelous things, but at a cost we have not really understood. Can we maintain the achievements of this technology, yet get back in touch with ancient wisdom, which includes a deeper understanding of the marvels of our bodies and of the earth? All of this recovery is surely part of our professed theology of creation and Incarnation.

Otis related a touching point about his son who had spent time at the Zen Center I had visited in San Francisco. The son had asked his father what his lineage was, meaning his spiritual lineage. Many of us would be hard put to show by our lives what our religious heritage was. The most serious spiritual leaders I know are searching out this question.

> The power of leaders in other religious traditions is precisely this: they live what they believe and they can offer anyone a simple experience of that living faith by certain kinds of practice. At the Zen Center, one learns to sit and explore the whole inner spiritual journey from egoism to a confident relationship with God. What simple practices do we put before our people? People seem to mature not so much by intellectual knowledge, important though that is, but by simple, daily practices. A monastery is set up to focus on such daily practice. Even there we can be confused and at times, uncertain. What of the people, faithful though they may be, who must live out their lives in this world?

Otis was trying in several ways to give his people actual spiritual experience. He had done this by sharing a walking, meditative, journey with groups of people. It reminded me of one of the themes described at the beginning of this adventure. Life is a pilgrimage to, and with, God.

I also had the privilege of talking to the Bishop's wife, Elvira. She is an exceptionally sensitive, feeling kind of person. Her perceptions are quite different from her husband's. She recognizes how difficult it is for a feeling person, and a woman, to discover her own spiritual way. In our time, the recovery of the woman's way is part of the pain and of the potential power emerging in the Church. Elvira was exercising, dieting, writing a journal, and praying in various ways in an attempt to follow her own spiritual path. It was good to encourage her and to see in her efforts some of the richer resources awakening in the Church. She and the Bishop had to attend the funeral of a vestryman, and I had to move east. I left Salt Lake City knowing that there were others whom I would have to miss.

HIGH DESERT

The van had to work hard, climbing several thousand feet through the mountains east of the city; but once on the high desert in Wyoming, it sailed along. This time my music and prayer were accompanied by occasional views of graceful antelope in the distance and of some quite near the highway. The northwest desert country is also undergoing intense mineral development. Miles and miles of empty railroad cars await their turn to be filled with coal. New chemical plants appear in the desert like recently arrived space ships. Is this mixture of nature and high technology a glimpse of the future? Can we have both? That night I camped off the highway with a herd of antelope in the pasture behind me. The wide prairie space, the setting sun, the peace were meditative.

ZAZEN ON THE DESERT
In the morning I awoke with the approach of dawn. I decided to do the exercises I had learned at Esalen — modest joint and muscle limbering exercises. I never intended to use these exercises for the martial arts for which they were a preparation. I admit that when an early driver passed on his way to work, I felt somewhat self-conscious. At the end of my exercises I sat for ten minutes on the little cushion I bought in San Francisco. It felt good, just sitting quietly in the pasture before the rising sun. No doubt I am still in the romantic stage but I sense that being aware of one's body, breathing, and gently putting aside the distractions of the mind is good training. It is not so different from the usual discipline of Christian meditation, but for me the emphasis on the body is new. Of course, the aim of any meditation is to go beyond the body and the mind, but the "going beyond" is an art which must be learned. Simply focusing on the breathing is an important part of this art.

After my cup of coffee and an orange, I was on the road. The big mountains were fading behind me. Somewhere I crossed the Continental Divide, but it was unremarkable, just an extended plateau. Eventually I crossed into Nebraska. Here, north of the Platte River, began the famous sand hills. This is cattle country. The story is that when the early settlers brought their cattle up along the Platte River, there wasn't any fencing. In the winter some cattle strayed north and the next spring, they came back, fat and healthy. The ranchers realized that there must be water and feed in the hidden pockets of the sand hills.

THE ELDREDS
My destination was to meet with the Eldreds, the descendants of one of these early ranchers. Victor Eldred's father and mother pioneered ranching when there were few machines and fewer neighbors. Each ranch had to be its own village complex with all the necessary craftsmen right there on hand. This is the way of life that Victor inherited. He and his wife Martha now run a 122,000 acre cattle operation with modern machinery. For the fields he has all types of mowers, balers, and tractors. Checking water wells which would take a person on horseback several weeks is now done in a helicopter. Victor took me on one of his morning inspection rides. It was fun, moving effortlessly a few hundred feet about the ground, visually checking the water levels in the wells, watching a coyote getting a drink, seeing deer, enjoying ducks and waterfowl skimming the lakes in confusion at the appearance of this whirly-bird, and noting where there had been a fire the day before.

Victor was something of an inventor, having designed new machines to add to the basic tractor units. One mower had six mowing "arms" (I'm sure that's not the proper name). A phone call came to Victor at his desk telling him that an axle on one of his machines had broken. He commented that this item alone would cost $1,500. He was hoping to redesign the unit to avoid this problem. The amazing thing about Victor is not only his indomitable spirit in the face of constant ranch problems but his forward looking vision. He is not content to have surpassed his father in the use of machines. Now he is looking at solar heating systems, hydroponics (growing plants in water), investigating a plan to dam the creek to make fish ponds, and investigating every kind of new energy system available. He showed me a machine that harnesses the wind for electric power.

Victor is a man of faith. He and Martha belong to the local Episcopal Church but their interest in matters of faith ranges across and beyond denominational lines. Both of them have investigated various ways of healing. For instance, they visited the faith healers in Manila who "open the body" for surgery or healing with their hands. This is documented but not explained by people in the normal medical profession. This medical work in Manila comes from an ancient tradition among the people who are now Roman Catholics but who use primitive wisdom as well as simple faith techniques to do their extraordinary healing work. Martha described how they "opened up" her chest and while she looked on, removed something that was interfering with her heart's efficiency.

Martha, herself, is an unusual person. She has survived out here on the ranch, 17 miles off the pavement, working closely with her husband, cooking for ranch hands, occasionally working in the fields, meeting every emergency — all of this with her own bright spirit. She, too, is a person of deep faith, something of a poet, and has many intuitive and feeling gifts. When people of differing gifts can live together in harmony, it is a marvelous example of grace at work.

Over a glass of herb wine, I listened attentively to the experiences of the Eldreds. (I had met them before and was acquainted with their sensitivity to the land and to the work of the Spirit.) They discussed their future plans for the ranch and some property they own in the nearby city of Alliance. They were getting older and wanted to see that their life's work passed into the hands of people who share their vision for conservation of energy and for the work of the Lord. Their children, now grown, a son and two married daughters, did not see themselves as continuing this ranch tradition. I commented here and there, sharing with them some of my own life experiences and the ways of God. We talked easily and excitedly. It is a joy to be with such people of faith who see their everyday life as well as their long range plans as part of God's work.

Sitting in my room on the morning of my departure, looking out over the rolling sand hills near the ranch house, I said Lauds. The prairie grasses, meadows, fresh morning air, and the soft glow of the rising sun, all seemed to touch a primitive chord.

> The earth is a beautiful sacrament of God. Can we keep it beautiful as we continue to exploit its resources with our new technology? If we don't keep this respect, we lose something of ourselves. What we do to the earth we do to ourselves. The Indians, previous keepers of this land, knew this well. Chief Joseph, the heroic Nez Perce leader, said, "The earth is the mother of all people, and all people should have equal rights upon it ...."

As I drove the 17 miles back to the highway, I made up my own psalms. The view before me wrote its own hymn of praise:

Wind blowing gently,
Waving the grasses,
God stroking His earth.
Antelope moving in the distance,
Sun shining and smiling.
Hills themselves seeming to roll.
Ducks skimming the water,
Sunflowers crowding the road
    Peeping in the front window,
    Drumming on the sides of the van,
Birds fanning out in front,
    Like flying fish.
Inside the van, harp music,
Opening me to the flow
    Of God's joy.

SIOUX CITY

The sand hills continue through most of Nebraska. It is a broad state. Finally I reached Sioux City, named for the tribe that once freely roamed in this area. I found a wayside camping spot and ate a simple meal. The western part of my sabbatical was ending. It was sad, but the memories, the people, are now mine forever.

> One of the lessons I learned at Esalen is that energy is stored in memories. One can recover that energy by touching the memory, and then use that energy for future challenges.

FOREST CITY

By 4:00 AM, I was awake and heading east; the van needed some attention. Forest City, Iowa, the home of Winnebago Industries where the van was made, was 200 miles away. It was fun driving toward the rising sun, saying Lauds, and watching the world come back to life. I arrived at the factory where my friend, Roger Lunning, who was in charge of Customer Service, put me on the work schedule. The van needed its 11,200 mile check-up. The cruise control was not holding its speed, the rear fender should be replaced, the rear bed reattached to the wall, a small light switch over the driver's head needed adjustment, the refrigerator door needed tightening, and that odd smell in the water system ought to be investigated. All of these little quirks had developed gradually as I drove across some 15 states, but I never had any major trouble. I had been remarkably free to travel, visit friends, enjoy the scenery, and stop where I wanted. I was grateful for this gift. Now it was time to give some care to this wonderful companion of my adventures.

The customer service department of the company is a genial place. People come and go, getting their units repaired and enjoying a friendly "traveler's rest" atmosphere in the lounge. I was given a special room where I could write letters and catch up on these notes. Because the repairs could not be completed in one day, I spent one night in Pilot Knob State Park where I had stayed on the way west, watching carefully not to park in soft ground. On my previous visit there I had been towed out of the mud. Fortunately, the weather was dry, allowing me an easy departure on the following morning. A few more hours back at customer service and the van was done. I always have to ask questions of the mechanics who do the work because they don't appreciate that I have to incorporate their discoveries into my understanding of the machine I am managing.

LABOR DAY WEEKEND

The drive eastward was now familiar. It is often said that the way home is faster. Perhaps the reason is because our imagination is no longer awake. Without imagination life becomes routine. When I stopped at a state park in Wisconsin, I discovered that it was full — as were all the nearby parks. This was Labor Day weekend. Oh, my! Well, time to start tapping one's ingenuity. I asked my intuitive self where an appropriate camping place was and pondered each turnoff of the road I passed. I turned off at a small airport and drove up to the hanger. I looked around. Not much activity. I was half-prepared to camp there when a couple came. They lived nearby, so I asked them if they thought it would be all right if I camped there all night. The man told me that just over the hill there was a little lake where no one would bother me. The entrance to this site was from behind the motel. I thanked him and went to investigate. Indeed, down a rather steep hill there was a lake, and I found a pleasant place to park. I fixed supper, said the Office, and after some reading, went to bed. Some time during the early evening I became aware of the gentle patter of rain. I consulted my inner wisdom. Is this going to be a problem in the morning? No alarm signal. So I went back to sleep.

The next morning everything was thoroughly wet. It had rained all night. Breakfast, prayer. Then to calculate my ascent. Should I back up for a running start up the hill? As I was making up my mind, I drove toward the dirt road. The van seemed to move easily up the first part, so I continued. Going slowly in first gear, it continued without a problem. It must have been the gravel base. When I reached the motel parking lot, I offered a prayer of thanks and sighed with relief. I parked in the motel parking lot and began to tidy up the van. I was definitely not in the West anymore. I could put away my moccasins. My compass would not be necessary. I'd have to get out better clothing. There were little things that ought to be put away on shelves. The candles on the upper shelf had all melted into one wax blob. Then there were all of those brown bags I collected each time I had bought groceries. I wanted to sort my books, those I would leave at the Abbey and those I would take east with me. I looked wistfully at my list of Western friends. Some I had actually seen, others I had missed. It all depended on how much time I had at any given place. There was some food on the shelves I had not touched, and there were clothes I had never worn. There were still a few systems in the van that I was approaching cautiously. Anyway, I was ready to return.

FATHER WIEDRICH

I was in Madison, Wisconsin, in the late morning, where I was hoping to find a person who at one time had been connected with the Findhorn Community in Scotland. This community had been one of the first to explore the connections between the various parts of creation. The person I was looking for was David Spangler who had left Findhorn and was said to be in the Madison area. I called the priest, Fr. William Wiedrich, at Grace Church, the large downtown church, and found he was conducting a funeral. I went to the church and caught him as he was about to drive to the cemetery. He said that he himself had tried to find David but had failed. He had to go to the cemetery but promised to be back shortly. So I went into the parish house where a reception had been planned and had some cake and punch. I casually asked some of the ladies if they had heard of David. One said she would be willing to help me track down his address. We looked in the phone book, called some numbers, got some curious responses, but finally found a person who had heard of David. But his phone number was no longer listed. So that was that.

In time, Father Wiedrich returned and after talking with various people, took me to his office for a chat. I offered him some of my insights. He put them up against his own situation. Again, I could see the pressure on the priest, or, in fact, on anyone in leadership. The importance of drawing the parish decision-making group into an honest and loving intimacy became ever more clear to me. And I could also see the pressure on a person who has some prophetic qualities. Can one person administer the ordinary affairs of the parish and still be sensitive to the enigmatic signs of the future? I felt he was trying. We hugged and parted.

DEKOVEN REVISITED

From Madison it is not far to Racine, Wisconsin. So by supper time, I was back with the Sisters of St. Mary at DeKoven Foundation. I wanted to compare notes of their own journey since seeing them last. Sister Dorcas was away at one of the hermit groups (a group of solitaries who live on one site and come together for some services and meals) I had passed by. But the other sisters generously gave of their time and talked with me about my journey, their own situation, and what probably lay before them. Not only do they live by prayer, but their faith must stretch to the practicalities of money and heating bills. I have the sense that such groups are probing the future in faith on behalf of the Church. Maybe in the future we will all be less materially secure. On Sunday I said Mass for them, had a few conferences, then left for Chicago.

RETURNING

I had to acknowledge that the closer I got to home the more ambiguous my feelings became. I was eager to see my brethren again, but I was also uneasy about what might have transpired in my absence. I had phoned regularly but that had provided only the essential facts. Would some of the old problems that eluded my ability still be there? Would the relationships have changed in any significant way? Was the money coming in? Had anyone else left? I knew that some of the brethren were going through difficult times in their vocations. How was the community handling the tension?

I arrived at the Abbey on Sunday evening when we take our supper in the recreation room with the guests and have a leisurely time until Compline. I had called ahead. Most of the brethren just looked up and smiled, waved, or nodded. Some gave me a hug. But after some 19 weeks of being apart we came together quite naturally. It was good to be back in my choir stall for Compline, and afterwards to sink into the corporate silence. There is indeed a strength in our life together.

In my absence, my room had been painted. The furniture having been moved to do this, everything was somewhat chaotic. However, I was soon asleep in my own bed. How comforting this is.

I did not rise at 4:00 the next morning. When I did come to, I had to sort things out in my room until I had it returned to some order. My office was somewhat confusing. One puts things here and there while working on various projects but when one has been away for a while, one forgets where they were put or why one put this piece of paper in that little niche.

I offered the brethren the chance to talk to me if they wished. At this time, the Abbey Letter was being prepared so everyone was fairly busy. Also, we were down in numbers. One brother was away, another was leaving for good, and the new postulants we had selected from the summer program had not yet arrived. Nevertheless, as I talked with the brethren it became clear that things were going well. Father Anthony, our Prior, had facilitated some important decisions. In our private talk, he noted some other things he still wanted to tackle. People seemed to be at peace and happy. That is a state a superior strives to achieve but accomplishes only periodically, and not always for understandable reasons. It is mainly God's work anyway. The question of louvers for the high windows of the church had been resolved; the library enlargement plan had been completed (libraries never have enough room); the fire damage at St. Denys (our guest house) had been repaired; and several rooms had been repainted. On the human level some relationships had deepened, some were getting more problematical. The usual. The money was fine. A generous gift had come from the Eldreds. No one was seriously ill. Br. David, in his long recovery from an earlier auto accident, was about the same. I slipped into the familiar harness and lived happily with the brethren for five days.

One day at Mass I shared one of the lessons I had learned at Esalen, how we can release energy within ourselves, and between ourselves and others. This must be something of the power the Lord exercised in healing and drawing others to Himself. Afterwards, one of the younger brethren came to me and quite simply revealed to me how at times I block energy in the community. There was a little sting in this feedback, but in general I was grateful for this kind of exchange. It is an example of what I say I want to foster in community. Can I be an equal with them in this process of growth?

My flight to Rome was only ten days away. My physician gave me my annual check-up and a flu shot, I had my teeth cleaned, and wrote a number of letters. By Thursday it became clear that I would be free to move on. One last check with the travel agent cleared up some confusion concerning my ticket to Rome. A stop at Battle Creek took care of a few items with the motor home dealer and then I was on my way, headed toward Ohio.

CHAPTER 17

THE EASTERN SPIRIT

TOLEDO

As I passed through Toledo, I remembered a difficult situation some years ago. I had been on my way to give a retreat in the Cleveland area and was no doubt preoccupied with that matter when I became vaguely aware of the car ahead of me. It was going fairly slowly, so I picked a convenient place to pass. Just at that moment the driver turned left, right across my path. I hit the car on the left rear fender. This destroyed any evidence of whether or not the driver had her turn signal on. I hadn't seen it. Well, we both limped off the highway, my car's front end smashed. When the police came, I was charged with negligent driving. Fortunately no one was hurt. My car had to be towed back toward Toledo to be repaired and I had to rent another car to continue on my way. In the retreat, I used this incident to show something about the unexpected events of life.

I returned to St. Gregory's with the rented car and it was weeks before I was able to pick up the repaired Abbey car. At that time, I went to the court and reported to the judge, who turned out to be a graduate of Notre Dame (a Roman Catholic university near South Bend, Indiana). He removed most of the penalty, but it was a drawn-out affair. A few items like this can make urban living wearing. It leaves you feeling helpless and angry — and tired. Now I relived all this, I tried to locate the exact spot where the accident had happened. I thought I would never forget that place, but I couldn't find it. It had disappeared, at least from my clear memory.

CLEVELAND

This time I got to Cleveland without mishap. My goal was to see the Austins, friends I had known in Detroit before Tom's business had moved them to Cleveland. Ann, his wife, had attended and organized some of my retreats. Soon I was on the 13th floor and found their apartment with its a lovely view of Lake Erie. Ann and I always move quickly to the questions on her mind, and she always has some fascinating ones concerning family and Church. We talked until Tom came from work. Philip, their son, came in and out of the room. Finally, we decided to go out for dinner, as Ann had injured her foot and didn't want to use it more than necessary. They took me to a delightful neighborhood Hungarian restaurant. We had to wait, but the food was good, the company lively, and our talk interesting. It was here that Tom asked my opinion about the use for a building next to the cathedral. He was Senior Warden and was trying to develop a policy (for the use of this property). I like nothing better than to speculate on a situation which offers opportunity for imaginative ministry — could the building be a training center — a community, an urban model? We talked about the neighborhood and how people would have to be skilled and loving to work there. Then we looked at the other end of the question: what would the city planner say? What would national planners say about this kind of urban question? We had a fascinating time.

I was aware that Ann and Philip were having their own good talk. Tom and I stopped and joined them. Philip was having a problem with one of the new teachers at the school. As he talked I was impressed with his ability to analyze the question from various sides. He was able to fault himself for some of his actions. This was an unusual family. Ann is the daughter of the late Bishop Hubbard of Spokane and Tom is an unusually committed person in his business and in the Church. I treasured my friendship with these people. We returned from the restaurant fairly late. Before I went to bed, I looked out the window, watching the lights of the city over the lake.

In the morning, with some extra time, I did my exercises and sat, yoga fashion, for ten minutes. This always clears my head and heart. Then we had breakfast. Ann was off on an errand. This gave Tom and me time to review the previous night's questions. I took the opportunity to show him how he could deepen his own spiritual life by reflecting on the wisdom and integrity the Lord had developed in him over the years. This confidence in God's work in him could take Tom deeper into prayer and strengthen him when he had to take a stand in his business or in the affairs of the Church. Tom listened attentively, the mark of his humility. We parted and I moved on eastward.

MYSTICISM

The drive on the freeway and turnpike was pleasant. I listened to some tapes by David Stendl-Rast, a Benedictine from Elmira, New York. These tapes were made at Esalen, another indication of the growing contacts between Esalen and traditional Western mysticism. Richard Price had told me about these tapes and subsequently had sent them to me. It was intriguing to listen to David talking at a secular conference center to a group of people, some of whom had left the Church and others of whom had never found it. He was skilled in presenting mysticism as the underlying basis of Christianity and of life itself.

YORK

By evening I had passed through some very beautiful countryside, still engrossed in the talk on mysticism. I arrived in York, Pennsylvania where I wanted to meet Fr. Kermit Lloyd, the Rector of St. John's Church and some of the members of the Elizabeth S. Bonham Mission Fund. They had given me generous support for my sabbatical van. To be near the downtown parish, I went to a motel. On Sunday, Fr. Lloyd kindly invited me to participate in the services. Some 60 people attended the 7:30 service, unusual for the early hour. I was impressed. The Church was begun in 1755 and had been part of the history of the Revolutionary War era. Not much of the original building remained, but something of the Spirit of those 230 years was still here. I spoke at all of the services and at the adult Bible class, and I found the people attentive. I always try to show the connection between the religious life and baptism. After the service I attended the Outreach Committee meeting and watched them juggle their limited resources with the many demands presented. It is heartbreaking to see such dedicated people trying to put their few fingers into the many holes in the dike. After the meeting, Father Lloyd, the Senior Warden, and his wife took me to lunch. We sat at a table at the country club and discussed the life of the parish. These were good people, doing the work of the Lord. There is not enough appreciation shown for the hard-working clergy and parishioners of our churches.

Eventually the talk turned to TMI. I had to ask what that stood for. I was told that it was the Three Mile Island nuclear power plant and we were only a short distance from it. Here was liturgy, life and death, human weakness fumbling with power far beyond human comprehension or control. The conclusion of their remarks was that the truth hadn't been told, the danger of "meltdown" was far greater than was acknowledged, and the problem had not been solved.

> This subject showed the dimension of the human problem before us. It tells me that we must explore the question of power deep within human nature before we can choose wisely about the external use and control of power. This is a spiritual question.

> Are we not being forced to develop our relationship with God *precisely* because incredible power is in the hands of people who see it as an instrument of their own wishes? Such power, misunderstood and misused, is now at a critical level. Power will make us face the ultimate questions of life: Where do we come from? Why are we here? Where will we go?

LAURA

After lunch, we parted and I drove north to Camp Hill. There I had tea with Laura, an old acquaintance through correspondence. We had never met. She was a single woman, now retired, a loyal member of the Church, and a long-time secretary for a New York businessman. Her mother and sisters had recently died. She was bravely fighting off grief. In tears she apologized for her feelings. I tried to make her accepting of her grief which was her love. I listened. She also struggled with the ending of a long relationship, business oriented though it was. Her love, tears, and smile touched me deeply. She had been suffering a backache, too. I prayed with her, asking her to let God's energy flow through her, easing her back, and her heart. We finished the tea and she said she was grateful for what we had shared. I promised to continue to pray as the next day she had a difficult interview. I left, admiring this very human and faithful person.

THE JAMESES

Not far from Camp Hill (and Three Mile Island), Charles and Helen James had retired. He had been the Rector of a fine parish in Michigan and at one time the confessor for our community. They had returned to a small town, Marietta, near where whey had both grown up. It was a charming little town with small houses reminiscent of the original Jamestown. I came into town about 7:00 PM and found their address. I discovered that very night they were preparing to move into their new (for them) house across the street. They were delighted to see me but shocked at the prospect of entertaining a guest. We all laughed nervously while I assured them that I could stay in the van. They showed me their new-old house, built by her grandfather whom Helen had visited as a child. They had worked hard to restore it while adding modern conveniences, but Helen admitted that coming "home" both to the house and the town wasn't what she had expected. It never is. Once we finish with the fantasy, we can go home and meet the reality of what is actually there. Charles was the Rector of the local parish. He was bringing considerable experience to this small town parish. He acknowledged that it was quite a challenge to open their minds to the larger issues in the world.

We sat on their porch and reminisced about Michigan, the Abbey, and mutual friends. Then we went back to the old house (how disconcerting to live in two houses!) for a meal from the freezer. Knowing that they had a busy moving day ahead, I excused myself early and went to the van, now parked in the backyard of their new house. I almost prefer my own, familiar accommodation to a strange room and bed. I slept well.

The next morning I went back to the old house where we had orange juice, fresh trout (the gift of a friend), fried potatoes, and coffee. Then I carried a few baskets of towels across the road. When the real movers came, I said goodbye. I knew the Jameses would be distracted and harassed.

THE JESUITS

My next destination was the Jesuit Center in Wernersville, west of Reading. I had read about their retreat program which struck me as an interesting development of the Spiritual Exercise of Ignatius Loyola, the Order's founder. A short distance out of town I found the old estate in which the Jesuits train their younger members and offer retreats. I was invited to Mass and was offered Communion, always a sign to me of the stage of renewal of a Church group. The celebrant, Father Bob Hatch, offered to talk with me after the service. I asked him my usual questions: How did the group handle conflict? Did he see a convergence of spiritual traditions, both within and beyond the Christian Church? And what kinds of growing experiences had this group known? This started us off in all kinds of directions. I could see that the American branch of the Jesuits was making an honest effort to incorporate Christian theology and tradition with contemporary human development insights. In short, they were learning some valuable things from the worlds of business and therapy. This coincides with my intuition that there are good things to bring to our tradition from these other fields. I obtained a pamphlet entitled, "The Group

Meeting as a Contemplative Experience." This was another connection. Unless we, as Christians, connect the events of our daily life with our deepest theology, we become split. Bob took me to lunch and then I said goodbye. It was a valuable visit. I want to stay in touch with these people. More networking.

OFF THE ROAD

Bishop Mark Dyer, the Bishop of Bethlehem, was on my list to visit but I also felt the urge to have some time alone. Solitude for my own thoughts, prayers, and catching up on some correspondence periodically claims my attention, and I had been with people regularly since leaving the Abbey. I needed to be a hermit for a while. So I talked to my inner person of wisdom and asked for a place to stay, just off the road. Perhaps this system only alerts me to pay attention. In any event, I spotted a large area where shale had been gathered for road work. It was separated from the highway by a high bank. Behind the bank was ample space overlooking the hills of eastern Pennsylvania. I drove into this area, tested it with my feelings, and felt comfortable. Having driven for a few hours, I had hot water (the engine heats the water system). So, being in quite a private place, I took my usual rinse and shower outside the van. I did a little laundry and then settled down to write some letters and catch up on these Notes. After dark I had a cup of soup and some peanut butter and jelly sandwiches, read the Office, did a little more typing, and to bed. How peaceful it was.

BETHLEHEM

In the morning in some nearby bushes, I could "complete my digestion" (as St. Benedict puts it quaintly), have breakfast, pray, and get ready to move. I love these quiet nights spent in the country. Back on the highway I put fuel into the van, checked the tires, and finally moved on to Bethlehem, "the Christmas City." The cathedral complex has something of a European appearance. There is a large cathedral church, an ample parking lot (which in Medieval times would have been a marketplace, a place for the mystery play, a place for the faithful to gather), and some older homes now made into diocesan offices. This had been a recent consolidation. Earlier in the century the wealthy parishioners had lived "up on the hill" and the working people lived down near the cathedral site. Now the Bishop, a former Roman Catholic Benedictine monk, has brought this all together. One can see how the communal experience of his monastic experience reflects itself in his policy for the diocese. Each week he sees a group of clergy for Bible study and sharing. He and his cathedral staff meet daily for prayer and open reflection on their life and their work.

> This emphasis on relationship around the Word is surely one of the key parts to life in the Church. How else can we understand the theology of the Body of Christ? And if it is not lived at the center of the Church's life, how can we expect the faithful to take the principle seriously? First, they have to see it in practice.

In the Bishop's temporary absence, I talked with Canon Rowley. He was in thorough agreement with the Bishop's policy. He had only been there a year, having come from Honolulu, where the mixing of races and cultures is the norm. It was something of an adjustment for him to confront the race problems of the mainland.

ESMA

Canon Rowley invited me to attend a meeting of ESMA, the Episcopal Society for Ministering to the Aging. Two women came from the nearby central office where they work in close association with the national church. They are setting up a computer service which will collect information on what is available for the aging. Then they will work with each diocese in any way that the diocese chooses. I was interested to see an actual program involving computers and ministry. And I was further interested to see how human the two representatives were. They explained to Canon Rowley and the local diocesan person in charge of aging that the ESMA office was run on the human family model. They chose to include their own human experiences, including grief and suffering, in the administration of their work. I asked them if they felt that this sensitivity to the human came from their womanhood. "No," they said. "The group includes men who are equally sensitive." Yet I believe that this is a more feminine quality which women have brought to the world of business. They had gone far beyond simply amassing information. They had seen the need for support groups for the aged, recognized the gifts of aging people as part of their resources, and realized that they would inevitably get involved in all of the complicated urban questions of legal rights, housing, insurance, and medical needs. But they were convinced of the need and were excited about the power of older people, once they were shown they had access to their own power of faith. I felt that this was an example of Christian ministry amplified with modern technology.

After the meeting I sat in the van for a while, had a peanut butter sandwich and some cranapple juice, and typed some letters. The Bishop came in from one of his clergy visits and we sat in the van and talked about the Church. With his training in traditional theology and his openness to renewal, plus his Benedictine experience, he had a rich set of resources to bring to his ministry. He was well aware of the challenge to the Church in trying to reach the unchurched. He noted Rahner's "Anonymous Christianity" — the mystery of faith in people who have no conscious connection with the Church. Sometimes the Church in its authentic work of revealing Christ's presence can show such persons that God is really within them. A healing word from Scripture, a Sacrament witnessed perhaps almost by accident (going to a friend's funeral), a touch of charity from someone — any of these can go deeply into a person's soul when the end of human strength has come. But we both recognized that some people or groups can commit themselves (no doubt unconsciously) to death. They can choose suicide. Even there, a person of faith can show them God's love by following them up to the very point of death. Then God Himself takes over. We parted, appreciating the focus that the Benedictine life gives to Christian faith and practice.

NOCKAMIXON

I drove south out of Bethlehem, waiting for a hunch about where to stay. I moved leisurely through farming country. Sometimes the roads were narrow and winding, a reminder that they were once used by wagons and horses. This was an older part of the country. Finally I came to Nockamixon State Park which was on a large lake. Surely the name came from the Indians. In the dusk I couldn't find a camping spot, so I just parked near the lake, had my supper, then a wash in the lake, and finally to bed. I was awakened around midnight by the ranger's flashlight. He said I couldn't stay there but that if I'd go to the nearby marina I could finish the night. I put on my trousers and drove the van to the marina and went back to bed. This has happened to me before and I am always a little embarrassed. I risk staying in places that are not specified for camping. So sometimes I lose, but my Scottish ancestors applaud me.

TEMPLE BELLS

The next morning I woke to the sound of temple bells. How delightful! But now what trick was my imagination playing on me? Oh, it was the breeze, tinkling hundreds of guy wires on the sailboats anchored along the series of piers. Still delightful. After breakfast and Lauds I phoned the Abbey. Fr. Anthony and I had to clarify a few items, but in general I had a good feeling about the community. Then I called Fr. Moore at St. Mark's in Philadelphia to prepare him for my arrival. He was still working on a place for the van so I agreed to arrive the next day. The rest of the morning and the early afternoon I spent in preparing to leave the van. I would not be using it for more than a month while I was in Rome and England. I drained the water. Why do they put the drain valves in such awkward places? Well, any mechanic is familiar with that question. But hands, even when you can't see, somehow can feel their way to the right spot among all the wires and pipes. Then I began the sorting out of what I would need for Rome, which would be fairly warm, and what for England, which in October could be anything. I made two piles: one for the European trip and one to remain in the van. In the end it all came out of the van in Philadelphia — for security reasons.

CHAPTER 18

BROTHERLY SPIRIT

NEW HOPE

Having an extra day and recalling that a friend, Father William Fox, lived nearby in New Hope, Pennsylvania, I began to head that way. As I drew near this charming old city, I noted the antique shops. Certain areas seem to foster this trade. It takes a combination of having enough old things around to restore and sell, and enough appreciative buyers who value them. But where was 135 Old York Road? I did not know that York Road was the toll road from Philadelphia to New York, that it appeared and disappeared along the way, and that it had been obscured in many places by large highways. The Holiday Inn desk clerk gave me directions. After intently looking for house numbers, stopping at an Episcopal Church for instruction, and going to the local post office for directions, I discovered that I was on Upper York Road. which wasn't Old York Road. After wandering around I did find it, drove into William's yard, and spotted him reading on his deck. I tooted the horn and he looked up, puzzled. I could almost hear him thinking, "Who in the world is this?" When I stepped out of the van and greeted him, he came alive. We embraced and sat down on the deck to exchange preliminary comments. Then he fixed a pot of tea and we got down to work. He and I had met before in very tense circumstances. He had been the interim priest of a large city parish in Philadelphia and I had been invited to come to do my workshop on the Body of Christ. As soon as I met the people of the parish, I realized that some of them did not welcome this teaching. Obviously there were a few who wished to remain in control. I went through the workshop, sensing more and more the hostility of the hidden control. In the evening, during this workshop, Father Fox and I would sit in his kitchen and ponder the mystery. He had come out of semi-retirement to do this job, and he was just waiting to get back to his life of reading and writing. When I preached on Sunday, walking up and down the aisle, I knew that it was both painful and exciting. Those who saw the meaning of the teaching eventually went to other parishes.

Since our first meeting he has pursued his writing, researching the connection between traditional theology and what is called the new physics. That is, he is examining how the new concepts in science, especially cosmology, force us to rethink the expression of our theology.

Force is not too strong a word to describe the effect of new views of reality on our understanding of God. The fact is that theologians use the same basic concepts and words that other people use to understand the world around them. You could rightfully say that theology is a specialized field. Yes, but the way that the average Christian hears that theology, whether it be in a confirmation class or a sermon, is colored by the ideas with which he lives his daily life. An example would be in the Bible which speaks of God being "out there" or "up there." That idea comes from a cosmology (the way we understand the cosmos) of those times. St. Thomas Aquinas' theological language is influenced by the cosmology of Aristotle. When we come to Newton and his physics we see a new influence on theology. Newtonian physics was based on clear ideas about cause and effect, about the solid nature of things (suggesting that unsolid things were therefore "spiritual" or unreal), about time and space as essential parts of the sequential nature of reality. There is no doubt but that theological concepts were colored by Newtonian physics. If one does this, God will do that. The Sacraments were understood in terms of an inner and invisible substance and outward accidents (like all things). Time is understood as the journey through this world (a place) to heaven (a place beyond). The new physics, arising from about the time of Einstein's theory of relativity, sees reality quite differently. Things are not solid at all. They are various forms of energy — matter equals energy — which only "appear" to us as solid because the energy system that makes them up is stable enough for us to give them names and have verifiable expectations. In addition the observer in this system contributes by interpretation to what he sees.

This is an extremely simplified sketch of a complex system of ideas. In any event, it is good that some people in the Church are examining this transition of meaning. It will, no doubt, take some time for these new ideas to filter down into the understanding of the average person's life, but we can see already that some concepts are outdated. When both of the superpowers possess atomic weapons, it is useless to think in terms of winning and losing. We are all involved in a "nuclear world" which does not permit anyone to be outside of it. The common cold may begin in one area of the world, but very quickly people on the other side of the globe are coughing. We breathe one another's air, drink one another's water, think one another's ideas, and carry one another's projected fears.

In the midst of this fascinating exploration between Fr. Fox and myself, a friend came in, bringing supper. Ed was a neighbor, a Roman Catholic, a successful businessman who was selling his restaurant and moving to England. It was amusing to observe how Fr. Fox and I, examining revolutionary new concepts, would quite consciously revert to "ordinary" common sense when Ed came in and brought up the affairs of the world — as most people perceived them. It will take a long time to convert our minds. I must admit, new or old ideas, Ed was a great cook, serving us an elegant meal amidst our speculations. Subsequent to our visit, Ed did indeed go to England, settled near Buckfast Abbey (Benedictine) in south Devon, and attended daily services at the abbey. Not an ordinary businessman after all!

PHILADELPHIA

The next day I left Fr. Fox and continued toward Philadelphia. I did try to see one more friend, Mrs. Welsh Strawbridge, whose family name appeared on various street and town names in the Horsham/Graeme Park area. When I called, she was not at home. So I turned south and decided to do what only a tourist would do, drive through the outer rings of the city, slowly moving to the center of William Penn's City of Friendship. As one would expect, it was a mixture of old and new examples of the long history of this city. Here a statue, there a slum area; here a park, there a weed-filled abandoned neighborhood; here a large institutional set of buildings, there a block of once grand houses; here a splendid avenue, there a back street filled with the junk of the poor.

> The modern city is a mixture that refuses to be brought together under any current economy or politics. It is a confession of all that is marvelous and all that is tawdry in our culture. Philosophers cannot heal the city, but they do have a role to play awakening us to new perspectives. Hurry up, Father Fox!

On the outskirts of the city I passed through Jenkintown which reminded me that in the early days of the Abbey's life, Mrs. Sumner Cross, Sister Scholastica we called her, came to live near the the monastery after the death of her husband. He had been a doctor to the DuPonts and other affluent people in the Philadelphia area. Nan, as her friends called her, had developed a quiet life of prayer and skillful sewing — which she considered as part of her prayer. She made exquisite vestments. When she came to know of St. Gregory's through Father Paul (one of our founding fathers), she offered to make vestments for us. She would quite blatantly tell some of her wealthy customers that they would have to pay double for her work. That made it possible for her to donate a vestment to us. She moved to a cottage near the Abbey in 1955 and continued her life of prayer and sewing. We were enriched by both. Of course, as a real Philadelphian, she sent back east to her favorite stores for hats, birdseed, and other essential needs in her life. She had style and class, culturally and spiritually. I thought of her as I drove through Jenkintown and prayed for her.

Gradually, I penetrated the city to its center where St. Mark's Episcopal Church is located. I had known Father Charles Moore since his days in New York, continuing to his time in Chicago where he had been the Rector of St. Giles in the suburb of Northbrook. I had known him, his children, and his gifted wife Sylvia, preached at her funeral, and provided the homily at his departure from St. Giles and for his installation at St. Mark's. He was a kindred soul. And by now he had acquired another of my friends, Father Phillip Bennett, as his curate. I drove onto the sidewalk next to the church, rang the bell, and soon was warmly received. Quickly we unpacked the van and took it to a funeral director's parking lot a few blocks away. Cars in the city are a problem.

I was given a room on the third floor of the old rectory (there was also a fourth floor). The rectory was part of the grand complex that made up this historic church which had been built some 140 years ago. The Wanamaker silver altar and reredos is only part of the grandeur of this church designed in 15th Century English Gothic style. But Charles and Phillip were very much in tune with new ideas. Some parishioners were ready for this; some were not. Not unusual. Charles and I had some time alone as Philip was not well. This gave us a chance to catch up on one another's lives. He and I had both come out of the Anglo-Catholic background. It was interesting to compare notes. Our journeys were different, but touched some of the same points — an easing away from non-essential "absolutes" in theology, a deeper awareness of the complexity of souls as revealed in therapy models, a strong perception that the future of the Church and the world are moving toward radical changes. We talked easily on these shared perceptions.

On Friday, the Feast of the Holy Cross, I attended the Eucharist. In the Lady Chapel with the Wanamaker silver altar we had a Rite II Service with a touch of charismatic singing. This seemed to be a nice blend of the old and the new. There is certainly something good about a gentle transition in the life of the Church — if the world will give us time for gentle transitions. That night we went to nearby Holy Trinity Church on Rittenhouse Square, another old parish almost as old as St. Mark's. They were celebrating the ministry of a new rector, Father John A. Smart. Obviously he was a warm and personable man. In the short time he had been at Holy Trinity, he had charmed many of his people and shocked a few by putting candles on the altar. The preacher gave us two images of Philadelphia: the old Black man picking food out of a garbage can (a familiar sight in the city) and the way of life in a high rise apartment. How was Trinity to minister to such a combination? Bishop Lyman Ogilby, a cadaverous person with a voice like Jeremiah, was in the sanctuary. Bishop Ogilby had survived the Bataan Death March in the Philippines in World War II. All of this provided the disconnected bits and pieces of Holy Trinity today. How to bring it all together? I hope that John, Charles, and Phillip can become friends. It will take a lot of friendship along with deep prayer and a sense of humor to bring such a parish into the 21st Century.

On Saturday, I moved the van from the funeral home parking lot to a more permanent place, the school ground of St. Peter's Church on the east side of the city. It would be there for some six weeks. I thanked the Rector, Father Lee Richards, and asked him what kind of prayer intention I could take to Rome and England in gratitude for this kindness. He asked me to pray for the renewal of his parish. Most pastors are aware of the vast changes that are coming to the Church; and they have a few tentative ideas of how this might be accomplished. But they stand in awe of the overwhelming task. They are in desperate need of a small, inner group which will venture with them. I promised to pray for Lee and for all pastors of congregations.

SUNDAY

Dressed in my habit, I attended the 8:00 AM Eucharist at St. Mark's. I preached a sermon on the heart as the inner place where we truly and fully meet life. I included some personal experiences. It went all right but there was not much response from the people. But at the 10:00 AM Mass, the same sermon, somewhat amplified, became a profound exploration of the hearts of those attending. I can only say that when I sense people responding, listening deeply, being touched by grace, I am able to enter into a holy exchange with them. It is as if both the preacher and the listeners were being taught by God. I could tell that many were touched. Afterwards their embraces and thanks showed. This is one of the most profound joys of a priest.

Later in the day, after lunch and a nap, Phillip and I listened to a cassette tape called "Solar Wind." The group of vocalists had studied Tibetan techniques by which the human voice is able to produce overtones and harmonics from a single note. It gives one the impression of basic, natural vibrations, earth music, primitive sounds. It suggests that musicians are aware of the profound changes coming to the world and that they are hearing the appropriate music to accompany this revolution. The Church's music will undoubtedly retain fine old tunes, but also be open to new music that reflects our new understanding of the world.

Phillip and I began to speculate on the life of the Christian parish today. Whether because of the music we had just heard or my own experiences on sabbatical, we moved easily toward ideas about workshops for spiritual growth. We recognized that the workshop is an opportunity for people to experience changes in themselves before they risk such changes in their actual life. They can then choose to incorporate some portion of the workshop teaching in their life as it seems appropriate.

> What type of workshop space is needed? How should such a space be furnished — or, not furnished? How would it be financed? There are many practical questions but the important point is that we all need opportunities to experience life and the Lord of the Gospel in new ways. With such experiences we can then more freely choose how to live our lives. Perhaps the Church should consider the role of workshops as a regular ministry for our conversion.

JULIE

That evening I was invited to Julie's apartment in the downtown section of the city. Julie is a lay employee of St. Mark's, a deeply committed Christian, and a skilled person in management. She was doing good work for the parish along with the two priests and the staff. It did not take us long, however, to come to a subject much on her mind. She was deeply concerned about a particular person on the staff, their conflict, and how to resolve this. As usual, the staff was aware of the situation but no one had the skill to deal with it directly.

This is a normal dilemma in parish life. I shared some of my own experience but tried to remain tentative. She needed to work such a conflict out with the Rector. But the importance of working such conflicts out, at the staff level, was reinforced for me. We need such skill throughout the Church. Julie's experience with therapy models helped us see various openings in this difficult question. We talked of other things and had a delightful meal while sitting on the floor around her low coffee table. I had to leave early so that I could finish my packing for Rome. I walked home, having an ice cream cone on the way, and pondered the pastoral questions on the administrative level of the Church's life.

On Monday, still wondering just what to include, I finished my packing. Rome would be warm; England, cool. In Rome I would be attending meetings with other abbots; in England I would be mainly in two monasteries. Yet in both cases, I would need some casual clothing. Then, too, I wanted my typewriter. No doubt I packed too much. I attended the Mass in the Lady Chapel, had a bite to eat with Charles, then went with him and Julie to the airport.

BOOK TWO

THE SPIRIT OF THE ETERNAL CITY

CHAPTER 19

KINDRED SPIRITS

TWA 260 AND 840

Flying today is relatively easy. But one has to be prepared for odd delays and inconveniences. Although I was to change planes in New York, I checked my main bag through from Philadelphia to Rome. The flight to Kennedy airport was on a pleasant sunny afternoon, over farms and briefly over the ocean. Then began the more complicated procedures for an overseas flight. I was early and had ample time to make a seat selection. I like being early as it gives me time to take care of little things without hurrying. In this case I could get some Italian money at the airport, enough to handle taxis and incidentals before I would be able to get the better exchange rate at San Anselmo's in Rome where the Congress of Abbots was to take place.

As the crowd began to gather for the flight, an announcement was made that they were overbooked. Therefore, if anyone was willing to take a guaranteed seat on an hour later flight to Rome, he would be reimbursed $200. My Scottish blood jumped at a further reduction in my expenses. That meant listing yourself with the gate attendant and then waiting until the last minute to see who actually turned up. I am not good at waiting but I was proud to discover that my sabbatical grace had given me less need to control situations. So, I waited. In the end my seat was not needed. But that meant that I was part of the scramble for the remaining seats. I wound up with an aisle seat instead of the window seat I had originally been promised. Oh, well. It would only be a seven hour flight. I stowed my typewriter in the overhead luggage compartment and began the tedious wait for everything to be sorted out before takeoff.

PHYLLIS

As I was sitting there, an attractive woman approached, smiled, and asked if I wasn't the priest who had attended Esalen. When I acknowledged that I was, she told me she was Phyllis, who had been there at the same time. Immediately, a flow of happy memories came back to me. We chatted until it was time to take off. What a real community had been formed in that short week. It reinforced the N.L.P. teaching that energy is stored in good memories.

We took off a little late but were assured that we would land in Rome at the appointed time. The routine is familiar to anyone who has made this flight. First the drinks, then the meal, next the movie, and several hours later, the dimmed lights for what sleep is possible. Because I was on an aisle seat, I could get up and move about easily. I was amused at my nonchalance, having made this flight five times before. The first time, all had been exciting: the printed menu as well as the wonder of flying at 37,000 feet. The couple next to Phyllis were annoyed at the smoke blowing their way and moved to another section. That gave me the chance to join her and talk about Esalen and what we had experienced. Then we spoke of her life. She was at a turning point. This had been her reason for going to Esalen. She realized that she had received valuable teaching and courage to face her new life — a life after a divorce, a probable change in her business, and a venture into professional writing. We had a great time savoring the excitement of life when one has the inner resources to face change with confidence. I found it easy to share something of my own situation, how I would go home and listen to my brethren to see what they had learned in my absence, and how in a few years I might not be abbot. She listened with a feminine strength that helped me view the various alternatives with even more equanimity. In my head I already knew that I had let go of much of my "career" expectations, but the sabbatical had given me time to let that knowledge filter deeper into my heart. Even if I was to remain abbot for an additional time, I would do the job with much more inner detachment and a greater sensitivity to what God was doing. It was further assurance that my life is in God's hands. It merely takes a long time to develop that trust — maybe a lifetime.

2:30 AM/ 8:30 AM

The movie was about an adventure of an English baby who had been take to Africa by his parents and, after their deaths, raised by gorillas. Purposely I had not rented the earphones and only took in bits and pieces of the story by watching the silent version. It had stirred odd dreams, interrupted by periodic waking. But at last, morning came. We were over France at 2:30 AM, U.S. time; 8:30 AM European time. I felt oddly unsettled. Fruit juice, a roll, and coffee were available. I pulled my typewriter down from its storage place and put on my collar. Actually I was traveling as a priest solely for the purpose of easing through Customs. What a motive! But I remembered a previous return flight from England when I had been smuggling a pork pie home to Eva Mercer, a British-born friend of the Abbey who lived in Three Rivers. She couldn't make the journey as she wanted and had expressed this wish. Like David's lieutenants in Scripture at hearing his wish for a drink of water, I was moved to heroic efforts to fulfill Eva's desire. But the process had involved me in a number of refrigerators and tricky maneuvers from England to Detroit. At the Customs clearance with the pork pie in my raincoat pocket, the young attendant, seeing that I was a priest, began to interrogate me on theological grounds. I was nervous about the pork pie, but not about the intricate marital questions he was raising. In the end, I pointed to the long line of people waiting to clear Customs and he waved me through. I didn't normally attempt to use the Church in such a fashion, but for Eva, all was fair. That much of my

Jesuit training remained. The end sometimes justified the means. When I fell on my knees in her small house and delivered the precious gift, she was delighted and had me tell the story several times.

In Rome, this time Customs was a painless process. On deplaning I found my luggage, walked through the aisle marked, "Nothing to Declare" and boarded the bus for the Termini, the transportation center in downtown Rome. A college age girl beside me asked me a few questions and I suddenly became an expert. At the station I gathered my luggage and then pondered the warning we had been given about unscrupulous taxi drivers who over-charged. As I was calculating, a cab spotted me and solved my problem by making it easy to accept his services. He agreed that it would only be about 8,000 lire, close to what the mailed out information had suggested. I agreed, trying to remember how much that came to in dollars — about $4.50. Not bad. But one has to develop a quick money translation system before buying anything or engaging anyone's services. Then there are different customs and rates for tipping. In this case, on arrival at San Anselmo, the meter only read 4,500 lire but the extra was for handling baggage. Anyway, I had arrived only a little late for the Congress which had begun that morning.

SAN ANSELMO

San Anselmo is the Benedictine College in Rome where studies are provided for young monks and others, too, in preparation for ordination or graduate work. It is also the center of the Abbot Primate, the coordinating Abbot who helps the various congregations (a group of abbeys with a Constitutional relationship) hold together loosely in what is known as the Benedictine Confederation. This is the worldwide organization of all Benedictines which provides the Benedictine world information while not intruding on the autonomy of the individual abbeys or congregations. It is a unique organization, based more on a common life under the Rule of St. Benedict than on any organizational structure. In this sense, it is close to the Spirit of the Anglican Communion — a model which might become operative for the whole Church as it seeks a way of sharing the Gospel with many cultures. As the Church evolves, this model could become more important. Abbots and Priors of abbeys around the world convene every three to four years for the purpose of studying some aspect of the monastic life and for the profound strength that comes from mutual support and friendship. This was my fifth Congress. After getting settled in my room, I quickly met old friends. Although I don't speak other languages, a smile and a nod are sufficient recognition. I was in time to join the brethren, and a few sisters, at the daily Mass held at San Sabina Basilica, a short distance from the College. San Sabina's is an ancient church with the curious arrangement of the choir, enclosed in shoulder high marble partitions, standing in an isolated position in the center of the church. I met the new abbot of Nashdom (Nashdom, being our founding mother house), Godfrey, and Mark, the new superior of Alton, another Anglican Abbey. Those who were not invited to concelebrate, the sisters, the non-Romans, and a few visitors occupied the outer choir. Finally, processing into the inner choir came the priests who shared the concelebration with the principal celebrant of the day. Today he was the head of the Sacred Congregation of Religious, a further reason for me not to consider receiving Communion. In Rome one is very conscious of the bureaucracy of the Roman Church. Today that body holds a conservative position, reflecting (or influencing) the present pontiff's point of view. It is a powerful system which has both advantages and disadvantages. I have learned to live with it, not to waste time criticizing it. "When in Rome...." The Mass was in Latin, which in this case allowed people from various nations and cultures to share a common language. But at home, most Benedictines use their local tongue. After Mass we walked back to San Anselmo's, greeting old friends along the way. I saw three whom I had met on my sabbatical, David Gerets of Pecos Abbey and Philip Lawrence of Christ-in-the-Desert. I also thanked Abbot Melvin Valvano of Newark Abbey for his gift toward my sabbatical. In general, the brethren saw the sabbatical as a positive event, many of them wondering how they might gain the same privilege.

MY ROOM
After lunch, always a talking occasion so that old friends can catch up on each other's doings, I went to my room for a welcomed nap. I was conveniently located up one floor from ground level. The rooms, usually occupied by students, are of a generous size, some 15 to 17 feet. They are furnished simply with a wardrobe, desk, plenty of book space, and a sink with cold water. This is most welcome. One can get hot water in the nearby bathroom (showers added recently) and thus keep up with simple laundry needs. Students, of course, are adept at improving the facilities of their rooms. I found a little heating element for making hot drinks, a tub for bringing hot water from the bathroom, clothing hooks at appropriate places, and more books than I could even browse. I was amused to find that the electrical outlet on the wall did not work. Italy was still the same. But I determined to nap before settling in fully.

At 3:45, after some light refreshment in the cloister, we entered the aula, the main meeting place for the Congress. This time they had screened off the sanctuary from the main body of the church and set up desks and chairs for the complicated translation system, now the norm for any international gathering. Behind the screened section there was still ample choir space to accommodate 230 superiors. Such is the normal size of many European churches.

LIVING IN CHRIST
The observers (of which I was one) and the sisters were seated up front near the Abbot Primate's seat from which the speakers delivered their papers. The first speaker was Father Ghislain LaFont, a monk of La Pierre-qui-Vire, France. He focused on the main theme of the Congress, "Living in Christ," from the point of view of life in the monastery. He noted the two poles of monastic life, community and solitude, and examined various connections and contradictions between them. Like the broader Christian world, history shows us that the monastic life has various expressions which may receive special emphasis in particular times.

From his talk and my own reflections, I came to these perceptions: it is clear that the early monasticism of St. Benedict's day was a far simpler kind of life. There were no grand buildings housing large communities. Daily prayer in choir, personal time spent in lectio (a prayerful perusing of the Bible), and farm work were the principle ingredients of the monk's day. This was a monasticism that gathered small groups of monks when the Roman Empire was losing its power. Then monasticism went into a kind of obscurity in the 7th and 8th Centuries, a time when chaos and turmoil reigned in the as yet undeveloped Europe. In 800 A.D. when Charlemagne came to power, his one aim was to stabilize the chaotic situation, making full use of Christianity. He chose the monks as a principal instrument for this work. Thus the monk became a teacher and an administrator for Charlemagne's policies. Europe was built with the monastery as an integral part of a system which saw Church and state as one. Monasteries required large and complex buildings to house hundreds of monks. This was a far different kind of monasticism than St. Benedict had imagined, and yet it was a natural development from his principles. As we know, Medieval Europe, magnificent as it was for hundreds of years, did not last, but the Spirit of the Benedictine Centuries remained deep in the soul of Europe long after the Reformation and Renaissance ended the Medieval world.

How does today's monk understand his vocation, when around him change is so radical? He retains certain timeless activities such as his choral prayer, his lectio, and his simple way of daily life, while adapting his ministry and service to newly recognized needs of the Church and the world. He remains a person of prayer, living in community. The little disciplines of daily monastic life, the way one eats, walks, talks, and works, become signs of human sanity and courtesy. Centering all of these actions on a simple attention to the presence of Christ, the monk treats the ordinary things of life with simplicity and reverence.

It is quite true that as human beings monks are wounded and insecure like everyone else. Sometimes they need an extraordinary measure of healing. Some break, or drop out. But it is the recovery of a balanced, human way of life that calms the overwrought condition of modern man and offers him a simple way to share the humanity of Christ. Through such humanness, when open to the influence of Christ's divine nature (Grace), he is drawn more deeply into living with Christ.

Such were some of the reflections that came out of that first conference.

ART

Although I frequently nodded off that night, I enjoyed a slide show which featured images of Christ from the earliest centuries through the 6th Century. This presentation clearly showed how art and culture influence each other. The images of Christ reflected the point of view of the times. Pictures or mosaics of Christ in glory coincide with political conditions of the emperor in Rome or Byzantium. This needn't be seen as a secular influence on religion, but rather as a combining of the two. According to Ephesians 1:23, one day Christ will have taken to himself all times and cultures. He will fill the whole world.

On Wednesday, just one day after my arrival in Rome, I slept through Lauds at 7:00 AM, but went downstairs in time for breakfast. The menu was hard rolls and butter, sliced meat or jam, cereal, and coffee or tea served in bowls. At first these bowls seem awkward, but you get used to them. You sit wherever you wish and talk with your neighbor at your convenience. There is a wide variety of personalities, even though all of them are in leadership. Along with the intellectuals one finds some with a deep affectionate nature. There are visionaries and practical types. Some appear to be sad — others are always clowning.

After breakfast I found the monk in charge of electrical repair, "on loan" from St. John's Abbey, Collegeville (U.S.A.), and asked him to do what he could with the faulty system in my room. Surprisingly, he had it fixed before lunch. That allowed me to use my adapter which reduces 220 volts to 110, permitting me to charge my razor's battery and set up my desk lamp conveniently. I didn't need any of my other adapter plugs, often required in a foreign country to fit strange outlets. I also bought some Italian postage stamps to be used on postcards (the Italians produce gorgeous cards of all of their famous monuments). Letters mailed through the Vatican Post Office have a better chance of reaching their destinations.

TRUE GOD. TRUE MAN.

The morning lecture was given by Father Pio Tragan of Montserrat, formerly a professor at San Anselmo. Fr. Pio's focus (under the main theme of "Living in Christ") was the Biblical and theological understanding of Jesus Christ. First, he presented his method which was historical-critical. This approach tries to use the best of modern scholarship, not accepting "pious tradition" unless it can be substantiated with solid evidence. For example, it is assumed that Jesus, in his human growth, gradually developed an ever deeper understanding of who He was. Those who emphasize His divine nature find this difficult to accept. But unless there is human development in Jesus' understanding, His humanity is unreal. Just how His two natures, human and divine, are combined in one person is not easy to comprehend. Theology has its abstract explanation of this mystery. Perhaps we have a glimpse of how this might work when we have a special touch of grace in our ordinary human experience. We know that occasionally our spiritual nature has come alive in the midst of our human experience. We dimly sense how two realities, grace and nature, can be experienced by one person. In any event, in reading the Gospel today, we bring a much richer view of humanness with insights from the psychological and human developmental sciences to our understanding of the Lord. It is a truism — the more we understand about human nature, the more we understand the divine, and vice versa.

After the morning refreshment break in the cloister — with soft drinks, weak beer, coffee and cookies, we convened in our language groups. Ours had American and English speaking members, but also a few Africans and some adventuresome souls who wished to work on their English skills. I am always amazed at the language facility that many Benedictines develop, whether from proximity to one another in Europe or their work in the mission field. In our group we tried to clarify the Christological questions before us but it became clear that we were not interested in theological niceties. Rather, we asked ourselves how we could communicate the reality of Christ to our communities, how we could understand Christ's real humanity, how we might see the meaning of such phrases as, "the unknown Christ" or "anonymous Christianity" when referring to the hidden presence of Christ in the secular world. If, as practicing Christian superiors, we had difficulty with the theology of Jesus Christ, what must the problem be for the average lay person? Of course, faithful people practice an authentic Christian life even when they can't explain it intellectually.

SHOPPING

I slipped away from San Anselmo's for lunch and tried to do some shopping. I had forgotten that most stores close about 1:00 PM and don't reopen until around 5:00. I walked through the streets full of Italians engaged in vigorous dialogues over the most ordinary affairs of life (no wonder they love opera!). I bought some Kleenex, some chocolate, and more colored post cards. I was back in time for the afternoon sessions.

After Vespers and supper, I talked with Abbot Godfrey of Nashdom. I wanted to get his impressions of the effect of the departure and marriage of Abbot Wilfrid (his predecessor), and to get news of my brother monks in our founding community. I was to give the community retreat and I wanted to get the feel of their situation. We also talked about a possible congregation involving the four Anglican Benedictine houses for men: Nashdom, Alton in England, St. Mark's Priory in Australia, and St. Gregory's in the U.S. There might also be a number of women's communities. We are not interested in a tightly defined or organized kind of congregation. That would not be true to the Anglican spirit or the variations of observance among us. But mutual support and sharing of resources could benefit each house without intruding on its life-style. We also discussed some personalities, some of whom had given considerable time and dedication to St. Gregory's before we became an abbey in 1969. Most of these notables — Abbot Martin, Dom Gregory Dix, Dom Maurus, and Dom Patrick — are now dead. Only Dom Augustine at Nashdom remains. There are deep ties between our communities, and the future promises a continuation of the relationship. This chat, renewing my memories of Nashdom, helped ground me in my monastic world — providing a focus for the larger spiritual movement of our time.

LITURGY

Thursday's main talk for the abbots, priors, and observers was on the subject of the liturgy, which, since renewal, has come to focus more strongly on the Pascal Mystery, the celebration of the death and resurrection of Christ. There are various fascinating spokes in the wheel of this theme. One can see the liturgy, the Eucharist and choral prayer in the wider sense, as part of the life of the Trinity, opened to us through baptism. Or one can explore the Pascal Mystery as a symbol of the whole human experience, gathered up and offered in sacrifice by Christ the High Priest. Still again, the actual forms of the liturgy can be examined to see if they effectively express Christ's life and Passion. There is also the aspect of the individual's personal growth as he participates in the liturgical life of the community. It was clearly acknowledged that lectio (prayerful reading of the Bible) is an indispensable ingredient of the liturgy. This may account for some of the problems on the parish level where the Sunday Eucharist is inadequate for the faithful in making up for a lack of Biblical preparation and a daily life of personal prayer.

It was recognized that over the last few centuries there has been a general loss of participation in the life of the Church. This shows itself most obviously in a drop in attendance. Liturgical theologians continue to examine this problem and produce as their contribution renewed rites with a clearer focus on the central themes of Christ's life, all of which are gathered up in His saving death and resurrection. But we must also recognize that the Western world in its intensely materialistic way of life has lost the sense of God, and therefore has lost the appreciation of liturgy as a normal way of being open to His presence. Or, to express it differently, the human energy and dynamic that used to go into worship is now poured out in "secular" pursuits (with all of the passion of faith now disguised in worldly zeal).

> From the human point of view one sees all kinds of substitutes for liturgy. A sports event in the West has some of the same ingredients of corporate worship: the gathering of people; the death-like tension which focuses on the athletes; the struggle; the victory — all of which perform a mysterious cleansing and releasing function for the participants. Or one can see a more grim version in the terrorist and war oriented incidents of our time. All misplaced energy tends to create victims offered in sacrifice. But, to what god? There seems to be an enormous amount of work needed before worship recovers its true place in the lives of faithful people. Modern man, alienated as he is, needs much healing before he can respond joyously to the central act of worship. Wherever the deep sicknesses of modern man, whether psychological, economic, or social, are honestly faced, man stands a much better chance of recovering the fullness of his humanity in surrendering himself to God in worship. Jesus' whole human journey gives us a clue to the pain and frustration involved in such a healing. We simply cannot do it alone. He has already done it for us, and continues to do it with us, if only we can connect our human journey to the life, death and resurrection of Jesus Christ.

SISTER JOAN

The whole dilemma of the liturgy was brought home in my luncheon engagement after Mass. Sister Joan Chittister, OSB, another observer, and I had met before. She is the head of a group of American Roman Catholic Benedictine nuns who have been experiencing a double emergence. Not only have they come out of their historical roles as teachers, cooks, nurses, and servants, but they have grasped the significance of the role of women today. Sr. Joan is a vigorous leader of this feminine movement. We had agreed to have lunch after

Mass so that we could talk and compare notes on the Congress. Sitting in the courtyard of a nearby hotel, she confessed that the only reason she had attended Mass was to keep our appointment. She was annoyed at the whole liturgical expression of the Congress. The stiff Latin rite, the heavy domination by the male priests who vested and concelebrated, and the refusal of Communion to non-Roman Catholics, all made her angry. As we sipped our wine and munched on rolls and jam, she jabbed resolutely at the Church's faults so clearly revealed here in Rome. She and her sisters do not accept this passively. They are taking strong stands on atomic questions, feeding the poor, appropriate uses of energy, the role of women in the Church, and on ways of sharing responsibility in community. One felt the passion of her anger, and it was clear that the feminine energy she so powerfully expressed is coming to the surface in the life of the Church. It will not go away. Some women like her have left the Church, others have moved to the sidelines. After listening to her, I did not doubt that some will remain at the center and make their witness. This represents a powerful force for future change — and will eventually affect the liturgy.

RELAXATION

Between such intense talks and exchanges there were many opportunities for light relaxation. During the two breaks in the morning and afternoon one could often get in a word with a friend about bus routes, how to use the telephone or about the weather. Rome had been unseasonably cool. The meals in the refectory were also happy times. One tried to calculate as one drifted to the dining room just where the various English speaking groups might congregate. The food itself was good. We usually had soup, a European custom. Then would follow several courses of meat and vegetables. The dessert was usually cheese and fruit. Wine and water were available. One learned not to take too much wine or the next event, even if it were a nap, would be affected. Then there were the accidental gatherings in the cloister where amusing anecdotes could be shared. (Why did the abbot of so and so move away when a woman sat down next to him in the dining room? HMMMMMM!).

ASCETICISM

The Friday lecture was given by Athanasius Polag, a German and a former abbot who had resigned. I remembered him from previous Congresses as a bright, independent, and very human kind of person. His assigned part of the theme was living in Christ from the ascetical point of view. That is, how do we follow Christ in an authentic human way? Asceticism, or discipline, changes with the times, sometimes trusting and sometimes distrusting human nature. Our fundamental theology of God has not changed but the understanding of human nature now available to us from the developmental sciences has deepened our appreciation of the complexity of the human person. I could not help but reflect on my Esalen experience. Life in community, while offering support for our human weakness, also requires self-denial. This common life is an important part of Benedictine asceticism in contrast to extreme practices of private discipline. Still, this common life must not be allowed to smother the uniqueness of the individual. Obedience is a very important part of monastic ascetical training, but must be exercised prudently within the context both of the common good and the personal good and growth of the individual. Personal growth and communal health (salvation) are both parts of the Gospel understanding of how we live in Christ. And Christ strengthens us to maturity, helping us acknowledge our failures, freeing us to be honest. To support this honesty and growth and keep the balance between personal and communal life, we need the help of an understanding community, especially the compassion and guidance of the abbot. He supports us by standing beside us in our struggles, not as a judge but as a friend who shares our pain and our faith. Through this kind of companionship the abbot and the community help free us from guilt and false fears. For it is inevitable that we must face new questions and new interpretations of the Rule. Today this is especially true when we are on the threshold of vast changes throughout the world. The only way we can move into the future is to be obedient to the Word in Scripture and to the Spirit in the circumstances of our life. The young are often inexperienced in faith testing and in the discipline of living in community, but the old have their share of burdens, too. They wonder why things cannot continue as before. Some (not always the young) strain toward new ideas, while others (not always the old) hang back in fear. Splits and factions can easily develop. There is some truth in both positions.

Asceticism helps us to temper our zeal for our own opinion and to listen carefully to our neighbor. We learn much about self denial by listening and serving others. This aspect of asceticism must be exercised especially on behalf of those who are weak, sometimes reaching heroic proportions when the weak break down under the strain of life. In such a case, all are up against the Cross. Reason and ordinary help do not change the condition. We are alone and helpless. This is the ultimate test of our maturity in faith and an opportunity for deep growth and union with the Crucified Lord. Even so, there are ways that we can strengthen one another in such trials. We can be present to one another in quiet compassion. God is not trying to test us so much as to move with us into more trusting love. The experience of the Cross, shared among the brethren, brings us to that Love which gave its very life for us. There can be no fulfillment of our human nature with its intense need to experience love without coming to the Cross — that place where Divine Love shows itself most clearly. This is the meaning of the discipline which seems senseless at the beginning. And when we practice the appropriate asceticism for our state of life and there are special kinds for each vocation (marriage has its full share), we are "surprised by joy," to borrow a phrase from C. S. Lewis. Joy is the escape beyond our little egoism into a larger life in which God is free to reenact his love in and through us. All of this focus on the common life reminded me of a talk I gave to a community in rather desperate condition. (Appendix 10)

After the lecture we had a little time which the Abbot Primate, Victor Damartz (formerly the Archabbot of the St. Ottilien Congregation), used for reports from the various congregations by the Abbots Presidents. These reports reinforced the idea for the Anglicans that we might form a congregation. How that would work was not yet clear. It seems unthinkable that such an Anglican Congregation might become part of the Roman Benedictine Confederation. Yet, there is such a friendly acceptance of Anglican Benedictines that it intrigues the imagination. St. Benedict lived at a time (5-6th Century) when there were no divisions, East or West, Roman or Protestant. He may still be working on an over-all monastic model which will provide the larger Church further evidence that there can be an ordered and responsible pluralism in Christianity.

That night after supper, Mark Gibson, Abbot of Alton Abbey (Anglican), came to my room and we talked about their community. I was to do their retreat after Nashdom. The preceding abbot of that community, too, had left a year or so ago, and had since married.

These departures have a message about the monastic life we should take seriously today. I feel that they are telling us that we need deeper love among the members. Not many have the fortitude to pursue the vocation in lonely and heroic isolation. Nor do I think that in most cases the Lord calls us to an individual kind of heroic loneliness. Yes, there are times and aspects of our monastic life which must be experienced uniquely by each person. But in the main, we are intended to share our lives as members of His Body. This is not well understood in our time, in a culture which emphasizes individualism and competition. Monks have as hard a time as any trying to live in Christ.

So Mark and I went over the communal history, the retreat, and other allied topics. We also consumed quite a bit of Italian chocolate in the process.

DIGESTION

I have to acknowledge that my normal digestive vitality was not up to par. With all of the wine, fruit, and oil with which the Italians cook, I usually have no trouble. But this time things were not working well. I became more aware of this part of my humanity because on Sunday, I was to preach at the Episcopal Church, St. Paul's Within-the-Walls. The theme that came out of the readings was about the gift of life. I was hoping that my "innards" would return to normal functioning by then so that I could celebrate that theme more fully.

On Saturday I slept through Lauds. I was not needed in the regular meetings because they were going to elect the Abbot Primate. This would probably result in an extended term for Victor as he was quite popular and effective. For example, one day early in the proceedings, I asked him if the Congress records showed how many times I had attended. He said that when the business of the Congress slowed down one of the secretaries could easily find that information. Later in the day I was moved when he handed me a slip of paper listing the dates of my attendance. He had looked it up himself. Such service to an observer spoke of an unusual spirit.

THE VATICAN MUSEUM

After breakfast I dressed in casual clothes and went out. By now I was getting reasonably proficient with a few of the bus lines. I caught a Number 23 bus and rode to St. Peter's. I didn't know exactly where to get off so I had to walk some distance before I found the Vatican Museum behind the basilica. Hoping to avoid the large crowds, I arrived before opening time. Once in the museum I followed the advice of others and hurried straight to the Sistine Chapel, passing many attractive displays on the way. Arriving at the chapel, with only a few others there to share it, I was at once overawed and disappointed. Here were the magnificent Michelangelo frescoes, high up on the ceiling, with his vital and fresh treatment of the human body in every conceivable posture, all depicting Biblical scenes. The movement, energy, dynamic, and realism of his treatment are astounding. I moved around and sat in various places, enjoying different perspectives. But the disappointing thing was that the colors were indeed somewhat dingy. One side of the wall was screened off. The Vatican received a generous gift from a Japanese donor and was in the process of restoring the colors to their original vividness. I am told they are bright, with strong contrast, more like Raphael. But I find that my years of a particular way of meditation have rather spoiled me for enjoying images of the senses, however beautiful they are. It's as if I cannot quite trust my sense experience. I remembered, too, that on the Myers-Briggs Inventory I test as strongly intuitive and weak on the level of sense appreciation. This test is based on the Jungian concept of four functions of our humanity: intuitive, sensing, thinking, and feeling. Each of us has a dominant function and therefore a weaker function. We had taken this test at St. Gregory's and I had found it helpful in counseling. Still, I knew I was in the presence of greatness. I spent over an hour absorbing the gorgeous power of these figures, most of them either nude or in flowing drapery which enhanced the beauty of the human body. Here, too, was a part of our Congress theme — the beauty of the human body. God did not hesitate to take this humanity to himself as the means by which he would reveal his glory.

Gradually I moved to other parts of the museum but all my energy seemed to have gone into the Sistine Chapel. There were other great artists represented in the collection and an overwhelming amount of Western history, artistically displayed. I am afraid I just couldn't give it all the attention it was worth. Museum fatigue.

About noon I left the museum and moved around among the shops which feature religious objects. One is both offended and intrigued by the number and variety of crosses, rosaries, holy cards, plastic statues, ash trays, that are available. I was looking for a few modest gifts for some friends. In particular, I had promised a brother, recently departed from the Abbey, to look for a memento from St. Clement's Church. I took the bus across town to the Colosseum area, but didn't make it in time. The church was closed. I had to wait a few hours, so I went into the nearby Esquilino Park. I am not sure of the history of this area, but a guess is that it had some connection with the Colosseum itself, possibly housing people who managed or were to fight in the games. But all is now in ruins and the grounds are mainly park-like. I bought a gelati, a delicious ice cream cone, and wandered through the grounds. In itself this was a view of Rome. A few drifters were cooking over little makeshift fires or sleeping by a bag with their few belongings. Over the centuries, Rome has seen itself as a kind of sanctuary for the poor. No one will disturb these people even when they take up positions that interfere with traffic or business. It is an intriguing concept and far from our middle class American way of thinking, although we have our share of homeless. Then there were lovers quite out in the open, unashamedly embracing, laughing, and enjoying their passionate interest in one another. Nobody seemed to pay much attention. This, too, was quite Italian — quite "un-Nordic." And there were the ubiquitous cats who thrive all over Rome. Some people quip that they are the descendants of the lions who battled the gladiators in the arena. Someone else said that they are now protected, having been nearly exterminated during World War II when they were martyred for the survival of the hungry. Now there are "cat ladies," dedicated women who regularly feed them.

Eventually, the church of St. Clement's opened, now run by some Irish Brothers. There was a large group of Irish pilgrims waiting for the tour. I merely wanted to look at the shop and find some mementos for my friend. On a previous night, I had seen the archaeological layers of various versions of the church, the first one going back to a Mithraic temple. The question which had first come to me in the Southwest of the United States returned to my mind: are there places of special spiritual focus which attract people, or are such places holy because there people of faith have continuously expressed their veneration for the Divine?

I walked back past the Colosseum, going in for a brief look. In my imagination I could see the crowds, human fighters, animals, the spectacles. In that ancient world life was cheap, death a companion of the armies, public life, and part of the amusement of the people. Are we really different today?

I walked all the way back to San Anselmo, as it is easy to want to see what is in the next block. Before one knows it, one has walked miles. I had a nap, ate supper with the superiors, then worked on my sermon for the next day. In the last week I had seen many fascinating examples of the gift of life.

ST. PAUL'S

Early Sunday morning, I was pleased to receive a return to my normal digestive process. Alleluia. After Lauds and breakfast, I set off with Abbot Godfrey on a Number 57 bus for the Via Nazionale. We both got off the bus at Via Napoli. Godfrey then walked to the Anglican Church near the Spanish Steps while I turned in at the Episcopal Church, St. Paul's Within-the-Walls. Father Douglas Ousley met me at the door with his two sons, John and Andrew. They were performing a morning ritual of going to the nearby coffee bar where refreshments were available. I was invited to join them. We made an interesting group — a priest with two children and an abbot. The neighborhood people knew Canon Ousley, the only married clergyman in their experience.

St. Paul's congregation is partly local English speaking residents and partly tourists. Various races and languages reveal the mix of the Anglican Communion as they met in the Eternal City. The music was familiar, the Rite from the new *Prayer Book*, and the ceremony more on a human scale than I had been experiencing all week. I preached and warmed to my subject, the gift of life. Afterwards, some people expressed deep appreciation. I was especially heartened by an African man who took both of my hands in his, looked me lovingly in the eyes, and thanked me. I felt that the Lord's Word had once again fed His people.

The congregation had a special blessing for a family who was leaving St. Paul's and returning to Massachusetts (the woman who mentioned this in the Prayers of the Faithful had come to Father Ousley for special instruction on how to pronounce this odd name of an American state). Afterwards, the people gathered in the courtyard to arrange transportation to a park for a parish picnic. I excused myself and went out on the street to wait for the bus.

THE ROMANIAN BEGGAR

I was approached by an unkempt man who had taken up his station near the front door of the church. He had been pointed out to me as a Romanian beggar, one of the many homeless who live on the streets of Rome. He spoke to me in a strange tongue. I knew what he wanted but I was not moved to give him anything. How is one to know what is legitimate charity? He repeated his request several times. I did not respond. He left. I had some qualms of conscience, especially after preaching on the gift of life and the need to support it whenever it presented itself to us. Later in the Congress when we heard reports on the poor I had more guilt feelings. But I honestly didn't know.

On my return to San Anselmo's I had lunch, a nap and wrote some post cards to family and friends. It is a pleasure to send these beautiful Italian post cards back home.

On Monday, just a week after arriving in the Eternal City, I was finally getting into a comfortable rhythm of life. I had caught up on sleep, my digestion was working, and I was enjoying good company and interesting reports from all over the Benedictine world. Our morning lecture this day was given by Bishop Matthew Schmidt from Brazil, formerly a monk of St. Benedict's Abbey in Atchison, Kansas. He had gone to Brazil to a daughter house of St. Benedict's and had been made a bishop. In his talk we moved away from the quiet cloister, away from theoretical systems of Christology and Sacramentality. He talked about the needs of the poor in South America. He spoke also of Fr. Boff, a South American who had been summoned to Rome to report to the Sacred Congregation for Doctrine regarding a book he had written. South America was witnessing an intense struggle between what North Americans would call the democratic free enterprise system, and Marxist Communism. It is extremely difficult for us to see the picture clearly. But it is clear that a people, predominantly Indian, multi-racial, and poor, were now moving out of a way of life forced upon them by European conquerors. And the Church which had brought the faith to this land was caught in the middle. The political and economic numbers are disturbing. Hunger, poor housing, ill health, and inadequate education are the norm for two-thirds of the people of the world. The United States and the Western world in general, a small minority of the world population, consume far more than their share of the world's goods. And Latin American governments do not have the history of common law, business, and middle class living that we enjoy through our English heritage. Corruption, inflation, and military force are the common experience in South America. Bishop Matthew went so far as to say that the monk must become political, not in the sense of holding office but in deciding and acting upon appropriate Christian positions.

The Monk and the Poor.

> What is the monk to do? He must somehow remain a monk, living his life of prayer, worship, study, and work. But in his service to others, in monastic hospitality, in his missionary tradition, he has precedent for real ministry. He must be realistic in discerning structures of sin in the culture, those systems of money and privilege which keep the poor underprivileged. But he must move beyond theory and do something practical for the poor. And in this service he discovers again that the poor have much to teach the monk. They show us a deep appreciation for persons in contrast to our preoccupation with things. They show us simplicity of life. They maintain dignity while living in actual poverty. We often just talk about poverty as a monastic virtue. They share with one another in deep charity. They must obey the inexorable law of power while we enjoy considerable freedom. The monk is recalled to an early part of his history when he was used by the Church to evangelize Europe, before he too became a part of the power structure. Now he is freer to serve. But it takes real discernment to see the world situation realistically, and true courage to take a Christian and monastic position. This discernment and courage are being called forth in South America. Western Christendom seems tired and theoretical by comparison. When South America works out its own kind of "Catholic Communism" will they evangelize us?

Later in our language group discussion we heard some interesting reports from the various superiors on how they were actually serving the poor. All monasteries have some kind of hospitality to guests. This is often difficult to exercise when some of those who come to us have mental and/or drug problems. Many North American abbeys give away large sums of money and resources. They support good works around the world. Some have even taken to challenging atomic power, ecological irresponsibility, and corporate myopia. Sr. Joan, representing the emerging feminine consciousness, was especially impressive with her community's report. This is an example of how a minority group, coming out of its former role of submissiveness, can remind others of their Christian duty. The Bishop's talk was a disturbing contribution, a necessary one, a prophetic one. We were stretched. The danger of being split between prayer and activism is real. The monk cannot give up prayer. But neither can he abandon fellow pilgrims, many of whom live far more heroically in faith than the monk. St. Benedict wrote his Rule at a time of cultural disintegration. We seem today to be at another such crossroad. It will be intriguing to see the monk's role in the present world crisis. It is in fact a spiritual crisis and the monk represents that inner self that is open to God.

A.I.M.

In the afternoon session we had a report from a part of the Confederation which offers aid and information to new monasteries and convents in the young Churches of the Third World. This was further confirmation of the monk's place in the present world. For example, in 1900 there were about 13 monasteries in the Third World. Today there are more than 250. The Muslim world and China are obvious examples of places where it is difficult to found a Western monastery. One might question the worth of a monastery in a place where the basic needs of human beings are in question. A house of prayer provides an important sign that, essential as it, we do not live by bread alone. We were told how to work through the different secretaries of the A.I.M. to send needed supplies to these new monasteries. We at St. Gregory's have done some of this according to our resources. We support St. Mark's, our daughter house in Australia. It does help to keep us detached from our abundant privileges when we are in contact with people with far less.

ZEN BUDDHISM

As a continuation of this A.I.M. report, one of the abbots, Simon Tonini, the Abbot General of the Silvestrian Congregation, gave a most interesting report on an interfaith event. In 1976 the Secretary for non-Christians (in the Roman Catholic Church) asked Western monks to explore non-Christian monasticism. Thomas Merton was interested in this request. In 1979 some Asian monks visited Europe. This was followed by 17 monks and nuns from five Western countries going to Japan. There they visited several Zen monasteries and learned by living experience what Eastern monasticism teaches. In particular they learned to sit in Zen fashion. I remembered my own experience at the Zen Center in San Francisco. Abbot Tonini made the point that Eastern monasticism is more than just technique. By practicing simple disciplines, like sitting, one is gradually released from illusion and evil. This is exactly the point of our Western training in monasticism. To discover such common ground is a hopeful sign for the future relationships between East and West. The Zen monks felt that they had met the heart of the Western world far beyond the West's preoccupation with business, science, technology, and democracy. This raises the question, is Christ somehow present in all religions? Rahner and von Balthasar, among other theologians, now use such phrases as "the anonymous God," the God who hides himself in all religious traditions, and "the anonymous Christian," one who responds to God, however he understands Him (constituting what the theologians call the baptism of desire). This common human experience of God shows that the monk is a universal type, a representative of every person in the journey to God.

That night at supper, surrounded by friendly abbots, I opened up the question of Communion. If we are to explore our relationship with non-Christians, what about our relationships among divided Christians. The abbots around me were surprised that Communion had not been offered to me. They witnessed to their growing practice at home of inviting all baptized Christians, especially in mission countries. But here in Rome, they recognized that the Institutional rules dominated. I accept this and have lived with it all my monastic life. But I wondered whether some tragic world event would finally awaken us to the relative insignificance of so many "problems" (like Communion) of the Western world, be they secular or religious.

LAY MONKS

On Tuesday, the Abbot of Prinknash, Aldhelm Cameron-Brown, gave a most interesting report on the lay monk question. (This reference to Prinknash called up our Anglican Benedictine history. Our parent abbey, Nashdom, developed out of a remnant who did not join the Roman Church when the Caldey community, once Anglican, became Roman Benedictines. That Caldey community became the basis of what is now Prinknash Abbey. We had pleasant talks when I met Abbot Aldhelm. Of course, we were both later generations on both sides.) In his report, he was touching on the vexing question of the lay brotherhood. All former lay brothers have now been integrated, that is, offered the chance to say the full choir Office, given Chapter rights, and considered full monks in every sense of the word. That being the case, there now are only lay choir monks and ordained choir monks.

> But are there still people who would like to be monks and spend less time in choir and study, with more opportunity to work — even living and working outside the monastery? (See Oblate question below.) With all of the advantages of having one class of monks it does seem a legitimate question. There are a variety of gifts and emphases in the monastic life. As the culture tends toward ever greater diversity, we are going to get people of more divergent backgrounds. A lay person today is usually at least as well educated as a priest. And ministry is being progressively shared with lay people. It is a question that will probably stay with us for some time.

SHOPPING

It was often a welcome relief to go shopping after such heavy sessions on serious subjects — items we couldn't fully comprehend much less resolve in one Congress. However, looking back over many Congresses, at least one discovers a focus on the roots of the monastic life, roots that produce ever new expressions in each age.

But out on the streets of Rome, the mind must shift to the immediate problems of getting the right bus, often referring to one's pocket map (feeling awkward and like a tourist), pondering whether to search for a purchase. Even a small item like a towel requires some work. Where are the department stores? What is the Italian word for towel? Is it really worth trying to do all of this? Maybe one should just sight-see. Part of the fun of it is simply to wander the streets — some of them busy modern streets filled with traffic, others old medieval streets that reveal what it must have been like hundreds of years ago. Even with modern plumbing these old streets are filthy. What would they have been then? No wonder that the Black Death or other great plagues periodically swept Europe. Oh, there is the Coliseum! Maybe let's get off the bus and have a gelati and think this out more leisurely. Often, I did just sit by the side of a busy part of the city and watch it all.

MORE CANON LAW

After such an outing, one is more ready to tackle theology. At this point in the Congress, we had a lecture on canon law by Father Polycarp Zacher, a Cistercian from Yugoslavia. Father Polycarp offered some interesting points not previously mentioned in my brushes with canon law through the talk at New Melleray. The new code reflects Vatican II recommendations, namely that Scriptural and theological support be provided for principles in the law. One can see that the whole organization of the Church had drifted into a somewhat self-defined and isolated system. The Church was in danger of becoming a dwindling religious institution. Pope John XXIII's intuition moved him to bring the Church back into contact with biblical thinking and with the world of today. The new code of law required that Benedictines, among others, should submit new Constitutions for each Congregation which reflect these new points of view. Admirable as this is, the cumbersome, ecclesiastical, machinery still labors to handle renewal. So, the discussion in the Congress had to take into account minute details of law which seem to an outsider (and to many loyal Roman Catholics, too), to stifle the Spirit. For instance, the new code still associates authority with the clerical state. And this, at a time when the vocation to priesthood is still in critical condition.

> A question: When the vitality of the Church shifts to the Third World as it continues to do, how will monasticism accommodate itself to those different cultures? In one way, the monk is less affected by current social conditions. But in a very real way, St. Benedict adapted the monastic tradition to meet the needs of his time. We are in one of those times in history when adaptation will inevitably take place. It takes persons with deep faith and a genius for discernment to do this work well. At least the new code is in touch with the universal theme of the monk — following Christ in the Gospel. But how this will actually express itself in the 21st Century is an intriguing question.

OBLATES

On Wednesday the second session was taken up with the question of oblates. The archabbot of Beuron, Hieronymous Nitz, presented the report. He had been in charge of oblates at his abbey and had questioned many other abbeys on this matter. His paper showed the ambivalent situation of the oblate today. An oblate is a person who wishes to live according to the spirit of St. Benedict, while living out his baptism in the world, possibly in the married state. Such a spirit encourages the oblate to live as simply as possible, making time for prayer and Scripture reading, seeing work as part of ministry, and maintaining a connection with a particular Benedictine house as a spiritual home. In the whole renewal of the life of the Church arising from Vatican II, Benedictine life has been affected and with it the vocation of the oblate. So there are oblates with "traditional" piety, and there are oblates with "renewal" piety. About a hundred years old, the oblate movement is facing its own renewal because it is intimately connected with the renewal of monasticism. There is no question in my mind that there is a place for oblates, persons who live in the world but who do value St. Benedict and his spirituality. It will be one more aspect of the Church's life which must undergo painful adaptation. Oblates will help bring a spiritual perspective to current issues in the world and bring valuable feedback from the world to the monastery. Undoubtedly some oblates will understand this and be the foundation of the oblate movement in the future.

The Abbot Primate asked for some remarks from one of the English superiors on the lay community at Worth Abbey in England. This is a Christian community that lives near the Abbey and attempts to model its principles on the spirit of St. Benedict. People come and stay for a few months or even a few years. They work nearby, but live a communal life of prayer and sharing. This is another model of support Benedictines could offer. No doubt many more would use it if it were available. Toward the end of the Congress, a statement was prepared to express the appreciation and support of the Confederation for the oblate program.

THE ANGLICAN CENTRE

After the morning sessions the three Anglican abbots went to the Anglican Centre (notice the spelling) near the Piazza Venezia. This piazza is dominated by the Victor Emmanuel memorial, commemorating the unification of Italy (if that is in fact what happened — Italians are exuberant and diverse in their temperament.) It is grand, pretentious, and monumental but it doesn't measure up to the good taste, balance, and style of the early Roman monuments. However, it serves as a handy landmark when you are wandering around the city. The Anglican Centre is maintained to provide a place where Anglicans and those interested in things Anglican can gather, just a short distance from the piazza, up the Via del Corso. It is a suite of rooms made possible by the generous help of an Italian lady who is sympathetic to Anglicans. A resident chaplain lives there (at the time of my visit, Canon Howard Root and his wife, Celia). We arrived in the neighborhood and then wandered around looking for the address. A doorman from the building found us and put two of us in the elevator. The other had to wait until we had gone up to the fourth floor and returned the conveyance. For Americans used to modern technology, this was an amusing experience. We were met at the door of the Anglican Centre by Howard and Celia and ushered down a long hall, past displays of things English and a library to a pleasant living room. We had a light wine and immediately began commenting on the Anglican world by naming people we knew here and there. Of course, we discussed Rome and the Holy Father. There is no doubt that the Church of Rome fascinates all Christians. This is the Church from which we all came (except the Orthodox) and possibly, if we can find a new way to live together while retaining our denominational traditions, the one within which we can experience a reunited Christendom. The ecumenical question goes far beyond European history, but as Westerners, the Catholic-Protestant problems are our immediate concern. We moved to the dining area and had a delightful meal — small portions of a variety of dishes, each course separated from the others by a gracious space. All in all we had a very pleasant time, feasting on things edible, thinkable, and talkable. Two hours later we excused ourselves and returned down the quaint elevator. I used the stairs and beat the other two. They told me that for some unaccountable reason, it had stopped in mid-flight.

On the street I left the two Anglicans and did some more shopping. I found it was quite easy to get lost. Few streets are clearly north and south or, even straight. They wander and meander according to some historic logic which is not clear now. But you come across many charming little places — some you wish you could find again and others you hope never to rediscover. It would take several lifetimes really to know Rome.

AN ATTEMPTED SUMMARY

On Thursday, just two days before the end of the Congress, Father Elman Salmann from Gerleve Abbey, was appointed to pull together the Christological theme. By its very nature the theme had taken us over the whole of creation and all of history and human experience. Father Elman was a professor and a German. The translators were soon sighing heavily from their booths as he labored through abstract theology and crossed tenuous bridges between the divine and the human. He also attempted to discern the times, the better to see how the Church might show the God-Man, Jesus Christ, to present day people. Fr. Elmann made a valiant attempt, but only succeeded in confirming our original perception that Christ is more of a mystery now than ever. But for Christians, He is still the central mystery of God's revelation of His divine life and love.

A few insights about our times caught my attention:

The world is in a kind of collective dark night. Such darkness is confusing and even frightening. Some of the violence and chaos of our time can be attributed to the loss of each culture's tradition by which it lives out its understanding of the meaning of life — its myth. In this loss, people tend to become anonymous, uprooted, lost. But the face of God can still be seen in such anonymous pilgrims. They look for food, homes, clothing, security, community, love, and meaning. In fact, they look for God. And as always, He identifies in a special way with the poor and the anonymous, wandering with them, cut off from the signs and the traditions, religious and secular by which His presence was known in steadier times. In our time, God is hidden in the lives of the lost (by no means not only the poor). What a challenge for the Church: how to reveal His presence!

A further insight:

> God, revealed in His triune glory, is the center of reality. Man cannot define himself or God solely by his earthly existence, good or bad. God defines Himself according to His own existence. But in Jesus Christ, God reaches out to man compassionately, unchangeably loving, and effectively. For man is not lost to God, only to himself. When man comes to himself and really stops to consider his condition as the prodigal son in the Gospel story, he longs to return to that Love for which he was made. So we need not despair of the life of the Church — that earthly presence of Christ — but we dare not be complacent about its human and sometimes scandalous weaknesses. In our time, the Church may well be approaching a judgment. We tremble, but we know that our Judge is Love. Sin loves separation and isolation — which in our honesty we know we cannot accept. It is death. We want to live. As life draws us forward, we face judgment, we face pain. And we hear a Divine voice whispering in our soul, "Do not be afraid. I am with you."

We shudder at the emerging truth. The glorified Christ is God. The abandoned, dying, Jesus Christ is God. This is more than we can understand. We can only surrender to this huge mystery of love.

For the monk, such a surrender comes back to practicing the simple way of life given him by the Rule. Sometimes it may not seem to connect him realistically with life in today's world. Or, it may become clear to the monk (as well as the ordinary Christian) that simple obedience to his baptism is his connection with the God Man, Jesus Christ, in whose hands alone lies the salvation of the world. At times this kind of faithful obedience may appear to leave us in a backwater far away from the world's events. At other times we may find ourselves tumbling out of control in the mainstream of violence and chaos. In either case, our center, our heart, our simple faith keep us anchored. The flesh, as usual, is weak, but is renewed by a Spirit not our own.

STATEMENTS TO COMMUNITIES

Arising out of Bishop Matthew's impassioned report on the Third World, a statement on peace was requested and developed by a small commission. (This document is included in the Appendix 9). At least the statement will give abbots something to show their communities, some practical result of our two weeks of work together and something on which a group of monks can examine their own integrity in regard to peace. We knew we were not addressing such a statement to important political bodies. We were talking to our own communities and those for whom were are spiritually responsible. To be honest, humble, and faithful is the best one can do in a world full of terrible pain and anxiety. But we trust that the Lord will use our best for His purpose.

VARIA

In the afternoon of the last working day of the Congress, the Abbot Primate pulled together various matters, reports of the different Congregations, information we needed for our departure, and so forth. This he called "varia." Included in this were several statements from the Orthodox representative, from the nuns, and from me as the spokesman for the Anglicans. I had performed this task before, but this time I felt more relaxed and even playful. Although I touched on some important matters, I didn't feel I had to convince anyone or add more theology to the already overburdened abbatial minds. I gave a copy of the text to the translators. This reduces the creative spontaneity, but it helps assure that something of what you intend will get across. As a fifth time veteran, I enjoyed my assignment more:

> Dear Father Abbot Primate, Sisters and Brothers in St. Benedict, and all who have made this Congress possible:
>
> On behalf of the Anglican observers, I wish to thank you all for your hospitality, a true experience of sharing the risen Lord present in you all — especially our common Abbot. [Here I turned toward the Primate's chair and allowed the assembly to show by applause their genuine appreciation for Abbot Victor's fatherly guidance].
>
> This is my fifth Congress. It is a school for superiors, a special recycle (a term used at San Anselmo's for updating courses). As the Rule says, we should not be dismayed at the cost of maintaining equity and charity — for this Congress community is made up of matters from all over the world.
>
> Through Christ and the Spirit who draw all baptized people together, St. Benedict has his own ecumenical movement. He never experienced Christ as divided. Some of you have non-Roman Catholics as oblates. We have some Roman Catholics who belong to us as oblates as a witness to our common unity in the Lord and St. Benedict. My prayer was for unity when I met the Holy Father yesterday. We remember the blessing of his recent visit to Canterbury. [Here I indicated to the translators that I was departing from the text.]
>
> I reflected on the sad condition of our Swedish Lutheran brethren (the Primate had read a letter from them indicating that of the five members of the community, three could no longer tolerate the interference with

religion by the Swedish government and had become Roman Catholics, two others had remained loyal to the Lutheran Church. Yet they remained in the one community and understandably experienced great strain). and raised the question, "How long do we continue with our Reformation arguments and Church structures which separate us?" [I returned to the text.]

And I am happy to acknowledge my appreciation to the American abbots who invite me to their annual workshop meetings.

If canon law is a burden for some of you — we Anglicans stand ready to offer you an alternative — primordial chaos (laughter). This is where God began once before.

The way the world is going, we Religious in the First World may be the minority one day. However, as the Viennese say, "The situation may be hopeless, but not serious." That is, doing what we can in our monastic vocation, we trust God. We enjoy His glory, enjoy the gift of life, serve Him as we are able, and try to enrich life for one another.

WOMEN

All through the Congress the brethren were aware of the presence of the nuns as observers. The European ones were dressed in traditional habit, most of the Americans were in some version of ordinary street dress with crosses or other community insignias. Sr. Joan was the most vocal, but others also expressed themselves. The variety of positions of the women became clear. Some were content to be dependent on the men for chaplains, teachers, advisors, etc. And others, mainly the Americans, were not. I sensed that the whole feminist movement in both its political and spiritual aspects (some would say there is no difference) is working within the Benedictine world, too. I doubt that it will go away. I would even predict that eventually ordination of women will come to the Roman Catholic Church. I don't know when but I think it is inevitable. It seems to be part of the equalization process going on throughout the world. It is part of justice, raising minority groups to equal dignity with majority groups. It is part of the renewal of energy, bringing feminine energy into human affairs on every level, and it is part of the utilization of human gifts. It will be interesting to see how the Roman Catholic Church handles this question. I suspect it might end by allowing women to administer the Sacraments without calling it priesthood. Thus, everyone will win. (Appendix 11).

There were other matters: a report on the process of beatification for Abbot Marmion (something which Anglicans do not do), a discussion in our small groups of the possible theme for the next Congress (set for 1988), small changes in the rules governing San Anselmo, and so forth. The Abbot Primate reserved the closing address for himself. He simply enumerated all those to whom we owed things: the secretaries, bursar, translators, student servers at table, employees and brothers, members of Commissions, lecturers, moderators, guests, observers, abbots, priors, and superiors of Monte Cassino, Subiaco, and Norcia for receiving the abbots for a visit, and for the use of San Sabina Church. It was an impressive list showing what a complex operation a Congress is. And the Primate was especially grateful for the support we had given him as evidenced by the generosity some had shown in support of the financial needs of other monasteries and in accepting changes here and there which the Primate felt were needed. It is remarkable there were no power plays or serious challenges to his position. It was a good experience of how the Benedictine model works at its best. In gratitude to God we sang the Salve Regina.

THE LAST SUPPER

After Vespers that night we went to our last supper together. Abbot Victor invited me, Abbot Godfrey (Mark had left by this time), and a few others to share the head table with him. Unfortunately, Abbot Godfrey was off in a telephone booth negotiating his ticket for the next day. I sat on the Primate's left, a sister on his right. He was skillful in moving back and forth between us, changing languages in the process. I am always impressed with anyone who can use several languages. They become the effective persons in today's world, bringing people of many cultures closer together.

After the meal I went to my room and began the process of packing. The gifts I had bought, some of them large posters, all had to be integrated into my luggage. In the end I decided to add an extra piece of hand luggage. Then I cleaned up the room, putting wash tubs away, books back on their shelf, and returning lamps to their original position. I put a note, some chocolate, a bar of soap, and some Italian postage in a little pile on the desk as a gift for Max, the student from South America whose room I had occupied. I slept the last night in my lovely room on the Aventine Hill. But I determined that if I were to be a student there I would ask permission to supply my own pillow. Mine had been lumpy. Still, all in all, it was a happy place to live — both my room and San Anselmo in general. One could be grateful for the inspiration which prompted predecessors to found this college for Benedictines.

DEPARTURE

I awoke at 5:20 AM. After shaving I put the few remaining things into my luggage and carried everything downstairs. How heavy my bags had become! It was a sharp reminder of my hernia operation some years ago. Then, I waited for the arrival of Abbot Alfred with whom I had made an agreement. We would reduce the taxi fare to the airport by going together. Abbot Godfrey had left separately. Well, the appointed time came and went and, there was no Alfred. Then the group began to gather for the trip to Norcia, the last excursion of the Congress. One of them asked me what I was waiting for. On hearing, he explained that Abbot Alfred lived at a nearby hotel, had probably waited there, and then left. A small detail that Alfred had failed to tell me. So now, I asked each departing group if they were headed toward the airport. To underline the sadness of leaving, it began to rain. Finally I found two Germans going to the Termini. Well, I could improvise. At the Termini, we had the usual problem with the fare. The meter read 11,000 lire but we settled on 18,000. It was the baggage that always pushed the price up.

On the airport bus I carried my bags, a suitcase, briefcase, typewriter case, and a plastic shopping bag. The ride out was rather dreary. At the airport, with all of the signs in a strange language, I jumped off at the first stop and raced along the corridor looking for a luggage cart. I was not going to carry all of those bags through the long process of ticket clearance and Customs. I couldn't find one. It dawned on me that the bus could leave with my luggage. I raced back and found the bus. I jumped on and asked the driver for my luggage. He groaned. The bus was ready to leave. Then a porter, sensing my problem, asked where I was going. When I said England, he told me that I should go to the next stop, the international building. I reboarded, feeling embarrassed as the passengers looked impatiently at this inept traveler.

At the international building all was much easier. I found a luggage cart, the Alitalia ticket booths, and after discovering that the "business" section was really first class, finally got cleared at the economy window. Customs was simple. Again, I admit that for this purpose I was wearing my clericals. Later, friends told me that in England it would make absolutely no difference. Having checked two bags, I could now easily manage the briefcase and the plastic shopping bag. No one questioned me when I passed through Customs under a sign clearly reading, "ONLY ONE CARRY-ON PIECE OF LUGGAGE." Italians are not that consistent. I looked through the duty-free shop, but it was mostly liquor and cigarettes, so I bought nothing. A couple of abbots were waiting near the departure gate. And we waited and waited. Even after we were admitted into the special waiting room, we continued to wait. At 10:00 AM, the departure time, there was no sign of any personnel or activity that would suggest departure. So, we continued to wait. I heard comments that Atlitalia was notoriously nonchalant about schedules. About an hour later we got through the doors and onto the ramp where some buses waited to take us out to our plane. Once on board, I was directed forward to the first class section. A mistake, I thought. But I sat down in the comfortable two seat section assigned to me. Some of the remarks made by the ticket agent in Rome came back to me. She had said something about the no smoking section being sold out and something about going to the business class. I assumed that would mean paying more and so had not responded. Apparently she had put me there anyway. So, I had the very posh (as the English say) treatment of first class. I was given a newspaper, had a special lunch, and, of course, there was much more room than in the crowded economy section. I looked around and saw well-dressed, well-mannered, people. I thought how much easier it is to be privileged. But if you are used to it, you probably don't even notice it or have much appreciation for those who must live without it. My reflection on being in the first class section gave me a small sense of how pleasant the world can be — why not enjoy it for the brief time available. So, I enjoyed it for the rest of the flight.

BOOK THREE

SPIRITUAL ROOTS

CHAPTER 20

OUR NASHDOM, OUR HOME

HEATHROW

In two hours time we landed at London's Heathrow International Airport, one of the busiest in the world. After passport clearance I found a cart, located my luggage, and fell in with several other priests, again shamelessly using the collar to avoid a time consuming and messy examination of my baggage. (Not that I had anything to conceal. It was just that everything was so neatly packed.) We moved through the corridor marked, "NOTHING TO DECLARE," and soon were into the public area where I spotted Dom Gregory. He was the monk who had spent a month at St. Gregory's Abbey just after I had left on my sabbatical. It would be interesting to hear his impressions of America. I bought two chocolate bars and changed my lire into pounds. We found the car and were soon on the motorway. Nashdom is only about twelve miles west of the airport so we just had time for a short talk. But in that time I was able to catch up on the mood of the community since the departure of its previous abbot, Wilfrid, and to begin to collect impressions of the mother house as background for the retreat. I had not prepared much for the retreat, feeling that I needed a sense of where Nashdom was before deciding what emphasis would be helpful.

NASHDOM ABBEY

The former country house of a Russian prince and his American born wife, designed by the famous British architect, Sr. Edwin Lutyens, became in 1926 the new home of the Benedictine monks after they had left Pershore, a house on the grounds of a medieval monastery. This community was the remnant that had remained loyal to the Church of England after some had gone to Rome. They moved to Nashdom (Russian for "our home") and made the elegant house and gardens into a working monastery. For instance, the grand ballroom is now the chapel. Not only was the intention of the founding fathers to make a place for the Benedictine life in the Church of England, but they prayed for reunion with the Church of Rome. As Benedictines and as a symbol of unity, the Nashdom brethren adopted the Latin Rite used by Roman Catholic Benedictines at that time. They picked up their monastic usages from books and contacts with continental and English Benedictines. It was all very daring, unusual, and suspect, to attempt such a revival of

Benedictine life in the English Church. And Rome at that time was fortress-like. England as well as Europe had a long and painful experience of Catholic/Protestant conflict. This was the context in which Nashdom began its life and developed its friends for some decades. During this time, some talented persons, including Dom Gregory Dix, made their contributions to the life of the Church.

Then came Vatican II. The Catholic world, with a good deal of wrenching (which is not over) shifted into a new position. The Roman Church came to see itself anew as a pilgrim Church, a penitent Church, a servant Church, opening up to all people everywhere. Many of the objectives of the Anglo-Catholic group in the Anglican world now appeared in the Roman Catholic Church: vernacular liturgy, emphasis on Scripture, greater use of the laity, more shared authority. In many ways, Nashdom's particular position was no longer needed. In a way, the prayer had been answered! Now what was Nashdom's position to be?

The community went on with its Benedictine life, seeming to grow and prosper. But changes in the world, of which Vatican II was but one sign, continued to erode old patterns of life and their companion institutions. The West was losing its dominant role in the world and with that loss the Church was inevitably involved. Then a very personal and painful event occurred at Nashdom. The relatively young abbot resigned and got married. Very quickly, the real situation of the community revealed itself. They were down to 18 in number — nine of them over age 70 — with no monks between age 50 and 65. Many both within the community and outside wondered if it could continue. Nashdom was in something of the same crisis as the Church, and the Western world. A cultural down-cycle that had been developing for centuries was now unavoidable. The culture was dying.

Nashdom elected a saintly elder, Dom Godfrey, as Abbot. I had been with Dom Godfrey in Rome. Now I must ponder the community retreat. I felt honored but unsure of my approach.

Having arrived after lunch, Dom Gregory and I ate alone in the elegant pillar-supported dining room with windows which open out onto the south lawn. A large English oak was monarch. A row of Spanish chestnuts, planted from nuts brought back from the Peninsular Wars, had only recently been replaced. After lunch Dom Augustine, the man under whom I had spent more than half of my monastic life, came into the room. We embraced and I quickly measured the change in his appearance. He was 80 with remnants of the vigor I remembered, but thinner and with less spirited eyes. We went to my room in the novitiate (where I would have a sink and access to a shower) and chatted. We exchanged greetings from common friends and then he felt moved to tell me the details of the previous Abbot's departure. He told it straightforwardly, but I knew how it had hurt him, since he had groomed Wilfrid to be his successor. He left for an appointment and I took a nap.

The Office of None was said at 4:15. The chapel is now fairly square with two sides of the choir facing each other over a hexagonal altar with a modern metalwork corona suspended overhead. The guest area forms a third transept, making an overall kind of T-formation. The altar candles, throwing their light through the corona, form interesting designs on the ceiling. After prayer, we had tea in a room off the refectory, where I met old friends. I had not been here since my return from the Congress in Rome in 1980. There were a few new novices. I was particularly pleased to find Dom Francis as Prior. He is a thoughtful, loving person. I knew I would need his help from behind the scenes. The somewhat somber presence of the older monks was perceptible.

DEPRESSION

At tea, one of them was quite noticeable. He had a vacant stare. Knowing him from previous visits, I invited him for a walk. Once on the grounds, he quite naturally told me of his depression. It was not something totally new but it was heavier to bear in old age. We talked about his childhood, periodic episodes of depression, and the regime his doctors were prescribing. I didn't want to intrude but I saw a chance for some healing prayer. We stopped along the row of Spanish chestnuts and prayed that the Lord would reveal himself to the brother just at the point where he had suffered in his childhood so that he would be assured of a Brother (the Lord) who would go through this depression with him and eventually heal him (not necessarily in this life). I felt that this was a symbolic introduction to the Nashdom community. Over the next few days, my uncertainty about my ability to help the community rose and fell and periodically rose and fell again. It was a healthy reminder of my own limited capacity and a clear sign that whatever I could do would mainly be the Lord's work.

After Vespers we had supper in the main dining room with classical music instead of reading. It gave one a hint of other times when a musical ensemble accompanied the meal for the Russian household and its guests. Then we went upstairs to the common room for recreation. Only a few were present. Life was definitely quieter this time. I attended Compline at 8:30 in the chapel, staying on afterwards to watch the shadows from the candles. I was alone with my many thoughts. This was going to be a different part of my sabbatical. But for all Nashdom had done for St. Gregory's, and indeed the Anglican communion — giving us our Benedictine life and nurturing it for years — I was glad to do what I could. It was like suddenly discovering that your parents are old — very old.

SUNDAY

We arose in time for 5:30 Matins. Although there are only a few voices who can really carry the music, the Office here is largely chanted and sung. At breakfast I rediscovered a large can of lovely English marmalade. There was no limit, and this on toasted dark bread and a cup of coffee made a wonderful beginning to the day. After Terce (Third Hour), we had a concelebrated Mass (priests vested and standing around the altar with the main celebrant). As a concelebrant, I never had done this in the Roman Rite so formally and had to watch the others carefully. (Nashdom retained this privilege because of its Benedictine association.) It brought back memories of my early days in the monastery when everything was mysterious and holy. (St. Gregory's, too, had once used the Roman Rite in Latin.) But the main purpose of worship was there — to thank God for His gift of life renewed in His Son.

THE GUEST LOUNGE

After Mass, I wandered into the guest lounge where coffee was served and the monks and guests could mingle. I spotted Norman Davey, the community architect. He had designed the addition where I lived which is no small venture when one considers the reputation of a Lutyen's building. Many years ago when as a young Prior I first visited Nashdom, he had offered some architectural ideas for St. Gregory's. I was eager to find out how he was thinking now. Over coffee we talked and rambled through many subjects. It soon became clear that the state of the world was affecting his ideas on building architecture. He was advocating an even simpler version of monastic buildings, maybe without the traditional cloister. This coincided with what I had seen at some of the smaller communities. Norman was active in Church circles. This brought before him the weaknesses of Christianity today. His reflections reinforced my own that in the complex world in which we live, Christians must be simple, honest, and realistic without losing touch with the Divine mystery.

> We don't know what the future patterns of life will be. But we do know that many past patterns no longer work. The important principle seems simply to focus one's life and the basic life of the parish on the Lord so that He Himself can create the new forms in us. This is what St. Benedict did and the emerging way of life became a pattern for many centuries in Europe.

THE CONFESSOR

On Monday, and for the next few days, the Confessor for the community was in residence. Normally the brethren make their confession to priest members of the community, but experience has shown that occasionally it is helpful to have an outside confessor. Derek Allen is an experienced priest with his own parish and has had considerable experience with Religious. I was grateful to have the opportunity to talk with him and to check out some of my impressions. He agreed that Nashdom was indeed going through a critical time. I encouraged him to think of a group of outside friends who might share this time in Nashdom's journey in a discreet and supportive way. Communities need what sick or older folk need, friends who give them perspective and help. It is an aspect of the hospice ministry.

HAIRCUT

One day, Dom Francis came along with his haircutting kit. I simply sat in my chair in my room with a large cloth over me and he used the one length clippers. How easy it is to keep to one monastic hair style. In the various cities I see all kinds of hair-dos — long, short, punk rock, whatever. I'm just too lazy even to envy any of these styles.

TWA

I wanted to confirm my return flight, but first I needed to master the phone system. After some instructions, I gave it a try. All sounds on a strange system were confusing. Was that a busy signal or was it ringing the number? How did you do long distance? Was London long distance? Eventually, I got through to TWA and confirmed my flight. I also asked for a special seat reservation. That hadn't worked on my flight coming over, but I thought I'd try it again. In the back of my mind I had a vague premonition that it wasn't going to work this time either. Oh well!

INTERVIEWS

The brethren were all cordial and some of them — mostly the younger ones — wanted to talk seriously. I was happy to provide a fresh ear, and it helped me gain a better idea of the state of the community. However, over the years one learns to let each person present his view on the situation, inwardly knowing that this is a mixture of objective fact and subjective feeling. But it is all part of the picture. I could sympathize with the older ones who really didn't have the energy to consider radical solutions and I could also relate to the younger ones who knew that some changes had to occur. The sad thing was that none of us had been trained to listen to one another and to discern God's will through an honest exchange. This is generally the case throughout the Church. I saw more clearly the need for a trained outside facilitator.

EXERCISES AND SITTING

The simple exercises I had learned at Esalen, plus the Zen sitting, became important parts of my day, helping to provide some balance to the mental activities of prayer and the analysis of the community. Too, I was more appreciative of the body as a message center. But the main point of the Zen sitting exercise simply is to focus on being where one is. I find that this kind of focus is an important grounding to much of my preoccupation with planning and looking ahead.

MARGARET

Every monastery has good friends who support it with their prayers and their acts of kindness. Some of these are women who help bring a feminine quality to a male community. Margaret is one of those for Nashdom. I had met her years before through Abbot Augustine. She has visited St. Gregory's and she had been part of the group that took Abbot Augustine and myself to a Swiss chalet and the Oberammergau Passion Play before we went to Rome for a Congress. She had been a good friend of Eva Mercer, a similar kind of friend for St. Gregory's. I am sure that privately they often compared notes on the monks. Eva is now dead and we miss her.

I was pleased one day to find that Margaret could have me over for lunch. After Mass, she picked me up in her small English car and drove me to Marlowe, a small nearby town. I always ask for a map when I am driving. It helps me to orient myself. Margaret just drives. Anyway, it is fun driving through the English countryside, often on narrow roads and with peculiar traffic patterns at crossroads, and round-abouts, all very interesting or harrowing, depending on your nerves. On a previous visit, Eva and I had rented a car and driven west to Cornwall. I enjoyed it, got used to driving on the left, and I only nicked one car (an English driver sits on the right hand side — and so has a tricky calculation to make when passing on the left).

At Marlowe I changed a few dollars into pounds. Then we went around to visit Margaret's friend and housecleaning lady, Fordie. She had "come all over strange-like" and was now in bed. Margaret fussed around Fordie and her husband, a dour gentleman who didn't lend much cheer to the situation. We said a prayer and then left for a glass of wine at Margaret's. We talked and talked and talked. She knew Nashdom pretty well (from her point of view) and she went back and forth between annoyance and pity. I listened and learned more.

THE GEORGE AND LION
Then we went down town to a nice pub, the George and Lion. It looked very old with wooden timbers properly worm-eaten and embedded in the plaster of the long ceilinged dining room. But alas, it was all a reproduction. However, the food was good — lamb cutlets, French fries, a vegetable, rolls, and cheese and biscuits for dessert. We talked more. We returned home, had another glass of wine and finally Margaret took me back to Nashdom.

THE YOUNGER ONES
After tea that night, I had a meeting with the younger ones, that is, those under age 50, professed and novices. I tried to cheer them up and encourage them to ask for access to a trained outside person to help them learn how to talk openly with each other. Also, it was obvious that these brethren didn't have too much in common. I could see that pulling this group together was going to be hard work.

WEDNESDAY NIGHT PRAYER GROUP
The next few days were spent going through the normal monastic day from rising about 5:15 AM until bedtime around 9:45 PM. I realized this has been the background for my inner life for some 36 years. And what has been going on within?

> I have been digesting the extraordinary meaning of the Lord's promises that we are forgiven and that we are free to love God and our neighbor. I have had help in learning this good news from friends, other monks, certain joyful groups in the Church like the Charismatics, and often from

being close to souls on their own inner journey into freedom. So, here I am at age 63, still enjoying the monastic life as a context within which I am able to experience God's love. It is my great joy to share that with others. And when in return they can share their own experience, I have an experience of intimacy with God and with others that is overwhelming. It is what most people would call the intimacy of marriage. At times, I have wept with this poignant joy. But in between there is the hard work — just like marriage.

So at this time I was simultaneously working out the retreat addresses, pondering the state of Nashdom, and wondering how God would work His healing love.

PETER LANG

Independently of my prayers and reflections, Abbot Godfrey in his own concern for his community had talked with other abbots at the Congress. One in particular, from an English Roman Catholic Benedictine community, had recommended an Anglican clergyman, Peter Lang, as a helpful outside resource person to work with a troubled community. Abbot Godfrey had invited Peter to come for a preliminary talk and I had been asked to join them. Peter had been born in Zambia, but had come to England and had been educated here. After ordination he had held several parish jobs, but eventually had found an attraction for counseling. Presently, this is his full time vocation. He is fairly tall, lean, with an unusually gentle manner. He also has a dignified way about him which comes from an inner center of compassion. I liked him and felt comfortable with him. In the Abbot's study, the three of us discussed the reasons for inviting Peter, gave him a quick sketch of the community's state, and would have gone on to some practical matters, but Peter interrupted us. He told the Abbot that as he listened to the recounting of the Nashdom situation, he was close to tears. This told me a lot about Peter's humanity and the genuine compassionate feeling he would bring to his work. We discussed various aspects of the possible communal workshop. He also asked to talk to the Novice Master. Nothing that he said later changed my original impression of him.

We concluded that the Abbot would present the community with the possibility of a first meeting with Peter and his assistant (on hearing more fully of the complexity of the situation of Nashdom he had asked to have his assistant work with him, at least initially). I walked Peter to his car and told him some of my own experiences with workshops at Esalen. We quickly fell into an excited exchange about the human potential movement, books, people, places. It was a relief to be able to talk openly about my own hopes and to see the possibility of such a person as a resource for Nashdom.

10 ACORNS

On Sunday, after the concelebrated Mass, Dom James introduced me to one of his woman friends who comes to Mass frequently. She had collected ten acorns. I had asked for these on behalf of Br. Bernard who wanted to plant some at St. Gregory's. I wondered how I was to get them through customs, but took them gratefully. After all, I had smuggled other things successfully. Perhaps this would be a further symbol of life transplanted from Nashdom to St. Gregory's.

THE ELDERS

Sunday night after tea, I met with some of the elder seniors at my request. I presented them with some impressions which had arisen in my mind after a week of living with them. I had to say clearly that there were certain signs of death (not news to them) and that I strongly recommended getting someone from the outside to help them work through this difficult period. At the end of my talk, there were a few questions but I felt that these elders were either numbed by their situation or felt that there were no real problems. Most people are reluctant to bring outsiders into their private life. Is this from guilt or fear of change — or anxiety over losing control? Some of the brethren felt that God would rescue them if they just kept up their prayers. I wondered if they were right. It contradicted everything I had experienced in the last few years. But fortunately I didn't have to force my views. We stopped our exchange for meditation and Vespers.

The brethren made a decision to invite Peter Lang and his assistant to do a preliminary session. This was hopeful. It meant that in some sense the monks recognized their crisis situation. It is always embarrassing to admit to oneself that help is needed, but such an admission is the beginning of openness which permits new insights and strength to come to a community.

Margaret came to Mass today and I conveyed to her my need of some extra strength in the form of chocolate to get me through the retreat. She readily complied and I was given several bars of Cadbury's, "chocolate grace," as I called it.

THE RETREAT

At 5:00 PM, we began the retreat. I opened with an examination of the Trinity. Our knowledge of the Trinity comes from Christ's comments in the Gospel. From various references He shows us that the members of the Trinity are persons, equal with one another, have a relationship, and enjoy unity of being. Emphasizing that these truths were given to us by the human person, Jesus Christ, allowed me to develop my version of what the Congress had looked at, Christology from the human side. The Church has often explored the divinity of Christ, but at this time in world history, it seems important to understand more deeply the meaning of Christ's humanity. I knew this was difficult to convey, especially as the implication points toward our own humanity. I wondered what some of the older members of the community would think. And of course, one can never tell how people are receiving a retreat by looking at them. They can have the most misleading expressions on their faces. The conductor must just go on. That night after Compline, I had a large piece of chocolate.

INCARNATION

On Tuesday, the second day of the retreat, we looked more specifically at the doctrine of the Incarnation, the divine Word made human. From my own monastic journey, I offered some personal experiences as a commentary of my understanding of Christ. Even though I was providing Scriptural support and quotes from the Rule for my comments, I was uncertain how all of this sounded to the brethren. I used the Benedictine vows of Conversion, Obedience, and Stability to look at the essential human steps of growth. Under the aspect of Conversion I looked at the inward journey from the ordinary, common sense, center of one's life, toward the deeper, the true, hidden center where Christ is free to be the Lord of our life. Under Obedience I looked at the painful work of subduing that ordinary center of one's life, that ego center, to the will of Christ. It is a labor as the Rule tells us, but also a liberation. And under the aspect of Stability, I looked at the connection between stability of place and stability of heart. Abbots, of all people, are not famous for stability of place. That is, they often are out of the monastery for one reason or another. In this condition of life, not unlike modern people living in the world, how does one achieve stability of heart?

> By prayer and faith one must connect the daily affairs of life in all of their variety with God. The heart is the place where this connection is made. As one moves about and is moved about by life's circumstances, one must stay in touch with the heart. The more heart-centered one is, the more stable one becomes.

As I looked at examples from my own experience of living in faith, I became more convinced of God's compassion for us. We are very complex creatures. He alone can understand the process of opening our humanity to His divinity through Christ.

Outside the addresses, one person who came to talk, James, gave me some intriguing insights. He was doing a lot of personal work through images. This is a method which allows a person to move beyond a personal memory or an event by working with a scene in the imagination. Just as the Church has discovered that certain truths can best be communicated through images, e.g., presence of Christ in the Sacrament of Bread and Wine, so, too, we discover that images often contain a valuable truth, often hidden, about our lives. We find out more about ourselves as we prayerfully muse on inner images. I enjoyed working with James. He came often and we found ourselves to be kindred spirits.

HOLY SPIRIT

The third address was concerned with the Holy Spirit. That is, I tried to discover possible works of the Spirit in our time, preparing us for God's work. I noted how hard it is to penetrate human awareness. The prophets went to extraordinary lengths to get people to listen. The Lord had to wrestle with the Hebrew mind. A recent visitor to Israel told me that even now certain sects of Jews were opposed to an Israeli government because it would be too "secular." They would even prefer a Muslim regime. Such is the strength of an ancient

Hebrew tradition. The early Church made use of the Greek mind to help explain the mystery of the Trinity and the Incarnation. Today, we are up against the same problems of opening up human minds, perhaps making use of an unlikely new ally, the world of science. What we discover from scientists like Fritjof Capra (The Tao of Physics); is that Newtonian mechanistic systems of thought (seeing reality made up of solid building blocks) are outdated. Scientists today see reality as flowing energy, everything interconnected. All is part of a holistic unity. In this new view, man as the most conscious part of reality becomes the mind, nerves, and soul of creation. The Fathers taught that man is indeed the priest of creation. Such Patristic teaching has now reached an incredible fulfillment.

> Is the Spirit teaching us that all reality is spiritual energy and that we need to be in harmony with the life of the Spirit? The monk, as a person of prayer, a contemplative, has a special role of openness to the Spirit, showing it to be a normal way of life for all people.

The last two talks were on the theme of the Pascal Mystery, the death and resurrection of Christ. Here I was not only intent on reviewing the work of Christ on the Cross, but also on looking more closely at the death cycle in all of life, and in particular in the life of Nashdom. I looked at some specifics of the early vision of the founding monks: their Anglican Benedictine vision, prayer for unity, contributions in liturgy (especially that of Dom Gregory Dix), music (Dom Anselm Hughes), and, spiritual direction (Dom Bernard Clements, Dom Benedict Ley, Abbot Martin, Abbot Augustine, and others). I noted how the life of Nashdom had been lived out in the post-Victorian era, in the time of two World Wars, a time of vast changes in both the world and the Church as expressed in the Vatican II Council.

> Discernment is everything, knowing when to continue a certain vision, or when to evaluate and renew it. This is the art of following the Crucified One through death into new life. How difficult it is to know when the Spirit has moved to a new chapter of life.

The final address focused on the Resurrection. I tried to complete the thought begun in the preceding talk on death. I traced the Anglican Benedictine vision into some possible expressions for the 21st Century. The world is in every practical way, one world. Whatever the future is, all human beings share it. One consequence is that every racial, national, and religious achievement will be handed onto the future as an essential part of the heritage of man. Nothing is to be lost. The role of the Anglican Church and a Benedictine monastery within it is now in the context of the larger world. So an Anglican Benedictine community has a certain quality of faith to offer to the final religious body which gives to the world its soul. Whatever form the universal Church takes in conjunction with other major religions, there will be a role for the monk.

This role of the monk will preserve the essential tradition of openness to God primarily through worship, but also in teaching that openness to others. In our time, we are seeing the emergence of a cosmic, one-world spirituality. The place where the monk explores this spirituality is in his community, but the community then becomes a sign of what the whole world is intended to be. In St. Benedict's mind, the monastery is both school and workshop. In Western history, the monastic community became a practical model for building Europe. Now some form of that model is needed as an effective sign for the world.

One thinks of the turbulence of St. Benedict's own times. That turbulence is here again. Not just Benedictines, but all religious communities have an important responsibility in working out a balanced way of life for the future. This will mean that monasteries can be workshops where all of the skills to foster life and avoid death can be taught and shared. The one world must have a spiritual center, and many local centers to show forth that spirituality.

As I finished the retreat, I wondered what some of the older brethren were thinking. Most of them had not come to talk to me so I had little idea of their response to my thoughts. The younger ones were either enthusiastic, or gloomy about the possibility of working with the older brethren. I had some words of appreciation from some, but mostly just silence. That is not necessarily negative — it is English. Well, one must just leave it at that. It is God's work. That night I packed as much as I could so that the next day I would be ready to go to Alton Abbey.

On Saturday I was appointed to be the main celebrant at Mass. I had watched the Mass for a couple of weeks, but I am not a person who notices details. Still, I was surprised at how relaxed I was at the prospect of saying Mass according to the Roman Rite for these people about whose inner feelings I was still unsure. Over the years, I had made some progress with my nerves. In fact, it was a peaceful Mass and I was able to warm it up here and there with some smiles, an occasional look at the people, some slightly improvised texts where I was on my own, all the while staying fairly close to the rubrics. And I noted the quiet joy of some of the younger ones.

LEAVING FOR ALTON ABBEY
After coffee I said goodbye to various people. Then I waited in the guest lounge for Abbot Mark who was to arrive at mid-morning. At 11:30 I called Alton Abbey. He had left and was on his way. Various people drifted by and inquired about my plans, the delay, and the possible explanations. Finally, at 1:00 Mark showed up. Twice he had gotten lost — not really hard to do in England. We had a late lunch at Nashdom, chatted with the Abbot, and left for Alton, a town in Hampshire. The drive was pleasant and we had a good talk about the community I was about to visit. Mark stopped to purchase some cheese for a party they were having that night and I needed more chocolate. After shopping, we arrived at Alton Abbey.

CHAPTER 21

THE ENGLISH SPIRIT
AT ALTON ABBEY

THE PARTY

I had arrived on the day that they had their annual music festival and party, a gesture of goodwill to local people. One of the Abbey's friends had arranged to bring from London the Verona Ensemble, a small orchestra. The group was composed of professional and semi-professional musicians. Chairs were set up in the church, the altar moved and the orchestra of nine violins, two violas, two cellos, a double bass, and a cembalo (a small harpsichord) was set on the raised portion of the sanctuary. All was finally decent and in order. At 7:00 PM the concert began. It was grand to have live music in spite of an occasional mistake. The program included selections from Albioni, Bach, and the ever-popular Four Seasons of Vivaldi. This lively and joyous music was delightful and the audience appreciative. At about 9:00 we retired to a dining room for a buffet meal. Noticing the long line, I immediately went to the dessert table of cheese. I could eat a meal of cheese alone. With a glass of wine I chatted with various people who soon detected that I was from the States. I had many pleasant conversations. In general, I have found British people friendly with Americans. I left the party and went to bed with the music still ringing in my head.

THE SERMON

The next day, having been invited to preach by the Abbot, I gathered my thoughts on the general theme of the wedding feast. It all came together in the short homily in which I was able to remind those who had been there the night before that we already had a rich image of a feast, musical and social, in the concert. I compared this to the joy of life. The king in the Gospel story was rightly upset when those invited to the party were not interested, some even violently mistreating his servants. He rejected these ungrateful people and filled his banquet hall with common folk. I encouraged the listeners to offer thanks through the week for the gift of life. The sun was shining, the atmosphere still seemed to ring with the baroque music, and the Mass was simple and happy.

Afterwards, I was invited by Don and Jean, a couple with two teenage boys, to take a drive in the country as they delivered a friend, Nora, back home. At Nora's house we were invited for coffee. But first we had to see the horses. We had to hear the story of how Sally had upset Nora's sister by pulling the cart up a steep bank and overturning it. One story after another introduced me to the life of middle class folk in the countryside of Hampshire. But I became aware of the good sense and perception of Don and Jean. They were Methodists but on occasion had begun to visit the Anglican Church and had discovered the Abbey. They found the mystery of the Catholic life of the monastery intriguing, and had also found the monks quite human and likable people. I asked them many questions about the state of religion in England. It all seemed to come down to the quality of leadership. They in their own life were a remarkable example of a Christian family. He is a psychiatric nurse; she is a teacher. They live their faith naturally with the family which includes her father. They are vitally, painfully, happily involved in everything going on around them. I felt blessed in their presence.

ALTON ABBEY

This community, now one of the four Anglican Benedictines, began its formal life as the Order of St. Paul in Calcutta in 1889. At that time, the Community maintained houses in Calcutta, Rangoon, and Barry Docks in Cardiff, as well as a ministry in the East End of London. The original work was in providing recreational facilities, moral welfare, and improving working conditions for the men of the mercantile marine through political activity. In 1895 it moved from London to a plot of land in the country near Alton, Hampshire, and continued to meet the needs of destitute and out of work sailors, eventually establishing a retirement home for them. In Alton, the Community began combining more monastic features with its work.

THE CHURCH

The church, as designed by Sir Charles Nicholson, is the most traditionally monastic in style among men's communities in England. Although never completed to the original plans, the church may be called early Gothic. Additions to the conventual buildings in later styles have still maintained a cloister plan.

As we went in and out of the church building, a brick and flintstone construction with pitched roofs, I became aware of how cold it was. Even though I wore a cowl, and finally a sweat shirt underneath, I was still cold, and it was only mid-October. I wondered about the older men. No question of why the medieval monasteries carefully planned their churches to shield the buildings from the north wind and help create a cloister that caught the sun. Even so, in England the sun is not that dependable. Winter services here must be a real penance.

On Monday we began Matins at 6:15, followed by meditation and then Lauds. Breakfast followed. I was delighted to find marmalade again for my toast. With coffee this was great.

As I moved through the day, getting to know the brethren better, finding my way around the monastery, clarifying the schedule, I realized how hard it is to come to a new community. One is self-conscious and awkward. By the same token, one notices much that later becomes routine. Once you get to know the life and the people of a Benedictine house, life becomes comfortable and secure. This has advantages; but, it also has a disadvantage of fostering a spirit of complacency. Such a spirit is particularly hazardous when the Church is going through deep changes.

In settling in, I found some large picture books of travel, architecture, and natural wonders. I find these restful after I have given retreat addresses, talked with the brethren, and kept up with affairs of the day. In this case I was particularly enjoying a book on Rome which helped me understand more of the history and art of the city I had but lately left. With the help of Brother Francis, I had also located a low stool which would serve for my Zen sitting sessions. I was pleased to find this exercise becoming part of my daily routine.

WIVELROD

That afternoon, after a nap, I took a walk and found an intriguing road sign, "Wivelrod." The road was narrow and little traveled. An intriguing invitation. I walked between high hedges and looked out on rolling fields. Some of them had sheep, most were newly plowed and harrowed. All had the familiar flintstones bordered by shrubs and trees. Once in a while I tried to identify a bird, but I was not confident after finding out that what I called a chickadee was actually a tit, or something. Some of these fields in their stone-fenced out-line no doubt went back for centuries. I came upon four men from the Abbey, out for a walk. This retirement home for men, something of a successor to their original ministry of taking care of retired sailors, is now not so populated. I asked the men which way was north. They all pointed in different directions. So, I continued to walk my winding road and enjoyed what came around the bend. Nothing very unusual met me until I reached a cluster of farm houses. There a big black dog with hair bristling and teeth bared threatened me. The woman who had been with the dog called authoritatively. I didn't know what else to do so I just kept on walking. The gentleman of the pair, dressed in very British riding gear and field coat, congratulated me on my composure. The dog returned to them. We passed. And that was about as exciting as Wivelrod ever got. Later I learned from one of the monks that the name was a corruption of Weaver's Rood. There had been a rood, that is, a wayside cross, at the town of Weaver. It was an even nicer walk when I was told later that I had probably crossed over some ancient Roman ruins which have been found in this area.

THE RETREAT

That night I began the retreat. They wanted nine addresses instead of the five I had given at Nashdom. I simply divided the talks and filled in here and there with more details or sto-ries. As the retreat went on, I became aware that the talks were changing subtly to fit a dif-ferent community. The theology and the Scripture references were the same, but the more personal remarks shifted to meet the group of people I was slowly getting to know. But I could also see the similarities, the isolation from one another (the way we were all trained), the difficulty in talking frankly, the fear of one another. Is there any way to change this? I had offered to meet with the community in the afternoon for an open session of exchange, but this idea had not been accepted. I promised myself to talk to counselors to learn more about helping people break through this inhibition.

In the time between talks, I was available for private interviews. One young monk came and talked out his doubts about remaining at the Abbey. I listened and tried to help him clarify what he had in fact already told me. Long ago I learned by an unhappy experience not to talk someone into staying in the monastery. In talking with this monk I gained a new insight into the situation in Ireland which had been his family home. I heard firsthand reports of what it is like to live in a violent society, and how complex the problem is, going back centuries, now made all the more difficult by various groups exploiting the situation for personal ends.

Another monk with whom I talked, one professed for some four years, revealed a great sadness at the community's inability to talk. Sadness over poor relationships seems to be a recurring theme in many religious houses. But the offer to help them learn the art of "speaking the truth in love" (Ephesians 4:15) is usually met with resistance. Is this typical in the Church at large? We must get past this problem for it cripples us in our faith, joy, and ministry.

On Tuesday I said Mass according to the Roman Rite and found it orderly, balanced, and objective as liturgy. I would wonder if it allows enough spontaneous response. The Abbot Primate in Rome had made the remark in his opening address that we need to make the liturgy more our own. Now I could see what he meant.

As the retreat moved from Trinity to Incarnation to the Holy Spirit, I longed for some feedback. But there was little. This is often the fate of the conductor. He would like to know if he is communicating. Meanwhile, those receiving his presentations are focusing on their own lives. One just trusts that something positive is being accomplished.

ST. LUKE

Thursday was the Feast of St. Luke. I took part in the concelebrated Mass. I prayed for more healing, St. Luke's specialty, but had no idea how it was to be done. On Friday, the last full day of the retreat, I became preoccupied with my return to Nashdom. The more complex question was whether I was supposed to stay longer at Nashdom as some of the Nashdom brethren had requested. It would mean changing my ticket, paying more money, and rearranging my plans in the States. But I was willing to wait and see.

DEPARTURE FROM ALTON

On Saturday I said the Mass. Afterwards we had coffee in the common room. The brethren were quite warm, but no one really commented on the retreat. Well, yes, Fr. Michael said that he wanted to question some of my theology. I wished he had. My bags were packed and Abbot Mark drove me back to Nashdom. This allowed us to continue our talk, begun the night before. In this talk I felt at least that someone was using me for some honest feedback. Abbot Mark is intelligent and loving. He was quite open about his community, its past, and his hopes and apprehensions. It is not that I feel I have any great advice to offer. Although I often do have some experience to share that is helpful, it is more to the point that when a person fully reveals himself, that he is ready to move to another set of insights in life. To remain closed and secretive is to remain stuck in one's present situation. Of course, to share one's inner thoughts one has to have access to a person who will keep confidences.

Once back at Nashdom we were in time for lunch. Abbot Mark borrowed some vestments for his coming ordination to the diaconate. (Although he was Abbot, he had not as yet been ordained — a condition not entirely without precedent in the Benedictine world. St. Benedict himself was probably not a priest.) I would likely be gone by the time of Mark's ordination. We said goodbye. I had enjoyed him in particular and looked forward to further meetings. This would no doubt take place as several of us were considering some kind of written exchange among the four Anglican Benedictine houses.

Then I went to my room and began the awkward procedure of collecting my things for my intended departure the next day according to my original plan.

PETER AND MARTIN

At 2:00 PM, I joined the Nashdom brethren for the initial meeting with Fr. Peter Lang and Martin Little, his assistant. We were to explore how these facilitators would work with the community, and whether afterwards the brethren wished to continue such work. I am sure that there was considerable tension among the monks, although not on the surface. Peter and Martin were well aware of such feelings, having worked with various groups and families under stress. For them, this was the normal working condition. They offered some preliminary remarks, promising confidentiality on their part. This is important since the process would inevitably disclose some sensitive areas in communal life. They also requested to be told if anyone could not hear anything that was being said, or if someone did not feel comfortable in doing any of the exercises or responding to any of the questions. They closed these preliminary comments with the important observation that it was our common task to discover what God wanted Nashdom to do, and how best this might be achieved. This was an important statement since some of the brethren, I am sure, felt that they might be put through a psychological exercise with no particular purpose other than to open up the communal situation — a condition that deeply troubled some. The theological purpose of Nashdom's life had been accepted by the two therapists. Now, could the intricacies of the human condition be explored?

In their group procedure, the next step was to invite each person to give some basic information — his age, length of time in the monastery, any offices he had held, what brought him to the monastic life, and what he saw now as the future for himself and for Nashdom. As Peter asked each one of these questions, sometimes clarifying a point here and there, Martin was writing. This would help them get the feel of the community. After the process was completed, I offered the observation that some of the information the brethren had heard was probably the first time they had ever known such facts about one another. Several agreed. This reinforced the fact that people can live together in a group, even a Christian group, and not really know one another. There was many a poignant remark that an attentive ear would pick up. But the therapists did not follow these up in much detail. They were getting to know the people and letting the people become secure with them.

Then they gave the group an exercise. We were to pair off with someone whom we felt we did not know very well and discuss the tasks and the problems of Nashdom. The brethren did this quite comfortably, perhaps even with some relief. At last they could face important questions in the presence of two people who, while outside the emotional state of the community, were committed to help them. The pairs put their findings on large sheets of paper and fixed them to the wall. Then we wandered around the room and looked at each sheet. There were many similarities. This, too, was helpful — getting the situation out in some objective fashion.

The next exercise further opened up the condition of Nashdom. We were to get into groups of four and explore what we thought would happen in three years if everything remained about as it now was. This exercise was repeated with the figure of ten years. Here one could see the obvious. With no vocations and a number of deaths, the monastery would probably not be able to remain at its present site and would have to find a kind of nursing home accommodation. Of course, this was depressing but it brought out into the open what many were fearing inwardly. The follow-up was to look at Nashdom as if things had improved, an exercise in hope and positive imagination. This relieved some of the tension.

We had a break for None and some tea, giving Peter and Martin a chance to reflect privately on what they had heard. When we reconvened there were some frank and somewhat painful observations on the part of some of the brethren, aimed at other individuals. This showed that the setting had been made safe for some honesty. Peter and Martin did not let this process go very far. They made the point that each person had his own point of view and that this point of view was unique to that individual. Others had quite different points of view. This showed that without checking our perceptions of one another in some objective fashion, we were all churning with impressions about one another which were partly true and partly made up. Obviously trust could not develop in such a situation. This is a normal problem in community.

As Peter and Martin drew this first meeting to a close, they thanked the community and did it very genuinely. They made it plain that if the group were to continue in this process there would be times of pain. People should not be surprised at this nor wish to back out of the process because of it. They suggested that in Nashdom's state, important decisions should not be made and they offered the community the basic choice of remaining as at present or choosing to be creative about the future. Then they asked if the brethren wanted to decide whether to continue working with them. In the face of general agreement, but some hesitation, they recommended a wait of a week. Their sensitivity and carefulness for the freedom of the group and each individual in it was impressive. This built trust. And that is where it was left.

Sensing that I would probably be leaving soon, several of the monks, especially the younger ones, came to me. We had some marvelous, poignant talks. I felt as if I had been taken very deeply into the community, not only by those who confided in me. By a look, others had shown me that we had shared the mystery of the Lord's presence in the monastery. I talked with the Abbot and a few of the other seniors, but I didn't get any kind of signal that I should stay — however much they wanted me to be with them as long as I could. So I concluded that I should keep my scheduled departure on the next day. I returned to my room and found a brother waiting with chocolate and a candy bar. One more love touch.

SUNDAY

I attended Matins and Lauds the day of my departure. I picked up several icons done by one of the monks from the Abbey shop. These are holy pictures of Our Lady, skillfully and beautifully mounted on plywood. They were professionally done. I asked the monk who mounts the icons to include a modern picture I had found in Rome of a young girl and child. My gift bag was growing. I now had four pieces of luggage to bring through Customs.

During the opening lines of the Introit hymn, I found tears in my eyes. I loved these brethren. The celebrant's sermon went on longer than I could fit into my tight schedule, so after the Communion I slipped away, picked up my bags, and went with Dom James to the car. I had missed saying a last goodbye to the brethren and to Margaret Raynor who had come especially to see me. Well, such is life. We hit one bad traffic spot and I wondered if I would miss the flight. What an intense snarl of people and traffic around an airport. But, I did catch the flight and found myself leaving London at 11:30 AM — with my window seat (away from the sun).

FLIGHT 755

We actually took off at 11:55 AM. This would be a different experience since we would be flying during the day, trying to catch the sun. Although it was a bright, sunny day, we soon lost England in the scattered clouds. I tried, as I have tried before, to catch a glimpse of Nashdom since it was on our flight pattern. It was down there somewhere with part of my heart. Why would I want to become attached to something that was sure to be painful?

We were promised an easy flight of some seven hours at an altitude of 37,000 feet. I changed my watch back. Then began the familiar "liturgy." First, the drinks. I was sitting next to an attractive young Irish woman, the bride of an American soldier. I felt like celebrating my European venture. I offered to buy her a drink.

"No," she smiled demurely. "It makes me dizzy."

I suggested a mild sherry.

"No, thank you."

So I had an creamy chocolate Irish liqueur, followed by the meal, then the movie. It was a fantasy about a young American meeting a mermaid offering opportunities for some nude backviews, discreet and natural. I only caught bits and pieces of the story and dozed occasionally. Finally, we were awakened for Devonshire cream and cakes. With the experience of a veteran, I brought my overheard luggage down before the landing.

BOOK FOUR

THE FAMILIAR SPIRIT

CHAPTER 22

THE SPIRIT OF FRIENDSHIP

PHILADELPHIA, USA

We landed at 2:07 PM, just seven hours and twelve minutes from take-off. Outside it was 70 degrees. Chilly England had been left behind. Customs was easy and soon I was outside on the street waiting for an airport bus. I missed one and so had one and a half hours altogether at the airport, somewhat ironic in comparison to the time spent in the air. It gave me a chance to watch various passengers returning from Aruba with the inevitable native art which looked odd here. Finally I caught the bus and with the aid of a taxi, arrived at St. Mark's. There was Phillip on the the sidewalk chatting with a friend. It was 4:30 in the afternoon, in another world. After taking my bags up the two flights of stairs to my room where I had left my other luggage (which I didn't want to leave in the van), I showered. That night Charles, Phillip, Julie and I dined at a nearby restaurant. It was expensive, leisurely, and a pleasant ending to the European portion of my sabbatical. What memories! We returned to the rectory, had some cognac I had brought from the duty free shop and looked at the presents I had gathered for them — a little jeweled cross for Julie, some posters from the Sistine Chapel for Charles and Phillip. None of these were expensive, but I again discovered how pleasurable it is to give to others. As the evening wore on, not too late for them, I eased mentally into a quiet, dazed, half awake state. Finally I went to bed, a long 22 hours after starting the day at Nashdom.

BISHOP DIMMICK, R.I.P.

The next day I slept until mid-morning. I took it easy for the day and I was surprised that I didn't have severe jet lag. I called home and learned that our Bishop Visitor, William Dimmick, had died. He had served the community from 1976 until the time of his death, October 19, 1984. In the two visitations he had conducted (times of external review of a community's life that occur every 4-5 years), and in various informal ways, he had given us fatherly counsel and loving oversight. He had also had a full career, beginning with civil rights matters as Dean of the cathedral in Memphis, moving to a large parish in Connecticut, then becoming Bishop of Northern Michigan, moving on and working for Bishop Anderson of Minneapolis while keeping residence at the ecumenical quarters at

Collegeville (a Roman Benedictine abbey), being interim dean at Seabury Seminary, and finally moving to Alabama where he was to be Assistant Bishop. However, several heart operations had finally caught up with him. Still, he preferred it that way. It seemed like a further sign of the closing of a chapter in our Abbey's history. There is always grief at such losses — an important cleansing in preparation for a new chapter.

ADJUSTING

Other matters at St. Gregory's were about as usual. There had been some departures which are always sad, but not unusual. I felt excited at the prospect of bringing more wisdom to my role as Abbot, but uncertain as to my ability to convey it — hoping to prepare St. Gregory's for the vast changes I felt were coming to the Benedictine life. Amidst these feelings, I called around Philadelphia and made some appointments to see various people.

On Tuesday I bought some mailing envelopes which Julie used to mail the other gifts I had brought back from Rome for friends and benefactors. I hoped the gifts would convey my gratitude for their part in my time in Rome and England. It had all been part of the sabbatical gift. That afternoon I took the subway to New Jersey, just across the river, to meet one of our oblates, Ben Haines. He does some AA rehab work, has an antique business on the side, and knows various monks at both Nashdom and St. Gregory's. We talked over the whole puzzle of the religious life. He felt that the clerical question was central to the modern problem in the Church. I knew what he meant, but I couldn't quite convince myself that this explained the situation in the Church. Still, each person's perception has some validity.

MAC

While Ben was making a stop at a local bank, I sat in the car. I was amazed to watch several people walk up to an outside station on the wall of the bank, push some buttons, and in less than a minute have some cash, an envelope, and some kind of a read-out on their financial condition. That is part of the modern information revolution.

We met Ben's friends, John and Dorothy, and had a lovely supper at a restaurant. Before Dorothy came, the talk hovered around AA themes since both John and Ben had experience with that movement. Again I was impressed at the fundamental truth of the AA Steps. Coming to a realization of one's powerlessness was essential to any spiritual recovery — with or without the addiction problem. I wondered if I really knew that fully for myself. I understood some of the effect of growing up with an alcoholic father, but I was not reading Twelve-Step literature regularly or attending any meetings. And I wondered whether Christians in general understood how primary a healthy sense of powerlessness is for all people. After Dorothy arrived, she entertained us with one story after another. She was a librarian and a keen observer of life. And she was a superb story teller.

Around 9:00 PM, Ben drove me back to Philadelphia, on the way showing me some of the prominent buildings. Philadelphia is laid out in a masterful, 18th Century plan with broad avenues connecting parks and squares in five sections of the city with something of Franklin's spirit of 18th Century order still prevailing. It is also the city of tolerance. The first official Roman Catholic Mass was said here. And street people who live over steam vents are allowed their place.

ROBERT

On Wednesday I went west of the city to visit Robert, one of the recently departed members of St. Gregory's. I had brought him some gifts from St. Clement's Church in Rome since the name he had used in the monastery was Clement. We had lunch in a Burger King and went over the situation surrounding his leaving. It was nothing extraordinary. The Novice Master felt he didn't have a vocation at St. Gregory's. But my heart opened to this young man as he described his home situation with an alcoholic parent, his work making hoagies all day long (a hoagie is a kind of meat and vegetable sandwich popular in this area), and his hopes for another chance to serve the Lord. It was sad. I offered him some comments from my experience and said I would be glad to hear from him, even an angry letter if he felt moved, so that he would be free to move forward in his life. My ride home through the slums of West Philadelphia reinforced the sadness in my heart for Robert and the uncertainties of the human journey. My fantasy is that I will become a billionaire and fix everything. Only — it wouldn't, of course.

HOLOGRAMS

Partly to cheer myself up and partly to see something of the city, I stopped at the Franklin Institute. It was full of the kind of mechanical machines that Franklin would have loved. He and others in that time played with inventions and machines, as if they were the final answer to human problems. Perhaps computers occupy that hope today. I am sure there is a computer museum somewhere, housing huge things that today have become much smaller. However, the new toy that had caught my fancy was the hologram. I looked at some in the museum and had some explanations given me. I couldn't understand it all but two things intrigued me. A hologram is an image of an object which can be projected into space. There it floats. As you walk around this floating image, it changes colors. It can even go through changes in movement if several images have been projected in sequence, something like a movie. If we are beginning to discover these images in the air, projected though they be, are there other images, floating, undiscovered, or unrecorded? Someone has asked whether the universe might be a hologram, projected from the mind of the Maker.

Another aspect of the hologram that stirs the imagination is the fact that the glass plates through which the image is projected can be broken into pieces — and each of the pieces carries the full image. From this fact we begin to see a connection with our own physical cells, each of which carry (in this theory) the full image of our personhood. Then again, perhaps the person carries the full image of the whole of the universe. We can see why today's physicists are seen as mystics. Their discoveries are carrying our minds to the edge of the infinite.

After absorbing as much as I could of the museum, I visited their shop. No holograms. I asked and they said that they had previously stocked some simple examples of the hologram, but not now. I was determined to keep looking.

SUPPERS

Charles, with Phillip as a kind of apprentice, cooks marvelous meals, most carefully prepared. The salads have a delicately flavored dressing. The vegetables are just slightly undercooked, al dente. Served in candlelight with a glass of wine, such meals often draw one into thoughtful and hilarious comments about life. Cooking and eating can be an art — really an extension of the Eucharist.

BISHOP WHITE

On Thursday I went over to St. Peter's Church, one of the oldest in the area, to give Father Richards, the rector, a small gift of gratitude for keeping the van. I took the opportunity of checking on the van and it was intact. The motor turned over immediately. What a dutiful friend!

Talking with Father Richards in his study, I noticed an old portrait. It was Bishop White. In 1772 he was the assistant minister in what was known as the United Churches of Christ and St. Peter. All this was under the still-operative Anglican jurisdiction. However, Mr. White (according to the usage of that time) was busy planning the measures for the reorganization of the Church in Pennsylvania. This work led to the union of all the Anglican churches as the future American Episcopal Church. When the Rector fled to England, escaping his arrest for praying for the King in a public service, Mr. White was in charge of the multiple congregations. After the Revolution, England having accepted the inevitable loss of the colonies, Mr. White was consecrated Bishop of Pennsylvania in Lambeth Chapel in 1787. He remained bishop and rector until his death in 1836, and indeed became a significant guide for the emerging Episcopal Church. As I looked at his portrait, I mused at how the Church situation had changed since then. Today the Anglican Communion continues to be stretched into a world wide Communion, and into relationship with all religions. Toward this, Bishop White took an important step.

ST. MARK'S

At noon one day at St. Mark's, with Charles and Phillip taking advantage of my presence to go out together, I celebrated the Mass. It was good to be at the altar and to have so many reminders of the past in the architecture of this old church. The congregation was small, but it ranged from Joe, a street person, to people from the fashionable suburbs.

VOTING

This day, October 25th, I filled out my absentee ballot for the Presidential elections. It was puzzling to know whether our democratic process is really working, or are we simply infusing the process with subtle brainwashing, media techniques which leave people uninformed and unaware of the real situation.

> The hope is that there is enough diversity in the United States to prevent any one group from totally manipulating the public. I believe we are not sufficiently attentive to the political education of the average citizen. The system should put one in touch with his local neighbor for a thorough discussion of all sides of a situation. Granted we have to overcome the inertia of the middle class to take political responsibility. As the world situation gets increasingly worse, we should treasure this gift of freedom.

THE POSSIBLE SOCIETY

On Friday evening, Charles, Phillip, Julie and I went to a conference given by Jean Houston and her team — all of them focusing on the richness of human nature in every culture — and looking ahead to the future. She is one of the people mentioned in *The Aquarian Conspiracy*, a futurist who worked with Margaret Mead and others, trying to apply our new knowledge of human nature to education. She is giving herself to conferences across the country, teaching people the meaning of the information revolution now occurring. This conference took place outside Philadelphia in a motel with a large meeting room. There were some 600 people attending. Her basic theme is that by learning how to use more of our human potential, we can bring the possible, the world of our dreams, into more reality. While she does not support any one religious way of life, she is fully conversant with the major religions and draws on their major tenets to show that wisdom is universal. After tracing the essential changes from the industrial, nation oriented, rationalistic and male way of life toward the service, international, and holistic way of life (a common analysis from many of today's social commentators), she went on to give us exercises which would help us recover more of our human nature's latent gifts. The use of the word "recover" is a conscious reference to "primitive" people who knew how to use their human gifts more extensively, before we became reliant on ideas and machines.

One of her exercises had to do with shifting one's center from the head to the stomach. Although it sounds rather foolish, it shows us how head-centered we have become. The shift doesn't mean that we don't use our heads, but that we learn to live more from a center within, located more in the center of our body. A few exercises — breathing fully from the stomach, walking, meeting people, driving one's car, more from this belly center shows us how it relaxes, brings balance, and keeps one's motive from being too aggressive and self-centered. Try it! The shoulders drop naturally. The muscles relax. Strain is reduced. We see more of everything around us. We gain perspective between our immediate goals and our long range potential as a human being. Try it today, especially at some moment of tension.

Another exercise activated our less dominant side. For instance, most people are right handed. As has been recently discovered, their dominant side is the left brain. For these people, the left hand and the right brain are less active and skillful. For left handed people it is the other way around. In any event, one can exercise the less dominant side of oneself and bring new capacity to that side — a pianist, for example, does this automatically. We can learn simple exercises and increase our range of skills. Such an increase is simultaneously integrating our full mind. It is now known that the muscles, nerves and the mind interact. A tightening and constricting of one part of our human nature constricts all of the other parts. This is the principle underlying the psychosomatic concept or the holistic idea.

> We are indeed one being and we need to learn how to live in harmony with ourselves, others and all of creation. Love your neighbor as yourself is the Gospel. Today this is the essential challenge before the world as we approach a new level of human integration and consciousness.

In between instructions and exercises, Jean's team of musicians and actors led us in simple dances. Physical movement helps us understand more completely, understand with our whole being what our head has assimilated.

10:00 PM came quickly. We drove back to Philadelphia discussing what we were learning. We were not entirely uncritical, being somewhat professional ourselves in the education field, but we knew we were seeing a very human and experienced person at work.

THE WIZARD OF OZ

On Saturday we returned to the Houston workshop for a full day's work. Jean was a good story teller as you would expect of a good teacher. She had many anecdotes and stories from various cultures to share with us. As her central story, a truly American myth, she used the Wizard of Oz. This story provided her with plenty of examples of universal human situations. Dorothy is an ordinary American little girl, living an ordinary, rather dull life. Then a cyclone hurls her into another world. Dorothy is able to take giant steps into her own potential while releasing various characters from their limitations. Eventually she overcomes the wicked witch and sees the friends she has acquired on her fantastic journey happy and fulfilled. Can this be our story? Yes, just as the Gospel story, a much more profound reality, can be our story. Jean was reinforcing the power of story, and the possibility of human fulfillment.

LITURGY

As the four of us watched and participated in Jean's teaching, we became aware of the dynamics of her work. There was teaching, acting out of the teaching, witnessing, a kind of altar call, confession, a certain breaking open of the truth, a sharing of the truth, moments of communion, tears, and joy. It followed patterns of what we would call liturgy, but it centered on its own message, not the Gospel. Still, it was unmistakably powerful. Is there a universal liturgy?

THE CHILD

One of Jean's teachings had to do with the child, our own childhood, and our lingering child still within us. In our time, the importance of childhood has been rediscovered. Now we know much more about the influence our childhood has on our adult life. If we had a peaceful birth and a happy childhood, we are apt to be secure adults. If not, later in life we are afflicted with all kinds of anxieties. A reassuring part of the wonderful discovery of our time is that we can go back to that unsure child and nurture, comfort, and lead it beyond the damage. We can be a stronger adult for having a healed child within us as our companion. I would be a stronger person today if someone had helped me move through my hurts as a child, received from growing up with an alcoholic father. But the joy is that it is never too late. In fact, there is no reason to be trapped in sorrow or hurt from our past. We can move past it, not just in spite of it, but with inner healing and greater integration. I feel that this work of healing is a very important part of the ministry of the Church. Many more people will need training. The best will be people who have been healed themselves.

The four of us were tired by early Saturday evening and elected to leave before the session was over. We knew we would not be back for the Sunday session since we had our own liturgy to do at St. Mark's. But it was a remarkable experience. I felt that I had been reminded of some of the teachings I had received at Esalen. I bought Jean's book, *The Possible Human*, intending to study it at leisure.

SUNDAY

With good feelings and stimulated responses from our Jean Houston workshop, we took up the Christian liturgy for the parish. St. Mark's uses the new *Prayer Book* with care and warmth. I preached at both the 8:00 and the 10:30 Eucharist. The people of St. Mark's are always appreciative. It is a joy to serve them.

During the coffee hour I was invited to a special meeting of the vestry. The question of opening the church buildings to the use of a gay group had raised the whole question of responsible sexuality in today's life. This is particularly real for an inner city parish whose membership is composed of many single people. I admired Charles and the vestry for their courage and honesty in facing this question. They did not come to an easy answer on this complicated question. I was able to offer a few reflections from my monastic experience.

Although I live in a celibate community, I am aware of the interconnection of all parts of our humanity. This includes all of the emotional, intellectual, and relational aspects of sexuality. As human beings we cannot put this part of our life out of sight. We can only seek to live responsibly with our sexual impulses. Monks attempt to redirect that energy into prayer, communal life, and ministry to others. But it requires constant work, humility, and a strong faith in God's love as the all-containing power of our human passions.

I encouraged the vestry to monitor all of the groups now using the church facilities so that they could say they were informed and responsible for all that was going on in the parish. I even encouraged them to visit some gay meetings to become better informed. Awkward and complicated as many of the issues before the Church are, I feel that the rector and vestry of every parish need to face these questions honestly. As the parish leadership matures in its ability to handle these difficult questions, it improves its capacity for ministry as the governing body of the parish. Some people feel that the priest should handle all of these matters, but I incline to a shared authority approach.

After the meeting, by now 2:00 PM, we had a quick lunch and while I took a nap, Charles and Philip attended a concert of choral music in the church presented by a local college.

CHAPTER 23

THE REFLECTIVE SPIRIT

THE LAST NIGHT

By about 7:00 PM, the four of us who had spent so much time together on the weekend came together in the rectory for a final meal. I had spent two very happy weeks with these people, one before and one after my European trip. They were special friends. I asked for some time during the cocktail hour. I wanted to acknowledge the specialness, mused out loud about what we were, what we knew, what the future might be. This sounds pretentious but I feel that good friends need each other and need to be more open with one another. The future, which to some seems ruled by large forces beyond our understanding or control, can be affected by persons of faith, sharing and strengthening one another. So, I opened this part of the evening by thanking them for their friendship. Then I touched on some particular qualities of each one, trying to draw out what I felt were their gifts and some of the hidden things awaiting development. Again, this sounds uncomfortably pretentious. Still, I am willing to take such risks because we often realize too late that we have not spoken of the real issues of life with those whom we love. I invited Charles, Phillip, and Julie to respond and give me feedback on myself. It was a rich and rewarding time. It must have succeeded in establishing a deeper intimacy between us for toward the end Charles looked at me and pointed out that he had resented that I had not really shared my tears, feelings, weaknesses, myself. Charles had known me for many years and I trusted his observation, but the sting of reproach was there. But I knew that Charles' love had found a sealed off part of my childhood. The sting came from the release of the tourniquet. The moment passed. We moved on to a delightful meal. Sometimes the conversations would return to our previous sharing level. Finally, at too late an hour, we said good night. Julie had to go home.

DEPARTURE

The following Monday was the feast of the two apostles, SS. Simon and Jude. It also was the time when I left Philadelphia. My luggage, much more than I could comfortably fit into the van, was all packed and sitting in the rectory hallway. I had a quick cup of coffee and then walked the dozen or so blocks to St. Peter's to pick up the van. I drove it back and parked on the sidewalk in front of St. Mark's. This is standard procedure in the city as there is simply no room for all of the cars. I began loading. Charles and Phillip showed up to help. In the midst of this, I told them how much the previous evening had meant to me — including Charles' remarks which I could still feel deep within. This told me they were true. Only someone who loved me could have offered that kind of insight. Charles had not wanted to hurt. He was only responding on the level that I, myself, had opened up. I thanked him. We hugged and said goodbye.

I drove across town and found my way to the freeway — that modern instrument of travel that allows us to leave a place quickly, musing on the deeper happenings as we flow along the highway. Philadelphia and St. Mark's had been an important part of my sabbatical journey.

FATHER FOX

In a couple of hours drive to the northeast, I was back in New Hope, Pennsylvania for lunch with my friend Father Fox. I could report to him on my visit to Rome and England, plus my conference with Jean Houston. Over a sandwich and a glass of milk we talked about the implications of the concepts of the new physics. William is working on the theological expression of these concepts.

> It will take many minds, and much faithful imagination, to work it out. But it is coming. It must. To arrive at world peace we must have a single set of human values — probably not a single theology. Those values must not suppress different cultures. In fact, it will help each culture to recover the best of its own tradition. We can trust that the best will build peace, a rich, vital multi-cultural peace.

As window washers and friends came to Fr. Fox's house, I excused myself. I wanted to try to find Newark Abbey in Newark, New Jersey.

CHAPTER 24

THE INNER CITY

NEWARK ABBEY

By the time I reached the Newark area, it was dusk and I was swirling in an unknown complex of freeways. I called on St. Benedict to guide me. I remembered that the Abbey had elected to stay with their high school in the inner city. I headed for the tall buildings of Newark. I found a street phone and tried to look up the number. No phone book. This is normal for phone stalls on the street. But a delivery man came along and he had heard of the Abbey. He directed me and in a short time, I found it. I went into the church just as Mass was ending. I saw Abbot Melvin and touched him on the shoulder. He turned, lifted his eyebrows first in surprise, then in recognition, he smiled. He had sent me a gift for my sabbatical. This touched me as a special kind of charity. With an Italian background, he combined warmth with a perceptive insight. He and his community would need all of their gifts and abilities, plus an extraordinary kind of faith to help them chart their course in the inner city. Here was the Benedictine way of life surrounded by the chaos and tensions of a modern American city.

After the van had been securely parked behind the Abbey gates, I was given a room in the guest apartment. The monastery buildings were of different vintages, some going back over a hundred years. As individual members of the Abbey chanced upon us, Abbot Melvin introduced me; I noted their warmth. Something of the cost of electing to stay in the city had awakened a quality of life in these brethren. Later I was told that the Abbey had looked at its own possible death and had come through to new life. Facing death always brings the gift of new life. Deciding to stay in the old buildings, they had remodeled them. White walls, wooden stair railings, more openness, occasionally walls of brick, old works of art set in light-filled niches are touches that bring new life to old buildings.

A young novice, Michael, was assigned to show me around. Then we sat in a room to chat before Compline. Gradually he told me his experience in an all Black school in Brooklyn. He had been threatened, beaten, and advised to leave the school. But he chose to stay. At his graduation he received a standing ovation. I felt that this was a worthy, if grueling, preparation for a life of sacrifice as a monk.

The next morning we had Vigils and Lauds at 6:15. These men were combining the demanding work of education with their monastic life. This was the tradition of most American Benedictines who came to this country to serve the spiritual needs of immigrant peoples. After breakfast, a young senior in the high school was assigned to show me the school. I was struck by his courtesy, intelligence, and humor. A fine young man. As the students, mostly Black and Puerto Rican, gathered for their daily meeting before attending classes, I was introduced to them. I had noticed how difficult it had been for their Black leader to get them to quiet down. In a short talk, I brought this to their attention and tried to show them the opportunity they had in coming to a new respect and courtesy for one another. The sirens and slums surrounding the school showed them that the old distrustful and competitive system did not work. I admit using some street talk techniques. After a few minutes I sat down, and they clapped. What a challenge it would be to teach these "street smart" youngsters the "Spirit smart" resources for life.

The Abbot had to go to a funeral, others went to work, and I was headed for New York. I was impressed with Newark Abbey and the toughness and adaptability of St. Benedict's way of life.

THE GEORGE WASHINGTON BRIDGE

In about an hour I was on the George Washington Bridge, approaching the great city of New York. I forget which great European visitor to the States remarked that this bridge was a miracle of engineering and imagination. It is truly very beautiful, lyrically poetic in its steel grandeur. But once over it, one is plunged into the exciting, dirty, teeming, crowded, energetic Manhattan. I was headed for Absalom Jones Priory, a branch house of the Order of the Holy Cross (Episcopal). I found the address on 148th Street, a brownstone house like those on the rest of the block, and many more blocks in Manhattan. I met Clark Trafton, the superior of the Order who most of the time resides here at this city Priory. After putting some things in my room on the third floor and having a sandwich, I decided to make a quick visit downtown to look for those tantalizing holograms. I had heard that they were available at several places. I had a little over two hours before an appointment with two young college students. What naivete! As it happened, one of the brothers, Michael, was going downtown, too, and offered to introduce me to the subway. I appreciated this because I had never learned much about any subway — let alone the New York one which combined several systems. We took the D train to 59th Street, transferred to one that took us to 42nd Street, then I was pointed to the final train that would take me to my address. All went well. I found the address, saw some interesting holograms, but found them to be fairly expensive. Then with about 45 minutes left, I headed back to the subway. Without my companion, names and numbers began to swim in my head. Sometimes I asked directions only to be given a smile and a comment in a foreign tongue. Finally, I did get back on the D train, "EXPRESS" it said, but at Columbus Circle it stopped. Then a voice came over the intercom, "Out of Service." A loud groan from the crowd, vulgar comments and curses, told me it was true. We all piled out onto the platform and waited. The next D train was jammed to capacity, but some aggressive travelers pushed on anyway. I waited. At last one came that I could squeeze into. I looked at my watch. I was already late for my appointment.

PETER AND GRIFFIN

I arrived back at 145th Street and walked quickly to the Priory where Peter and Griffin were waiting. They were gracious. We made a cup of tea and sat in the kitchen. I had known Peter from his family's visits for several summers to St. Gregory's Abbey. Now he and Griffin were students at Columbia where they were studying business. Both of them had found an oriental teacher nearby and wanted me to comment. Here I was again, a Western Christian, having to acknowledge that the mysticism many of our young sought was not clearly evident in the West, at least on the parish level. This is not a criticism of parish leadership, but an acknowledgement of what middle class people want — sometimes without knowing it. We talked for over an hour and a half. I was careful not to criticize the oriental master, nor to put him in competition with Western spirituality. I feel that I should encourage spiritual searching in whatever form it takes, and let the Spirit bring people to the tradition that serves them best. One could say that young people are naive, but that is the normal companion to all idealism. I believe in nurturing the idealism. Experience will temper it. At 6:00 PM we said Vespers with the monks, then Peter and Griffin left. I felt I had given them the best of my own spiritual understanding.

ORLANDO

As often happens in a busy inner city Religious house, all of the brethren were out for supper. They either do work, ministry, or attend classes. This is a calculated communal risk on their part. I didn't want to suggest any kind of criticism, knowing that they had thought it out. I recognized that even with brethren who spend a good deal of time together, the relationships are not necessarily better. We still have to learn the art of talking honestly with one another. In any event, Br. Orlando and I were left at the Priory. As I put the van in a nearby parking garage, he went out for some chicken and ribs and coleslaw. We had a leisurely supper and talked over many things. He had attended school for dyslexic people in Santa Barbara (dyslexia is a condition in which the eyes do not register images in the usual way). Before we knew much about this condition we thought that these people were simply slow learners or retarded. They suffered a good deal of judgment before the condition was understood. Br. Orlando in getting treatment, had met Jan Reid, my nephew Scott's wife. She was a teacher in a school providing treatment for this condition. I remembered that when I was in Santa Barbara, she and Scott had mentioned a member of a Religious Order in her class. Now I was eating supper with him. Small world. I discussed with Orlando my observation that when we are healed in a particular way we are often being shown our ministry. He would be the best kind of person to help others with this kind of problem. Other brethren, returning from their duties, drifted in and out of our conversation. We enjoyed a little TV and went to bed.

LITURGY IN THE CITY

The next morning I joined the brethren for prayer and Mass. At 6:30 in the morning there was not much noise. But the city can often provide an interesting "choir" for the liturgy. I remember being in Detroit once with the Little Brothers of Jesus. Mass was being offered in the evening and the background noise was more than chaotic, it was violent. One could hear shots, shouts, and cars banging into one another. A small Black boy, attending the service, looked wide-eyed at the priest and the few guests sharing the service. We just offered it all up as part of the death and resurrection of the Lord.

DR. HOLDER

After breakfast I collected my things from my room. I wanted to leave that afternoon but first there was the chore of moving the van. I had brought it out of the garage and double parked it on the south side of the street. According to the custom, I had to move it at 11:00 AM to the north side, and contrive not to get blocked in by others who were allowed to double park. It was a game that the whole neighborhood played. It was just another example of how awkward living in the city can be. One of the brothers was out on the front steps surveying this procedure. Another neighbor, a Black medical doctor who lived next door, was there calculating when he could move his car. Part of the game was to anticipate the move so that you could get a preferred parking spot and still not get a ticket. The doctor, the Brother, and I fell into conversation. It soon became apparent that we had the same politics and world view. I was impressed and pleased to find such a balanced mind in a person whose race had experienced long standing persecution. He had every reason to be bitter and cynical. We talked about the poor, the violence in their world, the misuse of power by those in authority, the need for fair minded people with a constructive world view. By 11:00 we moved our cars and said goodbye. It had been a good philosophers' club. Maybe we need more time together like this.

MORE HOLOGRAMS

By phone, I had discovered a hologram museum, way down in the Soho part of lower Manhattan. This time I only had to get one train and it was not a busy time of the day. We sped by all of the stops I had seen the day before but this time with no trouble. In a half hour I was at Canal Street. When I came out of the subway, I met a different world. It was a warehouse district with stores lining the main street. Everything was very cheap. People in the neighborhood were a mixture of business suit types, some Orientals and Latins, and what looked like a wild set of costumed performers (only they were just dressing in their normal neighborhood attire). It had the air of a circus. I admit it was more interesting than the upper portion of Park Avenue, but I know it could be dangerous, too.

I found my address, an adapted warehouse. Soon I was viewing the film story of the hologram, then I went through the displays.

> It is too soon to imagine how the hologram will fit into our life, but it is definitely another piece of the new science which requires that we change our thinking.
>
> In a hologram, what is real — the original image, or the projected image floating in air? What is the reality of our whole media and image-based world? And yet, real or unreal, it is a normal part of our life.

I ended up at the museum store where they had displays from mere toys all the way to pieces of art selling for several hundred dollars. I knew it was premature for me to look for a particular kind of hologram, but I was getting myself ready for the future. What I have in mind is a hologram that can be positioned in a dimly lit room, projecting abstract images into the middle of the room, with quiet meditative music as background. In developed meditation one moves beyond images. But this could be a preparation exercise, quieting the mind, taking us beyond the turmoil of the day. I bought a few inexpensive items and went to the nearest post office. I mailed a set of toy-like holograms to Fr. Fox and to Charles and Phillip in Philadelphia. One day I felt we would all be enjoying sophisticated versions of these new-age toys. Think of the computer, now in desktop portable size. I hear that credit card people are already incorporating holograms in their cards. It won't be long.

My return on the subway was uneventful. But I had time to ponder the graphic art, the graffiti some would say, now entirely covering the subway cars, inside and out. One could view it as art, looking for some expression, or as a kind of violence. It had a weird, Halloween-like mood to it. It is so characteristic of our age that we are almost getting used to it. I wonder if the classical buildings of Rome had graffiti on them?

Back at the Priory I had a simple lunch, said goodbye to Clark, and drove north out of the city. I wanted to replace a headlight that was not working. I stopped at a gas station and found they could supply and install the light. I was mildly stunned at the price of $22. But I was told that this is normal for the new type of headlight in which the bulb and the reflector glass are all incorporated.

A ride up Broadway showed me another lively part of Manhattan. Here again was the circus. It looked happy enough. If only we could subtract the drugs from this scene. But drugs are an integral part of the economy of such neighborhoods. Finally, I located the entrance to the George Washington Bridge. Going back over it, this time with no toll, was the conclusion to my brief adventure in New York. I had enjoyed it. But what of those who must live there day in and day out? I am told that one learns to shut out the disagreeable part. But then in the shutting out we lose some of our sensitivity to life. Who knows how much it costs human beings to live in the city!

CHAPTER 25

THE SPIRIT AT REST

GOING WEST

It was late in the day and I was heading for a state park in western New Jersey. I realized that I merely wanted to get out of the city. Since my return from Europe, well, really since my coming East, I had missed the space of the West. I still had more people to see on the East coast, but I wanted to have some time to unwind. I had to get used to the van again, I wanted to type these notes, and I wanted to slow down. I could feel the end of the sabbatical approaching. I needed time to think about it slowly, evaluate it, store it more deeply. I found Voorhees State Park and spent the night. How peaceful. My introvert side rejoiced.

ALL SAINTS

As I began the Office the next day, I realized that it was the Feast of All Saints. I would be celebrating it very simply, greeting the ordinary people of my travel day as unrecognized saints. The fall of the year has its own mood. My sabbatical was approaching its own fall. The state parks were closing. Long lines of geese were heading south, their plaintive cry inviting one to follow. I decided that I would at least drop southward into Maryland. The hills of western New Jersey, eastern Pennsylvania, and northern Maryland slowed me down. The van certainly could not get its usual good mileage.

I found another state park open, Rocky Gap, Maryland, with a hot shower room where I could bathe and do my laundry. How refreshing! I did more typing and read some of Jean Houston's book. One of her initial exercises, breathing from the stomach, was already helping me in moments of stress. As I was reading after dark, a knock on the van door introduced me to the hunter's world. Some hunters had been locked out of the camp and wanted to borrow my gate key to get back in. I gave it to them. It reminded me that this part of the country had grown up with a pioneer spirit of the hunter, some hundred years and more ago. The "good ole boys" still have that spirit. I went to sleep in the peaceful forest.

ALL SOULS

For those accustomed to the liturgical cycle of the year, the Feast of All Souls is the next observance after All Saints. This is a time when we remember all the dead. I thought about my parents, William and Ethel, my two deceased brothers, some children in our family who had died at an early age. Then I thought of those who had died by violence. The death of Indira Ghandi, a few days before, was a prominent one. Margaret Thatcher recently had just missed death. There were millions more and there were the added millions who were dying by starvation or mentally dying through oppression. One had to step back from all of the horror and see it as the Fall of the Year, a natural harvesting of souls in the Lord's cycle of time here and time eternal.

> We do what we can to make this world just and peaceful. But we trust in an eternal world in which justice and peace will be everyone's experience. We cannot give up our labor here, we dare not give up our hope for eternity. Our Christian faith blends these together.

For the next few days I wandered around in the country. Sometimes I sat in the van and typed. Sometimes I walked. I found National Parks with the heated washrooms still open. On Sunday I said Mass over an extended time during the day. I have done this before. I would begin with the readings, then take some time to ponder them. Then I might do some practical things in the van or take a walk. Next I would take up the intercessions and later the Offertory. Finally, after lunch and a nap, I came to the consecration of the bread and wine. De Chardin wrote an account of his Mass for the World. I won't pretend to have his informed mysticism, but I do find it meditative to join the Lord and all of the faithful in this timeless offering.

During the Mass I thought back to Charles Moore's remarks: I didn't weep, I didn't share. Other friends who love me have verified this. For all my workshops on human growth, I still need to recover my feelings as the people at Twin Town Alcoholic Treatment Center showed me. It is painful, but it also connects one with deeper aspects of one's humanity. It is in this connection that we become more fully human and therefore more open to grace. "Grace builds on nature" is a classical statement on the relationship between nature and grace. I have my own experience of how this works.

CHAPTER 26

HEARTHFIRE SPIRIT

RETURN

On Tuesday, November 6th, election day, I returned to the urban part of my schedule. I drove out of the mountains where the hills were dusted with a light snow and picked up a freeway heading north to the Washington area.

HEARTHFIRE LODGE

One of the conference centers on my list to visit was Hearthfire Lodge. This is part of a larger group known as the Fellowship of the Inner Light. This sounds gnostic, unfocused in religious tradition, but vaguely spiritual. All of these things are true of places like New Harmony, Sky Hi Ranch, the Transpersonal Psychology Center, Jean Houston's workshops, and now this Fellowship group. Too, I note that they tend to work with some of the same ideas which they either borrow from one another, or as they would say, "discover simultaneously." What intrigues me about these places is that they are honestly and very seriously exploring the capacity of human nature to grow, discover new resources within, create a better life. We could say that there is a certain naivete in supposing that human nature has its own resources to do this. But that would do an injustice to the best teaching of these groups. What we Christians express clearly in a theology of God, they tend to leave to a more vague set of concepts. An example is AA (Alcoholics Anonymous) referring to one's Higher Power. What one cannot deny is their honesty in searching for spiritual growth. Perhaps Grace is not added to nature, but is hidden within it. Sometimes I feel that we traditional Christians take our human growth too much for granted, congratulating ourselves on our orthodox theology.

At Hearthfire I found a small group of men and women running this lodge, an old farm and plantation-looking building on the outskirts of the small town of New Market, Virginia. I had no appointment, but was taken in quite courteously. I was given a room, but they apologized that the heat had not yet been turned on. I had supper with the group and recognized something of the same spirit — a group of young, idealistic people searching for a teacher, wisdom, and a way of life that would respect all of the great spiritual traditions — both East and West. They were happy, eager, and sensitive.

THE ELECTION

After supper I turned on the TV and watched the election returns. I am not an avid student of politics and so was not prepared for such a landslide in favor of Mr. Reagan. Of course, the unique Electoral College system we use in this country veils the popular vote which indicated that Mr. Mondale only trailed the President by a third. That is not so devastating.

But in offering various figures and reports on all facets of the election, the commentators revealed a rich over-view of American life. How strange that the Republicans had kept in better touch with the majority of people than the Democrats. How disappointing to see Americans choosing their own welfare no matter what the rest of the world needs or thinks (of course, the Republicans honestly think they are serving the world with their policies). How alarming, to me, to see the young, college age people choosing Reagan. How eerie to see issues such as poverty, minorities, women, justice before power, etc., all failing to catch the American response. It is a conservative, political and religious mood, not only here, but in the powerful nations of the world. I wondered how the ideas that are taught in the conference centers I visited will become credible and practical. American politics has very little capacity for vision, the future, compassion, and statesmanship. It is geared to the majority as they are now. We can only hope that the Russian leadership will not stiffen any more and decide to confront America. Fumbling on the edge of atomic threat we might somehow win the gamble and gain some time for far-seeing leadership on all sides. What an astounding work of the Spirit to have the super powers subsequently break away from world-threatening confrontation. The human experiment deserves to develop more of its potential.

I went to bed about 11:00 PM. The next day, aided by the electric heater provided, my room was fairly comfortable. But out in the hall on the way to the bathroom I could tell that winter was coming. Of course, I was in a higher portion of Virginia than the coast. I said Lauds, meditated awhile, and then joined the group as they gathered around the dining room table. Sharon, one of the leaders, began the morning session with a review of their current theme: The Forty Day Journey Within. As she was doing this, breakfast was being put on the table. We all helped ourselves to oatmeal, honey, milk, and some special jello with nuts in it. Then Dave, another leader, went through a meditation in which he asked us in our imagination to go to a quiet place of beauty, and there to have the conscious and unconscious parts of ourselves talk together, forgive one another, and offer love to one another. This done, Divine Love was invited into the inner place to offer love to both our conscious and unconscious parts. Then a list of positive statements, prayers, aims was read. I was aware that the oatmeal was getting cold but I dared not be rude to the group life. With all of these groups, I saw that as the common denominator they are using images and exercises to heal undeveloped or hurt parts of the human person and to draw that healed person into greater hope for a richer life of love. This is all centered on some kind of concept of the divine. Perhaps it is a natural mysticism, but today it has a strong appeal to many people. Maybe it is a preparation for a recovery of traditional religion. If so, I think it will influence traditional ways with a new appreciation for the complexity and potential capacity of human nature. It will be interesting to see the convergence of traditional and current spiritualities. Elements of traditional theology and humanistic psychology have already crossed over the barrier that formerly separated them. Traditional theology often has little practice attached to it; it is an intellectual exercise. Humanistic psychology has much practice and exercise, but little theology. Are they not parts of the same spiritual wisdom? A simple example is the liturgical use of the kiss of peace. There, the members of the worshiping congregation send a signal to one another, a signal of love, respect, appreciation.

The Hearthfire group, still eating and exchanging, moved into a Hebrew lesson. David was teaching them the way to form the Hebrew letters and something of the meaning of these letters. The others had pens and ink and were practicing. This was a specific way to learn something of the religious tradition that had formed Israel — a true part of our Christian heritage, and a specific practice.

Finally, after about an hour, people began to drift away to work. I stayed in the kitchen and talked with a young Englishman who had been with the group for two years. No novice was more interested or committed. I returned to my room to do some typing, waiting for the return of the teacher of this community. Was this Fellowship another version of a secular monastery? They profess a clear spiritual faith. It is not solely Christian, but its pluralism is an example of one kind of gathering place for people who do not want a single religious expression. I believe there should be room for such groups.

PAUL SOLOMON

I looked out the window of my room and saw him. This was the man, an ex-Baptist minister, who had founded this Fellowship. He was well acquainted with people like Jean Houston, Findhorn (a new age community in Scotland) and Esalen. A network exists of people who combine various religious traditions with the new findings in humanistic psychology. I went downstairs and introduced myself, explaining that as the father of a community I knew he would have people in community to see first. Like other people in this field, he has been in various parts of the world. He had just flown in from Spain and Switzerland where he had conducted some lectures and workshops. This suggests to me that, in fact, there is a growing number of people who are aware that we must learn how to recover our religious roots and respect various cultures and religious traditions. I returned to my room and some typing until Paul was ready for me.

About 11:30 AM, Sharon told me that Paul could see me. I went to his office and told him how grateful I was to have a few minutes on his return. He was gracious in discounting my scruple. Still, I wanted to discipline my time. People who see many others can be consumed by them. I simply asked the questions and listened to his replies. He was articulate and charitable, affirming his respect for all religious traditions. He said that he had met many Christians who couldn't be free of a single interpretation of the Bible and therefore were not able to explore its unique meaning for themselves. He explained that in fact a person could accept the literal meaning of the Bible and also find a mystical meaning for themselves on their own journey. Today this is what many are seeking. This is the reason that these communities are attracting many seekers. Of course, in our time there are probably many more fundamentalist seekers. This is part of pluralism. Let us respect them.

Paul also spoke about the need to help people find the right kind of mysticism for their own journey. We can understand mysticism as the normal, human yearning for the infinite. It might be connected with a well developed religious tradition (such as Christianity), or it might be aligned with an undeveloped search for the divine as in many of the cults or the youth movements of our time. In either case, it is hopeful that responsible readers are emerging to guide people in their search. And it shows the major religions that they dare not neglect their own mystical tradition. Paul gave me the names of people and groups in the Detroit and Chicago area who are part of this networking. I am sure that some of these people will be beyond my own tradition of Western Christianity, but I feel it is worthwhile to know about them and to meet some of them.

Having covered my questions with Paul, I excused myself and sat down to lunch with a young man who was visiting for a few months. He was Irish and had all of the fire of that people. How good that he is getting some guidance so that his fire doesn't just burn itself out. We had thick lentil soup and a tuna fish sandwich. Then I left, grateful to have found one more member in the loosely connected group of searchers.

CHAPTER 27

THE HISTORICAL SPIRIT

SHENANDOAH VALLEY

In driving northeast up the Shenandoah Valley, I was aware that this was historic country. Memorial highways to early national leaders — Washington, Monroe, Madison — recalled the birth events of America. How amazed these early leaders would be to see the development of the country that only existed in their vision, faith, and imagination. A lot has happened in 100 years. Off to the right, parallel with my route, was the Blue Ridge Skyline Drive. I had driven some of it many years ago when I was showing Dom Patrick from Nashdom Abbey some of this country. The fields around me were uneven with stone outcropping. It was not an easy part of the country to farm.

HOLY GHOST ABBEY

My next objective was the Holy Ghost Abbey, a Cistercian monastery at Berryville, Virginia, on the Shenandoah River. I have always found that contemplative groups are a mixture of very old style ways of living the monastic life and some exciting openings to the next level of mystical discovery. Thomas Merton was an example. We at St. Gregory's have become fairly well acquainted with a number of the Cistercian brethren because their microfilm center is in Kalamazoo, Michigan. There they gather annually for meetings of scholars and monks and nuns. Some of them often come down to St. Gregory's for a visit. One year, for old times sake, we had Latin Vespers, and shared wine and cheese on the lawn. Among others, I had met the ex-abbot of Berryville, Edward McCorkell. Now, I wanted to check out some of my reflections with him.

I found the Abbey, a farm with a plantation-like building on a hill. Obviously it had been a gift to the Order. They simply adapted the pillared mansion to their own needs. I found the guest master, Br. James, in a little gatehouse. He was quite cordial but explained that Fr. Edward was in retreat. I respected this and decided not to remain. As I drove back down the entrance road, a brother, fussing with some farm machinery, waved. These Cistercians have a simple tradition of silence, work, and liturgical prayer. Some of them are a simple combination of straight-forward manhood and faith. Others, in probing the mystery of God are quite intellectual, sophisticated, articulate, and far-reaching. I have never felt called to live that life, but it always moves me whenever I meet it.

WATERFORD

I continued to Leesburg, Virginia, and called my friend Brown Morton. Many years ago, I had met Brown in Rome. Since then, he has been ordained, but at that time was working full time for historical preservation agencies of the government. I had always found him a ready companion for the journey of the Spirit. He was not in his office in Leesburg, but a call to his home in the nearby small town of Waterford (which dates back to the 18th Century) provided me instructions on how to get to their home. Brown's son, Robert, had given me general directions, but wandering around on the back roads allowed me to taste more of the flavor of the pioneer life. When I came to Waterford, I thought I was in an unrestored Williamsburg. Some work had been done, but nothing compared with the more famous restoration. One is immediately struck by the scale of the 18th Century buildings. They are smaller and packed closer together along winding streets. It is all much closer to a human scale. In a car (and especially a van) one is frustrated, trying to negotiate tight spaces. But walking, one experiences a sense of relief, a recovery of being allowed to be human. The 18th Century had not yet learned how to overwhelm the human scale with machines and super-sized buildings. Charming, but doomed! Affluent people wanting more of that nostalgic ambiance, moved into such villages, restored the houses, drove the prices up, lured the development, and in the process changed the mood of the place which had originally attracted them there. Meanwhile the townspeople and nearby farmers had become angry at this invasion. Another Eden lost.

BROWN AND MARGARET

My friend Brown and his English-born wife, Margaret, lived in one of these old houses. After inquiring of some local people, I found their house. No one responded to the knock. Finally I pushed the door open and called for Robert. There was no answer. So I went in and surveyed the living room area. The ceilings were lower, old wood and brick were the natural decoration. The windows and floors were uneven and the doors small. Improvised wiring revealed how modern people had brought the dwelling somewhat up to date. I found a book of Merton's poems and settled down to wait for someone. Eventually Robert and his friend Evan tumbled into the room, continuing their friendly tussle from the street. I introduced myself and these 13 year olds did their best to recover their behavior for the sake of the adult in their midst — but, it was a strain. Periodically as they chatted with me, they hit one another, went through various mock arguments, and showed their deep affection for one another in boyish competition. Besides themselves, their attention was given to a box of tricks they had just received in the mail. There were plastic fingers one put on which had apparently bloody gashes streaked along them, buzzers to shock an unsuspecting handshaker, plugs to insert in the exhaust system of the car to make it wheeze and whistle on starting up, and, the most exciting item, large bladders to be blown up and hidden under seat cushions to produce an absolutely vulgar sound when sat upon. One could watch these two vaudeville clowns, untrained but with the same unerring instinct for earthy humor, playing out the last of their unrestrained youth. Soon they would enter the tunnel of higher education, serious aims for life, marriage, or inner city single living, having to squeeze their zest for life into small and smaller moments. Too bad. I enjoyed the show.

Then Margaret came in, looked at me in surprise and graciously smiled her acceptance of another unplanned event. She was lively, unorganized, and passionate on human issues. As the car was unloaded and various requests made of the boys, she shared her views of the recent election, local projects she was involved with, the plight of the lonely liberal, interspersed with urgent reminders to the boys of their duties. They gradually submitted, brought in the groceries, built the fire, and fixed us all a ginger ale. Then the two dogs bounded into the room, pouring out their love on one after another, adding one more element of energy to this lively family scene. Finally, Brown came in from his work. He is a big man, warm-hearted, very physical and passionately spiritual. These qualities come together powerfully but not abrasively. The disordered life of the family unfolded before me. Brown had canceled a meeting to be with me. Margaret was having a group from the parish at the house that evening. Evan had forgotten to follow his mother's instructions and so was dependent on the Mortons for supper. Margaret made some preparations in the living room for her meeting. The boys now had two masters directing them, but all flowed along through the evening. Brown, the two boys, and I had a delicious meal of thin strips of meat, onions, green peppers, mushrooms, and ginger seasoning all cooked in a wok. This was added to some noodles for a satisfying meal. Then the boys were deputed to do the dishes while Brown and I went upstairs to catch up on our news and views.

I was impressed with the complexity of his life — the life today really of any intelligent person. He had to hold together family life, a business (private practice in restoration work), and his priestly work as assistant at a nearby parish. It never goes together smoothly. It lacks that zen quality of balance and wholeness. I could see that for the average person living in our Western world, it was an intense job of ordering this complexity. This means selecting and simplifying. Again, I felt that the art of spirituality was to bring order into this complexity, centering it on God. I still think someone should write a no-nonsense book on urban living, including all the normal, practical items like running a household, cars, insurance, education of the children, time for the adults to talk, exercise, diet, review of one's work, study, neighborhood, health care, connection with a parish, and a regular process of review of life (looking at the interactions of one's inner life with family, business, and parish lives). It is a struggle to maintain these connections because life never fits together smoothly. It is not supposed to.

> We live in this complex world, constantly looking at it and through it to God. This is an exquisite art. Those who attempt such a balance at once find themselves at the foot of the Cross and in touch with the glory of God. And they inevitably become victims of the world's disorder, sometimes attracting the anger and violence of those who are not surviving. This vocation is fully as demanding as that of a monk. I stand in awe of those who must take it up every day.

TRESPASSO

Brown asked me if I would be willing to share an exercise he had learned from a friend, (an example of a small piece of humanistic psychology). Willing to look at all kinds of experience, as long as its purpose is to grow and discover more about life, I agreed. The name of this exercise is "Trespasso." It sounded like something from the Spanish speaking world but Brown did not know the origin. Two people sit, facing each other, each one holds his hands in such a way that the hands are cupped together, one up one down, with fingers touching lightly. Then the hands are separated and the other person's hands (who has done a similar action) are engaged. Thus, my left hand, turned up, touched Brown's right hand which was turned down over mine. Our fingers touched lightly. The other two hands were in a similar position. I was directed to look at Brown's left eye while he did the same to my left eye. I was told that I could disengage at any time, speak if I wanted, scratch or sneeze, or do whatever I wanted. But the main point of the exercise was to bring us together gently, intimately and soundlessly. We began. And as in sitting zen fashion, I soon became aware of all kinds of inner twitchings of body or mind. But with patience, the body and the surface part of the mind settle down. Then begins a curious and surprising series of experiences. One becomes aware of many levels of oneself behind the facade, some pleasing, some startling. I felt many things: exposed and invaded; peaceful and weak; and supported and vulnerable. I was also aware that I was penetrating (moving gently into) Brown's inner life. This was not a mental or rational exchange. It was a quiet merging of feelings, a touching of the mystery of each other. Occasionally, Brown had tears in his eyes. I remembered that Charles had said that I don't weep. I tried to give myself permission to weep. Nothing happened. The point of the exercise was not to make oneself do anything, just to be silent and inwardly open with each other. I remembered the breakfast session at the Hearthfire where we had been led into a dialogue with our unconscious. Here, with Brown, I felt that at times I repressed my unconscious and I tried to talk reassuringly to that part of me, acknowledging my neglect or injury to my hidden self. Then the roles switched and I sensed that I might be in the unconscious and Brown was looking at me as my conscious self. All of these perceptions were more like floating images, coming and going, with no apparent connection or sequence.

After maybe fifteen minutes, Brown spoke and said, "It's like dancing." I shared that at times I felt my face blurred and I was looking at him from within my own mind. I also noted that I seemed to look beyond his own face. He agreed that we had been together in a nonverbal, gentle kind of sharing. We slipped quietly out of our touching contact and sat for a while, talking of our experiences — at this moment and in general. I shared Charles' observation with Brown. He said that he could see both the powerful peace with me and the needy weakness. There was no judgment in his reflection. It felt very healing, releasing me from trying to hide any part of my life. He went on to look at some of the dilemmas in his own life. I was able to exercise my intuition and offer some comments. Some of these seemed to be helpful.

Trespasso had enabled us to be together in a noncompetitive way. This kind of sharing can even happen when people meet over words or ideas if they will only let go of the ego-centricity. Often our relationships are a clash of personalities, each intent on winning something. In one way or another, I felt we all need these kinds of exercises to experience what it is like to be with another person, almost within them. This is really not trespassing, more like moving toward mutual inner sharing with permission. It was now after 11:00 PM and we parted to go to bed.

The next day the circus began again. The parents going in different directions, Robert preparing his own lunch, the dogs in and out, the maid arriving and looking at the household with a calm eye of acceptance. Brown went off to work. Margaret and I talked for awhile on various issues. I admired her generous attitude but noted her vulnerability. Her liberal point of view had just been voted away in the national election. What could we learn from this landslide vote? For me the lesson was that the liberal and religious point of view must also be well informed and have practical skills. Idealism is not enough. The child within us would like this world to be a nice place to play in. If we are honest, we recognize that while we were in our childhood, we got hurt, abandoned, invaded, rejected, and abused. As adults we often try to recapture our childhood innocence — hence our naive idealism. What is needed is a conscious return to the hurt child within — an acceptance of that child in its hurt — some comforting from the adult side of ourselves — allowing for a slow healing and growth for the child. Then the adult becomes more whole. This allows us to be idealistic and capable of the practical skills to effect those ideals and it shows us how God brings good out of every human experience, even the hurtful. About 9:00 AM, I departed, having enjoyed my brief but rich experience of Waterford.

FREDERICK, MD

I declined the suggestion to use the backroads, beautiful as they undoubtedly would be, and chose to go to the main highway, north to Frederick. I wanted to visit Gary Gillard, a priest and teacher at the Maryland School for the Deaf. He had been a frequent visitor at the monastery and knows our Br. Bernard well. As in many other cases, I had to start from the phone book to find the person I was looking for. After a number of inquires, I found my way to his address which was in a new suburb. Unfortunately, no one was home. I found a neighbor who let me call Gary at work. He said he would come home from work for lunch and let me in. That was fine, and I sat in the van doing more paper work. I always had the financial books to bring up to date, the van diary, my personal notes, thank you's to write, and various little chores to keep my small home livable. Gary came home and we went into his new, three bedroom home. In the short time he had, he showed me how to do my laundry, where to find the ingredients for a simple lunch, my room, and an invitation to attend a concert in Washington with him and his former senior warden Louise. I agreed, wondering what kind of suit and tie combination I could put together. He returned to work and I made myself a little corner for my things, showered, laundered my clothes, took a nap, selected my evening ensemble, and typed a note to the Mortons. Soon it was 5:00 PM and Gary was back with Louise, one of those loyal churchwomen who keep the local parish going through whatever kind of crisis. She was now retired and Gary was taking her on a rare trip to Washington for an evening's entertainment. While Gary was in the house doing a few chores (the same problem of balancing one's home needs with one's work and leisure life) Louise and I talked about her life, nursing experience, and work in the Church. Again I saw how irreplaceable these people are. Priests come and go, loyal laypersons hold things together. I talked to her about the healing of memories in the lives of abused children. She had worked with children, but was uncertain whether she wanted to leave her retirement for this ministry. As she had had knee surgery, she was somewhat limited in moving about. But I had planted the idea of a potential healing ministry in her imagination.

CHAPTER 28

SPIRIT OF LIBERTY

KENNEDY CENTER

Although we were some 50 miles away from Washington, we moved along easily through an intricate series of freeways, all selected smoothly by Gary who has driven them many times. We arrived at the Kennedy Center for the Performing Arts, which is on the Potomac River and near the Mall. It is an Edward Durrell Stone building, but grand as it is, already appearing dated. It is always hard to keep materials, in and out of a building, fresh and attractive when they are used constantly by the public. We parked in the underground and went up to the roof for a cafeteria supper. The view looked out on the Mall, the Lincoln and Washington Memorial, and the White House in the distance. This is one of the best designed cities in the world, the work of the orderly 18th Century mind of Charles L'Enfant. Like Philadelphia, it has a series of wide avenues which connect circles and feature a prominent setting for public buildings. London and Paris, for instance, cannot attempt such order, having had medieval (and earlier) origins which put the emphasis on the cathedral or the palace. The concert itself featured two works; Beethoven's so called "Emperor Piano Concerto" and Prokoviev's "Fifth Symphony,"— it was a rich experience of sound in a well-designed hall.

> Why is listening to a live orchestra such a fine experience? It must be because there is actually more sound (lost in recordings) and a real interaction with the audience. Do they become "members" of the orchestra?

I am afraid that I periodically nodded, only to be awakened by a particularly vigorous portion of the music. Both pieces had their share. Afterwards we met (having had to sit in different places due to my last minute ticket purchase) at the car park. The way home was just as easy. But by the time Gary and I had chatted about the Abbey, he had done a little word processing job for his next day's work, and we had a cup of chocolate, it was again after 11:00. The urban pace is demanding. So, to bed!

Over breakfast the next morning Gary drew a map for my return to Washington. The trick was to avoid the rush hour traffic. He left for work and I soon followed, my map in my hand. As I entered the closer environs of Washington, I often glanced at my map, trying to remember comments that Gary had made. Once off the freeway, I had the maddening problem of trying to read the street signs. When I become president of the universe, I will enlarge all road signs. I missed one street sign and wandered around a residential area for awhile. Here, the 18th Century mind had not penetrated and the curving streets, blind alleys and unfamiliarity with the directions, soon had me quite confused. This was nothing to downtown Washington. After awhile, I recovered my plan and soon arrived at my destination, the Cathedral. I wanted to talk with Tilden Edwards, Director of the Shalem Institute, located on the Cathedral grounds. I already knew that I probably couldn't see him on such short notice, but I thought I would set up an appointment. I found the Institute in the Hearst Building, talked with the secretaries, had some coffee, and chatted with Gerald May, a member of the staff with whom I also wanted to talk. The Institute was combining traditional Christianity, East and West, with the insights of modern psychology. This is just the trail I had followed on my sabbatical journey. While waiting for Tilden to arrive, I looked at their library. How tantalizing! I craved to know all that was sitting on those shelves. But the realistic thought came to me, I could never know all of that. I was not an intellectual and had not been given to exhaustive searching in books. Why torment myself with that possibility? But by intuition I could sample traditions here and there, and pick up the main outline of ageless wisdom. I wished I were closer so that I might take one of their courses. Yet, I could also see the real opportunity I had before me. In the monastery we can combine the practical tasks of communal living with the leisure to pursue the wisdom of monastic spirituality. In the midst of these reflections, Tilden, who was between meetings, poked his head in the door and we made an appointment for another day. I reparked the van, now in an authorized place, and went to the Cathedral.

I don't have the facts and figures before me, but it is an impressive modern Gothic structure with old and new works of art. One becomes aware that a cathedral is a very public place, a space to meet for many kinds of people whether they be in or out of the Church. Sometimes Church people today get uncomfortable when non-Church groups use a cathedral. Agreed, there are some limits beyond which a Christian community should not let itself be used. But think of the medieval cathedral, the scene of mystery plays, an open market in the courtyard, a place where minstrels sang, a public place in every sense of the word. There is a sense in which a cathedral belongs to everyone.

As I walked the aisles and absorbed the vaulted glory of the main structure, noting the side chapels, niches, shrines and crypt, I was moved again to see the cathedral as an expression of the Body of Christ. I must admit that I cringed somewhat on seeing some women dressed in purple gowns and Canterbury caps who were acting as guides. I remembered a previous encounter with one of these people who, with the best of intentions, inquired of a friend and me while we were kneeling in prayer, "Can I help you?" Well, no doubt the human part of the Body of Christ is odd and peculiar everywhere. It is all part of the great compassion of the Incarnate Lord. This time the ladies did not ask any questions. I ended up at the gift shop, bought a few cards and an inexpensive copy of the *Prayer Book*, and went out on the grounds to look at the current construction. Cathedrals are never finished. I was reminded of a story about a medieval cathedral. A visitor asked the workmen what they were doing. Each one explained the specific job he was doing — cutting stone, making choir stalls, carving gargoyles, etc. The visitor came to a very humble workman who was simply clearing away rubble. When asked what he was doing he answered, "Building a cathedral." This man more than the others, knew what he was doing.

I went to the van, had a snack (one of the great advantages of traveling this way), and then began my approach to the inner city where I had agreed to spend a few days with Father Daughtry and the people of St. Paul's.

WATERGATE

I had instructions how to get to St. Paul's, a parish that had contributed two brethren to the Abbey. I did well until I got downtown and the traffic got heavy. Whether it was the sudden appearance of the famous Watergate Hotel or the combination of north/south east/west and diagonal streets I don't know. Anyway I missed my turn, knew it a block later, and started a wild set of improvised maneuvers calculated to get me back in the right neighborhood. The trouble was that I didn't know which was north, south, east, or west. With my city map in one hand, I tried to think, drive the van, and read obscure signs. Often I would want to make a turn only to find that it was a one way street going the other way. After a half hour of wandering around, I began to get oriented, found my way to the right neighborhood, and at last located the alley entrance to St. Paul's parking lot. Whew! I was pleased that the church was located in a reasonably safe place in which to park the van.

The parish sexton let me in the rectory. I unpacked a few things and in due time Father Daughtry arrived. We had known each other for many years and in the early part of this sabbatical, I had shared the Benedictine Experience with him at New Harmony, Indiana. Jim, who had broken his hand in a recent car accident, quickly put me at ease, gave me a room, and provided a wonderful base both for Church life and for exploring the city. I took a long nap and joined him and another house guest, John, for supper at the rectory. After a leisurely meal I excused myself, took the parish leaflet to my room, and began to ponder the coming Sunday's lectionary on which I was to preach.

On Saturday I attended Morning Prayer and Mass, a daily event at St. Paul's. Here was a parish as regular in its prayer life as a monastery. During the morning I settled in more and caught up on my notes. I used the phone to make appointments with other friends in the Washington area. After lunch I took a long walk, longer than I had planned. But a city is an invitation to keep on walking. The Lincoln Memorial was not far away. There was Lincoln within the classic Greek styled building seated on a marble chair, larger than life, and looking down on us. A constant flow of people moved around him. His spirit was there. I read the Gettysburg Address carved in the south wall of the memorial. Was it the stone that made the lines seem so strong, or was it the lines themselves? I pulled out the parish leaflet and read the lessons again, looking for connections. The opening lines of the Address struck me: "Fourscore and seven years ago, our fathers brought forth on this continent, a new nation, conceived in liberty and dedicated to the proposition that all men are created equal…" Here in this setting, on one end of the grand Mall near the historic

Potomac, the American experiment in democratic government, "...of the people, by the people, and for the people ...." became fresh again. But one wonders how to preserve such ideas, and keep the quality of the lives of our great men real in the minds of each new generation. Politics is a never ending process of communication.

VIETNAM MEMORIAL

Our national politics broke down during the Vietnam War. In the first place, it wasn't clear why we were there and it produced a terrible national ambiguity of conscience. The Vietnam Memorial was a short distance from the Lincoln Memorial. As I walked toward it, I remembered that this was the weekend of Veterans' Day. Already on this balmy Saturday, large crowds were gathering at the unique and controversial sculpture. A gradually inclined walk led one alongside slabs of black marble on which the names of some 58,000 dead veterans were carved. The height of the slabs increased as the walk progressed along the gentle slice in the earth. It seemed like a very long grave. If I had seen it without any people I might have missed its full impact. Widows wept quietly beside a name; children stood wondering, unable to comprehend what war meant; flowers were stuck in the cracks between the slabs of marble; some people were making rubbings of a name; veterans in various kinds of uniform cried openly; others just looked or drank beer. The veterans and the curious observers mingled. The feeling was intense. Having had my own encounter with war as a member of a B-17 bomber in World War II in the Air Force in England, I was thrown into my own pain. I did not actually shoot anyone or drop any bombs but the whole calculated destructiveness of war made me angry. What was the power of our egos that brought us back again and again to such violence — with such a human cost to millions, not only in lives, but lives crippled. I was deeply depressed. Occasionally, an improvised sign would signal the location of a particular military unit where members gathered, beer in hand, to catch up on one another's news since the War. Later, I read in the newspaper that some generals had made friendly overtures toward these veterans, trying to undo the hard feelings that had developed about them. Some said that they lacked courage and commitment. Others said that this was a totally new kind of war. There is no doubt that a world conscience is developing on the question. These men were caught in the middle.

I emerged at the other end of the walk, coming slowly up to ground level. I moved along the Mall to the reflecting pool with benches, and finally to people flying kites. The tension drained away. I put my anger and depression back into my inner sanctuary for prayer. The sculptor/artist is to be congratulated. The Memorial makes it possible for many people to experience the effect of war with the focus not on some heroic figure, but on the names of those who have died or are missing.

As I moved toward the distant Capitol, I remembered another capitol, Rome. What grandeur! What human weakness brought it down to ruin! Now this capitol! I came to the Washington Monument — that thin spire of tapering rock. Apparently, it took over a hundred years actually to finish this memorial to the Founding Father. Lines of people circled it, waiting to go inside. Outside, people wandered around, families ate their snacks, kites flew overhead. The Mall seemed to draw one on. I found out where the National Art Gallery was. I wanted to see the very modern new east wing by I. M. Pei. When I arrived, it was closed but I peeked in. Architectural space itself had become part of the display. I regretted the closed doors but I had missed other sights along the way in this sabbatical. I took what came.

Across the Mall I spied the Aerospace Museum. I had been told that it was spectacular and I wanted to see if they had any more holograms. It was almost closing time when I entered. Primitive flying machines and huge, modern, commercial craft hovered overhead, hung from the ceiling. Impressive. The museum shop was closed but an attendant told me that they used to have holograms, but no more. I would have to wait for this new toy to become more available.

By this time it was dusk and I headed home. Should I take a bus or walk? Washington is one of those cities that invites the walker. It is a living museum in itself. At one point ,three Asian youths approached me for directions. On my city map, I was able to show them where they were and where they wanted to go. I felt I had repaid others for the many directions I had asked in a strange land and I felt good showing them some American friendliness. I passed an ice cream store and went in. The store itself was an interesting piece of architecture. A row of old houses had been converted into stores, preserving their original lines and materials. Behind them, connected with glass and steel corridors, was a high-rise office building. It was a respectful way to join the old and the new. A large coffee flavored cone and a cookie were a refreshment after miles of walking. Back at the rectory, I warmed up some lasagna from the refrigerator and went to my room to ponder the sermon, "All Men Are Created Equal."

On Sunday I preached a brief development of the theme of equality. Where does it come from? From the Trinity where the persons are equal. Lincoln, consciously or unconsciously, was presenting a Christian theme. Democracy itself was an evolution in time of the timeless being of God. But how hard we have to work to remember this gift.

Later at the family Mass, I was able to combine this theme with a baptism. Germain was a small Black child. He was surrounded by family and friends all waiting for the baptism. I left the pulpit and talked to the congregation about baptism as the way in which God lifts us into equality with Himself. Actually, thinking about all of the people in the world, most of whom are not baptized, I was trying to understand how there may be equivalents of baptism in other religions. But for now, I talked about baptism as we experience it in the Christian Church. At one point, I picked up Germain (who was very well behaved) and walked around with him. I pointed out that this child would not know what baptism meant unless the people of his family and the congregation taught him. How could they do that? By touching him. This was the language of belonging he would understand best before he learned to read and think like an adult. This graphic example of the Church's teaching was effective. People need to experience what they are taught. I had said the same thing in St. John's Church, San Francisco.

After the third Mass, Jim and his house guest, John, and I went to a nearby restaurant to recover from the exhausting work of the "day of rest." Afterwards a good nap completed the reward.

LINDSAY

On Monday morning, after Morning Prayer and Mass and a cup of coffee, I had an appointment with a parishioner, Lindsay. She had studied diet and exercise; I wanted her ideas on how these might be applied in communal life. She gave me more information than I could absorb, but I became more convinced that diet and exercise are essential parts of our life. They should be included in what we often call a Rule of Life, a spiritual program to help us stay open to the indwelling of the Holy Spirit. The cardiovascular system, the muscles, and the joints are all important parts of our body, and it is the body which is the Temple of the Spirit. Lindsay also has some training in human development beyond diet and exercise.

> Our love for our neighbor and for ourselves needs exercise, too. An active Christian would say that worship, prayer, and ministry are exercises in love of God. But we have not been as clear about exercises on behalf of our own growth in proper self-love and love of our neighbor. I am sure that the Church will make many mistakes in developing an appropriate practice around this human growth area, but I am also sure that we must learn. Workshops, lectures, books by therapists, physiologists, psychologists, and other responsible students of human nature need to be integrated with theology. But we must do the exercises and integration. Where Christian doctrine and human growth exercises are combined, a powerful spiritual program can result. This, I am sure, is the work of the parish in the future.

HENRY AND SALLY

I walked a few blocks and came to the house of Henry and Sally Breul. Henry is the rector of St. Thomas' Church. Some years ago, this church burned and Henry persuaded the congregation not to rebuild. They worship in the parish house. Henry is a member of Associated Parishes (a group dedicated to renewal in the Church). He is convinced that celebrating the Eucharist without too many signs and symbols (liberating us from an excessive dependency on externals) is an important freedom for today. He concentrates on making neighborhood residents, a mixture of racial and ethnic folk, aware that the Church belongs to them. Sally, his wife, says that it is Henry's sermons which make it all work. He was trained as a sociologist and has continued his reading in theology and secular studies. St. Thomas' parish style is very different from that of St. Paul's. Can't we have both and still more kinds of parishes? We had a delightful lunch on TV tables as we explored all kinds of fascinating ideas. I had a third appointment that day, so I left the Breuls and returned to St. Paul's.

JEAN

I was picked up by Jean, a woman with whom over the years I have had an extensive correspondence. She took me out of the city into Virginia, just a short distance away. Her house is situated among some of the affluent and important personages of the Washington area. At one time, Erlichmann of Watergate fame lived here. But then, Washington is like that. Everyone knows someone who knows someone else who works for someone else who is connected with… and on and on the web develops. Anyway, Jean, a single parent, rearing five children, was making an heroic effort to do everything — her nursing work, running the household, and keeping it all centered on the Lord. It is not easy. I sense that any of us who attempt this Christian life suppose that God will somehow make it easy. We are inevitably disappointed, even tempted to lose faith. God is not the servant of our egos. We are His servants. Learning this is what is meant by dying to self. We talked about the various aspects of her life.

> In such conversations, I try to learn something of the unique quality of the other person, including their worst fault, as they understand themselves. I don't believe a spiritual director is meant to change a person as much as he is invited to strengthen what that person already is. And the fault? This is often a clue about that person's uniqueness. That fault, redirected to the proper object, becomes part of that person's love of God. I also try to encourage a person simply to enjoy God and let Him enjoy them. The relationship between a parent and a child often provides a good example. What parent would not prefer to have the child show trust by coming to the parent, no matter what the issue? Is God that kind of parent?

I have to acknowledge that such exchanges with persons who are honestly seeking to do God's will is always a blessing for me. Jean drove me back to St. Paul's with the gift of a little sack of carrots from her garden for my next trip in the van.

BILL AND SALLY

A quick shower and a short nap. Then I drove Jim and John (the house guest) out of the city to the home of a parishioner, the Hardys. Another couple, the Harrisons, joined us and we had the usual before-dinner drinks, then a marvelous meal sharing the mutual birthday celebration of the two wives, Jean and Sally. Finally we looked at the pictures of the Hardys' last trip to Turkey. It seems that the ordinary people of the world get along fine. It is the governments that disagree and manipulate each other. By 11:00 PM, after a very long day, I broached the embarrassing question of departing for home.

SHALEM INSTITUTE

I said Mass the next morning with Jim carefully shepherding me through the Missal. It had been a long time since I had used that particular altar book. True, I began my priestly life using a Latin Missal but that seemed a hundred years ago. It was a pleasant flashback, but it didn't seem to connect with the contemporary world so well any more. After Mass, I packed the van, said goodbye to Jim and John, and headed back toward the Cathedral. There I had an appointment with Gerald May, a member of the staff of the Shalem Institute and a psychiatrist. And of all things, he grew up in Michigan not far from the Abbey. Now, many miles from Michigan and many years later, we were to meet. I appreciated Gerald's caution that we should not misunderstand the role of psychology in the Christian life. It must remain secondary. But given that priority, can much of our new information about human nature enrich our Christian life? He gave me names of people in the Midwest who might be resources for human growth for the members of the Abbey. I continue to ponder how I can work such resources into our normal life without alarming the brethren. But I am so convinced of the worth of our deeper knowledge of human nature that I know I will be shown the way.

Later that day, I had an appointment with Tilden Edwards, the other staff member whom I had come to see. I recognized in Tilden the gifts of intuition and feeling. I could tell that each of my questions elicited deep searchings. It's not that his head could not have tossed off good answers, but he used his heart to filter the answer. I could tell that he had worked hard to keep the head and heart in balance. He gave me a new name, Parker Palmer, a Quaker, whom he thought I should meet. Since he was in residence outside of Philadelphia and not far away, I decided to try to include him in my journey. I pledged to Tilden that we should keep in touch, "networking" as some say, because something profound was brewing. The Spirit's presence leaves unmistakable signs.

CHAPTER 29

THE UNSETTLING SPIRIT—
A TIME OF CHANGES AND GROWTH

BALTIMORE

Having been in Philadelphia, New York, and Washington, I was now going to a fourth big Eastern seaboard city. Today one can go in and out of a large city on the freeway and hardly see the place in the old way. It used to be possible to penetrate the rings of a city and gradually let it educate you with its history, people, customs, flavor, and mood. I never really saw Baltimore. I went around it on the belt system and went to a small town on the outskirts, Brooklandville. There I found old St. Paul's school, founded some 150 years before from old St. Paul's parish downtown. I went to an elegant mansion on the grounds where the headmaster and his wife, John and Mary Ordeman, live. The mansion was built by Charles Carroll (the singer) for his daughter, Mary Caton. The house had the feel of a grand manor house. The Ordemans lived rather simply on the second floor. There to meet me was Father Bill Workman, one of our oblates, the real reason I had come this way. He had formerly worked at the school and now was an assistant priest at the downtown parish. He and the Ordemans were good friends. I was given a room and then sat down with Bill to see how things had been going. We chatted about many things and people some of whom we knew mutually at the Abbey and elsewhere. Then we had supper with the family. Afterwards, as Mary was doing the dishes, John was puttering somewhere, and Jessica doing her homework, Bill and I got the chance to talk again. This time it came out. He was very upset that John had been asked by the School Board to leave, and with no real explanation. This was unjust in Bill's mind and it deprived him of some very dear friends. I was not competent to review this decision, but I could appreciate Bill's feelings. I know that I must one day let go of being Abbot and that would be painful. We came to the conclusion that Bill must be faithful and also remember his own experience with helplessness, a concept that led him to sobriety and inner stability. Again, I was moved by the power given to a person when he meets the death question in his life, and finds a way to let God take him through it. Bill said good night and went home.

Mary came in and we talked. From her point of view the dismissal was painful, but her faith told her how to handle it. She was more concerned with John. We talked about the death and dying journey. She was already working in hospice groups. Two important concepts emerged, self-respect and honest connection with one's feelings. Feelings often lead us to discover our anger and our resentment. Without knowing this, a true response to a loss of goodness in our life, we are apt to cover over the truth with a pretended attitude of "it doesn't matter." My childhood survival taught me well how to do this. Under that is cancerous cynicism and self-doubt. So to avoid such cover-up one has to acknowledge one's feelings and find a way in faith to continue to respect oneself. Mary understood all of this. She is a person of prayer.

I went to bed in my elegant room, mentally rearranging it, as I always do, to my own use.

The next morning was bright and clear. I could look out on the Maryland hills toward the city which I would not see on this trip. I went down the hall to the kitchen for my coffee. There was John making his own breakfast. I felt comfortable in bringing up the subject of his dismissal because Bill was a trusted friend. He quickly shared his own point of view. He was remarkably free of bitterness, but I stressed the importance of staying in touch with his feelings. Generally men are not as good as women in doing this. Is it because men experience more vulnerability at the feeling level? We think "on top" of our feelings; we are more cognitive. I know this in myself. John said that he could see this point of view and offered to work with Bill on a feeling inventory. I knew this would be objective, confidential with Bill, and helpful for John. He would then be more free to move on.

> All of life seems to be a journey, one of the themes of my sabbatical. Whenever we can step out of the journey and sort out our inner condition honestly and in trusting love, we are free to resume the journey with a clarified vision.

John left for work. Mary fixed me breakfast and we talked more. I felt I had come at a significant time in their lives, and that I had been able to help them clarify the issues before them. In faith they could easily put it in the context of their trust in God. This is the beauty of Christian strength. And it is always a nurturing experience for me — receiving some of the grace that passes through me to others.

THE HERMIT

Soon I was back in the van and on my way toward the Philadelphia area. Through a phone call the previous evening, I had secured an appointment with Parker Palmer, the person recommended to me by Tilden Edwards. It was a pleasant day to drive, crisp outside, but in the van warm and comfortable, leaving me free to negotiate the freeways, say the Office, and muse on my recent experiences. The van had allowed me the flexibility of being a missionary at times, and in between, a hermit. It was a marvelous way to process life.

> There is a hermit inside all of us, a place where our personal faith sorts out the rough and tumble of life outside us and looks for the presence of God in it all. I realized that my sabbatical had opened my hermit self to a

rich circus of experiences in the world, giving me further assurance of God's love, and confirming my original call to be a monk. I did not belong totally to this world. I was meant to live on its edge, helping others see the Divine presence everywhere.

PENDLE HILL

Soon I was in the greater Philadelphia area. I went into a rest stop, had a snack and did some typing. At about 2:30 PM, I drove to the address I had in Wallingford. I found a lovely stone house in the half-urban, half-suburban, mix of what is typical of most large cities. Parker Palmer lived with his family in this house in the Pendle Hill complex, a Quaker school and conference center. It brought back my own experience with the Quakers when as a student from Dartmouth, I spent some weeks in Mexico, working and studying with a Quaker work group. I respected these people and have come to see that their integrity of the inner life is an absolutely necessary ingredient. The Catholic emphasis on Sacrament and outward sign is the other ingredient. Today these two aspects of life are coming back together. It is not surprising then to find a person like Parker being familiar with Thomas Merton and Henri Nouwen (who had written the preface to one of Parker's books).

In a pleasantly simple living room, we began our conversation with a cup of tea. It was not long before we were sharing and comparing ideas on faith, monasticism (in which Parker had a genuine interest) and the state of the world. I found him to be "simpatico." He gave me a special phrase, "nurturing solitude for one another." This is very close to the monk's heart. How extraordinary to find this concept in a fully occupied teacher, author and family man. But it is not extraordinary. It is coming up in many places as a necessary alternative to modern noise and activity. He also noted that salvation cannot be achieved by group interaction. This was a sensitive point with me because it is precisely here that I found my own communal experience to be ambiguous . But I understood his reservation. Group interaction cannot be allowed to stand for the absolute in life, for God. This was Gerald May's point, too.

As we talked, I became aware of Parker as a person: tall, gentle, aware, very compassionate, yet committed to certain values. He listened, too, always the mark of a truly prayerful person. His words came out of a deeply integrated personality, a humanness quite gracefully open to God. "Naturally supernatural" is a phrase I had heard before. I felt it applied here.

His varied experiences in community and education had led him naturally to an appreciation of the Benedictine formula — work, worship, prayer, lectio, and community. They were monastic values which he had discovered to be true for himself. In a few years, he was thinking of moving to a monastic community and continuing to live out these values with his family. It was a theme I had thought about a lot. But I had never been able to put it into actual effect at St. Gregory's. There are groups and individuals near the Abbey who appreciate its life. Here was a man who intended with his family to explore such a venture.

I posed to Parker one of my constant questions when I am with a person of depth and faith. How do you handle conflict? He was not quick with the answer, a mark of a wise person, but cited some Quaker ways. They practice a method of silent worship (that is not exactly the phrase he used). In that silence, anyone is allowed to speak. However, they must speak from their heart; speak in the largest context of their faith; not argue with anyone else; not discuss or dialogue; just speak and let it rest in the minds and hearts of the group. Such a process, Parker said, opened the group to its deepest understanding and allowed everyone to know the members of the group in their best faith stance. This did not contribute directly to the solution of an immediate problem, but it put all problems in the context of the group's hope in God. I remembered a similar comment from my interview with the Director at Sky Hi Ranch. This seemed to me a more profound kind of group interaction. Perhaps the essential point is whether the group is centered on God.

Parker gave me two of his books. I promised to send him *RB 1980*, the commemorative book the Benedictines had put out on the occasion of the 14th Century of St. Benedict's birth. I had been in Rome for that occasion where we had speculated on the future of the monastic life for the 21st Century. It made one aware of the depth of the monastic tradition and of its continuing place in the life of this world.

We touched on the delicate point of consensus in group decisions. It is not a matter of democratically coming to a majority position, but more a matter of allowing the group to come to a mature mind on an issue, then being very careful that any minority opinions are comfortable in supporting the main mind of the group. If not, then the group must wait for a more prayerful searching of the question. It is a process delicate in the extreme. In a crude way, some people can obstruct the common life by withholding their agreement. Or the group can force its mind on unresolved individuals. It supposes a real life of faith and prayer. Of course this is the limitation of our political democracy. The human person, without some practice of faith, is no less tyrannical than a king or a dictator. So much for the great vision of the 18th Century forefathers. But our political experiment was an important step for the world. And it is still being worked out politically in various places that have never known such a way of respecting individuals. (Who could have foreseen the explosion of democratic energy in eastern Europe in the late 1980s?) The religious person knows that democracy has a much deeper spiritual implication. That is the new ingredient going on now in various religious groups. We can even see Vatican II as an incorporation of certain democratic ideas.

Parker's wife and teenage children came in during our parting conversation. They brought their own noisy and disruptive exuberance. I was all the more amazed that this man could discover monastic qualities from his family experience. Perhaps the discovery came out of the need for solitude, a rare ingredient in a modern family experience today. Perhaps a monastic quality can be lived in the family when there is respect for each person's inner spirituality and certain time for family prayer and celebration of God's presence. I realized what a gift I have in my monastic vocation, and that the monastic and marriage charisms are two sides of the same divine revelation.

As we parted we knew that we must meet again. We were part of the unorganized network of people who were exploring the way forward for people of faith. It is a way that requires deep personal integrity. Some of what one sees on TV is too extrovert and manipulative to provide a long range base for the Church. Our Christian, Catholic, experience is a reliable base, but it needs considerable personal application of its own principles of "growing up in Christ." I knew I had met a person who was living this truth.

I left Parker, worked my way westward through the Pennsylvania hills and after dark eventually came to French Creek State Park. I do not like to arrive at a place for the night after dark, but in this case I was the only one there. So it was easy to find a place near the heated bathroom and settle in for the night. Again, what a relief to have some solitude.

NEW DIRECTIONS

The next day, the weather still telling me clearly that Fall was here, even fading into winter, I drove onto the turnpike and headed west. By mid-afternoon I was in the Pittsburgh area. I called David Hemmerling, head of the New Directions, a scholarship program for worthy young men who have the aptitude for a college education but not the finances. David raises the money for these scholarships and also instills in the students a sense of religious and moral values. They live together in a former convent next to a Catholic church in Whitney. It is just across the highway from St. Vincent's Archabbey, the Benedictine Abbey that originated in Bavaria in the last century. The young men from New Directions attend St. Vincent's College.

David and I had talked on previous occasions, he had brought the young men to St. Gregory's for a visit, and we had shared dreams of how the Benedictine life could be adapted to the New Directions' program. We had not come to any conclusion. As I arrived, he and Michael, a former member of the student program who had stayed to become a member of the staff, were just finishing a meeting with a family who were interested in selling some nearby farmland. David was indeed looking for a site for future New Directions buildings. The family was impressed with the New Directions program and would prefer that the family farm be used for this kind of a worthy cause. No agreement was reached, but I recognized that David was putting together the various pieces that would one day make up a fully functioning organization. I also knew that it is heartbreaking work. No sooner is one piece in place than another piece of the plan falls apart.

Over tea, David and I sat at the dining room table and talked more. I could see that he was refining his vision through the actual experience he gained. He had been at it for some 14 years. He talked about his fund raising efforts. This is hard work because one has to evaluate what the donors' expectations are, and whether in fact, one can meet those expectations without departing from one's vision. It is not easy to be honest in such a complex endeavor.

Then he talked about a new opening for Asian students. This would be a fascinating challenge, but some of his board members would not be comfortable with it. For example, labor unions do not favor foreigners in America, and David has financial support from some unions. So it goes. Vision and compromise are uneasy companions.

We also discussed how monasticism might be part of the influence New Directions offered to its students. I support this idea in general, but have a lot of reservations on its actual implementation. The monk, his habit, other-worldliness, and separation from certain kinds of human activity, are signs of one part of Christianity, but how to incorporate these signs into the formation of the active youth who intends to live in the world is not as obvious. Many monasteries with schools face this dilemma. Today the conservative swing is moving parents to place their children in religious schools where they believe that they will receive some discipline, a deeper appreciation of their culture, and some religious training. The fact is that the Church's educators recognize that they are not turning out students who retain religious values. Perhaps the obvious fact is that it is difficult to instill religious values in a young man who must then compete vigorously in a materialistic culture. Even so, the effort must be attempted. In our conversation, a theme that came often to David's mind was the concept of toughness of character. How is it instilled in young men?

Our talk was interrupted by an invitation to go to supper. A woman who is a close friend of New Directions invited us out, so I quickly showered and pulled a slightly better shirt out of my wardrobe. We went to a nearby inn, a restaurant that had been a place of hospitality since the pioneer days. We had a good meal and lots of banter back and forth. I could see David and Michael in a different setting. It was fun to be with them — all the more so since I knew of their serious commitment.

At about 9:30 PM we returned and much to my surprise, David summoned the eight boys in the program to a conference. I would not have intruded on their studies or their free time, but David posed the question of toughness. What did they think it meant? We had all kinds of answers and they honestly tried to penetrate the meaning of toughness. Occasionally, I would add a thought, but I didn't want to be too academic or to exclude any of their ideas. It became clear that most of their thoughts had to do with personal survival or career. They couldn't be blamed for soaking up the themes of the culture in which they lived. Privately, I pondered how God and religion might be at the center of their life. We quit at 11:30 PM. Perhaps it is the mental wrestling that is the most useful exercise at this stage of their life.

The next morning, Friday, I let the students get off to school before appearing. David and Mike prepared a lavish breakfast of juice, omelettes, sausage, toast, jelly, and coffee. I knew I wouldn't need any lunch that day. We continued our talk. I could see that David's energy focused naturally on getting New Directions established. He was ambitious; I knew the feeling. I had pushed hard for my vision of St. Gregory's. Some of it had been actually accomplished, much had not. One has to fight disappointment. My sabbatical had healed most of that hurt and given rise to more possible goals — also opening up some new dreams. But how does one tell all that to a younger man? David and I agreed that we needed each other. It was an older person with more experience letting a younger man with great visions share his dreams with a friend. I loved David. I love any person with a dream and the energy to pursue it. The American poet, Robert Bly, speaks of the need of the young men to have older men as mentors:

What lies on the other side of an unfulfilled dream? What happens when the energy drains away?

But you can't say to a dreamer, "Be careful!" You can only say, "Think as hard as you can, love as hard as you can, pray as hard as you can, and if it doesn't work, laugh as hard as you can."

I hope that David and I can practice tough love between us. As I departed, he gave me a round tin of chocolate-covered peanut butter nuggets. I prayed that one day his dream would taste as sweet.

CHAPTER 30

WINDING DOWN —
DISCERNING THE SPIRIT: TEACHING

WINDING DOWN

As I drove along the freeway into Ohio, I knew that my winding down plan was forming in my mind. I am not a person who can stretch out an ending. I am already working on the next step: to distill the many impressions I had gained on the sabbatical and share them with my community. After listening to my brethren, I would know better where St. Gregory's was going and what my role in that corporate journey would be. I was not anxious, but I needed time to sort things out. I stopped in a motel that night as the temperature was dropping to 30 degrees and the state parks were closing.

In the motel I began to finish up these notes, to balance my books, write some thank you's, and make some lists of things I wanted to do on my return. I am a great list maker. I suppose it helps me handle large amounts of detail within the huge vistas of my own dreams.

In between doing my paper work, I turned on the TV and found the movie station. It was hard to turn away. Herbert O'Driscoll, formerly the Director of the College of Preachers and himself a great storyteller, says that the movies are the enactment of the dreams of the public's unconscious. The stories, no matter how banal, draw us into their movement. We are always looking for "our" story, and there are bits of our story in every story.

> Our Lord told lots of stories. The story lets you find yourself in one character or another, or, in all of them. The story lets you discover your own story.
>
> I saw the story of the journey in many versions. I saw my own sabbatical journey. My notes are a little of my own story. Our life is a story, if you can become aware enough to see what it means. The Gospel shows us the man, Jesus, who reveals the meaning of our story. It is the story of every person. From listening to the story we find ourselves involved personally and more clearly with our choices in life.

On Saturday I began to sense my final plan. I would make two more stops — one in Flint and one at the motor home dealer in Battle Creek. As I drove north into Michigan, the weather became colder, grayer, and, oh dear, there were little streaks of snow now and then. In Flint, I called the home of Barbara and Al Koegel, some friends who had supported the sabbatical. They were not home. I called their store (one of Barbara's hobbies) and their daughter who worked there gave me directions to drive there. At the furniture store, I sat in the kitchen and typed on my notes. At 5:00 the daughter said she was closing but that she would drive me by her parents' home. I could take my chances.

We pulled up to the door and they answered the bell. They had just returned. I fumbled my way through an explanation that tried to make them completely free to have me as an overnight guest or not. They were gracious in the extreme, as all of my friends have been. I brought in a few bags. We chatted, had dinner, and then I was taken to a concert by the Flint orchestra. This was the second time I had worn my suit and tie. Flint's orchestra is one of those smaller groups that shares a director with another city. The players are paid, but not a full salary. The music was good; the violin soloist superb; and the conductor eager and joyful. Again a live orchestra is much more rich and sparkling than recorded music. It was a grand evening. I only nodded during the last part of the vigorous Strauss piece. Al's mother, 96 years old, was there. What a story she has, having begun her life in 1888. And what changes she has seen. We went home and said good night. It was 11:30.

FIRST PRESBYTERIAN CHURCH

I had already decided that if I stayed the night with the Koegels I would attend Church with them. I had met Barbara at retreats and quiet days I had conducted in Michigan. They had also had considerable experience with some of our mutual friends in the Charismatic Movement: Mike Schulenberg (once the rector of the Episcopal Church in Flint); Graham Pulkingham and the people at Redeemer Parish in Houston; and, Messiah Parish in Detroit. Now the Koegels were attending the Presbyterian Church. It is quite usual for people to move around among various denominations, going where they are fed. We went to the 9:30 worship service. It was probably like most mainline Protestant services. There were hymns by a large, vested choir, prayers, a children's gift procession (for Thanksgiving), ushers, a collection, and a sermon. It was the sermon that caught my attention. The pastor, forty or so, spoke about overcoming disappointment with gratitude to God. In his sermon, he spoke of his personal feelings of disappointment and revealed a good deal of himself. Here were elements of the insights into our humanity I had observed at various conferences now appearing in the teaching in Church.

Later on, after the service, I attended a class on gifts of the Spirit. The point of the class was to help us discover our own gifts. Here was a kind of human workshop, based on the Gospel.

I was dressed in my monastic habit and returned people's smiles and shook hands with those who introduced themselves. In such simple ways we bond with other human beings. I felt I was among friendly people and that the denominations were indeed coming closer. I could feel the groping, listening, yearning for more life. Had the touch of death in the city and in the world alerted us to the preciousness of life? Some, of course, didn't look at me at all; they looked down, looked away, remained unsmiling. I couldn't blame them. The monastic habit is not calculated to relieve tension, unless you know its meaning and history. That meaning and history have not been an obvious part of our American life. Americans know only the problems surrounding the Reformation. But I sense that we are finished with those problems. Or else we have such huge new problems that we can no longer hang on to the old ones. Even the TV commercials employ the jolly friar.

The pastors themselves were genuinely friendly in their greeting. And of course they were busy with their people. Barbara and I left and drove out to the country club.

THE COUNTRY CLUB PATRIARCH

Barbara's father had reserved a room for a family gathering. I had been included because I was Barbara's and Al's houseguest. Some 20 people, related to one another in one way or another, came together for the brunch. I watched the patriarch loving his family. He greeted them, moved from one to another, brought them to the table, even pushed a bit when some lingered, and announced the purpose of the meeting which was to enjoy the family. Then, he prayed. It was a good prayer — inclusive and grateful. Then we went off to the buffet to select our food from the great array available.

I listened to the people around me. I answered questions, trying not to overwhelm them with theology or seriousness. They listened politely, sometimes questioning me further. The most interesting parts of our conversation took us deeper into new insights in human potential, healing, and teaching. Barbara's sister, a teacher, sat next to me and wanted to know more about healing children. All the while the patriarch talked to one or another member, again greeting them, touching them, inquiring about their health, family or job. He was strong and faithful, but a little like the chairman of the board. I thought of my own father. The Victorian model was not dead. It had many good qualities.

The family finally caught up with its own gossip, enjoyed the meal, and began to leave the room. The patriarch, sensing this, asked me to give a blessing. I was happy to acknowledge the gift of family life. As we moved out of the room, the patriarch came to me and told me more of his own Christian work. He was on a Christian board with Roman Catholic leaders and well-known men in the religious field. Here was a concerned and committed Christian.

Driving home with Al and Barbara, I opened up the question of the credibility of the patriarch. We agreed that he had many good qualities, but that his generation had never taught him to know or reveal his own inner weaknesses. These were to be carried privately, and concealed as well as possible. That was the model. I remember my own father, finally coming to his children with the recognition that he was an alcoholic. This was a shattering revelation for him, and, for us. Although we had lived with it for years, no one knew what to do with his pathetic confession. We did not know how to love him. We could not overcome our anger. Today, I would have embraced him, loved him, and walked with him through that part of his life. I did take him to AA meetings, but I never knew what he thought of them. He never said and I never asked. Such was the style of fatherhood and leadership, of that time.

> I think we have just put another one like that in the White House. Reagan is the old model. He is even the child of an alcoholic. Probably we are not ready to support the new model, the leader who shares his weaknesses with his community. Together the leader and community can find their strength, not in themselves, but in God who shows us marvelous new resources when we share our weakness. This new model is scary and exciting. When will Americans be ready for it? When they are —he or she will show up.

This small family vignette showed me the transition from the 20th Century to the 21st.

Back at the Koegel's house, I was invited to stay longer. Although I considered the alternative, I felt the pull of my final plan. Departing seemed right. I gathered my few things from the bedroom, put them in the van, then came back to Barbara and Al. I tried to tell them how much I admired them. They had been heroic in their faithfulness, taking weak people into their home, walking with their own children through difficult times, following charismatic leaders into ways of real sacrifice. Here was a new kind of middle class American couple. They enjoyed the best of what America offered, but they remained centered on God. Nor were they critical of others. They just went about their life with God, listening, serving, taking in unexpected visitors like myself. They had learned to enjoy life with God, painful as it can be at times. It is exciting and unpredictable, taking one deeper into the mystery of death and resurrection. One does not always feel up to this life of faith. Sometimes the urge to draw away is strong. But the call of God is simply too strong and real.

I had given Barbara a small gift from Rome, a little cloisonne broach. I gave them both a hug and left with the only real gift I had: the assurance of my prayers and the clear hint that God was preparing all of us for a new sharing of His love. The disruption and violence of our times were but the surface reactions of people and races in pain. I said that we must stay in touch so that we, together, might better discern the Lord's new way.

THE LAST NIGHT

Back on the freeway with a full tank of fuel, I made my way southwest toward Battle Creek and the motor home dealer. I had traveled some 14,010 miles in my faithful van. Now it needed its 15,000 mile check-up. I wished I could almost have a service of recognition and gratitude for this marvelous machine that had accompanied me through many adventures.

To provide a few headings is to see the seven month journey in quick review:

23 states, some of them two or three times, plus the District of Columbia;
2 foreign countries, Italy and England;
20 parishes;
20 religious houses, convents or monasteries;
12 conference centers;
8 bishops;
6 cathedrals;
4 National Parks;
several music concerts, museums, monuments, a 21st Century city (Arcosanti), an American Indian Commune, a ranch, a prison, and a California mission.

Through it all, I had prayed the Office, said Mass in the van or in the homes of family or friends. It had been an extraordinary extended meditation. Is this what life in the Spirit can be?

As it turned out, the motor home dealer couldn't take me, so I continued on to the Abbey.

I swung into the Abbey's garage parking area and noticed one of the tires. It was almost flat. Perhaps I was feeling something like that, too. I went into the refectory and met a few of the brethren at tea, some nodding, some giving me a hug. Vespers followed soon afterward. I received a blessing and took my place in choir. It was good to be back with the brethren, saying the Office. I offered thanks in my heart for this wonderful gift, a gift of a lifetime. But how to communicate all this to the brethren without discounting their journey for the last seven months. I felt somewhat blank — loaded with impressions, afraid I could not share them, and uncertain of how to re-enter.

Over the next few days, I caught up on the news of the brethren's lives, unloaded the van, and began to sort the lumps of correspondence waiting for me. It would take time to re-enter but I was determined to see my cell, office space, and conference room anew, and simplify wherever possible. It was a great opportunity to see my life at the Abbey washed with the colors of my sabbatical experience. If I were to attempt a summary of that experience what would I say?

CHAPTER 31
THE SPIRIT'S REFLECTION

SUMMARY

Life is indeed a pilgrimage to God. I found the Spirit everywhere and all along the way. God was my companion, teaching, guiding, sharing His creation and friends, no doubt often laughing at and with me — enjoying the journey, too. My heart often found the sanctuary, friends and special places of a "presence," filling me with gratitude for the sabbatical journey. It was a gift to me through my brethren and the friends of the Abbey. It awakened me more deeply to the glory of the gift of life — and to the Giver. Being open to the Giver of life is the source of peace. (Appendix 3).

I experienced again the variety and the beauty of America. It is an amazing country, profound, overwhelming, even stirring up deep anxiety. In some three centuries, this land has seen people come from all over the world and develop it from a raw, pre-colonial frontier to a mega power. America is awesome; her responsibility is large — both promising and frightening. Being in Italy and England helped me to recall our roots in the Western culture. Perhaps most Americans never think of this. Even so, our task is to continue to nurture those roots, and to discern the next step in our human growth — a growth no longer simply Western. We are a people of one world and we must live and grow together. With many cultures and religions, this is an overwhelming responsibility. Can we find the way to peace so that the rich traditions of all human beings can compliment one another? We have just come to a precarious political balance with the people of the far East. Now, there are signs of unrest in the Middle East, South Africa, and mid-Europe.

We cannot end up in one super-culture. It must be an orchestration, not a world "noise." Closer to where we live in our local parishes and dioceses, my intuition suggests that we can and must accommodate to this rich complexity — now represented by people of many traditions and generations that hardly understand one another. Pluralism sounds formless. Diversity with a common humanness and Spirit sounds better. There can be a soul at the center, the life of Christ's Spirit. His Spirit is indeed the inspiration of all that is good everywhere. How can we simplify the life of the parish so that people of many backgrounds do not stumble over one another's culture? Can many small groups in the parish be allowed to explore various kinds of spirituality — classical Western, Eastern, AA, holistic health, journaling, meditation, exercise and diet, Biblical, Sacramental, environmental well-being, justice for the poor, inner-transformation programs, healing of memories, world peace, and many more? If a particular way of spirituality promotes health and growth, then Christ and the Spirit must surely be there — even if not named directly. Bringing all of this spirituality to the Eucharist could make it a celebration and a feast of extraordinary richness.

What is the place of the monk — and the ordinary baptized person — in this search for comprehensive spirituality? Spirituality is a combination of the wisdom gained from the human journey (biblically enriched for us Westerners) and real conversion — moving beyond the self center (Luke 9:24). Christians understand this conversion as a gift from Christ and His Spirit. The monk explores this gift in his daily life on behalf of all human beings. The monk also makes this exploration with the aid of large spaces of silence, the forgotten language of communion with the Divine. In silence one must come to peace and harmony with oneself and with God's compassion. Otherwise we cannot stand ourselves and we soon give up the silence — and faith. For we discover in ourselves all of the selfishness behind the world's violence and exploitation. We must be honest about this little self, but discover the Divine love of the Redeemer ready to forgive, heal, and lead us out of our selfishness. Monk or ordinary baptized person, we must all learn this painful lesson. It is a contemplative lesson. By being open to God's love in the complexity of our own life and in the world around us, we come to that steady stance before God which discovers the Divine as our center. Then His healing power and direction can flow freely in and through us.

At this time in history we desperately need this contemplative way of life. It is a gift which God longs to give us. It was a gift to St. Benedict. His Rule made that gift available to our Western culture. That same contemplative gift was made to other cultures and religions. It is given to all people. It is now time to receive a renewal of that gift, a way of simple openness to God for all people. This need not contradict any particular culture or tradition. In fact, it will verify it on the deepest level of our human and spiritual experience. Today, a number of life observers such as Ken Wilbur are using the word contemplative to describe the next stage of human growth — a stage beyond ego-centeredness. What the mystics have always known must now be made available everywhere to all persons.

I saw the yearning and the hints of spiritual desire all through my sabbatical journey. Now it is my privilege and my joy to nurture this contemplative opening wherever I find it. And it is everywhere, especially in those persons who have come to a dead end in a too mental, ego-centered, way of life. The art of opening up to God is mankind's next vocation. Let us share that calling, for it comes from deep within our hearts and deep within the Divine Heart. It is the work of the Spirit, joyously loose in the world.

Postscript:

Since writing these reflections a number of situations described in this account have changed, some of them considerably. I have included several items which occurred after the sabbatical. The emergence of the democratic movement in the world in the late 1980s, the feminine issue within the church, the allusion to new international conflict, and Giamatti's views of sports and religion all were evidence to me of the continuing Presence and movement which I saw and experienced. I have chosen to leave the original thought intact, dated as it is in some instances. This sabbatical was a one time glimpse of the vast mystery of life. The glimpse is gone, the outward form has gone back into the cosmic kaleidoscope — except in the memory, but the hints and clues about the mystery of the abiding wisdom and work of the Spirit remain.

APPENDIX

APPENDIX 1

WEEK OF REVIEW
JANUARY 23-27, 1984

Statements regarding Fr. Abbot's sabbatical:

I. Statement regarding Fr. Abbot's Chapter rights during the sabbatical.
    Registered in Chapter Minutes.

II. Twofold purpose of the sabbatical:

A. To allow seniors a time after 28 ½ years under the direction of Abbot Benedict for an alternative leadership style. Fr. Anthony was the seniors' choice as an interim leader. He should be allowed, within the Rule, his own way of governing. Negotiation and obedience are the two main factors in our tradition.

    1. This means that no important decision need be left for Fr. Abbot's return, unless there is some other good reason for doing so.

    2. Fr. Anthony and the seniors are free to:

        a. change the committee system;

        b. sell any portion of the land;

        c. change obedientiaries (department heads);

        d. reduce the number of meetings;

        e. limit outside engagements;

        f. resolve architectural and building questions;

        g. adapt the Constitution.

    3. The intention of giving the seniors this freedom is to allow them the experience of a different way of governing the community, and to make an intelligent decision at the time of the offering of resignation of the present abbot in April, 1986.

    4.   Some practical needs:

        a.   a secretary for architectural/fund raising affairs;

        b.   a replacement for the pastoral function of the abbot with guests;

        c.   a method of saving questions for agreed-upon days when the abbot will telephone the Abbey;

        d.   a form thank you, and a system for answering the abbot's mail;

        e.   a folder with names of people in on-going projects;
- architecture,
- fund raising,
- Foundation.

B.   To give the Father Abbot a chance to reflect on his role as abbot — with his emphasis on intuition and over-all long-range planning and group process.

    1.   To look at the advantages and disadvantages of being superior for more than 28 years.

    2.   To do some research on trends in the Church and the Religious Life for the future.

III. To grant interviews with the brethren in preparation for the sabbatical, in order to remove misunderstandings so that all are free to live without resentments.

IV. Father Anthony's statement:

A.   On Decision Making: to follow Chapter Three of the Rule — the superior assesses the input from the Community and then makes his decision. The democratic process of voting is permissible but not preferred.

B.   On The Wednesday Night Forum (discussion group): it provides an optional way for the monk to practice part of his vocation. Other options include developing a monk confidant; or going directly to God. However, as a result of the isolation it produces, the latter can debilitate the vocation.

C.   On The Monk as Member of Community: the monk is a Christian man with a community obligation of charity. At times when he does not possess that charity, the monk should absent himself from the meeting, etc., until he can resume an appropriate composure.

APPENDIX 2

SOME THOUGHTS ON THE POSITION OF SUPERIOR OF THE COMMUNITY

BY FR. ANTHONY; JANUARY 23, 1984

I. One of our problem areas, in my opinion, is that of decision making. I take Chapter 3 of RB as the working norm. In a community of our size, however, I should think that when the brethren are to be consulted, the junior part of the monastery should almost always be included. There will, of course, be a few questions which the seniors only should handle. With the appointment of obedientiaries and their assistants, and with consultation with all the monks, each should be able to realize that he shares in the management of the monastery.

The Superior hears all the opinions, and then *He* makes the decision (unless he wants to delegate that decision to another). I suppose there may be times when a vote could be taken, but the act of voting has its own inherent weaknesses as a fair system, and in effect, we have voted if the opinion of the community is heavily in one direction or another. Then the Superior makes the decision. That decision need not be the majority feeling expressed in the community, but it may often be so; in any event, it is his decision, made to the best of his ability.

II. The Wednesday Night Forum presents one way to exercise an essential part of one's vocation. If this group — which certainly should remain optional — is not a congenial setting for a monk, he should try to find another way, e.g., a monk-confidant, with whom he can talk over his inner problems and tensions. Normally this would seem to be the Novice Master for novices, the Junior Master for juniors, and the Abbot for seniors; but it would not be at all unusual to find personality differences which would seem to demand other persons fulfilling this function. If a monk finds that there is no one to do this for him, let him trust that God can do this directly; but he should realize that many vocations turn odd when lived in this type of isolation.

III. We are a group of adult Christian men, who are trying to live the life of Benedictine monks. Some are members of a monastic chapter and the rest are testing their aptitude for that responsible role. Therefore, contentious, childish or irascible behavior at meetings or anywhere in public should not be tolerated. No punishment need be given; the person simply absents himself until he can again assume his community obligation of charity.

APPENDIX 3

EXCERPT FROM CONFRATER'S LETTER,
SPRING 1984

You will read in the next Abbey Letter, soon to reach you, about my sabbatical. I will be away from the Abbey from just after Easter until Advent. I will be visiting various monasteries, convents, spiritual centers, parishes, and some friends too, posing this question: How have you learned to live in peace? Peace is intended to carry the Hebrew quality of a full humanity, growing and being shared with others. Wherever this peace is alive, I expect to find clues about the way of life for the future, a future which will be an intense conflict between chaos and faith. For I suspect that the stress and strain we now experience in this world is only the beginning. At the end of my pilgrimage I hope to gather some notes around this question to share with you. I will also return to my community which will have learned some valuable lessons too. We can compare notes and perhaps clarify our own way of living the Benedictine life. I encourage you to ask yourself the same question, How do we live in peace…?

Abbot Benedict

APPENDIX 4

"ON SABBATICAL"
REPRINTED FROM THE ABBEY LETTER, SPRING, 1984

From Easter until early Advent of this year (1984), I will be on sabbatical. Let me tell you how this developed.

A few years ago I realized that I was approaching 65, the age at which the constitution of the Abbey calls for the abbot to offer his resignation. The abbot submits his resignation, and the seniors (monks in life vows) vote whether or not to accept it. If they decline to accept his resignation, he continues as abbot for a few more years, when the process is repeated. Or the abbot may insist that his resignation be accepted for the good of all concerned.

The prospect of the beginning of this process two years from now started a train of questions within me. Would a 65-year-old superior, having served a community for over 31 years, have necessarily finished his fruitful time of leadership? How would I myself know when it was time to give up the office of abbot? Another vocational question came up, although it was one which did not seriously enter into my considerations: Would I permit my name to be entered as a candidate for bishop in a couple of diocesan elections? I do not feel called away from my monastic vocation, so I declined the nominations. All these things led me to consider the idea of a sabbatical leave.

A sabbatical year, in the Old Testament meaning, is a time of release from debts, a chance to begin anew. It occurred to me that I was at one of those moments in life when freedom from ordinary obligations was important if I were to discern God's will for me and the community for the future.

One purpose, then, of my sabbatical, is to give the community an opportunity to manage its affairs without me. Father Anthony, our prior, will be in charge. He and the other seniors have the freedom to rethink any of the Abbey's present policies. They could change our system of committees, for example, or sell some of the land (an asset to which I myself am especially partial). They could slant in a different way our methods of sharing authority in the monastery. I think it is important for the seniors and the other monks to have such an experience if they are to discern what is best for the community two years hence.

Another purpose of my sabbatical is to give me a chance to reflect, out of harness so to speak, on my life after nearly 36 years in the monastery, more than 28 of them spent as superior. As various writers have recently pointed out, it seems important that one know when one enters the age of wisdom (not necessarily possessing it, of course). In the last active stages of life, goals suited to a developing career are left behind. Americans seem generally slow to see that there is a special meaning to life in old age. When and how does that venerable wisdom come? This will be part of my search. And I am genuinely curious about the future of the Lord's Church in today's world. I want to travel across the States and visit a number of monasteries, convents, and spiritual centers to see if I can catch clues to the work of the Spirit. Osage Monastery in Oklahoma, for example, is active in East-West exchanges. Surely the attempt to understand one another across cultural lines is vital in our time. I will also go to Rome for the Abbots' Congress and to Nashdom Abbey, our mother house.

Friends have generously provided a small motor home to make my travel easier and to allow me often to remain in my "monastic cell," now on wheels. And then, there will be times of plain fun. I am a person who likes to roam state parks and forest preserves. My only embarrassment in my plans is that I can't possibly drop in on all of our friends. I can only count on your understanding if you discover that I have indeed passed close by you and did not stop. You will know that I did so regretting the difficult choices that limited time imposes.

You can be assured that your letters will receive careful attention. Fr. Anthony will be opening my mail. If there is some matter on which you want absolute confidentiality, you can prepare a separate note, so marked, and this can be forwarded to me. I will have designated mailing addresses, and I will phone the monastery frequently.

If indeed I am approaching the age of wisdom, I should not be surprised to learn that, while the community had a valuable experience in my absence, I did not learn anything radically new about God. I may find some hints about the future, but I don't expect to find anything totally different about the God of the future. I will remain a person of prayer in my traveling cell. I will be meditating on the One who is at one with his creation and simultaneously utterly beyond it. To be compassionate in the presence of God in people and silent in the presence of the Infinitely Silent One is the aim of the contemplative life. I don't need to travel to find God. But in making this pilgrimage, I will surely find out more about divine love. Different perspectives reinforce the enduring truth.

In any event, I hope to share with you in these pages some of the insights I gain. Perhaps I will stimulate your curiosity about your own life. It seems true to me that we are witnessing, often in violent forms, the breakdown of our culture. For persons of faith, it is important to focus on God's plan, to trust that he is indeed shaping a new way of life for this planet, and to be excited and confident about taking one's place in that plan. Even if you can't manage a sabbatical, take some time for a mini-pilgrimage. And more important, choose daily to enjoy your pilgrimage Partner. Blessings.

Fr. Abbot

APPENDIX 5

THE TWELVE STEPS

These steps can be a way of recovery for individuals and for families from any kind of addiction, as well as for members of Alcoholics Anonymous:

1. We admitted we were powerless over (_____), that our lives had become unmanageable.

2. Came to believe that a Power greater than ourselves could restore us to sanity.

3. Made a decision to turn our will and our lives over to the care of God as we understood Him.

4. Made a searching and fearless moral inventory of ourselves.

5. Admitted to God, to ourselves, and to another human being, the exact nature of our wrongs.

6. Were entirely ready to have God remove all these defects of character.

7. Humbly asked Him to remove our shortcomings.

8. Made a list of all persons we had harmed, and became willing to make amends to them all.

9. Made direct amends to such people wherever possible, except when to do so would injure them or others.

10. Continued to take personal inventory and when we were wrong, promptly admitted it.

11. Sought through prayer and meditation to improve our conscious contact with God as we understood Him, praying only for knowledge of His will for us and the power to carry that out.

12. Having had a spiritual awakening as the result of these Steps, we tried to carry this message to others, and to practice these principles in all our affairs.

APPENDIX 6

LIVING THE RULE OF ST. BENEDICT

PAPER GIVEN AT A BENEDICTINE CONFERENCE IN NEW HARMONY, INDIANA, 1984

The title of this paper permits me to be very personal. As of 1984, I have lived under the Rule of St. Benedict for nearly 36 years. Living only in one monastery, St. Gregory's Abbey, I have served as Novice Master and as Guestmaster at different times; as Conventual Prior for 14 years, and as abbot for an additional 15 years. In a small community, just now reaching a steady number of 20, this is not an unusual record. I don't intend to offer an academic commentary on the Rule, but rather one monk's personal struggle with, and appreciation for, the vigor of St. Benedict and his Rule. My feelings as well as my thoughts will give us all a way to understand our baptismal vocation, yours and mine, in the Christian life. For this baptismal vocation is the very essence of our humanity, stretched to its infinite dimension. To be human is to be open to the Divine. St. Paul expresses it this way, "For by grace you have been saved (made whole) through faith; and that not of yourself, it is the gift of God" (Eph. 2:8).

HISTORY

Very briefly, we may note that the Rule comes from a long tradition of ascetical living that predates the New Testament. I am not even considering the monastic tradition outside Christianity although that is a valid study. An Abraham, a Moses, or an Ezekiel give us glimpses of a personal faith journey, lived out at an interior depth which suggests the monastic quality of searching for, and living with, God. John the Baptist may have lived in a particular community, the Essenes, which expressed certain monastic elements for that time (poverty, chastity, obedience, shared goods, and a common life of prayer). Finally, our Lord himself, in his celibacy, simplicity of life, and obedience to the Father, exemplifies the supreme model for the monk. One should quickly add that He also provides the supreme model for all baptized persons, whatever their vocation.

In the Book of Acts, we see the emergence of a Christian life which was centered on faith, on community, on prayer and sacrament, sharing of goods, and on ministry (Acts 2:42-47). It is easy to trace the evolution of this early pattern into the life of the Desert

Fathers, those heroic, and sometimes neurotic, pioneers of the monastic and hermetic life. Certain figures like St. Pachomius, St. Anthony, and St. Basil clarified and codified the monastic ideal. It should not surprise us then to realize that St. Benedict (480-540 AD) inherited a rich and mature monastic tradition. In fact, we know that he took a pre-existing rule, established previously by a person known only as the Master, for the basis of his own version of a guide for monks. With this rich monastic heritage it was possible for a spiritual genius like St. Benedict to reshape the monastic life without distorting its ideals. The result is a Rule which is famous for its balance of inspired direction for unlimited growth in sanctity and a common sense understanding of the average person (Chapter 73). At the end of the Prologue, St. Benedict writes, "And so we are going to establish a school for the service of the Lord. In founding it we hope to introduce nothing harsh or burdensome. But if a certain strictness results from the dictates of equity for the amendment of vices or the preservation of charity, do not be at once dismayed and fly from the way of salvation... for as we advance in the religious life and in faith, our hearts expand and we run the way of God's commandments with unspeakable sweetness of love."

PERSONAL VOCATION

Without attempting to trace the history of the Rule in Christendom — except to note that certain periods of the Medieval era were known as the Benedictine centuries — I will now offer my reflections from my own experience. In the summer of 1948 at the age of 27, I came to St. Gregory's, then a newly founded Priory of Nashdom Abbey, an Anglican Benedictine monastery in England. I was a lay person with ordinary parochial experience but no real understanding of monasticism. From California, I drove my model A Ford across the desert, having left my family and friends in some uncertainty about my decision. With my skis poking out one window and my guitar propped up in the back seat, I arrived in Three Rivers, Michigan. The nine year old Priory and the new postulant were both idealistic, naive, and inexperienced. But there was the Rule and its tradition to guide us. I did not know that St. Gregory was the Benedictine pope who sent St. Augustine to England in 597. I was unaware that St. Augustine used the Benedictine model in setting up his episcopal See, a fact that gave a Benedictine, some would say a monastic, shape to the English Church from the 6th century on. So I did not understand that my life in the Episcopal Church was already deeply affected by the Benedictine emphasis on liturgy and community. I only sensed that the two fully professed American monks, Dom Paul and Dom Francis, at the little farm house priory, and the novice, Br. Joseph, along with myself and another postulant, were involved in a way of life with deep spiritual roots. (Dom was a title for a fully professed monk — not used so widely today.) I had a college degree from a Jesuit university, my previous education at Dartmouth College having been interrupted by World War II where I served in the Air Force. I also had good health and an exuberance of youthful energy and self-assurance. All of this was to be stretched beyond what I could imagine. But then I innocently prayed that I be given a life far beyond my own capacity. The Lord answered that prayer generously — or put the prayer into me. What attracted me to monasticism was the ordered life of liturgical prayer, community life, and time for private study and reflection. I slowly discovered that prayer, personal and corporate, was the appropriate medium for my intuitive bent to explore the mystery of life. And community was the context in which I could understand what it meant to be in the Body of Christ. Quoting the Psalmist, St. Benedict in the Prologue asks, "Who is the man who will have life, and desires to see good days?" I believe that I came to the monastery in response to that question, and to have access to a way of life in which I could give myself wholeheartedly to God. A small group of people, living the Rule, provided me with the opportunity to fulfill my deepest longing. But I had no real comprehension of how much of my human self was in that longing. And my older sister, my parents having died, who came to check out what her little brother had gotten into, was convinced that the monastery was a total mistake for Dickie!

COMMUNITY

Here is the bittersweet mystery of the common life. It does indeed offer a person a time-tested way of living for God in a spiritual family. But people seldom achieve the ideal of community they carry in their imagination. And their ideals vary considerably. However, after 3 1/2 decades, I still believe that it is possible for a cenobite, that is, a person who "lives in a monastery and serves under a rule and an abbot" (Chapter 1) to have a reasonable hope of finding true happiness. Monks and nuns are not special kinds of people. They are those who, in the mystery of God's love, are willing to live out their baptism by a rule of grace. In this sense, the monastery is a small version of the Church, where the monk stands for all the baptized. The monastic emphasis expresses one form of the irreducible elements of humanness and grace, looking beyond time for fulfillment.

But the price of maintaining such a vocation is far greater than I suspected. The price is the pain of a slow death in the way we understand ourselves. This sounds exciting when read in a book, but it is an agonizing transformation that requires a clear faith that we share the Lord's own death and resurrection. And this death and resurrection, His and ours, is the norm for all people. The Epistle to the Romans (6:4) comes to mind: "...when we were baptized we went into the tomb with him and joined him in death, so that as Christ was raised from the dead by the Father's glory, we too might have a new life."

For a middle class American with a circumscribed experience of family life (an addictive father and an atypical family of five boys and a girl) this living out of one's baptism became, and continues to be, ever more exacting. New depths of one's humanity, its gifts and brokenness, continued to be revealed. And as married people can attest, individuals discover different aspects of hurt and joy in one another, come to wisdom in different ways, and reach the essential level of powerlessness at different times. Each person's complexity is revealed in the rough and tumble of family life. And yet this common life is the very context that St. Benedict uses for the spiritual maturing of his monks. I had no inkling that there was a lost childhood within me, buried under a continual striving after great aspirations. The child of an alcoholic or dysfunctional parent learns to survive by not talking, not feeling, not trusting. This survival pattern then becomes, no doubt unconsciously, part of adult life. But the tension of such a suppressed childhood creates stress in human relationships and fuels exaggerated ambitions.

BR. JOSEPH

I remember the strange journey of our Br. Joseph. He was the first American trained monk to persevere at St. Gregory's. He was the one who, on my arrival when I had gone into the quonset chapel to pray and offer my life to God, beckoned me outside to help unload a truck of building materials that had just arrived. In such a simple and direct way, using a very practical Br. Joseph, did God begin my monastic education. Well, somewhere, somehow, in the ensuing years, under the pressure of holding his humanity to the faith, he emotionally broke. He had what the doctors called a schizophrenic episode. But they acknowledged that they were not sure what that meant. After times in and out of the mental hospital, after years of living a limited monastic life, of being treated as a "sick" person, he became an intriguing combination of psychic unbalance and faith, held together precariously in the Benedictine community of his profession by his early training, by the mysterious force of life, and by the love of his brethren. And through it all, he retained his humor. One day, toward the end of his life, he broke into profanity, a very untypical expression of frustration for him. A younger brother remonstrated mildly with him, saying that swearing didn't do any good. Br. Joseph replied in simple logic, "How do you know?" From such human examples, one grows to appreciate the practical compassion of the Rule in Chapters 36 and 37 as it makes careful and loving provision for the sick and the old.

OBEDIENCE

Obedience, as described in Chapter 5 and throughout the Rule, is a central quality of monastic life. As a young monk, I lived under several priors at different times and under one abbot in England. How tempting it is to appear to be obedient, to conform outwardly, and still manage to gain advantages for oneself. And when the abbot is in England, for we were a dependent Priory for some 30 years, one can hear these kinds of arguments running in one's head, "How would he know, he's not an American," or, "I would like to see him handle this character," or, "I hope he doesn't hear about this because I am improvising wildly." Fortunately, I had an understanding abbot in England. But the "job description" of an abbot is awesome. The Rule says that the abbot "…holds the place of Christ," (Chapter 2). One has to meditate for years on how Christ rules and study the various checks and balances in the Rule, before one can bring wisdom to such an office. In fact, an abbot is powerless without faithful monks. In Chapter 71, the Rule says that the brethren are to be obedient to one another. Obviously St. Benedict is much more than a legalist. My experience with Americans has shown me that the brethren often approach obedience either as children facing a demanding parent, or as teenagers, rebelling because that is the only way they know how to assert themselves. Why? That is not clear to a young person. Only slowly do we all learn that by obedience we move beyond the ego, the ordinary self, toward charity. It is a way of loving God and our neighbor. St. Benedict in his realistic understanding knows that at first it will be a labor (Prologue), but in time it will be an effective escape from the tyrant within and a freedom to love others. Our Lord himself, according to the Epistle to the Hebrews (5:8), "...learned obedience from the things which he suffered." It is a way of growth for all of us. Growth involves not only attitudes but an incredible development in the whole person. Spiritual growth stretches our humanness including our neural, muscular, and cellular life to indescribable dimensions. When this growth is taking place in community, the spirit of the common life can be sweet and exciting, although much of it is hidden. And when there are experienced deans (Chapter 21), and a good Prior (Chapter 65), both of which it has been my privilege as a superior to have, the corporate life can be a hint of heaven.

Occasionally, obedience becomes heroic (Chapter 68, If A Brother Is Commanded To Do Impossible Things). The impossibility is usually not intended. It just arises out of peculiar situations that get out of reasonable control. There were times in my life as a young Prior when I literally had no one with whom I could talk — or didn't know how to ask for help. Such pressure stretches us beyond our ordinary human limitations. We wonder if we possess real control of our lives, from some common sense center within. Yes, we do but it is limited. And inevitably we try to manage and fulfill our lives by our own power. This never works. Do we have true access to God's power? Definitely, but this is available only through surrendering ourselves to God. Everyone faces this according to his vocation. Such a surrender feels like a death. Surprisingly, it proves, if we truly surrender to God, to be a way into more life. So an abbot and his brethren are on a dangerous spiritual journey that invokes feelings of oppression and anxiety at times, and at other times great excitement. I never guessed how much childhood damage I was bringing to the exercise of obedience.

THE ABBOT

In former centuries, the spiritual leader was often the most educated person in the group. So he was the priest, the cleric, the gifted one, the person in authority. There are still strong traces of that paternalism in the Church today. But in a contemporary monastery, all of the brethren are educated and many have extraordinary gifts. And life today is far more complex. This Abbot does not intrude, for example, on the computer world, although he appreciates the vast changes it is making in the world. Obedience now becomes more of a corporate process by which the brethren seek God's will as it is revealed, yes, in a given tradition (monastic in our case), but revealed also in a bewildering set of new circumstances. Of course, there are times when the abbot must make a decision, simply to help the community get past a dilemma. But the deeper questions remain, waiting for sensitive and mutual discernment. St. Benedict is right up to date in Chapter 3, On Calling The Brethren To Counsel. This may mean a long and mutually exploratory process between the abbot and an individual, or with the gathered group. Such an exploration takes real skill on everyone's part. Priests are not the only mediators. The one who can help the community develop communal skills in listening, talking courteously, showing respect even when there is strong disagreement, waiting in humility, dealing with anger — this person is meditating, making Christ present at the moment.

My own brethren sometimes get impatient with meetings. I think that this is the natural result of our clumsiness in discernment. We have just taken the Myers-Briggs test, a test which, without passing judgment, reveals each person's gift and weakness. Such a test is an example of how a modern insight into human nature can enrich ancient wisdom. Once one knows oneself and one's brother in this "given" sort of way, it is much easier to understand one another. And with understanding comes compassion. One is not so surprised, or overwhelmed, when someone's weakness, even darker side, is "dumped" on people nearby.

It is obvious why it is important for a community to exercise prudence in selecting its abbot (Chapter 64). Our Constitution, a governmental document that each monastery draws up for itself, requires that the abbot submit his resignation at age 65. In 1986 I will be at that age. So at this time, I am taking a sabbatical, both to give the community a real experience of an alternative style of leadership, in this case under our Fr. Prior, and to give myself a time out of harness in which to reflect on my own spiritual journey. I am taking this opportunity to visit various monasteries, convents, parishes, and other spiritual centers to see if I can discern signs of the direction Christian life will take in the future. For there are plenty of signs that the world is finishing up its present chapter, and moving into an as yet unknown new way. Violence always marks such a transition. It is not unlike the turmoil in which St. Benedict himself lived in the 6th century, a fact which prompted him to withdraw from the world and to center his life as a monk on God. He had no intention of reforming the world. But the result of his focus on God, according to a well-established tradition, created a Christian form of community which in fact did provide a model for much of the shaping of what we today call Europe. His Rule was a form of the Gospel which helped convert the Western world.

DEATH AND NEW LIFE

Our Christian wisdom tells us that there can be no real conversion except through death. The life of a human cell would be instructive, and a study of the DNA imprint on cells reveals a fascinating stamp of the source of life. But we are mainly aware of our conscious life. So we must deal with the death of our limited understanding, of human nature, of attitudes which create enemies, some of whom now have nuclear power, of life without love. Death in the world leads us to confront divine love which wants people to be friends with God and with one another. To move through death into love, we must share our lives and our faith and ironically, we must share our death. For it is through weakness, honestly acknowledged and shared, that the Spirit of the living God works to bring us to new life.

Part of the death we must transcend is our sexual selfishness. Chastity is the responsible use of sexual love. For the monk living as a single person in community, such responsibility helps him absorb sexual energy into work, charity, and worship. This is not an easy achievement, no easier than the very conversion of our self-centeredness into the wholeness of our new self. But the witness of chastity, celibate or married, is a sign that sexuality is a gift of God's love, to be returned to Him in worship. Married love is one form of that worship. Celibacy is another. Both forms of love glorify God. Celibacy must turn its human longing into loving God more directly. Loneliness, endured in faith, becomes one kind of intimacy with the Divine, an intimacy which focuses our deepest longings — longings, deeper than the flesh or the ego. Chastity as responsible sexuality finally becomes a freedom to receive the "longing" of God. For God is lonely, too. He longs for our love. Can a person, single or married, endure loneliness until such freedom is achieved? That is each person's journey in love.

HUMILITY

This may be a timely place in this paper — and in our time — to consider the virtue of humility which St. Benedict emphasizes so strongly. In the opening phrases of Chapter 7, On Humility, St. Benedict quotes Scripture, "Everyone who exalts himself shall be humbled, and he who humbles himself shall be exalted". Here again, we have the human dilemma: cling to the most precious center of our life, our very self, and fail utterly to fulfill our life; or submit ourselves to God in faith, through a process ordained by God and His Church, and trust that we will in fact come to the true fulfillment of life. This is a profound and eternal dilemma. But it is most acute when we come to moments of anxiety, personal or corporate, when our natural instinct prompts us to hang on all the more tightly to the only thing we have, our very self. A recent experience in our community provides a dramatic commentary.

One of our monks who does outside ministry slipped gradually into an alcoholic pattern. We did not notice it in the community. Eventually, friends who loved our brother, and who were skilled in what is called an "intervention," came to the monastery and received my permission to discuss the matter with him. Because of their love and their skill, and such skill requires that there be irrefutable evidence but no judgment, the monk acknowledged his condition. He was in fact relieved. He went off to an alcoholic treatment center. Their skill and compassion is a remarkable example of a modern healing process. Since that process strongly encourages the family to participate in the healing, another brother and I spent a week at the treatment center. We formed a small support group of people who were there on behalf of members of our family receiving treatment. While receiving an education on the nature of alcoholism as a disease, it slowly dawned on us that we ourselves were being asked to recover. From what? From living unlovingly and unconsciously with a member of our family who was in fact very ill.

The therapist asked me, "David, how does it feel for you to be here?" I corrected her, saying that my name was Benedict. "Sorry," she said, "you remind me of the last abbot we had here. You abbots are all alike." Well, in trying to answer her question I fumbled considerably. Finally she said, "You don't know how it feels." I realized that we had shifted attention from getting information to some personal involvement in the question of addiction.

By this time I was annoyed with her and her questions. But with love and skill she helped me return to my own childhood and to recognize that growing up with an alcoholic father had indeed taught me to survive. And in this survival we learn, mostly unconsciously, to cling to ourselves. Such surviving includes learning not to feel, not to talk, not to trust. With shock and dismay, I gradually saw how deeply and blindly I was hanging on to survival patterns learned in childhood. And now I was employing this pattern as an adult, as a Christian, and as the abbot of a community. I had to recover. This was a recent experience of humility for me.

Surprisingly, the teachings on humility in the Rule are very close to the Twelve Steps of AA. The Spirit has been saying the same thing in every age. Let go and let God. But it is not only self-will we must let go of, but of deep and unconscious damage, including anything unforgiven. We are inclined to think that our past and our childhood with its normal deaths and resurrections are our own business. But whatever we are is part of our life with others. As St. Paul says, "...we are members one of another" (Romans 12:5).

> How we come to peace in our small Christian groups is precisely how we will come to world peace. Humility is living in harmony and truth with the earth, with all human beings, with our human nature, with every living cell everywhere in the world.

WORSHIP

St. Benedict does not expect us to achieve a humble condition overnight or with a few virtuous intentions. He gives his monks daily exercises. First, there is the Work of God as he calls the liturgy. He spends Chapters 8 through 20 on this subject. Whatever one feels like or wants to do, the work of God comes first. This brings the monk back again and again to the essential purpose of life, to praise God because He is God and for the gift of life. But it can also grate on one's nerves at times: the same psalms, the same brethren (who often sing flat), the relentless rubrics which control our feelings and subjective wishes so that there is in fact an orderly way of corporate offering — all of these press upon our fragile human condition. The monastic choir is a great training for focusing and elevating one's life. Perhaps a mother of children or a man running a business can appreciate the ordinary work aspect of a monk's prayer. The world will never come to its fulfillment until it recognizes its responsibility to praise the Creator. Is that likely to happen soon? No matter, the monk is a sign of that truth.

PERSONAL PRAYER

The monk's personal prayer derives much of its content from the liturgy and from lectio, a daily perusal of the Bible. From reading and reflecting, he gradually progresses toward a few simple concepts or even a word. Repeating such a word (e.g., Jesus), can lead a person into depths of silence where one is simply aware that God is. This is a true experience of God, although it is far beyond the senses and even the mind. And it is of no immediate practical use in daily life. It may bring one to a deeper sense of peace, but it is not "useful." If it were, we would be back in the world of the ego, the place where I am in control. Such prayer takes a lifetime to develop. And people travel this path in different ways. St. Benedict speaks very little about how to practice personal prayer. He assumes that it will arise naturally from living responsibly by a Rule centered on God. Of course, he provides times of silence and privacy. The exercise of discovering God in prayer is accompanied by a parallel discovery, the discovery of oneself.

What part of me argues that to experience God, I must see, taste, touch, hear or smell Him? It is that ego center. What part of me rattles on with clever arguments arising from my conflict with someone? It is that wounded self. What part of me dreams great fantasies of achievement, for God of course? It is that self that seeks exaltation, on its own terms. Why does my body always itch or tighten up in tension when I have decided to pray? It is my body's attempt to keep me at the physical level. Why do I get depressed when reading books on prayer? The reason is that I have not come to a kind of self respect that dares to let God be my friend, exactly as I am, with my peculiar way of loving Him.

Prayer will eventually lead us to reject both God and ourselves, or to smile, swallow our pride, and accept both in love. Now, one can see the adventure of the hermit. With a full understanding of his place in the Body of Christ, he enters deeply into that dialogue between the Father and the Son which by grace raises him to the height of friendship with God. Intimacy with God is the greatest gift of the divine love. But how much easier to talk about loving God than to do it.

GOOD WORKS

Another arena of the monk's life is his work with the brethren. Sometimes this is exciting when we are able to cooperate and achieve the order and harmony of a small village. Monasteries, in history, have often been complex clusters of buildings and operations. When there is peace among the occupants, they are signs of the redeemed life. At St. Gregory's we are gradually developing various departments: the sacristy which stores all the things used in worship; the Chapter room where we work out communal decisions, and sometimes relationships; the library where monks and guests can find a wealth of reading to help them in the search for God (as well as novels, books on travel, humor, art, and poetry); the common room where we have recreation with records, tapes, letters from friends, current periodicals, and great attention given to the cats — those creatures of apparent indifference who nevertheless provide endless entertainment; the kitchen where our daily food needs are prepared as well as great feasts provided for special occasions. Then there are administrative offices where we wrestle with all of the modern problems of housing rentals, insurance, tax questions, and the like. Another department is our publishing office. Our Abbey Letter is, of its kind, an admired monastic journal. Also, we do much of our own maintenance, landscaping, and wood cutting. There are the very important departments of formation (Chapters 58-60) in which the young monks are trained, not easy today when the tradition is being reviewed and reformulated; and the guest department which ministers to a steady stream of visitors and groups.

What blessings pour out of our life when our daily life and work are infused with the joy and peace of Easter. This quality of peace and joy, which arises from an observant community, gives to the Benedictine life a sense of celebration. It is the Kingdom now. But what frustration if the community slips away from the hard work of daily awareness of death and resurrection.

Many of the problems that come to my attention as abbot have to do with work conflicts. This is especially true of Americans who were raised on a work ethic. Your worth is what you do. It is a hard struggle to learn to employ the Instruments of Good Works as listed in Chapter 4. These are mainly works of faith and attitude rather than works of practical use as a modern person would view them. And it is deeply humiliating to realize that what we say in the liturgy does not always penetrate the heart. It is not unusual, if we are honest, to discover that we have two theologies, two Gods. A community is truly blessed if it has a cellarer (Chapter 31) who indeed can be "like a father to the whole community." For the successful mediation of problems and people in conflict requires a fatherly compassion. It takes divine tact to remind a hard-working practical American (Chapter 57) that his tools and the materials he is handling are in truth part of the vessels of the altar (Chapter 31), part of communal worship.

POVERTY

Benedictine poverty (Chapters 33, 54, 55) is not a way of being deprived. Rather it is a way of celebrating creation. And yet it is a demanding task to distinguish between a mindless affluence (the spirit of our age) and a spirit of celebration which is ready to share with others. St. Gregory's has an annual operating budget of more than $275,000. This budget supports the use of all forms of modern insurance, credit cards, electric typewriters and computers, three cars and a motor home (in which I am making this sabbatical pilgrimage), tractors and farm machinery, well-supplied workshops — and now a building program which exceeds three million dollars. How can a modern monk in the West talk about poverty? He can, in fact, dare to do so if he is constantly aware of the dangers, the egoism, in the possession of many things. If love of God and of neighbor infuses the use of many things, then the secular world is given a model of a redeemed world. But it takes a faithful community to achieve the kingdom of heaven on earth.

In contrast, there are people today, and not all of them from the '60s, who live an extremely simple lifestyle as a witness to the spiritual power of poverty. There are millions who live this witness by necessity, their starvation pointing to the results of a consumer-centered culture in the affluent parts of the world. Violence and revolution are, at base, a cry for justice. St. Benedict (Chapter 34), again quoting Scripture notes: "distribution should be made according to need." This principle touches the world's condition directly.

Monastic poverty in a religious house in the Western world can only be lived out in a painful consciousness of the world situation. An attempt to be simple while living in the affluent West is a daily trial of conscience. To hear the TV news regularly, is to be confronted regularly. It is this very trial of conscience that will, in time, help to create a one-world aware-ness. Nothing short of that will bring us to the necessary decisions regarding justice and peace. At St. Gregory's, we tithe 10% of all major gifts given to us. The monastery, following the principle of distribution according to need, can be a prophetic sign for the world.

DISCIPLINE

Being painfully aware of the world helps a committed Christian to see discipline in a new light. We should not discipline ourselves in order to feed an inner desire to be in control of our lives. Discipline means being the disciple of the Lord of the Universe and of all of His people. Discipline prepares us to serve. St. Benedict spends Chapters 23 to 30 and 43 to 46 dealing with the inner discipline of the monastery. But the monastery, or any Christian community, can now be seen as a microcosm of the shrinking "global village," as Marshall McLuhan's phrase goes. So the principles of discipline in the Rule, established for the wel-fare of community, can be instructive for the world. Watching the maneuvers of govern-ments and their diplomats, one sees them struggling desperately for some kind of balance of power in the world community. Can it be achieved without attention to justice and to the source of life itself? Can compassion be brought to human affairs except through the source of compassion, God's love? Compassion, balance, and moderation are all marks of the Rule (Chapter 70).

Yet, in this world community, we are faced with pluralism in religion and culture, and with large portions of a population with no faith. Serious commitment for the sake of the world order and justice can lead to martyrdom. Martyrs are not necessarily wise or well-informed, but they give their lives for God's purpose as they understand it. Think of the martyrs, on both sides, in Central America, Africa, the Near East, and China. We are prob-ably heading into a time when we, too, must live our lives more simply for God and for the welfare of the world community. St. Benedict (Chapter 49) speaks of the Lenten quality which should mark the whole life of a monk. It would seem that the world is moving toward a long Lent.

SILENCE

To face a world in turmoil can produce opposite reactions in people, even in the faithful. They can decide to support some action aimed at reducing injustice. Or, they can gather their resources on behalf of their loved ones and dig a protective hole somewhere, trying to enjoy for a while the good things of life which do not seem abundant enough to share with others. Monastic silence seems to miss the point of both positions. But in silence (Chapter 6), properly employed, the monk is going beyond action and escape. He is going to the source of action, to adore. In the stilling of his human, and sometimes neurotic, impulses he opens himself to the One Who is pure act. Such exposure is painful. For silence shows us a God Who seems content with injustice in the world. Silence also exposes us to our own selfish action. We want to change things and people to suit ourselves. We must either give up silence — and the modern Western culture has largely done that — or penetrate its secret more deeply. Silence can make way for the revelation of divine love. In silence we experience God's patience with all that is wrong in creation. God's patience is revealed to us in the Crucified God on the Cross (Ephesians 2:16). He takes responsibility. He doesn't wait in eternity for us to change ourselves and the world. He bears the results of our choices in His Body, in His very being. He makes Himself vulnerable to all of the pain and hurt of every human being everywhere. And He shares that very being of love. He invites us into His weakness (Col. 1:24, Gal. 6:17). In silence we listen to the silent God Who will not judge the world (John 12:47). His love is His only judgment. Awe-filled and trusting silence is our openness to that love.

One time, conducting a retreat for an Archbishop and his diocesan bishops, we came to the question of trust. The Archbishop, perhaps because he was nearing retirement, became very honest. "Benedict," he said, "do you mean that I am supposed to trust my brother bishops? Well, I don't. I have a file on each one of them with plenty of problems."

I closed my Bible and remarked, "Brethren, I can't bail us out of that." So we waited, and the silence was oppressive. Finally, together, we began to fumble with the answer. We can't, and don't trust one another. But God trusts us anyway. Awesome! What love! In the strength of that love we are moved to commitment.

VOWS

The Benedictine vows, (Chapter 58) stability, conversion, and obedience predate the later version of the evangelical counsels. But the same qualities of poverty and chastity are contained in the Benedictine vows. In a time when commitment and perseverance are disintegrating, all vows seem either outdated and unreal, or blindly heroic. We at St. Gregory's have had our share of departures. At first, these seemed a gross breakdown in personal integrity. Now we have a far more compassionate understanding of the complexity of human choices under stress. We are also gaining a deeper appreciation for the support that the community must give to an individual. Is this not true of baptism, marriage, and priesthood? So the question of vows involves the deep, nurturing, interaction between a monk and his community.

GUESTS

Guests (Chapter 53), are both a blessing and a burden for a monastery. I am happy to acknowledge my deep personal debt to guests. For in the confiding of their lives to me, I have understood my own life more completely. They have lived out parts of my life which I did not recognize or want to accept. And in the God-given compassion I was allowed to share with them, I have been healed of some of my own childhood wounds. What greater joy is there than the sharing of a healing touch of God's love. Then there are the special friends outside the monastery who accepted me as the particular human being that I am. Being a monk, a priest, an abbot can be a heavy load to carry. One can be the target of the unrecognized and unclaimed hurt of others, unconsciously projected. What a relief to have a few friends who do not engage in such painful transactions! How much of my own understanding of life I owe to my loving friends I cannot even measure.

GOOD ZEAL

Chapter 72, On The Good Zeal Which Monks Ought To Have, is a suitable theme with which to close these reflections. Zeal is a powerful force when it is purified of selfishness. And when so freed, this zeal is infused with a deep joy, the joy of the Lord. But of itself, a Rule cannot guarantee such spiritual maturity. That process is hidden within the mystery of the human heart where the person and His God work out their relationship. St. Benedict respects that truth in the last Chapter 73, in which he acknowledges that his little rule for beginners is only the threshold of an unlimited spiritual adventure.

We may reflect today whether it is time for another simplified version of the Gospel adapted for communal use? Ordinary people need a way to share their humanity and their faith. There is a deep spiritual hunger, akin to the yearning at the time of the Gospel, for an escape from an imprisoning collective form of life into a more just and peaceful celebration of our glorious human share in creation. Witness in our time the revival of all kinds of religious expressions, some of it strange and unfamiliar. Witness the religious fervor of the Islamic world. Witness the secular form of violence that is tearing the world apart. Within this fervor there is a universal longing for happiness. But that longing is mixed with darkness and light — a mixture that will prevail apparently to the end of time. For Christians, Christ is the light, the Omega point, of creation's story.

People of faith believe that we are on the verge of a new breakthrough chapter in this longing. And in the world of scientific exploration, awesome discoveries herald that new chapter . What is a laser beam? What is a computer chip? What place does imagination and faith play in the cure of cancer? How far out does space go? How far in can we see into the human person? The great minds and spirits of our time are networking, not in an organization, but in a shared vision. But can they ever overcome evil? Not likely, unless they are people of faith.

Now we are back to the essential monastic quality of faith, lived out by the monk on behalf of everyone. There is something of this monastic quality in everyone. The monk is a sign of the baptized person. The Benedictine Rule has served mankind for over 14 centuries. Will it inspire a Rule for our time, a simplified way of living the Gospel for the complex person of the 21st Century? Will it prove to be one of the universal documents for all time? St. Benedict, pray for us.

APPENDIX 7

A TALK BY ABBOT BENEDICT TO THE SENIOR MEMBERS OF A RELIGIOUS COMMUNITY

Brethren, I bring you greetings from St. Gregory's. I apologize for yet another meeting, but I have some impressions which I wish to bring before you. These are my own. I am not speaking for your superior or for the younger members of the community. I offer these, as well as the retreat that will follow, as some measure of recognition of a shared style of vocation in the Church.

I have read the Bishop Visitor's [the special bishop who represents the community to the whole Church] charge. I have listened to a number of you. I see certain signs of life, and some of death. I have some sensitivity in discernment through my thirty years as a priest, through my work as Chaplain General for a community of women, and through my experience on the Advisory Council for Religious. I am sixty-three years of age, and have been a monk for thirty-six years, twenty-nine as superior.

The signs of death (not to overlook the obvious signs of life) are typical of individuals or groups undergoing a death process. We may note that death is a Christian event and can be experienced with faith and dignity. It is not my intention to analyze the Kubler-Ross signs of death: denial, anger, bargaining, depression, but rather to look at a way forward into life. Let's consider two possible plans, and you must test my proposals by your own faith and experience.

PLAN A:
Do nothing. But I sense that there will be between one and five departures in the next year, perhaps including an older member of the community. Of course, you inevitably have natural deaths. Then there is the question of whether you even want to keep the novitiate open. But I encourage you not to use valuable energy in brooding or guilt. You need all of your energy.

PLAN B:
1. Recognize the likelihood of departures allowing yourselves genuine grief over these losses, and prepare yourselves to conserve your energy and peace.

2. Work with an outside person who can help you:
   a. preserve your dignity and freedom of choice;
   b. preserve your trust that God is working with you;
   c. preserve your self-respect as Christian Religious. You have a valuable experience in a venerable tradition. You have a solid place in the Church and you have many friends and oblates.

3. Be ready to hire workers if necessary, maybe intern oblates with a serious intention to live the Religious Life who are not free, for one reason or another to make the full commitment. Then the monks can conserve energy and continue to live the life of prayer. Consider a smaller house, or houses.

4. Gather a special group of outside friends, the Visitor, clergy and laity, who will share this special time with you.

5. Give your superior, who knows you, a real chance to lead you — allowing him to point out certain faults which are debilitating to the community, so that your best faith and energy are available to discern and comply with God's will.

I apologize for the obvious in these suggestions, but they are my honest evaluation — and they may serve to stimulate your thinking. Thank you for sharing your life with me at this special moment of grace.

APPENDIX 8

SERMON

DELIVERED AT CHURCH OF ST. JOHN THE EVANGELIST
SAN FRANCISCO, CALIFORNIA

AUGUST 19, 1984

In the name of the Father, and of the Son and of the Holy Spirit. Amen.

I am the Father Abbot of St. Gregory's Abbey, a Benedictine Monastery in the Episcopal Church located in Three Rivers, Michigan. I'm on sabbatical right now so I'm making a swing through the continent to see what the Lord is doing.

This morning God is doing a workshop in the parish Eucharist. And I'm not the leader but I'll comment on what I think God is opening up for us. It's a workshop on separation. In the readings [Isaiah 56: 1-7; Romans 11: 13-15, 29-32; Matthew 15: 21-28], you heard Isaiah talking about foreigners and Paul talking about pagans, and then we have the Canaanite woman who is herself in the eyes of the Jews a separated person, a foreigner and a pagan.

Now that doesn't sound like a very attractive workshop. But of course the Lord doesn't want to leave it there. To get into the Lord's workshop, let's get in touch with a memory. A memory is where we store a lot of energy, especially if it's a good memory. So I'd like to take just a moment and invite each one to remember a time when maybe you were a foreigner, an outcast, and someone found you, or maybe the roles were reversed and you found someone who was "outside." If you feel energy when you recall that memory, you are already in the workshop. Sense how the Lord as expressed in the Collect is the sacrifice for everything that is separated, a bridge that connects. In the Hebrew understanding, sin is what is separating, so in feeling the energy in the good memory, you touch the Lord's love and his genius for bringing back the separated person.

Paul says that we are imprisoned in disobedience. I'd like to connect that with our thoughts this morning, imprisoned in a bad memory of being separated. And if we are so imprisoned, we feel separated from the Lord. What we're looking at is how the Lord works, going back and forth between good memories and bad memories, healing our experience of separation.

Sometimes we choose to stay in a prison of separation because we are familiar with that world. It's more comfortable. We know what our response should be. We know our role. Somebody comes along and says, "Cheer up, you know the Lord loves you."

"Don't cheer me up! I know who I am." Well, I'll leave you to play that game if you want to, because the Lord is not forcing anyone. But it's good to know if you are playing such a game. We may be choosing our prison of separation. If so, then we need to know that our choices send a message to the unconscious. Eventually the unconscious dutifully repeats what it has been told. As we live out these messages from the unconscious, we may not realize that we have lost some free choice.

The Lord wants to open the door of that prison and he's doing it through the story of the Canaanite woman. Let's go through the story slowly and carefully. The Canaanite woman is a foreigner to the Jews, an outsider. You'll remember in the Bible that the Canaanite people tried to destroy the religion of the Old Testament people as they came into that area. They used all kinds of fantastic temptations, so the prophets got very upset with the Canaanites. The prophets had to protect their people. So there's a bad memory on the part of the Hebrew people about Canaanite people. They suffered, and would not allow anyone try to bring a Canaanite into the life of the people of God. Now you may see more clearly how memories work?

The Lord in the Gospel intends to dissolve that memory. The Canaanite woman who is desperate for the healing of her daughter comes to him and shouts — I mean she's not reticent any more, she's not being middle class, she's shouting, she really means it. He doesn't say a thing. Now if I were the Lord at that moment, I would have accepted her immediately. No, he wants something deeper. He doesn't say anything because he's working very deeply inside the Canaanite woman and possibly inside us. So when we shout and cry to the Lord and he doesn't say anything, try to remember the story. When the Lord is silent he's reaching deeper within us.

Now the disciples, being loyal followers, want to get rid of this problem. They say, "Look, she's making a racket, let's get rid of her, give her whatever she wants and get her out of the way because we've got more important things to do."

The Lord explains to the disciples, and he's working with them, too, (and us) as well as the Canaanite woman, "I've only come to the people of Israel." That sounds like a nasty thing for a priest to say when somebody comes for help. Be patient. The Lord is reaching deeper. He is resurrecting that bad memory in the minds of the Israelite people and he's saying to the woman in effect, "What are you doing here? I've only come to the Israelite people. Who are you? You're an outsider."

Well, we often feel we're outside. Now for a moment try to think about the possibility that we make up separation. We're the kind of people that make up stories and myths that everything is broken, everything is separated, everything is painful. And the Lord is trying to liberate us. He says, in effect, "You don't have to live that lie. My mercy is bigger than your story about being separated."

Well, the woman is really working hard and she cries, "Help!"

This is the opportunity that a good pastor would utilize, but this man, Jesus, is going deeper than just trying to get somebody into the church, or to get a new pledge. His accusation cuts deeply and he makes a reference to, "I shouldn't take the food from the people of God and throw it to the house dogs."

Any respectable Canaanite woman would have left at that moment. What he's doing is reaching beneath the prejudices, the fantasies that were separating her from God. He's working deeply within her (and us) and he's trying to touch something. He knows He has her attention because she is desperate for her daughter. Her desperation keeps her glued to Him in this encounter and that's what he's working with. She makes a very clever reply. She responds from her own heart: "But even the house dogs are allowed the scraps from the children's table." Jesus recognizes her heart's response.

At that moment He realizes that she has removed the fantasy, the image, the memory of separation. She has stayed with Him and he says, "Your faith will heal your daughter." That's the kind of faith that will not accept separation, alienation, or brokenness as normal. That's what the Lord wants us to accept, too. I don't know what your agenda is for this coming week, but I'm sure God will present you with a lot of things that appear to be broken, separated, alienated, unconnected. Watch yourself play with one or another memory and with one or another invitation to faith.

In Isaiah's meaning, justice is when someone is brought equal, justified. The Lord has made the Canaanite woman equal to Himself in a way through his mercy. He has broken through the disobedience of doubt.

Now let us refer for a moment to Jesse, who's going to be baptized this morning. I want you to use the opportunity of being in church with him to communicate to him, to show him that he belongs and is accepted. And if you can't communicate this with words — touch him. How old is Jesse? Three. Jesse's three. He will not understand words. He wants to know that he is accepted by the way you touch him. That is the only way he can understand baptism, by the way he's looked at, by the way he's touched, by the way you hold him. Then he knows in his three year old language that he belongs and is accepted, welcome, wanted.

Just three years ago Jesse left a magnificent body where he had wall to wall peace, food delivered on schedule, total acceptance and then the landlady said, "Out!" What a terrible experience, and he's yearning to get back into a body where he will know he belongs. This parish is the Body of Christ. Show Jesse that he's safe again.

You adult parishioners know that you are in between Rectors. You, too, are stranded in a way, aren't you, separated from the complete parish life. As good as your present pastor is, he's not the permanent one. The Lord, of course, is the pastor here, but He needs human representatives. So you feel a little bit strange, incomplete, without your permanent pastor. I know there's a search process going on. You are temporarily locked into a kind of separation. You can feed on that and you can say, "Oh, poor St. John's. We're alone; we need a pastor." Do you hear yourself building the myth? Separated, alienated, unloved. It's a comfortable convenient myth.

Your new priest, whoever he is, is going to come into the parish feeling the same way. Alienated, separated, uncertain. "Who are these people? Will they love me? What is that look in their eyes? What are their unspoken thoughts? What does it all mean? Acceptance or rejection?" He's going to be loaded with ambivalent feelings. You will have similar feelings. I hope you can break through this awkwardness, perhaps with the help of your Canaanite friend. Reach out to your new Rector, signal to him, accept him. We are funny little people, so separated, but we are in the Lord. He has accepted us completely. Can't we live in that acceptance?

It would be fun to carry this workshop on all through the week. I'll leave that to you. In the Eucharist, we'll complete the rest of the workshop, for the Lord says, "You are my people. You are my body. I feed you with my body. I give you my body. You and I are one. I have no separate life. Whatever happens to you, happens to me. And what happens to me happens to you." That's the lesson of the workshop. You may spend this week, many weeks, or the rest of your life working on that. When you feel separated, go back to the Canaanite woman and let her teach you that the Lord longs to be merciful. The greatest gift that you can give God is to let Him love you.

In the name of the Father, Son and Holy Spirit. Amen.

APPENDIX 9

MESSAGE OF THE CONGRESS OF ABBOTS TO THE BENEDICTINE COMMUNITIES 1984

We have been meeting together over the last two weeks for the Congress of Abbots, and we have been reflecting on the Lord's question: "But you, who do you say that I am?" (Mk. 8:19). It was our replies to this question that prompted us to address a special message to all our Benedictine communities. The problems which we have been examining constitute a call for us to a serious self-examination; and they can be summed up in the following questions:

- what is Christ saying to us Benedictines today?
- what does Saint Benedict demand of us today?
- what do other people, both in and out of the Church, expect of us today?

We are living in a world which is full of conflict: there is tension in society and in the world of politics, and violence is rife in all its forms. We Benedictines living in our monasteries hear the echo of all this conflict, and we cannot pass over it in silence; rather, we must work for peace. We do this on several different levels: through our prayer, and through becoming more conscious of human needs, as well as through concrete action, in the measure called for by the specific vocation of each individual monastery and the means available to the individual monk or nun. We are all the more under an obligation to strive for peace because the word Peace — "PAX" — has over the course of the centuries become the motto of our Order. In our search for peace we are going back to the last legacy which Jesus gave to his disciples, and to that peace which has been promised to us as a gift of his Spirit.

1. Peace in ourselves: to persevere in patience, to make progress toward reconciling the conflicts within our bodies, our hearts, our souls and our minds: this should be our program, and it demands that we engage in a genuine asceticism day by day. As a result, our way of life can become in itself a form of service which we offer to our fellow men and women, and we shall find our own inner fulfillment in the joy of the Spirit.

2. Peace in our communities: by fostering mutual respect, goodwill and readiness to forgive. We must struggle against all hidden forms of violence, injustice and jealousy. The proven way to achieve this goal is a genuine community life, as provided for in our Rule and traditions.

3. Peace among our fellow men and women: in the first place, by helping those who come to our monasteries to experience peace. We welcome them without respect of persons, but we practice, nevertheless, a special preference for the poor, for the old and for the young (RB 53,15; 4,71; 37,1). We wish to respect the specific mission of each individual monastery, and we wish to practice the virtue of discretion; but we also wish to affirm our support:

- for the elimination of all forms of poverty, whether overt or hidden;
- for the integration into society of those who are pushed out on to its margins;
- for better relations among all groups in society;
- for recognition of the cultural rights of all races and peoples;
- for non-violent resistance toward blatant injustice, all forms of extremism, and the crime of war;
- for all efforts to foster disarmament and peace.

4. Peace with material creation. In the past, Benedictines were often successful in developing a balanced attitude towards nature, and a sound appreciation of the value of material things. In the present age, too, our work has to be carried out, as far as possible, in a way that both respects the value of creation and also furthers the development of the human race. Unbridled consumption, wastage of raw materials and the destruction of the ecological balance; these are evils that need to be countered by a responsible attitude towards material creation, as well as by a new appreciation of the importance and dignity of the contribution made by human labor. Our material possessions, our buildings and our cultural inheritance ought to be quite clearly at the service of humanity.

5. Peace with God. Peace in all the areas we have mentioned will only become possible if we are prepared to make our peace with God, ready to let ourselves be redeemed by him, ready to allow him to make use of us. This applies to all men and women, and it applies to us Benedictines too. It is God who offers us the gift of reconciliation with himself, and it is his Spirit which operates to create unity within the monastic community; it is He who opens our hearts to the problems of our contemporaries, and it is He who is the one Lord and the true goal of creation. In our "Opus Dei" we have a special symbol of our communion with the oppressed. In the psalms, the voice of the poor and oppressed is raised in protest; and this voice of protest, in spite of its powerlessness and its lack of success, will never cease to call on God, the guardian of righteousness and the defender of the helpless.

May Jesus Christ our Lord, the "Father of the age to come, and prince of peace" (Is. 9,6) renew in us the gift of the Spirit and lead us into the ways of peace. May he find us on the side of those who have served him in the despised, the suffering and the persecuted (cf. Mt. 25, 31-45). This is how we seek to answer his question: "But you, who do you say that I am?" (Mk. 8, 29)

APPENDIX 10

COMMUNAL PROCESS FOR CONFLICT RESOLUTION

Over the years that I have been working with various groups and families, I have come to a few general principles regarding conflict resolution.

If there are periodic emotional explosions by members of the group then three factors probably are at work:
1. long standing frustrations are being vented;
2. these frustrations often reflect (real or imagined) a sense of injustice;
3. reasoning doesn't always help.

These explosions reveal our dependence on one another and yet our need for a healthy independence. Coming to the right balance probably will have to wait until the group is well established in its own recovery (as in 12 Step work).

The explosions and strong reactions to them (even silence) are not necessarily aimed at one person. We are looking at a family system. Without knowing quite how, or intending to do so, we often reinforce frustrations in one another. The whole group suffers when one person is frustrated.

In helping the group move from emotional tension toward discussion, it is helpful to realize that different persons may use "language" in different ways. For example, in Myers/Briggs categories, an intellectual person and a sensate person use words differently. The "listener" must know (or learn) these languages, and show respect for each person — helping the group to learn this same discernment. This will build understanding and help the group regain confidence. Some people may be so accustomed to their own language that they literally cannot "hear" other languages.

Working with the communal process toward recovery will take time. Virginia Satir's work is a good reference. One can at least offer choices to the group:

> not allow emotional explosions
> OR
> find a way to reach the real issues with each person.

forget about painful events,
OR
deal compassionately with a genuine cry for help.

pretend you speak the same language,
OR
develop help for the group to learn different languages.

avoid explosions and the people who react that way,
OR
teach the group the skill of exploring the issues, showing respect to
all concerned.

APPENDIX 11

APPRECIATION AND REFLECTION
DELIVERED TO CONGRESS OF ABBOTS, 1988

In the following Congress of Abbots, 1988, in which the theme was "The Holy Spirit and the Monastic Life," I offered this reflection as part of a thanksgiving (on behalf of the Anglican observers) to the Congress for their gracious hospitality. The presence of Roman Catholic women superiors, also observers, along with several painful misunderstandings around the feminine issue — gave this reflection some intensity.

I wish now to speak for myself, offering a few reflections on the work of the Spirit of the Risen Lord, and yet a work of some surprising new unfoldings. The Spirit was there at the beginning of creation — our own and that of the cosmos — bringing ever new and varied images of the divine into reality. Some of our trouble today results from a loss of the covenant with nature, beginning at the moment of our conception, and thus affecting our whole relationship to our bodies and to the earth. With the loss of that covenant, we lose the passion of the Spirit for the unity of all creation. Hence the violence and the pollution. But the Spirit, in new insights of mysticism — coming from some of our scientists — reminds us that the very cells of our body, in all their diversity, yearn for salvation, health, unity. Let us go into the heart, then, the place where we ponder the mystery of life, and learn of some fascinating initial sacramental experiences, pre and birth, with the Spirit we have all had — and "forgotten."

A. We received our first baptism into the body of the living — in a woman.
B. We heard the first music of the Spirit, charismatic and wordless, next to the heart — of a woman.
C. We experienced contemplation, our first experience of God, totally, open, married, and centered in another — in a woman.
D. We received our First Communion, the body and blood of life — from a woman.
E. We experienced Benedictine Vows, Stability, Conversion, and Obedience — in a woman.
F. We were Confirmed in the Spirit, anointed for Christ's death and Resurrection at birth — by a woman.

G. We made our First Confession and received forgiveness — from a woman.

H. We learned our First Catechism, Love — from a woman.

Surprises? Yet all part of our experience of the Spirit in the first stage of our life. It is good for us to remember such beginnings, our own, and that of all creation. The Spirit was brooding over it all — and will rejoice with us at our fulfillment and the completion of all creation. The masculine/feminine qualities of God were there at our conception, guiding and nurturing us all through life, and will be there to assist in our final birth into eternity. God is indeed All in All.

Abbot Benedict Reid, OSB

APPENDIX 12

TEXT OF CONFRATERNITY LETTER
MARCH 14, 1985

Dear Confraters,

I ended last September's Confrater Letter with these words: "I suspect that the Lord will be asking us to simplify our lives, to be ready for vast changes, and to be quite joyful in trusting Him. This is the basis of all true peace, I am sure." The development of this intuition, at least at the Abbey, is somewhat awesome. Simplification and changes have come to us in the form of many departures. Remaining at the monastery are the ten seniors (not counting Br. David residing in Grand Rapids) and one junior. I hasten to add that I don't think this was the result of my sabbatical absence. This is our share of the deep changes going on in the Church and in the world. I share some reflections with you in case you are seeing some of the same things in your own life. Much is indeed unstable these days. But if the Spirit is moving, then we need to discern where He is leading us.

Why do people leave the monastery? Discovering that one does not have a monastic vocation is in itself a normal clarification of vocation. In my nearly 37 years in monastic life, I have seen many, many, come and go. Most choose to leave, a few are asked to go. In the latter case, if they agree with us that it is God's will, then there is peace. If they do not agree, there is pain. Only time and goodwill can clarify our discernment. Not all depart for the same reason, of course. Some may leave because they are uneasy with the theological position of the Episcopal Church (ordination of women, for instance). This is always a matter for the individual conscience with which I never try to interfere.

A more subtle question, which we are just beginning to come to understand, is the difference between the contemplative style of life and the monastic. They are not necessarily the same, although they may be combined in one person. It seems to me that the Spirit is stirring up contemplative gifts in many people. Your own life may reflect this as you learn more about prayer and how to center your life on God. That is a genuine expression of contemplative living and can be combined with any baptismal way of life in the world. We are still learning how to distinguish between these two legitimate ways of faith. This whole discerning process, painful at times, is our part in taking responsibility, being as honest as we can, for the departures.

Some may leave because, in their own search for vocation, they do not find some important part of their humanity fulfilled. This possibility concerns me more than the others. There are enough of our brethren who would describe their departures in these terms to make me look seriously at our possible limitations. I see four areas in which we might explore this possibility. I put them before you to help clarify my own thinking, and possibly to help you discern the quality of your own vocation in your present setting. We are, after all, together in the Lord's Church, trying to be faithful to His will. I am convinced that we have reached a stage in history when we must be much more conscious of and accountable for the gift of humanness, fulfilled to the utmost by grace.

The first area of human fulfillment I note is the agreement between one's ideal and one's everyday life. Our monastic ideal is expressed mainly in our work of worship. We offer God praise, seven times a day in the time-honored recitation of psalms and scriptural texts, centered on the Eucharist. This is the arduous and privileged work of the monk. Tension comes when we compare our everyday life to this ideal. The pain of not measuring up can be eased by the conclusion, understandable enough, that we are only human. After awhile, this conclusion can become unconscious and we don't notice the discrepancy any more. The cost of such "forgetting" is that a vague sense of guilt may infect one's life, provoking unexpected outbursts of temper or moodiness. Or the other extreme is to be overly conscious of the discrepancy, concluding that we are not reconciled to the Lord because our life does not better reflect our professed ideal. Would it help us live in this tension, more consciously and with a sense of humor, if we found corporate ways of examining ourselves, with no judgment? Together, we might look for ways to close the gap between our ideals and our daily life, thus celebrating the practical use of grace. We might also discover the very real need we have of one another.

The second area I note is the human need to love and be loved. This applies to people whatever their vocation. "I am glad you are alive. I'm glad you are here." This is a signal we need to send to one another as we work together, as we adapt to one another, as we forgive one another (often without words). If we have seriously failed one another, and if this failure has not been resolved over the years, we may gradually fail to send that human message of love. Monks in particular, involved as they are with meditation and regular times of silence, may lose track of the importance of relationships. Celibacy too, with its special renunciation, requires that all the more attention be given to small acts of affirmation, the accepting glance, the courteous gesture, the gentle touch when a neighbor is "down." Perhaps older people were raised in a more robust way and did not need such assurances. Perhaps. I find younger people more vulnerable and more aware of their human needs than the older generation. We may be coming to a time of far deeper sensitivity — and that not too soon in terms of our care for one another throughout the world.

The third area I note is that of consciousness in the limited scope of communal life, that is, as an awareness of the whole of ourselves, our best and worst, plus our relationships. Strange to say, we may not always be realistic or honest about ourselves or our relationships, imagining ourselves better than we really are while losing touch with our worst. To become more conscious, we need the kind of tough love (spoken of in AA circles) that dares to give and receive love. This love brings reality before another person. And because it is brought in genuine love, without judgment, the other person can more likely receive it. And the other person must be free to give us the same kind of love, the truth about ourselves in God's love.

And finally, I note the place of mutual accountability. Granted, there are decisions and functions that belong to the one in authority. Still there is much of communal life that can be enriched by each persons taking his full share of responsibility in personal growth and in relationships. St. Benedict would see this as conversion. Most of us have not been trained in such accountability. I am responsible to my brother for my honesty, for my love for him, and my acknowledgment of my own weaknesses. I am not responsible for his choices, his moods, his problems. But this kind of accountability can only be learned in the rough and tumble of daily affairs. It is painful. A group of people learning this art must commit themselves to this painful work of conversion as part of their accountability to God. He has already demonstrated, perfectly, His accountability to us.

These are some of my reflections. Perhaps they may be of help to you. We must now digest the meaning of our small number. The abbot is doing pots and pans occasionally. We are learning a new dependence on the Lord, a new personal application of the Liturgy of Lent. Join us often in prayer. No doubt, the Lord has His own Easter hidden in it all. His peace is still a resurrection promise.

Blessings for Easter,

Benedict Reid, O.S.B.
Abbot

APPENDIX 13

"SABBATICAL"
ABBEY LETTER, EASTER 1985

"Life is a pilgrimage to God. It is also a pilgrimage with God. He is our traveling Companion." With these words I began the record of my sabbatical, a journey that lasted some seven months, from after Easter until just before Thanksgiving Day, 1984. My overwhelming feeling is that my sabbatical was a magnificent gift from God, from my community (who had to improvise in many ways during my absence), and from the many friends who supported it with their prayers and donations. It remains, even now, a profound blessing.

One way to suggest the extent of this gift is to offer a list, however inadequate to the experience, of the places I visited. I passed through 23 states and the District of Columbia, and went overseas to Rome and England. I was in 20 parishes and six cathedrals; I talked with eight bishops, visited 20 religious houses (monasteries or convents), and stopped at 12 conference centers (sometimes participating in a program). The list also includes an American Indian commune, a diocesan summer camp, a working cattle ranch, a state prison, four national parks, two concerts, and several monuments and museums. I saw many friends and missed seeing many more for sheer lack of time. In between all of these items there were many hours of saying the Divine Office and meditating, either in the most ordinary of circumstances (sitting in the van in a shopping mall parking lot) or in extraordinary settings (on the edge of the Grand Canyon). Then, too, there were the Eucharists I offered in the van or on a lonely mountain — or shared in a parish church.

My itinerary took me westward from the Abbey through Chicago, lower Wisconsin, and parts of Iowa, then back through Illinois and southern Indiana. After that, I headed west into Oklahoma, Texas, New Mexico, and Arizona. I had a leisurely visit with my relatives in southern California and then went up the gorgeous coastal route. After a stay in San Francisco, I returned to the Midwest through Nevada, Utah, Wyoming, and Nebraska. Following a brief stop at the Abbey, I went eastward through Ohio and Pennsylvania. Leaving the van in Philadelphia, I flew first to Rome and later to England. On returning to the United States, I made stops in the the Middle Atlantic States between Washington and New York City. All of this mobility, with freedom to stop and go as I pleased, was made possible by the live-in van. I could not have had a more accommodating companion.

Those of you who are acquainted with motor homes know what I mean. I encourage those of you who have never had this pleasure to try it, perhaps on a rental basis.

Our regular readers will know that I was aiming at two objectives on the sabbatical. I was giving the brethren a chance to think about the leadership of the Abbey for the future, since (after nearly 30 years as superior) I am approaching age 65, the time when the constitution of St. Gregory's calls for the resignation of an abbot (although the community need not accept his resignation). And I was looking for hints and clues about the future of the Church in this fascinating time when we have the potential either to end the whole human experiment or to move into one of its greatest chapters.

Overall, I was awed by the magnificent beauty of our American countryside and by the richness of our western culture, its roots going back to the unrecorded time of man's origin. One gets a glimpse of that cultural sweep walking the streets of Rome with its layered history visually represented in art and architecture. Ordinary people express their heritage in this grand procession of mankind, often unconsciously, as if it were their own private procession. The citizens of Des Moines probably don't think very much of the meaning and the French root of the name of their city. Nor does the manufacturer of the Winnebago motor home I was driving advert very often to the long scientific development, employing innumerable human inventions, involved in a modern vehicle. Cruising through the countryside in my monk-mobile, listening to Bach, munching on cellophane-packaged snacks, provided me a space and time machine of incredible freedom.

And yet, I couldn't escape the impression that this wonderful western culture will be enmeshed in violence and disturbance for the rest of the century — maybe longer. We are paying for so many mistakes of the past. Races have long memories, and now they are neighbors in the same world-village, possessing powerful machines which can be used creatively or destructively. Terrorists often cite, or act out unconsciously, grievances of past decades or even past centuries. In all of life, every wrong act must be redeemed, and sometimes at a terrible price. The shadow of the crucifix falls across the pages of the newspaper.

But the ordinary people — these are the remarkable ones. They go daily to work, they maintain a family, they support their local community, they wonder at the world situation, and they go on with their life. I met hundreds of them and they always touched me with their faithfulness. The bookstore owner who let me make a long-distance credit card call on his front desk phone was unassuming in his graciousness. The gruff U-Haul mechanic, swearing quietly as if he were praying, patched my bent fender efficiently. The 747 flight attendant, absorbing the loud reproaches of a non-smoker (who was himself smoking emotionally) kept on cheerfully with her duties. The state park ranger, apprehending me in a non-camping area at midnight, conducted me courteously to an authorized site. Sales people and gasoline attendants, workers and housewives, all do their jobs while governments and people of power push each other around in an ever-shrinking world.

Then there are the families. Staying together and raising children is a heroic vocation. I looked out on them from the sanctuaries of the parishes I visited. Mother and the young child she comforts, father and the bored teenager he keeps an eye on, all somehow participate in the eternal Sacrament emanating from the parish altar. And what human mysteries center on that sacred table! Many parishes are experimenting with one or another of the current renewal programs — Faith Alive, Cursillo, charismatic prayer groups, Bible study classes, midweek healing services, house Masses, meditation classes, hospice groups, and many more. The Church is working hard to give its people the tools to make their faith tough and effective. We will have to work harder, in my opinion. We have access to many professionally trained people in the parish and in the community. We need all of their expertise brought together in faith. Individuals and families need training in spiritual growth and in group life. Without such training we lose confirmands, fail to provide a strong communal context for married couples, and never touch the millions of unchurched.

In any event, the whole tenuous parish miracle is shepherded by the pastor and the vestry and faithful secretaries, who sometimes float in the glow of grace which attends the Lord's work and sometimes nervously count the empty pews. This "ordinary" miracle takes place every Sunday. I saw it clearly in a small parish in Iowa, lovingly tended by a woman priest. I saw it again in the Episcopal parish in Rome, St. Paul's Within the Walls, where a local congregation and international travelers, diplomats, and business people meet for Bread and Wine. How mysteriously powerful are these Sunday grace-workings for the peace of the world!

When I met a bishop or chatted with a member of his staff, I found hard-working people who, with all their heroic accomplishments, seem to be constantly rebuilding sand castles. If the parish needs to be training its people in many new practical ways of faith, how much more does the diocese need to be carefully monitoring its structures so that the overall model is the Body of Christ, not the business corporation.

The monasteries and convents I visited were living out their commitment to prayer according to their rule and tradition, but also pondering deeply the significance of human relationship within the common life, the art of using more of our human resources in the life of prayer (breathing techniques, centering prayer, healing of memories, Myers-Briggs psychological testing, attention to diet and exercise, Eastern methods of meditation). It is a time of extreme stretching, of trying to discern the legitimate extension of the tradition. Innovation is apparent at conference centers, which tend to explore the human potential much more freely. Workshops and counseling, tapes and books look unhesitatingly in every direction for clues about human development. Not all of these explorations are Christian, or even religious, nor will they all prove to be of lasting value. Still, I think that the Church must take their work seriously as a valid part of the exploration of the doctrine of the Incarnation.

It is impossible to squeeze all of my reflections, my experiences, my moments of joy, looking at the desert or the ocean, my visits with friends, my inner prayers and dreams, into a short article. Perhaps I have given you a touch of what this marvelous gift meant to me. Perhaps it may help you to clarify some of your own musings on your pilgrimage. All of life is our pilgrimage to God. And God is a wonderful traveling Companion.

— Fr. Abbot Benedict

BIBLIOGRAPHY

Bandler and Grinder, *Frogs into Princes*. Moab: Real People Press, 1979.

Berry, Thomas, *The Dream of the Earth*. San Francisco: Sierra Club Books, 1988.

Bly, Robert, "A Gathering of Men." PBS: Mystic Fire Video Distributors, 1990.

Boyd, Doug, *Rolling Thunder*. New York: Random House, 1974.

Boyd, Malcolm (ed.) *On the Battle Lines*. New York: Barlow Company, 1964.

The Book of Common Prayer. New York: The Church Hymnal Corporation, 1979.

Chifflot, T.G., O.P., Raymond Schaub, R. Turney, O.P., and Joseph Gelineau, O.P.,
The Psalms: A new translation from the Hebrew. The Grail: Collins Fount Paperbacks,
1966.

Conn, Joann Wolski (ed.), *Women's Spirituality*. New York: Paulist Press,1986.

Cox, Michael, *Handbook of Christian Spirituality*. New York: Harper and Row, 1985.

de Chardin, Pierre Teilhard, *Hymn of the Universe*. New York: Harper Torchbooks, Harper
and Row, Publishers, 1961.

de Mello, *Sadhana: A Way to God (Christian Exercises in Eastern Form)*. New York:
Image Books, 1984.

Doyle, Leonard J. (translated from the Latin), *St. Benedict's Rule for Monasteries*. St. John's
Abbey, Collegeville: The Liturgical Press, 1947.

Ferguson, Marilyn, *The Aquarian Conspiracy*. Los Angeles: J. P. Tarcher, Inc., 1980.

Friedman, Edwin H., *Generation to Generation*. New York: the Guilford Press, 1985.

Fry, Timothy, OSB, et.al. *RB 1980, The Rule of St. Benedict in Latin and English with Notes*. Collegeville: The Litrugical Press, 1981.

Grant, W. Harold; Magdala Thompson, and Thomas E. Clarke, *From Image to Likeness*. New York: Paulist Press, 1983.

Hanh, Thich Nhat, *Being Peace*. Berkeley: Parallax Press, 1988.

Heider, John, *The Tao of Leadership*. Atlanta: Humanics New Age, 1985.

Houston, Jean, *The Possible Human*. Los Angeles: J.P. Tarcher, Inc., 1982.

Ibraham, Ishak, *Black Gold and Holy War*. Nashville: Thomas Nelson Publisher, 1983.

The Institute for Research in Spirituality, *"Kairos,"* Coulterville, CA: Summer 1989, Vol. IV, 2.

Jampolsky, Gerald G., *Love is Letting Go of Fear*. New York: Bantam, 1981.

The Jerusalem Bible. London: Darton, Longman, and Todd, 1966.

Jones, Cheslyn, Geoffrey Wainwright, and Edward Yarnold, SJ, (ed.), *The Study of Spirituality*. New York: Oxford University Press, 1986.

Keating, Thomas, *Open Mind, Open Heart, The Contemplative Dimension of the Gospel*. New York: Amity House, 1986.

Kennedy, Eugene, *On Becoming a Counselor*. New York: Continuum, 1977.

Leech, Kenneth, *Soul Friend*. London: Sheldon Press, 1979.

Lewis, C.S., *The Screwtape Letters*. New York: Macmillan, 1943.

May, Gerald G., M.D., *Addiction and Grace*. San Francisco: Harper and Row, 1988.

Merton, Thomas, *The Asian Journal*. New York: New Directions, 1973.

Moon, William Least Heat, *Blue Highways*. Boston: Little Brown, 1982.

Nemeck, Francis Kelly, OMI, and Marie Theresa Coombs, Hermit, *The Way of Spiritual Direction.* Wilmington, Delware: Michael Glazier, 1985.

Neufelder, Jerome M., and Mary C. Coehlo (ed.), *Writings on Spiritual Direction, by Great Christian Master.* New York: The Seabury Press, 1982.

Peck, Scott, *The People of the Lie.* New York: Simon and Schuster, 1983.

Rahner, Karl, *Theological Investigations.*, Volume VI. Baltimore: Helicon Press, 1969.

_____ and Herbert Vorgrimler, edited by Cornelius Ernst, O.P., translated by Richard Strachan, *Theological Dictionary.* New York: Herder and Herder, 1968.

Sinetar, Marsha, *Ordinary People as Monks and Mystics.* New York: Paulist Press, 1986.

Soleri, Paolo, *Arconsanti, An Urban Laboratory.* Pittsburgh: Avante Books, 1984.

Suzuki, O.T., *Zen Mind, Beginner's Mind.* New York: Weatherhill, 1970.

Swidler, Leonard (ed.), *Toward a Universal Theology of Religion.* New York: Orbis Books, 1987.

Toffler, Alvin, *The Third Wave.* William Morrow and Co., Inc., 1980.

Tyrrell, Bernard J., S.J., *Christo-Therapy II.* New York: Paulist Press, 1982.

Underhill, Evelyn, *Mysticism.* New York: The Noonday Press, 1955.

Additional copies of *A Spirit Loose in the World* may be ordered from your local bookseller, or if it is not available at your bookstore it may be ordered directly from Harbor House (West) Publishers, Drawer 599, Summerland, California 93067 for $17.95, plus $3 shipping and handling. Quantity discounts are available to churches, dioceses, or other Christian organizations.